CAREER THEORY AND PRACTICE

Third Edition

To our families for their love and support
Bill, Merit, and Robert (JS)
Bob, Nick, Erin, Andrew, Patrick, and, most especially, Nolan and Elisabeth (NF)

CAREER THEORY AND PRACTICE

Learning Through Case Studies

Third Edition

Jane L. Swanson

Southern Illinois University Carbondale

Nadya A. Fouad

University of Wisconsin–Milwaukee

Los Angeles | London | New Delhi
Singapore | Washington DC

SSAGE

Los Angeles | London | New Delhi
Singapore | Washington DC

FOR INFORMATION:

SAGE Publications, Inc.
2455 Teller Road
Thousand Oaks, California 91320
E-mail: order@sagepub.com

SAGE Publications Ltd.
1 Oliver's Yard
55 City Road
London EC1Y 1SP
United Kingdom

SAGE Publications India Pvt. Ltd.
B 1/I 1 Mohan Cooperative Industrial Area
Mathura Road, New Delhi 110 044
India

SAGE Publications Asia-Pacific Pte. Ltd.
3 Church Street
#10-04 Samsung Hub
Singapore 049483

Publisher: Kassie Graves
Editorial Assistant: Elizabeth Luizzi
Production Editor: Olivia Weber-Stenis
Copy Editor: Kimberly Hill
Typesetter: C&M Digitals (P) Ltd.
Proofreader: Carole Quandt
Indexer: Diggs Publication Services
Cover Designer: Gail Buschman
Marketing Manager: Shari Countryman

Copyright © 2015 by SAGE Publications, Inc.

Printed in the United States of America

Library of Congress Cataloging-in-Publication Data

Swanson, Jane Laurel.

Career theory and practice : learning through case studies / Jane L. Swanson, Southern Illinois University Carbondale, Nadya A. Fouad, University of Wisconsin-Milwaukee. — Third edition.

pages cm
Includes index.

ISBN 978-1-4522-5669-6 (pbk. : alk. paper)

1. Career development—Case studies. 2. Vocational guidance—Case studies. I. Fouad, Nadya A. II. Title.

HF5381.S937 2015
158.6—dc23   2014007565

This book is printed on acid-free paper.

SUSTAINABLE FORESTRY INITIATIVE
Certified Chain of Custody
Promoting Sustainable Forestry
www.sfiprogram.org
SFI-01268
SFI label applies to text stock

14 15 16 17 18 10 9 8 7 6 5 4 3 2 1

BRIEF CONTENTS

PART III: APPLICATIONS

Detailed Contents

LIST OF TABLES AND FIGURES

TABLES

FIGURES

LIST OF ADDITIONAL CASES

Theory or Approach	Client Name (Age)	Race/Ethnicity	Page
Culturally Responsive Career Counseling	Norman (17)	African American	84
	Brenda (47)	Hispanic	90
	Justino (37)	Puerto Rican	91
	Monica (27)	Multiracial: Native American and African-American	92
Holland, Vocational Personalities and Work Environments	Judy (38)	White	106
	Johnny (44)	Hmong American	111
	Susan (17)	African American	113
	Cynthia (42)	White	114
Theory of Work Adjustment	Charles (early 40s)	White	125
	Phil (48)	Latino	131
	Melissa (32)	White	132
	Linda (18)	Korean American	133
Super	Karen (52)	White	146
	Walter (65)	White	154
	Maria Josefina (16)	Puerto Rican	155
	Deborah (33) and Trish (38)	White	156

Theory or Approach	Client Name (Age)	Race/Ethnicity	Page
Gottfredson, Circumscription and Compromise	Gary (16)	White	167
	Dorece (21)	African American	171
	Steve (39)	White	173
	Lori (45)	White	174
Social Cognitive	Ron (57)	White	188
	Jerry (32)	White	197
	Kamisha (21)	African American	199
	Jim (27)	White	201
Emerging Theories	Diana and Bill (mid 40s)	White	216
	Lian (23)	Asian international	220
	Ellen (50)	White	221
	Tony (19)	African American	222
Occupational Information	Elon (35)	African American	251
	Katherine (28)	Native American	252
	Daniel (43)	Asian American	253
Career/Noncareer	Julie (29)	White	263
	Jason (26)	Multiracial	264
	Beth (20)	White	266
	Alex (34)	African American	266
Summary and Integration	George (54)	White	276
	Tom (21)	White	285

ACKNOWLEDGMENTS

We express deep gratitude to the many individuals who have helped us with the first, second, and third editions of this book. First, our thanks to the career development scholars who provided feedback on drafts of the first edition: Nancy Betz, Helen Farmer, Lenore Harmon, and Mary Heppner. We also appreciate the feedback offered by experts in specific theoretical perspectives: Linda Forrest and Stephen Wester (gender), Rosie Bingham (cultural approaches), Gary Gottfredson and John Holland (Holland's theory), James Rounds and Howard (Tony) Tinsley (Theory of Work Adjustment), David Blustein and Mark Savickas (Super's theory), and Steve Brown and Bob Lent (SCCT). We thank Jeff Prince, John Westefeld, Mark Leitheiser, Azara Santiago-Rivera, and Chris Finn for feedback on case materials, and we thank the following organizations for providing the materials and scoring of assessment instruments: Consulting Psychologists Press, Career Development & Resource Clinic in the Department of Psychology at Southern Illinois University, and Vocational Psychology Research at the University of Minnesota.

We also thank the students in Nadya Fouad's summer 2008 Foundations of Career Development course at the University of Wisconsin–Milwaukee: Rosin Bergdoll, Melissa Brah, Lisa Engel, Donna Grady, Stacy Ludwig, Greg Mathias, Ginny Patton, Chad Peterson, Haley Pollen, Elizabeth Ojeda, Margaret Rhody, Shana Schloemer, Melissa Sell, and Elizabeth Wall. Professor Marty Sapp taught the same course in 2013, and we are grateful for his help and the comments of his students: Elizabeth (Liz) Baumgartner, James Holtz, Cara Hoth, Ernesto Matus, Tracy Murray, Sonia Pinero, Thomas Ploeger, and Lauren Roszkowski. The students in these two classes provided wonderful feedback on the second and third editions, helped us identify needed changes in the format and structure, and gave their perspectives on the breadth and depth of the cases. Similarly, Sarah Miller at Southern Illinois University provided her expertise and "fresh eyes" to a thorough review of the second edition. We appreciate their help.

We are deeply appreciative of the following individuals for their reviews of the second edition: Darlene M. Hannigan, LaSalle University; Margo A. Jackson, Fordham University; Mickey C. Melendez, The State University of New Jersey; and Donna E. Schultheiss, Cleveland State University. Chad Olle, Christina Wilson, Shin-ye Kim, Sherri Pfennig at the University of Wisconsin–Milwaukee and Kevin Tate at Marquette University provided invaluable comments on the third edition.

Finally, we thank "Leslie" for inspiration.

SAGE would like to thank the following reviewers for their contributions to this edition: Christina Jackson-Bailey, Adler School of Professional Psychology; Robinder (Rob) P. Bedi, Western Washington University; Theresa J. Canada, Western Connecticut State University; Gail A. Chester, Amberton University; Meredith J. Drew, Centenary College; Marie S. Hammond, Tennessee State University; Elsie Jones-Smith, Private Practice, Strengths-Based Institute; Ruth Riding-Malon, Radford University; Karen D. Rowland, Mercer University; Gerald E. Thomas, Springfield College; and Ginger L. Welch, University of Oklahoma.

PART I: FUNDAMENTALS

Chapter 1

Career Counseling:
An Overview

Ruth has been out of the paid workforce for 8 years. Her youngest son recently started public school, and she would like to find a job. Ruth has a degree in medical technology and worked in a hospital lab for 5 years before her first child was born. In her geographic area, the job market for medical technologists is poor, so she'd like to consider some other job possibilities. She doesn't know what other options are available.

Harry has worked in the human resources department of a large company for over 20 years. He had been satisfied with his job and had received good performance evaluations. However, he was recently assigned new job responsibilities that he doesn't feel adequately trained to do. Last week, he received a negative report from his supervisor, and he's worried that he might lose his job. Harry has been depressed and angry, and his wife is concerned that he's drinking too much.

Joel is a high school junior who doesn't have any idea what he will do after graduating. His parents want him to go to college, believing that a college education will provide him with opportunities they did not have. However, Joel's grades have been mediocre, and he really doesn't want to go to college anyway. His guidance counselor tells him that he needs to make a decision soon.

Each of these situations represents a struggle with some work- or career-related concern. Because work plays a central role in most people's lives, successful pursuit of work activities is crucial to psychological well-being. Furthermore, vocational issues and mental health issues affect one another in individuals' lives, and work is an important component of overall well-being (Blustein, 2008; Juntunen, 2006; Swanson, 2012). It is important for counselors to understand the crucial impact of vocational issues and to assist individuals in the choice and implementation of their career-related goals so that people's lives are enriched.

PURPOSE OF THE BOOK

The purpose of this book is to provide the reader with an understanding of elements of career counseling; hands-on, practical examples of how to apply career development theories to career counseling clients; career interventions in a variety of settings; and an appreciation of the overall importance of work in people's lives. We view the book as a bridge between career theory and career practice. In this third edition, we have included a number of chapters to help orient students to the interplay of work and mental health, the importance of incorporating a perspective about work in counseling and as a primer to career counseling. We added material to highlight the role of the economy and the changing nature of the workforce that influence the career and work decisions individuals make, initially here in Chapter 1 and then throughout the book.

The book is organized to facilitate the integration of theory and practice. Chapter 4 introduces "Leslie," the primary case example used throughout the book, and we apply a model of culturally appropriate counseling to Leslie's case in Chapter 5. We then consider Leslie from new perspectives in Chapters 6 through 11 to demonstrate how theories can inform the way in which counselors view and work with their clients. In addition to Leslie, a secondary case with an extended analysis is presented in Chapters 5 through 11. Three additional brief cases in each chapter offer the reader more opportunities to practice the application of theory and interventions to individual clients. Because many of the theories have unique definitions and constructs, each theory chapter in Part II also contains three pedagogical tools: a set of questions inviting readers to engage in personal reflection, a summary of the key theoretical constructs, and a sample of possible counselor's cognitions from that theoretical perspective. We also include personal reflections and counselor cognitions in many of the chapters in Parts I and II of the book, to invite readers to reflect on their own experiences and to guide counselors in deliberately attending to specific aspects of counseling.

We brought our own experiences as practitioners, researchers, and teachers to bear on our approach to writing this book. As practitioners, we believe that the theoretical orientation one adopts has a significant impact on how client issues are conceptualized and treated. As researchers, we know that the ethical delivery of career counseling must be based on sound empirical findings; this is highlighted in the Ethical Code C. 6.e of the National Career Development Association (2007), included in Appendix B. Finally, as instructors, we are committed to helping students make connections between theory, research, and practice in ways that are ultimately in the service of clients. We have attempted to incorporate all our experiences into the structure of this book by choosing theories that have received empirical support, by highlighting how the theoretical propositions influence views of clients, and by providing considerable case information for analysis and discussion. We have also observed that some students learn best by applying the material to their own lives, and thus we have incorporated invitations for personal reflection.

We also wanted to incorporate our commitment to integrating contextual issues in conceptualizations of clients' concerns. We both have spent our careers conducting research and teaching students about the need to consider a client's gender, ethnicity, socioeconomic status, sexual orientation, and disability status when helping that client make career decisions. An individual's choices and decisions, or lack of choices, are shaped by his or her gender, family, disability, sexual orientation, social class, and culture, which in turn influence his or her schooling, access to resources, and interaction with the larger environment. Consider, for example, a Latina high school student from a traditional Mexican American family growing up in an affluent suburb of Los Angeles. Her career choices will be shaped by her gender, her family's cultural values, and their expectations of her post-high school decisions. Their expectations may be influenced by their degree of affluence, their beliefs about gender and work, and the influences of the schools in their community. Her expectations will be shaped by her acceptance of her family's expectations and her ability to navigate expectations from her peers, parents, and teachers at her school. Her parents may feel that her post-high school choices are limited to options of which they approve, while she has been encouraged to "dream big" by her counselor. All these factors will influence her decisions.

Change the example above to an African American heterosexual male student in rural Georgia, or a White gay male in rural South Dakota, or a White heterosexual female in an inner-city high school in Boston. While all these individuals may choose to go to college after high school, the contexts for those decisions are shaped by their gender, family, race/ethnicity, disability, sexual orientation, schooling, and interactions with the mainstream culture in the United States. Fundamental to ethical practice is the consideration of clients' contextual factors, particularly gender and race/ethnicity. Readers will note the emphasis on the importance of context in several ways: Considerations of various contextual factors are integrated into each chapter, a specific chapter is devoted to cultural context in career counseling, and cases are included to represent the diversity of clients who seek counseling.

We wrote the book with two types of readers in mind. The first type is a student in a graduate-level course, such as theories of vocational psychology, foundations of career counseling, or practicum in career counseling, who is learning about theories of career development and how to apply these theories to clients. The second type of reader is an established counseling practitioner who wants additional resources to strengthen his or her delivery of career services or who is expanding the focus of his or her work to include career issues.

In this chapter, we begin with information about the changing role of the career counselor and the current labor market and several factors that will affect the future of work. We then focus on the role of theory in career counseling, beginning with a definition of *theory* and a description of types of career development theories. We then describe the theories selected for this casebook and discuss how to use theories, particularly as a means to develop hypotheses about clients. Finally, we discuss the development of hypothesis testing as part of career counseling.

WORK AND CAREER COUNSELING

What is work? The Merriam-Webster (2013) dictionary defines work as "the labor, task, or duty that is one's accustomed means of livelihood." Work is a critical part of the lives of most adults in the United States. Individuals make many decisions about work: whether to work or not work, what work to do, how to prepare for that work, whether to change jobs or careers, or how to cope with the loss of work. And any of these decisions may lead individuals to seek help from a counselor. They may need help deciding between two or more choices, learning how to make a decision, pursuing more satisfying work, finding work, or coping with the loss of work. Consider that, by the typical retirement age of 65, a full time employee will have spent some 80,000 hours working, and it becomes clear how central work is in people's lives. Blustein (2006) notes that work has particular psychological meaning for individuals, providing them with a means of survival and power, a way to connect to others, and finally, a means of self-determination and ways to express interests and passions.

This book focuses on the role of counselors in helping individuals with work and career-related decisions. We discuss other types of career interventions in Chapter 12, but most of the chapters focus on the practice of individual counseling.

Frank Parsons is credited with beginning the field of career counseling in 1909 with the publication of his book *Choosing a Vocation*. He wrote about his work with adolescent boys he was helping at the Breadwinners Institute in Boston, noting that "In the wise choice of a vocation, there are three broad factors: (1) a clear understanding of yourself . . . (2) knowledge of the requirements . . . in different lines of work, [and] (3) true reasoning on the relations of these two groups of facts" (p. 5). His method was to help the young men engage in self-analysis, help them uncover their preferences, provide some guidance and analysis as well as an outlook on the available options, and provide advice on how to find a job.

In many ways, his model continues to shape the work of the career counselor. Career counselors still help people understand themselves, understand possible work options, and how to translate that information into jobs and careers, but the role of the career counselor has changed as the world of work has changed. Career counseling as a profession is influenced by the economic structure and the role that career counselors can play in preparing individuals to enter and be successful within that structure. Parsons was trying to help young men enter the labor force at a time of considerable labor unrest and income disparity, and this guidance was seen as a way to decrease juvenile delinquency (Zytowski, 2001). Parsons was working within, and helped by, the context of the progressive reform movements in Boston at the time, but he was clearly a visionary in many ways. In *Choosing a Vocation,* he persuasively argued for a scientific approach to selecting one's work life, he provided a blueprint for training vocational counselors, and provided an amazing amount of occupational information on industries in the Boston area. In other articles, he also argued for a model to integrate vocational guidance into educational curricula (O'Brien, 2001). Many of his efforts form the basis of career interventions today.

In Parsons' time, the choice of a vocation was made early in life and was viewed as a successful choice if the person stayed in that job. Clearly then the work of the career, or vocational, counselor was most important in early adolescence. Over the past 100 years, however, the world of work has changed considerably so that now individuals move in and out of positions over their lifespan (sometimes not by their own choice), initial decisions are often made later than early adolescence, and there is a need for help at many transition points. Thus, the work of the career counselor has changed substantially over the years.

In the 1920s, 30s and 40s, career counseling became more prominent on college campuses, counselors were needed to help veterans returning from World Wars I and II, and counselors were needed to help individuals find work during the Great Depression. Parsons' first factor (knowledge of self) became a catalyst for assessment tools to help individuals know more about their interests, abilities and values, and those tools were used to help "match" the individual to a career. Career counseling was brief and focused on assessment. Career counselors provided information and earned the reputation of "three interviews and a cloud of dust" (referring to the Midwestern dustbowls of the 1930s). It could be argued that career counselors ignored Parsons' third factor to help clients "find true reasoning."

Donald Super (1953) used his presidential address for Division 17 (Counseling Psychology) of the American Psychological Association to outline the need to focus on the development of a career rather than just the one-time choice of a career. His theory, discussed more fully in Chapter 8, was developed in post-World War II America, when corporations were developing career ladders and occupational specialization was increasing. Increasing attention was paid to career as a lifelong process and to critical developmental tasks needed to make good career decisions. At the same time, in the late 1950s, the U.S. federal government became concerned about preparing students to compete on scientific grounds with the Soviet Union. The National Defense Education Act was used to provide funding for schools to develop guidance programs, particularly to provide career development services. Some $77 million dollars was directed to this program from the late 1950s through the early 1960s. This funding led to a tremendous increase in the number of guidance counselors in the United States and to the development of guidance programs designed to help students make good career and educational decisions (Flattau et al., 2008). Super's developmental focus began to be infused into guidance programs, and career development became a significant focus for school counselors.

Twenty years later, there began to be a general movement to attend to more psychological aspects of career decision making, rather than focusing solely on providing information (Herr, Cramer & Niles, 2004). Career counselors were still helping individuals make good career choices but were also encouraged to be good therapists. Divisions between career counseling and more general mental health counseling were explored in a special issue of *The Career Development Quarterly* titled "How Personal is Career Counseling?" As Subich (1993) noted in her introduction to the special issue, all the authors decried the split between personal and career counseling. The authors argued for a greater application of career counseling skills to workplace issues more broadly (Haverkamp & Moore, 1993) and a greater focus on personal identity and meaning (Davidson & Gilbert, 1993). Several authors also noted that, in essence, making a distinction between personal and career counseling trivialized the emotional aspects of making decisions about career and work.

More recently, career counselors' work has shifted in ways predicted by the authors of the special issue. Their efforts reflect the changing world of work, with more flux in the labor force necessitating many changes over the lifespan. Three decades of research on the role of gender, race, culture, social class, and sexual orientation, discussed more fully in Chapter 2, have resulted in much more attention to context in career counseling and the realization that work, and the factors that influence work choices, may differ across individuals. Career counseling is no longer viewed as focusing primarily on assessment or information giving about work options, because that was not meeting clients' needs, as we discuss in Chapter 11. Richardson (2012) issued a call for the field to be even more inclusive, from helping individuals choose careers to helping them "construct lives through work and relationship" (p. 191). She and other authors argue for a more holistic approach to career counseling addressing the entire range of work that people do in both the marketplace and in their personal care work (care for self and others). Today, career counselors are professionals who have specialized skills to help people make choices about their work and personal lives and the meaning of that work in their lives.

The National Career Development Association's (2009) *Minimum Competencies for Multicultural Career Counseling and Development* reflect the aforementioned changes to the provision of career counseling. The purpose of the Competencies is "to ensure that all individuals practicing in, or training for practice in, the career counseling and development field are aware of the expectation that we, as professionals, will practice in ways that promote the career development and functioning of individuals of all backgrounds" (NCDA, 2009). The nine competencies encompass the areas of career counseling that are deemed critical to effective practice. Career counselors must:

- Understand career development theory
- Be able to provide individual and group counseling skills in a culturally appropriate way
- Be able to provide individual and group assessment
- Be able to provide occupational information in a culturally sensitive way
- Be able to provide career programs for diverse populations
- Be able to provide coaching and consultation in a culturally appropriate manner
- Be able to engage in culturally appropriate supervision
- Act ethically and legally appropriate
- Be able to design and implement culturally appropriate research studies

In this book, we focus on each of these competencies (with the exceptions of supervision, consultation, and developing research studies).

CHANGING WORLD OF WORK

Theories of career development tend to be primarily psychological in nature; that is, they focus on characteristics of individuals that help explain the careers they enter, the ways that they adjust to work environments, or the processes by which they make career choices or changes. However, these theories do not exist in a vacuum: The larger economic and social systems in which an individual resides play crucial roles in the type of decision that is made or even whether a decision can or needs to be made at all. For example, when the national (or global) economy is booming, an individual may see many opportunities available and may feel little risk in deciding to leave a current job for one in another organization or field, or to pursue further education. On the other hand, when the economy is in a downturn, the same individual may see few opportunities and may not be able or willing to risk any work-related changes. When a labor market is relatively open (more jobs than workers), employers have to offer better salaries and other benefits to attract well-qualified workers; when a labor market is relatively tight (more workers than jobs), employers do not have to compete for workers and may decrease what they offer. These economic factors obviously influence an individual's career development, at particular choice points and in the progression of one's career over a life span, and we continue to discuss these factors as we consider specific theories of career development.

In the nearly 20 years since we wrote the first edition of this book, the world of work has changed fairly dramatically. We discuss labor force information in more depth in Chapter 13 but provide an initial overview of the current workforce and the projected changes in the workforce here. We want to help readers understand the major shifts in work that affect current workers and the future choices of clients making work-related decisions.

The workforce has become increasingly diverse, both in gender and in racial/ethnic diversity, in the past three decades (Bureau of Labor Statistics, 2012). Women are almost as likely to join the labor force as are men and stay in the labor force after they have children. Their wage relative to men, which was 62 cents to the dollar in 1979, improved to 82 cents to the dollar in 2011 (Bureau of Labor Statistics, 2012), although clearly, more work is needed to ensure equality in pay between men and women.

The entire population in the United States is increasingly diverse in terms of race and ethnicity, with nearly a third of the U.S. population identifying as some racial/ethnic heritage other than White. Examination of the 2010 U.S. census data indicates that Latinos represented over 16% of the population, an increase from 12% in the 2000 census (Humes, Jones, & Ramirez, 2011). African Americans were 12.6% of the population, Asian Americans grew from 4% to 5%, and 1%

identify as American Indian. This racial/ethnic diversity in the population is increasingly reflected in the labor force, with a greater percentage of new entrants in the labor force identifying as racial/ethnic minority individuals. Because the increase in U.S. racial/ethnic diversity is still relatively recent, 80% of the overall labor force identifies as White/Caucasian, but, as we note below, the overall racial/ethnic diversity of the labor force is expected to increase in the next 10 years.

It is important to note that, while there is more racial/ethnic and gender diversity in the workforce, there are still considerable gender and racial disparities in occupational distributions. In other words, although more women are working, there are still pay inequities within the same occupation, and women and racial/ethnic minority men are much more likely to be in lower paying occupations. For example, African Americans and Latinos are much less likely to be in higher paying management and professional occupations and more likely to be lower paying jobs in food preparation, custodial, transportation, and service industries (Bureau of Labor Statistics, 2012). Asian Americans are more likely to be in scientific and engineering occupations and less likely to be in many service jobs (Bureau of Labor Statistics, 2012).

The average age of the labor force has increased, as the large population of individuals born in the post-World War II years through the mid 1960s (the "baby boomers") is aging. The psychological contract between employers and employees, which stipulated employee loyalty in exchange for job security and retirement benefits, shifted in the late 1990s and early 2000s (Lent & Brown, 2013). Employers, facing increased global competition and an economic recession, restructured to have smaller organizations and fewer obligations to provide benefits or job security. This trend began in the private sector and more recently has affected public sector employees. The result has been much more of an onus on individual employees to be flexible, to be able to find new employment or careers throughout their lifetimes, and to save for their own retirement. Young workers will enter the workforce expecting to be responsible for their own career path and in fact, may relish the freedom it gives them to change and try new opportunities and roles. Older workers, however, may feel quite angry and at a loss at the changes in the workforce.

The recession of 2008 heightened the sense that the world of work is rapidly changing, and that changes will only accelerate with new technological advances. As we discuss more thoroughly in Chapter 13, the Bureau of Labor Statistics publishes yearly projections of the fastest growing jobs, the occupations with the most projected growth, and projections based on demographic changes (Bureau of Labor Statistics, 2011). It is important for counselors to understand and keep up with projected changes to help clients make good work-related decisions. We caution, though, that these are just projections, and often real-world events intervene to make the projections obsolete. For example, projections for an outflow of retirees from the labor force in early 2010 proved to be wrong as the economic recession of 2008 led many retirement funds to lose money and individuals decided to postpone retirement. Sometimes technological advances have far greater impact than previously thought, creating new jobs and changing others. Thus, it is important to be aware of labor market projections and economic influences that affect work and job opportunities but to keep in perspective that current economic factors are but one influence in people's lives.

DEFINITION AND TYPES OF THEORIES

A theory is a series of connected hypothetical statements designed to explain a particular behavior or set of behaviors. We have, for example, theories to explain how people solve problems (e.g., Heppner & Lee, 2009), to predict causes of stress in the workplace (e.g., Long, Kahn, & Schutz, 1992), or to describe how humans develop socially and psychologically (e.g., Erikson, 1968). Theories serve a very important purpose in psychology and in counseling; they help psychologists and counselors to conceptualize human behavior. In essence, theories guide us in making sense of very complex sets of information about how humans behave to help us understand them and to predict their behavior in the future.

One useful way to envision the role of a theory is to view it as a map (Krumboltz, 1994). Both maps and theories are representations of reality designed for a particular purpose to help guide the user's understanding of a terrain. Motorists use maps (or GPS devices) to facilitate traveling from point A to point B; counselors use career theories to help them explain a client's vocational behavior. Krumboltz notes that maps and theories can be useful for one purpose and not for another. Vocational theories, for example, are useful to help understand career choices but might be less useful in other situations.

Krumboltz (1994) also notes that theories designed to explain and predict complex human behavior must, of necessity, omit some aspects of behavior, distort other aspects to highlight them, and depict some unobservable conditions as reality. Thus, a vocational theory may include some variables that help explain career choices but may omit behavior related to interpersonal relationships. The theory may label some behavior to bring attention to it. The Theory of Work Adjustment (Dawis, 2005; Dawis & Lofquist, 1984), for example, has a number of unique identifiers for work-related behavior, such as satisfactoriness, to highlight those aspects of behavior the theory is designed to explain. Other theories have developed labels to highlight behavior leading to a career choice rather than to highlight behavior in a work setting. None of the theories explains all work-related behaviors, and in this way, theories distort the reality of the very complicated behavior related to making career decisions prior to and following the entry into the world of work. And all theories make some assumptions about internal conditions that are not observable. Super's theory (Hartung, 2013; Super, Savickas, & Super, 1996) includes an assumption that vocational choice is the implementation of the self-concept; this is not directly observable, yet it is a central tenet of his theory.

CLARIFYING DISTINCTIONS BETWEEN THEORIES AND THEORETICAL ORIENTATIONS

We have introduced several slightly different terms, which may cause some confusion: *theoretical orientation, career development theories,* and *career counseling theories.* The term *theoretical orientation* is most frequently used to describe one's general philosophical stance about the nature of personality and of therapeutic change, such as humanistic, cognitive-behavioral, or family systems. One's theoretical orientation interacts with one's view of career development and of career counseling, although this interaction is rarely discussed because of the manner in which we often compartmentalize career counseling and personal counseling, or career issues and personal issues within counseling. We revisit the issue of "career versus personal" in Chapter 14.

Our discussion about career-related theories has, thus far, focused on theories of career *development* rather than on theories of career *counseling;* yet they are not identical. Theories of career *development* were devised to explain vocational behavior, such as initial career choice, work adjustment, or life span career progress. The goal of theories of career *counseling,* on the other hand, is to provide counselors with direction for how to work with clients; these theories are more akin to theoretical orientation as defined earlier.

The distinction between theories of career development and career counseling is an important one. In fact, Osipow (1996) contends that no career counseling theory exists. There have been, however, several models for conducting career counseling, and we will discuss one model in Chapter 5. Moreover, there have been some efforts to apply psychotherapy theoretical orientations to career counseling, such as psychodynamic career counseling (Watkins & Savickas, 1990) and person-centered career counseling (Bozarth & Fisher, 1990), as well as efforts to more explicitly link career development theories to career counseling (Savickas & Walsh, 1996).

So a counselor might describe her general therapeutic theoretical orientation as cognitive-behavioral, her view of career development as guided by Holland's

(1997) typological theory, and her work with clients as following Fouad and Bingham's Culturally Appropriate Career Counseling Model (1995) of career counseling, with the central attention to the client's cultural context. These descriptors do not contradict one another, because they all influence how this particular counselor views her clients and affect her in-session behavior and interventions with clients. Counselors develop their theoretical affinities through exposure to different perspectives and through their own clinical experience.

We advocate that career development theories be used in career counseling to help practitioners determine the most appropriate and effective tools to help clients. This is an ideal situation, however, and one met with some skepticism by practitioners and researchers alike. Lucas (1996), for example, points out that "counselors insist on relevance, [and the theory-driven research published in] journals [does] not provide it" (p. 82).

The biggest concern voiced by practitioners is that career development theories explain pieces of vocational behavior, but no client ever walks into an office with just the exact piece explained by the theory. Practitioners contend that some theories do not adequately explain the career behavior of women, racial and ethnic minority clients, or lesbian and gay clients. They find that other theories do not discuss the interface between work and family or that they do not adequately address the myriad problems a client brings to counseling that include both career and personal concerns. This book does not specifically address the split between practitioners and academicians; there still remains the need for practice to inform science in a substantive way (Osipow, 1996). But we are suggesting that a counselor's solid theoretical grounding helps shape the way the counselor approaches the client and the questions he or she will ask. The counselor's preferred theory will also help determine the types of assessment tools used in counseling, as well as the interventions and techniques employed.

DEVELOPING HYPOTHESES AND A "WORKING MODEL" OF THE CLIENT

Each client who comes for career counseling brings a unique set of personal characteristics and life experiences. Yet a number of common dimensions can guide a counselor's work with clients. The specific dimensions of interest to a particular counselor will be determined by his or her theoretical orientation and the theories of career development and career counseling to which he or she subscribes.

One way in which career development theories influence career counseling is that they suggest hypotheses for further consideration and exploration. Walborn

(1996) describes a hypothesis as "an educated hunch that is grounded in theory" (p. 224) or that may emerge from the interaction between the client and counselor. Developing and sharing hypotheses with the client are critical components in any type of counseling or therapy, particularly in career counseling. Regardless of theoretical orientation, counselors have hunches about clients' presenting problems and what might be done to assist them. We demonstrate in Chapter 2 that many of these hypotheses should be informed by knowledge of the client's cultural contexts. Moreover, counselors "must be aware of where they are taking the client and, to do so, they must be aware of their hypotheses" (p. 225).

The language we use throughout this book reflects our focus on generating and testing hypotheses, and we strongly encourage the reader to adopt the inquisitive frame of mind that underlies hypothesis generation and hypothesis testing. The structure of the book offers many natural places for the reader to pause and reflect on (a) what is known about a particular client; (b) whether the reader's hypotheses have been confirmed, have been disconfirmed, or need further elaboration; and (c) additional hypotheses or speculations that the reader might make about a client. For example, in Chapter 4, Leslie's case history is first presented and summarized; then, assessment information is discussed and illustrated. The reader will form some impressions about Leslie based on her career history, so the reader can articulate those impressions before reading the section with Leslie's assessment results. Then the reader will review the assessment with his or her impressions and hypotheses in mind and search for confirming and disconfirming evidence.

Development of hypotheses begins with the very first exposure to the client, whether in person or through written intake case information, and is an ongoing process throughout counseling. Hypothesis development may need to be an explicitly conscious exercise for new counselors, but it becomes an automatic process as counselors gain experience. It is important for counselors to be aware of and be able to articulate the hypotheses that they form, whether consciously or unconsciously.

Refinement of hypotheses continues throughout counseling. Walborn (1996) suggests a number of benefits of continual development of hypotheses, including helping the counselor remain an active rather than passive listener, keeping counseling sessions focused, providing alternative interpretations of the client's problem, and fostering a collaborative relationship between counselor and client.

Counselors use all sources of available information to generate hypotheses. Moreover, counselors look for consistent themes across several sources of information as well as for inconsistencies between sources. For example, John's highest interest inventory scores are in the artistic area, and he reports that the course he enjoyed most last semester was art history. However, he is performing poorly in a photography course this semester. These bits of information provide both consistency and inconsistency, resulting in a hypothesis that merits further investigation: John enjoys artistic, flexible, creative environments as a spectator; he doesn't have artistic skills or abilities, nor does he enjoy producing art. How does the counselor then test this hypothesis? The most direct way is to simply offer the hypothesis to John to see how he reacts and to invite him to gather evidence related to the hypothesis. For example, John's counselor might comment, "You seem to have a strong interest in artistic activities but perhaps more as an observer or appreciator of art rather than as a 'doer' of art. How does that fit?" The goal is to help John discover something new about himself or to clarify something he already knows and help him integrate it within his view of himself.

Sometimes, a client already knows what the counselor offers as a hypothesis; for example, it may be quite clear to John that he doesn't have strong artistic skills but that he still enjoys learning about art. At other times, a client may not have thought about his or her interests and activities in quite the same way that the counselor has presented the hypothesis, and further discussion helps clarify information about himself or herself. It therefore becomes very important that the counselor makes it clear that the hypotheses are just that—hunches about the client that await further evidence and verification.

Counselors communicate the hypothetical nature of their statements via several methods. First, counselors use tentative language when offering hypotheses to clients so that they are not perceived as statements of fact. For example, a counselor might say, "I'm wondering if you might prefer selling ideas rather than selling products," or "It seems that you're most comfortable in situations where you clearly know what's expected of you." Second, counselors engage clients in a collaborative effort to develop and examine hypotheses, primarily by paying attention to the development of the counselor-client relationship. If the client feels that he or she is in a comfortable, collaborative relationship, then the client will be more likely to disagree with the counselor if the hypothesis is not accurate. The counselor might ask, "What do *you* think? How does that fit with what you know about yourself?" Finally, counselors need to remind themselves (and their clients) that they are offering hypotheses that are in need of further evidence and to search thoroughly for such evidence: "What other experiences have you had that support your pursuing an artistic career? How else might you 'test out' your interests and skills?"

Walborn (1996) argues that verbal disclosure of a counselor's hypotheses about the client is a necessary, but not sufficient, condition for effective therapy. The way in which hypotheses are shared with the client depends on the stage of counseling; the client himself or herself; the strength of the client-counselor relationship; and, perhaps, the theoretical orientation of the counselor. Within the realm of personal-emotional counseling, Walborn suggests that the presentation of hypotheses differs by schools of therapy. Humanistic approaches use reflection as the major technique because it directs the client's attention to something that the counselor deems important. Explicit disclosure of hypotheses is a fundamental basis of cognitive approaches, and hypotheses are most often related to a client's faulty cognitions. Finally, a variety of methods are used to disclose hypotheses in psychodynamic approaches, such as interpretation and catharsis. These stylistic differences in how hypotheses are offered and explored also may be seen in career counseling. For example, counselors using Holland's theory of vocational personalities might use a didactic style, and constructivist counselors would be likely to develop a collaborative approach to developing hypotheses with the client.

A final point is that counselors need to judge whether their hypotheses are accurate. First, the counselor must consider whether the hypothesis is culture bound. In other words, is the hypothesis appropriate for the client's culture and gender, or is it based on the counselor's own cultural background? Accuracy may be determined by the client's reaction to the hypothesis and by gathering further evidence to test its veridicality. Furthermore, Walborn (1996) suggests that the *process* of developing and sharing a hypothesis actually may be more important than the *content* of the hypothesis. In other words, one outcome of hypothesis testing is that the client learns self-exploration skills, which is important in and of itself.

A caveat about formulating hypotheses about clients: Hypotheses and "working models" should never be used to label prematurely, infer conclusions, or make judgments about clients. While it might be tempting for a counselor to think he or she has the client "all figured out," the counselor should always remain open to new evidence and be prepared to alter his or her view of the client in response to new information. Research examining how counselors form and test hypotheses suggests that counselors tend to pay more attention to new information that confirms their hypotheses at the expense of information that disconfirms their hypotheses. This research serves as a reminder that counselors need to consider as much information as possible (Garb, 1998; Pfeiffer, Whelan, & Martin, 2000; Spengler et al., 2009).

ORGANIZATION OF THE BOOK

The book consists of three sections. Career counselors, of course, need to be competent in a number of areas related to counseling, including understanding the career counseling process, conceptualizing a client's problem in a helpful manner, and being aware of various practical issues affecting career services. Thus, the three sections are organized to first, provide an overview and introduction to the fundamentals of career counseling; second, to provide an overview of theoretical perspectives to provide a foundation for client conceptualization; and, third, to provide some practical information on career interventions, world-of-work information and integrating career and mental health concerns.

In addition to this introduction and overview, the initial section (Part I, Fundamentals) includes chapters related to contextual factors influencing work related decisions (Chapter 2), using assessment in career counseling (Chapter 3), and the structure and process of career counseling (Chapter 5). We also introduce our main case of Leslie in Chapter 4, providing basic information about her context and work history. We build on the case of Leslie throughout the book as we consider her from a variety of different perspectives.

The second section (Part II, Theories) provides an overview and practical applications of career theories. The theories discussed in this book are attempts to explain some career-related behavior. Each theory overlaps with the others in some ways, but each has distinct constructs. In some ways, however, each theory may be viewed as attempting to explain different aspects of the proverbial elephant; depending on the theorist's vantage point, different aspects of behavior are emphasized.

Although there is considerable overlap among the major vocational theories discussed in this book, they each explain some unique work-related behaviors and thus are useful guides for counselors. Without a theoretical framework to guide us, we would find it very difficult to make sense of the information clients might bring to us about their work-related problems. To return to the map or GPS analogy, we consult a road map before we leave on a trip to know the best way to get to our destination; without a map, we may wander aimlessly. So a good theory helps us represent reality, understand behavior, and assist clients in understanding their behavior.

We chose several different theoretical approaches for inclusion in Part II of this book. Three of the theories have long histories of scholarship and recognition (Hackett, Lent, & Greenhaus, 1991): Holland's (1997) typological theory of persons and environments, Dawis and Lofquist's (1984; Dawis, 2005) theory of work adjustment, and Super's (Super, Savickas, & Super, 1996) life span, life space approach. The fourth theory, Lent, Brown, and Hackett's (1994) social cognitive career theory has achieved considerable stature in the past two decades. A fifth theory, Gottfredson's (2005) theory of circumscription and compromise, was included despite having less empirical support because of its appeal to practitioners and its explicit attention to early socialization. Finally, we include a chapter on emerging theories to highlight new approaches and perspectives.

A danger in presenting each theory separately is that this organization might foster a polarization of the theories, as well as the implication that one must choose a specific theory and not deviate from that choice. Nothing could be further from the truth. What we hope will become evident throughout the book is that each theory has some unique and useful perspectives to offer a consideration of Leslie, the primary case described in Chapter 4. Moreover, each theory may be particularly useful for a specific type of client, as evidenced by the additional cases provided in each chapter. Despite the organizational structure, we encourage the reader to think integratively across the theoretical perspectives, and we provide some assistance in doing so in the final summary chapter (Chapter 15). There, we model how we as counselors might approach a case from an integrated theoretical approach, and we summarize how each theoretical perspective added to our understanding of Leslie.

Finally, the third section of the book (Part III, Practical Applications) highlights additional competencies that career counselors need to develop. Counselors who focus primarily on career issues, depending on their setting, use a number of interventions in addition to individual career counseling. We discuss the practical issues and ethical concerns related to the career interventions in schools, higher education institutions, and community settings in Chapter 12. Chapter 13 includes a review of the types of available occupational information and the practical ways that world-of-work information is used in career counseling. In Chapter 14, we provide an overview of the importance of a holistic perspective of the client, and the frequent need to integrate career and noncareer concerns, but also provide some perspectives and guidelines on when a referral to another counselor is indicated. Finally, in Chapter 15, we summarize our approach to career counseling.

SUMMARY

We have presented the preceding issues in some detail, because each is crucial to considering how to apply theories of career development to real client issues.

We encourage you now to return to the three vignettes at the beginning of this chapter—brief stories of Ruth, Harry, and Joel. Imagine that any one of these people has come to you for counseling. What impressions do you have of each one? What do you think about his or her work or career concerns? What additional information would you like to know? How might you begin to address the concerns these people have expressed?

Now think back to a time when you had career or work-related concerns, such as an unsatisfying job, an inability to find work, or uncertainty about which career direction to choose. How did these concerns affect other aspects of your life? How did you resolve the concerns? Use the questions in Box 1.1 to guide your personal reflection.

BOX 1.1 Personal Reflection

- What have been some of the key transition points in my own career and work history? How did I make decisions along those points? Who influenced my decisions?
- What assumptions does society make about work? Do I agree with those assumptions?
- How have economic factors influenced my decision making?
- How has my context (gender, family, race/ethnicity, religion, disability status) helped shape my career decisions?

Chapter 2

Cultural Contexts and Career Counseling

Mark, a White career counselor specializing in midlife career transitions, has two new clients. The first is an African American lesbian from a conservative Muslim family who is seeking to change careers in her 40s. Mark has been trained to consider culture and so knows that he needs to have an understanding of the cultural values of African Americans, of career issues facing lesbians, and an understanding of the Muslim faith that may suggest conflicts between the client's sexual orientation and faith. He plans to ask the client which of her cultural contexts are most salient to her (race, sexual orientation, faith, age?) and where she is feeling conflict. He wants to know her career history and how discrimination may have shaped her choices and perceptions of opportunity.

Mark's second client is a White man in his 50s who is considering taking a new position in another company prior to retirement. Because they are the same race, Mark does not ask his client about cultural context. Because they are both men, Mark assumes that work plays a similar role in his client's life as it does in his own. Thus, he misses key information about the client's social class and upbringing and the importance of his role as a provider that would have helped him be more effective. The client was raised in considerable poverty in rural Nebraska, had to drop out of high school to support his family, and was able to work his way up the corporate ladder without the typical education his position requires. It is very important to him to be the primary provider for his family. His consideration of a new position is shaped strongly by the need for job security and fear of judgment about his lack of education.

These two cases highlight that all clients operate within a cultural context, which helps form their environments and their responses to the environment. Clients' contexts must be taken into consideration in developing hypotheses about clients because contextual factors shape clients' approach to work, the messages they receive about appropriate work, and the role that they want work to play in their lives. But, as we highlighted in the example of Mark, it is critical that career counselors first have a foundational understanding of the potential influences of context on their *own* perceptions and worldviews as well as on their clients' perceptions and worldviews. This is based on ethical practice (NCDA Ethical Code A: Professional Relationships, 2007), and is consistent with the "Multicultural Minimum Career Counseling Competencies" (NCDA, 2009) and the "Guidelines on Multicultural Education, Training, Research, Practice, and Organizational Change for Psychologists" (APA, 2003). The NCDA Career Counseling Competencies mandate that the competent career counselor "is aware of his/her own cultural beliefs and assumptions and incorporates that awareness into his/her decision-making about interactions with clients/students and other career professionals" (p. 1).

In Chapter 1, we asked you to reflect generally on how your context shaped your perspectives about work. Now, we ask you for a more careful examination. Consider the questions in Box 2. 1, which will help you think through the way your context has influenced your own thinking about work, the messages you received about what kind of work was appropriate, and the role that work plays in your life. It is important to gain self-awareness about your assumptions and beliefs about work so that you do not impose them on your clients, who may have different beliefs.

In this chapter, we discuss the need for an understanding of the implications of various contextual factors on work related decisions. By context we mean clients' psychological perspectives and worldviews that are shaped by their background, including such aspects as their culture, race/ethnicity, gender, social class, sexual orientation, religion, and/or disability status. Individuals' contexts may shape their decisions in several ways. For some, cultural values or family expectations shape the type of work they will choose to do or feel is appropriate. For others, choices are limited by real and perceived barriers, such as limitations due to racism, sexism, or heterosexism. Career counselors must have an understanding of the potential role of context in clients' lives. This is the foundation of culturally responsive career counseling.

BOX 2.1 Personal Reflection

- Fill in the blank with at least two occupations: Most _____ are men. Most _____ are women. Where did I learn those perceptions? How might these perceptions influence my work with a client who wanted an occupation that was nontraditional for her/his gender?
- Draw a family genogram (grandparents, parents/guardians, siblings, aunts/uncles, cousins) with each person's educational level and occupation. What are the common themes among the types of education and work for my family? What are my family's expectations about appropriate educational levels? What do the themes tell me about occupations that are acceptable (or unacceptable)? What messages did I receive from my family about "good" work? How might I guard against passing those messages about "good" or "bad" work to my clients?
- Are there some occupations that seemed possible for me to pursue? Are there some occupations that seemed out of the range of possibility? Has my race/ethnicity, gender, social class, or sexual orientation played a role in deciding whether or not an occupation is possible?

CULTURALLY RESPONSIVE CAREER COUNSELING

Culturally responsive career counseling is good for *all* clients. All clients come to counseling with unique biological, social, and developmental experiences that are products of the cultures to which they belong. It is also critical to note that belonging to a culture does not automatically mean that a client will display one characteristic or another. Rather, there is great heterogeneity within groups. Counselors need to be flexible enough to incorporate the cultural variables salient to the client. This requires that the counselor has developed multicultural competencies and is prepared for culturally appropriate counseling (Sue & Sue, 2013). While we discuss various contextual factors that may influence clients' work-related decisions, it is beyond the scope of this chapter to address all possible contextual factors that clients bring to counseling. We refer readers to Sue and Sue (2013) for general multicultural counseling considerations and Brown and Lent (2013) and Blustein (2013) for in-depth discussion of contextual factors related to career counseling.

A central tenet of culturally appropriate career counseling is that effective career counselors do not treat all clients the same, assuming their cultural experiences are uniform, but will approach each client as belonging to one or more cultures. For example, a client may be an Asian American man married to a White woman, working in a company headed by an African American and living in an ethnically diverse, middle-class neighborhood. He may feel that he belongs to several cultures; some may be more salient to him than others. His counselor needs to be aware of his multiple cultures and how they interact. His goals will reflect his cultural contexts, indicating which are most salient to him.

Culturally appropriate counseling requires that the counselor have knowledge and skills to work with specific cultural groups. A counselor working with Hmong clients in the Midwest needs to know the history of the Hmong immigration to the United States, the development of their written language, and their cultural norms and values. A career counselor working with a transgender client needs to understand the issues relevant to the transition from one sex to another and the workplace concerns of transgender individuals. A counselor working with a woman who is seeking to be an electrical engineer will need to understand the issues for women choosing nontraditional occupations. But while counselors need to know certain group-specific issues, counselors also need to be aware of several overarching variables that may affect many clients.

FOUAD AND KANTAMNENI'S THREE-DIMENSIONAL MODEL

To help career counselors capture the complexity and intersections of various aspects of identity and how they influence career and work decisions, we have adopted the three dimensional model proposed by Fouad and Kantamneni (2008) and shown in Figure 2.1.

The first dimension includes individual characteristics that influence work choices, such as interests, values, and abilities. These characteristics encompass the traditional areas that career counselors have emphasized: what a client is able to do, is interested in, and what choices are consistent with the client's values. We focus on assessing these constructs in Chapter 3, and, indeed the assessment of interests, abilities, and values forms the heart of much of career counseling.

But the relationship between individuals' interests, abilities, and values and the possible choices they consider are shaped by the second and third dimensions of the model. The group level variables in the second dimension encompass gender, race/ethnicity, social class, family variables, religion, sexual orientation, and relationships. Thus, individuals' work choices are influenced not only by their own interests, abilities, and values but also by the messages they received about appropriate and possible work based on those group-level dimensions. Some individuals, for example, would not consider an occupation in which the workers are mostly the opposite sex. Others might choose work that they would consider friendly to gays and lesbians, while still others might choose work in which they feel a spiritual calling.

Figure 2.1 Fouad and Kantamneni's Three-Dimensional Model

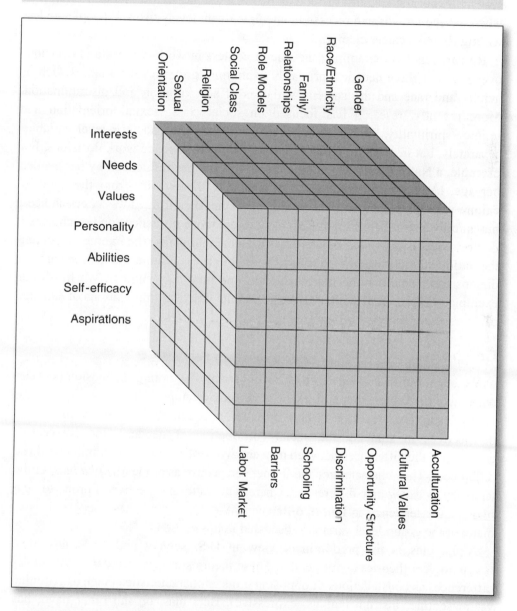

The third dimension is the broader society in which individuals live. Some individuals may feel they belong to the majority culture in the United States and their cultural values, such as achievement, recognition or helping others, influence their work choices and decisions. For others, the predominant values in their culture of origin differ from the majority culture, and these differences influence work decisions as well (including acculturation, discrimination and cultural barriers). This third dimension also includes the societal effects such as educational systems, labor market, and the economy. For example, as we noted in Chapter 1, when the economy is in a recession, unemployment levels rise and people are less willing to make career changes.

Researchers have examined the role of context in work choices and decisions over the past three decades, primarily examining group-level variables such as gender and race and the societal variables of acculturation and discrimination. More recently, research has focused on social class, sexual orientation and religion/spirituality. We discuss selected group-level and societal-level variables separately, but in real life, many aspects of context influence work decisions. For example, a Native American woman in her 30s may be influenced by her gender, her age, her Native American values and how those differ from the majority culture values. She may not know which are important influences on her choices, but an effective counselor will help her explore those influences on her choices.

The model portrayed in Figure 2.1 is a cube, highlighting the interaction among the various dimensions. More critically, although we assume interactions among dimensions, some may be more salient at one time than another. We finish our examination of context with a discussion of the practical implications of salience of intersecting aspects of identity.

Group-Level Variables

We begin our discussion of group-level variables by noting the tension between wanting to treat all group members the same and overemphasizing those differences. Hare-Mustin and Marecek (1988) provided a useful distinction on these two perspectives in studying the social construction of gender: One perspective emphasizes the differences between men and women, and the other minimizes those differences. They characterized the former perspective as prone to *alpha bias*, or the tendency to exaggerate differences, whereas the latter perspective is prone to *beta bias*, or the tendency to ignore differences. We can extend these perspectives to many of the group-level variables discussed in this section.

Alpha bias is the predominant view in U.S. society and underpins most psychological theories about gender. These theories propose fundamental gender differences as constellations of opposing traits or characteristics (such as feminine vs. masculine, instrumental vs. expressive). Beta bias, on the other hand, has received less attention but also exists in many theories of psychological development, particularly in the assumption that psychological development is the same across all races and for all types of sexual orientations. Beta bias is evident in theories and practices that attempt to treat men and women, and individuals of all races and sexual orientations, equally, yet may inadvertently perpetuate inequality.

One consequence of alpha bias is that observed sex or race differences may be overinterpreted as essential qualities, when they may be due to differences in the social hierarchy. For example, demonstrated sex differences in vocational interests, such as women's interest in social activities, may not be due to women's inherent relational nature but because social-type careers include lower prestige occupations that are more accessible to women. Moreover, by emphasizing between-group variability, alpha bias leads to minimization of within-group variability, such as the large differences in men's adherence to various gender role expectations. Thus, theories concerning gender tend to overlook differences among women and men that may be related to myriad factors such as race and ethnicity, age, disability status, social class, marital status, parental status, or sexual orientation.

Consequences of beta bias are more subtle in nature and, on the surface, may seem trivial. After all, what's wrong with arguing for little difference between men and women or different racial groups and therefore treating them similarly? However, ignoring special needs of women or men, or the influences of racism on psychological development of racial/ethnic minorities, may also underestimate differential allocation of resources and power and ultimately disadvantage women, men, or minority group members. Hare-Mustin and Marecek (1988) point out that "in a society in which one group holds most of the power, seemingly neutral actions usually benefit members of that group" (p. 460). In the realm of career and educational attainment, Betz (1989, 2005) discusses the "null environment" in which individuals are neither encouraged nor discouraged but simply ignored. The null environment, according to the originator of the concept (Freeman, 1979), has a greater effect on women because of the cumulative effect of negative messages about their pursuit of career goals. Heppner (2013) suggests that counselors be alert for women's implicit foreclosure of occupations because of gender biases and develop mechanisms to gently challenge those biases. By the same token, it can be argued that similar concerns need to be explored with men who foreclose on traditionally female occupations.

Gender

It is axiomatic to say that gender is important throughout an individual's life. Baby clothes and blankets are color-coded (pink for girls, blue for boys), toys are gender specific (trucks for boys, dolls for girls), and from an early age, boys and girls demonstrate (or are rewarded for demonstrating) different interests. It seems reasonable that these different expectations of behavior on boys and girls would result in different career choices. Until the 1970s, gender socialization practices traditionally expected girls to be helpers and boys to be prepared to be providers for their families. These different expectations led to separate career trajectories and decisions, with women either choosing not to work or choosing to stop in and out of the work environment as they took primary responsibility for their families. The effect on men was to considerably restrict their options and their ability to be involved with their families. Although the past five decades have witnessed dramatic changes in work force participation by women and greater options for men, the traditional socialization patterns and messages have continued to exert subtle influences on the work decisions of both men and women.

Many authors have argued that traditional theories of career development are really theories about and for White, middle-class males, so it is natural to focus our attention to how career theory and practice may better serve women. But clearly, men also are influenced by gender socialization and the gendered context in which they make career choices. Societal expectations of the male gender role and what types of occupations are appropriate for men may restrict the range of options of occupations. However, the enormous societal changes that have occurred for women brought about changes for men as well—in their conceptions of the role of work in their lives, in the expectations that are placed upon them by society, and in the structure of the family and interpersonal relationships. It is still important to note that gender socialization occurs for both males and females in this society, beginning from birth onward, through childhood, adolescence, and into adulthood.

Race/ethnicity

Just as gender has a strong role in career and work-related choices, so does an individual's race and ethnicity. We noted in Chapter 1 that there is large occupational segregation by race/ethnicity, as well as gender, with an overrepresentation of racial/ethnic group individuals in the lower SES levels and overrepresentation of White men in higher SES levels. The strong relationships between SES and educational attainment and occupational level have led to a continuous cycle of poor and poorly educated minority men and women (Arbona, 1996; Kenney & Walsh-Blair, 2012; Worthington, Flores, & Navarro, 2005). Discrimination has also played a role in keeping individuals trapped in this cycle. Overt sexism and racism are outlawed in the United States, but unfortunately, covert sexism and racism are still facts of life for women and racial/ethnic minorities and often limit the options that individuals may consider and restrict their access to a wide variety of opportunities (Byars-Winston, Kantamneni, & Mobley, 2012). In addition, the relationship between discrimination and poverty has a particularly disproportionate effect on racial/ethnic groups and single women, including negative effects of discrimination on mental health (Roberts, Swanson, & Murphy, 2004).

The statistics outlined in Chapter 1 show racial and ethnic differences in work choices, but what is less clear is how these differences in career and work choices occur. Are they a result of individual choices, shaped by interests and values? Or are these choices a result of compromises and perceptions of limited opportunities? We do know there are no racial/ethnic differences in children's career dreams and aspirations, but there are differences in the careers that children expect to do (Fouad & Byars-Winston, 2005), so we know that something occurs to circumscribe racial/ethnic minority children's dreams. More research is needed to understand the mechanisms by which race and ethnic group membership influences work decisions.

Relational and familial influences

Traditional notions of career development suggest that work choices are made individually. However, researchers and career counselors are increasingly acknowledging the role that relationships and family play in career decisions (Blustein, 2011; Richardson, 2012). Researchers have shown that positive family relationships can help individuals feel free to explore various careers while negative relationships can restrict behaviors leading to career exploration (Blustein, Schultheiss, & Flum, 2004; Richie et al., 1997). The role of family in influencing career decisions differs by culture and gender (Fouad et al., 2010), and it is important for career counselors to ask about messages that clients may have received from their family about work and careers.

Other relationships can be important in work-related decisions. For example, role models have been found to be influential, and Gibson (2004) suggested that identification with role models can be critical in career decision making. Role models could serve as mentors, as providers of information about career outcomes, and as supports in the decision-making process. In addition, social cognitive career theory explicitly incorporates role models as a source of self-efficacy and outcome expectation information (Lent, Brown, & Hackett, 1994).

Social class

Social class has long been discussed as a contextual variable but has just begun to be empirically explored as a contextual influence. As we discuss in Chapter 11, a major criticism of the field is that it has neglected the concerns of poor or working class individuals when compared to middle class or wealthy individuals (Blustein, 2006). Yet social class clearly is an influential factor in career development. Social class is fundamental in shaping access to resources and influencing career aspirations, development, and eventual career attainment

(Blustein et al., 2002; Brown, Fukunaga, Umemoto, & Wicker, 1996; Fouad & Brown, 2000). For example, lower income students are less likely to be raised in homes with enriched learning environments, less likely to receive career guidance and information from their parents, and less likely to have strong career expectations, which leads to lower career attainment (Fouad & Byars-Winston, 2005).

Societal-Level Variables

In general, the values transmitted via societal assumptions affect views on work, perceptions of possible choices and the overall career trajectory. It is important to note that cultures differ on a number of variables related to work (Gelfand, Erez, & Aycan, 2007). The United States is considered to be an individualistic society (Triandis & Gelfand, 2012), as opposed to a society more oriented to the collective (e.g., family, group, or clan). Societies also differ in emphasis on work as an end in itself (doing) versus work means to an end (being). The former is the traditional perspective in the United States, with an emphasis on the primacy of work. The latter puts work in the context of other aspects of life, such as family, friends, and leisure time. Societal values can differ in emphasis on achievement (what individuals accomplish) versus ascription (the family into which they were born). Societal values are often so deeply embedded that clients may not be aware of their influence on career choices, but it may be helpful to explore these values to gain a full understanding of the meaning of work in people's lives (Kim et al., 2006).

Difference from mainstream culture

The United States includes individuals from many backgrounds who bring values and perspectives from their own culture of origin, who may then encounter conflicting experiences and messages related to the world of work in the larger mainstream United States. Recent qualitative studies have highlighted this experience, as racial/ethnic minority individuals described having to navigate between two cultures (Gomez et al., 2001, Juntunen et al., 2001). Participants, all whom had successful careers, reported essentially developing a bicultural identity that allowed them to incorporate values from both cultures in making work-related decisions.

Two factors influence the way that individuals navigate between two cultures. The first is acculturation, which describes the way individuals change, accommodate, or adopt the cultural patterns of the "host" society (Kohatsu, 2005). Some individuals completely acculturate to the United States, some are able to be bicultural, retaining the cultural patterns of their culture of origin and adopt certain patterns of the United States, and still others are unable to accommodate or acculturate to the United States. As may be clear, the role of acculturation can be very influential in perceiving and obtaining work in the United States.

Discrimination is the second factor that influences how individuals navigate between two cultures. The potential impact of discrimination was illuminated in the racial/ethnic differences in employment and unemployment described in Chapter 1. It is difficult to tease apart the anticipated consequences of discrimination, limits in the perceptions of opportunities, and the results of overt discrimination. Nonetheless, discrimination strongly influences an individual's perceived and actual barriers in educational and occupational opportunities and ultimately an individual's work trajectory.

However, despite actual and perceived barriers, many individuals successfully achieve. Returning to the qualitative studies described earlier (e.g., Gomez et al., 2001; Juntunen et al., 2001; Richie et al., 1997) participants noted sources of resilience in the face of barriers, including support from their families, a strong sense of identity, and feelings of passion about their work. Bicultural individuals also have been found to be satisfied and have a strong sense of well-being, highlighting the strengths and resilience that comes with operating in two cultures (Quintana, Chew, & Schell, 2012). Career counselors are encouraged to ask clients about sources of cultural strengths.

Influences from mainstream culture

Individuals in the United States work within a society that transmits central assumptions about work in general. For example, U.S. assumptions include: "Everyone should work; Mothers should not work; All work is good; Some work is better than others; Working with one's hands is good; Working with one's mind is better than working with one's hands; Education ought to result in better work; Education ought to result in better pay." These societal assumptions shape expectations about work. The larger societal beliefs influence the perceptions of whether to work, how much to work, and which work to do.

As we noted earlier, the U.S. mainstream culture emphasizes doing rather than being; has a high value on achievement; is somewhat low on tolerance for uncertainty and somewhat low on power distance, or the distance between those in authority and subordinates (Gefland et al., 2007). These values shape policies around individual achievement, educational opportunities for all, and limited unemployment and family leave benefits. Educational policies and funding for schooling helps shape eventual career and work opportunities. For example, concerns about the science and math abilities of U.S. students relative to many other countries have led to additional funding for science, technology, engineering and math education. The recession of 2008 and increasing globalization have also influenced how individuals make work-related choices and decisions.

Individual, Group, and Societal Intersections

As we noted earlier, although we discussed each dimension separately, in reality they overlap and for many people it is impossible to distinguish the various influences on their decisions. Parental values are shaped by their culture of origin and influences from the mainstream society and are then transmitted to their children. The type of school individuals attend interacts with their social class that helps shape their opportunities to develop interests. It is not crucial that career counselors or their clients are able to pinpoint the origin of specific influences on clients' choices. Rather, it is important that counselors be aware of the many contextual influences that may affect clients' choices, and how choices may differ across clients because of their context.

It is also critical that career counselors be aware that while the various dimensions intersect and overlap they all contribute to an individual's sense of identity. More importantly, some aspects of identity are more salient at one time than at other times. Consider the following case:

> Amelia is a 25 year old Mexican American woman who was born in Los Angeles. She graduated from high school with a very high grade point average. Following high school, she worked for three years and then went to a community college to study to be a physical therapy assistant. She is the oldest of five siblings, lives at home, and often helps her mother take care of her siblings, so has been unable to go to school full time. She has three more classes to take and is now reconsidering her decision to enter this program. She seeks career counseling to decide whether to continue in the physical therapy assistant program, change to another program, or to transfer to another school.

If you were Amelia's career counselor, what sorts of questions would you have about her context? You might, for example, want to know more about her Mexican American heritage. How long has her family been in the United States, and how strongly does Amelia identify with her Mexican American heritage? Does she feel she has to navigate between two cultures, or is she feeling strongly identified with one culture or the other? What messages has her family given her about education and work? Did she choose to stay home to help with her siblings, and how does she feel about its impact on her ability to continue in school? You might want to know more about how she chose to attend community college and how she chose to become a physical therapy assistant. She did well in high school, so did she foreclose other options? And if she did foreclose options, what were some of the barriers she perceived? Were they financial barriers, or were they barriers due to perceptions of opportunities for women, or for Latinas? What influences are most important in her decision to change her major or career trajectory at this point? In other words, many of the group- and societal-level barriers may be interacting to shape Amelia's work and career choices.

Now consider the above case, but instead of Amelia, the client is Demond, an African American man, who lives in a small town in North Carolina. How does his gender and race influence your perception of the case and the questions you would ask? Would you ask different questions because he is a man or because he is African American? Does the geographic region make a difference to your assumptions, or that he is in a rural setting versus the urban setting of Los Angeles? Do you have the same questions about navigating between two cultures? Would you want to know more about the potential influence of discrimination instead of acculturation?

The cases above illustrate the intersections among the various dimensions of individual, group, and societal influences on work-related decisions. Often, we hear our students worry that this is too complex and that they may get the questions wrong. We do not mean to suggest there is any one way to ask these questions, or even that these specific questions need to be raised. Rather, we are reflecting the very real set of multiple influences that affect individuals' career and work decisions, because it *is* complex. Ignoring the multiple potential influences is, in effect, a beta bias, treating all clients as if they are the same when there are influences stemming from many group and societal level differences. More critically, this beta bias could result in ineffective career counseling. And the complexity is compounded by the fact that, while counselors need to be aware of the potential influences because of group and societal levels, not all those influences will be apparent or even important to any individual client. Some aspects may be more or less salient at any given time. Amelia's family may have lived in Los Angeles for many generations and she feels so acculturated she does not consider her Mexican American heritage to be salient to her decisions. Demond may feel that his gender is much more salient in choosing to be a physical therapy assistant than his race.

We suggest two ways to visualize the salience of various contextual factors on career and work-related decisions. The first is to use the cube model in Figure 2.1, while the second is to use circles within a sphere, which is discussed in depth in Chapter 5. Recall that in Chapter 1 we discussed the importance of counselors generating hypotheses. In general, your hypotheses form the areas you might want to explore further. Consider the dimensions of the cube in Figure 2.1 for Amelia, and identify the specific parts of the cube you might consider salient for Amelia. For example, these could include gender, race/ethnicity, social class, family, acculturation, and societal influences. What other hypotheses do you have and what else might you want to explore? Wilson likened the process of identifying aspects of the cube to windows, noting that "some windows are open" while others are closed (C. A. Wilson, personal communication, June 19, 2013). She meant that some aspects of identity are more salient to the client and the counselor in counseling, as represented by open windows. The open windows are clearly areas for further exploration, but you may also want to develop hypotheses about shaded windows if you feel they are strong influences on the client's decision making.

To further illustrate our point, consider the example at the beginning of the chapter of the African American Muslim lesbian in her 40s. It is not immediately clear which of these multiple, sometimes conflicting identities are the most salient to her: age, religion, sexual orientation, family, gender. Mark, the counselor in the example, will not know until talking with her, but he also needs to be open to listening to "which windows are open" and important in her consideration of various choices.

PRACTICAL IMPLICATIONS

A number of authors have made practical suggestions on how to incorporate context into career counseling, often from one particular perspective. For example, Betz (2005) encouraged counselors to overtly attempt to restore options that have been taken away from women through societal sexism and stereotyped socialization. Heppner (2013) further suggests that counselors be aware that both men and women may need help dealing with gender-related biases. Fouad and Kantamneni (2013), writing about race and ethnicity in career counseling, recommend that counselors ask clients about their families' expectations of their career trajectory. Juntunen, Ali, and Pietrantonio (2013) suggest that counselors explicitly assess how clients view their own social class and ask how that perception may be influencing their career choices. Prince (2013) notes that "addressing sexual orientation requires addressing sexuality, a particularly difficult topic for many people and one that polarizes religious groups and political parties" (p. 288).

While each of the above authors was writing from one aspect of context, many of their recommendations overlap. We were guided by their suggestions in making the following recommendations in incorporating context into career counseling (Betz, 2005; Fouad & Kantamneni, 2013; Juntunen et al., 2013; Prince, 2013; Whiston, Fouad, & Juntunen, 2013).

1. Gain awareness of your own biases and assumptions about the role of group- and societal-level influences on work and career. This is critical to ensure you do not impose your own assumptions and biases on others.

2. Understand that clients will differ in their awareness of various contextual influences on their decisions; respect their level of awareness and ability to articulate those influences.

3. Examine work and career options that go beyond traditional gender roles.

4. Help clients counter restrictive occupational stereotypes.

5. Help identify barriers so as to develop appropriate interventions.

6. Help clients identify family expectations and cultural assumptions that influence career choices.

7. When clients want to go against family or cultural expectations, help them discuss potential cultural consequences of countering those expectations. How will their families react? Help clients identify ways to address resistance.

8. Help clients identify the strongest influences on their decisions. What role did gender, race/ethnicity, sexual orientation play in those decisions? Were some choices foreclosed due to group or societal level variables?

9. Examine differences between aspirations (career dreams), expectations and goals. Help clients reconcile those differences, particularly if options were prematurely foreclosed.

10. Help clients understand how racism may have influenced their perceptions of opportunities, and how cultural values may influence career aspirations.

11. Encourage as much math coursework as possible, given its role as a critical filter in entry to many career fields. Explore clients' levels of confidence for math and possible ways to counter low math self-efficacy.

12. Stress decisions that keep as many options open as possible.

13. Help clients identify supportive others, including family members.

14. Help identify cultural strengths and interventions to promote resilience.

We have discussed the importance of contextual influences in this chapter. As we have noted throughout the chapter, career counseling is most effective when it takes into account the multiple contextual and cultural influences on career and work decisions. We incorporate this perspective throughout the rest of the chapters in this book, most specifically incorporating culture into a model of career counseling in Chapter 5.

Chapter 3

Testing and Assessment

Tristan, a high school senior, comes to see you as his guidance counselor. He did well on his ACTs, is receiving many recruiting e-mails from universities, and some have offered scholarships. He is overwhelmed by the attention and has no idea how to choose from among the offers. Tristan does not know what he wants to major in and has done well on all his coursework, so it's clear he could choose from among many areas of study. He is seeking help in exploring options and making a decision.

You are a university career center counselor. Alyssa is referred to you for help by her academic advisor. She is a second semester sophomore and has just found out she was not accepted into the School of Nursing at the university. Alyssa has dreamt of being a nurse since she was a little girl and is devastated. She did not do well in Organic Chemistry, receiving a D, but thought her grade point average of 3.15 would be high enough to compensate. However, the School of Nursing is very competitive and the faculty view high performance in Chemistry as a key predictor in selection of students. She does not know how to choose a new major; she is too depressed to choose classes for next fall and is considering dropping out of college.

Brandon seeks career counseling because he is very dissatisfied in his current career. He does not know whether he should seek another job in the same field or if he should enter an entirely different career. He is in his mid-30s and has been a civil engineer for a transportation company since he graduated from college. He has been very dissatisfied with the lack of promotion opportunities and the lack of recognition he has received from his supervisor. Brandon is not sure if he wants to continue to use his engineering skills in another company or if he wants to explore another career. He and his wife plan to start a family in three years, so he has a short window of opportunity to start a new career and wants help sorting out possible options.

All three of these clients could benefit from career assessment to help them make decisions. Use of assessment takes a somewhat broader role in career counseling than in counseling for other issues. In personal-emotional counseling, a test is primarily used by the *counselor* to make diagnostic decisions and recommendations. In career counseling, assessment is used primarily for the *client's* benefit, for self-exploration and self-understanding (Duckworth, 1990; Haverkamp, 2013; Watkins & Campbell, 1990). Because of this expanded role of assessment, it is particularly important that counselors be knowledgeable so that they may explain assessment results to clients accurately, clearly, and in the proper context. Indeed, the National Career Development Association and the Association of Assessment in Counseling and Education (2010) highlight eight competencies to choose, interpret, and communicate the results of assessment tools. These include being able to choose assessment strategies, identifying appropriate tools, administering and scoring assessment tools, interpreting results, using results in decision making, presenting statistical information about results, engaging in ethical professional behavior, and using results to evaluate career intervention programs.

This chapter focuses on most of the competencies that career counselors need in using assessment tools. We discuss issues involved in choosing assessment strategies and tools, including understanding technical aspects of assessments, developing an understanding of how to choose appropriate assessment tools, understanding the assessment process, and understanding the limitations of assessments. We then discuss several assessment tools we have chosen to give to the case of Leslie (in Chapter 4) as well as assessment tools that are publicly available. Many other career assessment instruments are available and useful for a variety of career issues; readers are referred resources such as *A Counselor's Guide to Career Assessment* (Wood & Hayes, 2013) for more information. We then focus on issues involved in interpretation of assessment results, before, during, and after the assessment process. Finally, we discuss ethical issues related to assessment.

THE USE OF ASSESSMENT IN CAREER COUNSELING

Seligman's (1994) classic text discusses the benefits and limitations of testing and assessment in career counseling. Tests can be used to answer *what* questions (What are Tristan's primary interests? What difficulties is Alyssa having in making a career choice? What are Brandon's possible choices?) and *how* questions (How do Alyssa's interests compare with other women in scientific fields? How do Brandon's interests fit with his values?). Tests are less relevant to answering *why* questions (Why is Alyssa having difficulty making a career decision? Why hasn't Brandon changed jobs?). The *why* questions may be sources of further hypotheses about the client to explore in counseling (see Chapter 4 for an illustration of using Leslie's test results to develop hypotheses).

Historically, assessment has been an integral part of career counseling. However, not everyone agrees that assessment should play a central role in career counseling—or any role at all. Some counselors argue that testing unnecessarily "pigeonholes" or "labels" clients, or that there is too much cultural or sex bias built into existing tests, or that assessment overemphasizes a counselor's expertise and therefore creates distance between the counselor and the client. Haverkamp (2013) proposed a useful framework for understanding different perspectives on assessment, which takes into account how career assessment may differ from other types of psychological assessment. She defined two dimensions underlying the use of assessment (see Figure 3.1). The first, horizontal dimension describes the *purpose* of assessment, specifically addressing whose needs are being met by assessment, with clinical or organizational needs representing the "expert" end of the dimension and client needs representing the "collaborative" end of the dimension. The second, vertical dimension describes the type of information that is provided by assessment, or the basis on which inferences are made, with one end being a traditional, data-driven, nomothetic stance and the other end being a contextual, intuitive, and idiographic stance. Combining these two dimensions creates four quadrants, each describing different types of assessment or different ways in which assessment is used. Career assessment clearly corresponds to the "client needs" or "collaborative" end of the dimension related to the purpose of assessment, and thus there are two quadrants of particular interest to career assessment. The first quadrant (upper right in Figure 3.1) includes traditional forms of assessment, which provide the client with objective and standardized results based on his or her responses to a set of items, using well-developed norm groups. Examples of this type of assessment include the *Strong Interest Inventory* and the *Minnesota Importance Questionnaire*. The second relevant quadrant (lower right in Figure 3.1) is referred to as "collaborative assessment" (Haverkamp, 2013) and includes idiographic methods of assessment. For example, card sorts have been developed for interests, skills, and values. Card sorts are used in session with the client (compared to objective or standardized assessment, which is likely to be done outside of session), with the goal of clarifying the client's interests, values, or skills.

Figure 3.1 Dimensions Underlying Approaches to Assessment

Data-Driven:
Empirical, Nomothetic

I/O Selection
SATs

Neuropsych,
School (LD)
Diagnosis
Career Selection

Clinician/
Organizational
Needs:
"Expert" Stance

Client Needs:
"Collaborative"
Stance

Selection
Interviews
Forensic/Custody
Evaluations

Collaborative
Assessment

Intuitive: Contextual,
Idiographic

For those using traditional assessment, the ethical use of psychological assessment requires that counselors be well versed in a variety of topics, including how a test is constructed, norm groups, fairness for female and racial/ethnic minority clients, and strategies for interpretation. Results of career assessment should be considered in the context of all other available information about the client. It is critical that counselors choose reliable and valid tests and know the limitations of the instruments that they choose. We briefly introduce the technical aspects of tests below, but we also recommend that readers consult sources designed to assist counselors in evaluating assessment instruments, such as the checklists offered by Kapes, Mastie, and Whitfield (1994).

SELECTION OF ASSESSMENT

Counselors using assessment tools have a number of decisions to make when selecting tools. Test developers should provide information to help counselors decide which tools will help their clients (Joint Committee on Testing Practices [JCTP], 2004). While test developers need to provide this information, test users are ethically obligated to use that information in selecting appropriate tests for their clients (Association for Assessment in Counseling [AAC], 2003a; JCTP, 2004). The first decision is to determine the *purpose* of the assessment. Career assessment may focus on helping clients make career decisions, including generating and exploring new options or confirming interest in a potential career area. For example, Tristan's counselor could give him inventories to help him further understand his interests and values, which would help him narrow down the type of field he might like to pursue and help him clarify the type of university he might want to attend. Career instruments may also be used to help individuals clarify needs and interests and predict satisfying occupational choices. Alyssa's counselor might help her clarify options other than Nursing that might be satisfying. Brandon's counselor could use a values inventory to help him further understand values and needs that are met as a civil engineer, helping him clarify if he wants to stay in the field or not. An interest inventory could help him identify a new field if he does decide to change careers. Finally, career instruments may be used to help understand and clarify concerns related to the career decision-making process. This could help any of the clients highlighted in the cases described earlier if they encountered problems with the decision making process itself. These different types of assessment tools are described more fully in the next section.

The second major set of questions in selecting career assessment tools concerns the *technical aspects* of the instrument, including reliability and validity. It is the responsibility of test developers to provide such information in test manuals, and it is the responsibility of test users (counselors) to evaluate this information (JCTP, 2004). Evidence of validity indicates how well the test measures what it is intended to measure and the appropriateness of inferences or conclusions drawn from test results. Evidence of validity for an interest inventory, for example, indicates how well the inventory assesses the domains of interests and how well it predicts career choice. Establishing the validity of an instrument is based on empirical evidence, meaning that the test has been evaluated through many investigations. Validity of interest inventories, for example, depends on establishing that the items assess the various domains of interests (typically the six Holland themes we discuss in Chapter 6) and that the items are capturing the entire domains of those interest areas. To give an extreme example, a counselor would not want to measure the interests of adult women with an inventory that was designed to measure interests of teenage boys. Validity of an instrument is critical to ascertain when choosing an assessment tool to ensure that the assessment results are an accurate representation of behavior or attitudes.

The other technical aspect to consider is reliability of the instrument. Reliability indicates how free the assessment tool is from error, how stable the results are over time, and how internally consistent the items are in measuring each construct. Evidence that an instrument has a high level of reliability enables counselors to have confidence that the instrument will assess behavior or attitudes in a similar way over time.

The third major set of questions relates to *social issues*: Is the instrument gender- and culture-fair? Is there evidence that the test developer has taken care to ensure that any differences among men and women or individuals from different cultures are due to differences in the skills or attitudes being assessed rather than to irrelevant factors (AAC, 2003b; Suzuki, Onoue, Fukui, & Ezrapour, 2012)? Test manuals should indicate information about the performance of men and women as well as various cultural groups on the instrument. Counselors also need to assess how similar their clients are to the norm groups for the instrument. For example, Brandon reports that he received very high ACT scores compared to a national group of high school juniors and seniors. However, consider if the comparison group was elementary school students, or students in one particular state, or professional athletes; the interpretation of his results would differ based on the group to whom he is compared. Thus, it is important for counselors to understand the norm group and to ensure that it is an appropriate comparison group for their clients. Questions they ask may include whether the group is balanced in terms of gender, culture, age, and geographic region, and what research indicates that the scores may be appropriate across groups. Again, this information should be available in the manual for use with the instrument.

TYPES OF ASSESSMENT

In the realm of career counseling, assessment types typically are divided into two broad categories (Betz, 1992; Whiston, 2005). The first category contains instruments that measure some aspect of individual differences relevant to career choice, such as interests, values, needs, skills, abilities, and personality. These instruments have been an important part of career counseling since its beginning. In fact, the development of vocational guidance was intertwined historically with the development of psychometric assessment, and some of these instruments date back nearly 100 years. The second category contains assessment of career-development process, such as decision making, self-efficacy, and career maturity (Rottinghaus & Hauser, 2013; Swanson & D'Achiardi, 2005).

Both types of instruments may be used as part of screening or intake so that the counselor can assess where the client stands on a number of constructs related to choosing a career. We now present a brief description of each of these constructs and how they are assessed.

Interests

Vocational interests are, without a doubt, the most frequently assessed construct in career counseling (Hansen, 2005, 2013), and clients may enter counseling asking for "the test that will tell me what I should be." Interests also play an important role in several of the theories discussed in later chapters, and the majority of measures incorporate Holland's typology (see Chapter 6) or a similar set of constructs. Several measures of interests are currently available and widely used, such as the *Strong Interest Inventory,* the *Self-Directed Search,* the *Campbell Interest and Skills Survey,* the *Kuder Career Search,* and ACT's *UNIACT.* Interest inventories also have been developed for specific purposes; examples include those on career planning websites. We discuss two interest inventories here, the *Strong Interest Inventory* (SII) and the *Interest Profiler.* The SII is commercially available from Consulting Psychologists Press, and counselors must be trained and qualified to use it. The *Interest Profiler* is free and available to the public at www.onetcenter.org/IPSF.html.

Strong Interest Inventory (SII)

The SII (Harmon, Hansen, Borgen, & Hammer, 2005) is a measure of an individual's vocational and avocational interests. Individuals respond whether they like, dislike, or are indifferent to occupational titles, activities, school subjects, and working with various types of people, and whether or not various characteristics are descriptive of them. It is important to note that the SII is not a measure of abilities but rather is an assessment of an individual's interests. The SII profile consists of four sets of scales: General Occupational Themes, Basic Interest Scales, Occupational Scales, and Personal Style Scales; each set of scales addresses a different set of questions about the individual. The General Occupational Themes assess an individual's interests in six broad work areas that correspond to Holland's (1997) six vocational personality types (see Chapter 6), reported in comparison with an individual's same-sex norm group. The General Occupational Themes are the most global scales and answer questions about work personality (e.g., What am I like? How do I like to work? What types of work environments do I prefer?). The second set of scales on the SII profile assesses an individual's interests in 30 broad clusters, which may represent vocational or avocational interests, answering the question "What do I like?" The 30 scales are organized in relation to their association with the General Occupational Themes and also indicate the client's level of interest compared with a same-sex norm group.

The third set of SII scales includes the Occupational Scales, which indicate the similarity of the client's pattern of likes and dislikes to men and women in 122 occupations, arranged on the profile according to their relation to the six General Occupational Themes. These scales answer the question "Who am I like?" based on the assumption that similarity to one's coworkers increases job satisfaction. Scores of 40 and above suggest that the client has interests similar to those of individuals in the particular occupation.

The fourth set of scales is the Personal Style Scales, which assess various aspects of work personality, more specifically addressing the question "What am I like?" First is the Work Style Scale, which indicates the client's preferred level of involvement in working with people. The second is the Learning Environment Scale, which assesses preference for learning by doing versus learning through books and traditional lectures. Third is the Leadership Style Scale, which measures an individual's interest in taking charge of others as a leader. The fourth personal style scale is the Risk Taking Scale, which measures the individual's level of interest in taking risks and in thrill-seeking activities. Finally, the fifth personal style scale is the Team Orientation Scale, which measures working on a task independently versus through teamwork.

The SII results also contain a set of administrative response summary indexes, which indicate the way in which the individual has responded to the items. The response total indicates the number of items that the client answered out of a possible 291 items. The remaining seven rows of numbers indicate the proportion of preferences that the individual chose for various portions of the SII items, divided among the *strongly like, like, indifferent, dislike,* and *strongly dislike* options. These percentages may be examined to determine the client's response style in completing the SII across the entire profile as well as within specific sections of items.

Interest Profiler

The *Interest Profiler* Short Form (Rounds, Su, Lewis, & Rivkin, 2010) is a 60-item interest inventory designed to measure each of the six Holland themes with 10 items per scale. This is a shorter form of the original 180-item *Interest Profiler* (Lewis & Rivkin, 1999). The *Interest Profiler* was developed with several goals. First, the developers noted that they wanted a brief, self-administered instrument that reliably and validly assesses Holland's RIASEC interest themes (discussed in Chapter 6). They were also particularly concerned about ensuring that the items span the varying types of work activities from highly skilled occupations to occupations requiring fewer skills. They were also concerned about including items that would be fair across cultures. The 180-item *Interest Profiler* is available in paper-and-pencil format and in a computerized form, but takes between 20 and 40 minutes to complete, and the scoring for the paper-and-pencil format is somewhat complicated.

A shorter, 60-item form was developed, is available at http://www.onetcenter .org/IPSF.html, and takes only 10 minutes to complete. The items were chosen and tested with the 1000+ individuals who were used to develop the longer 180-item *Interest Profiler*, with particular concern that the items reflect the complexity of tasks in that interest area. Individuals indicate if they *like*, *dislike*, or are *unsure* of each item; the total score is the total number of *likes* in each subscale. Individuals are then directed to occupations in their high interest areas in the O*Net database.

Needs and Values

The assessment of work values may be used to clarify a client's reasons or motivations for working, or what he or she expects to gain from a specific job or occupation (Rounds & Armstrong, 2005). Values and needs are central in the Theory of Work Adjustment (Chapter 7) and also are important to other approaches to career counseling. Measures of work values include the *Minnesota Importance Questionnaire,* the *Work Values Inventory,* and the *Work Importance Profiler* designed to be used with O*Net career exploration tools.

Minnesota Importance Questionnaire

The MIQ (Rounds, Henley, Dawis, Lofquist, & Weiss, 1981) measures 21 work-related needs, which are grouped into six value categories. An example of the profile is shown in Appendix A. The MIQ is available for purchase from Vocational Psychology Research at the University of Minnesota. Two forms are available: The paired comparison format presents each need statement compared to every other need statement (total of 420 pairs), and the rank format presents need statements in groups of five, asking individuals to rank order the need statements within each group. The latter takes less time to complete (15 minutes compared to 30–40 minutes). At the end of both formats, individuals indicate if each of the 21 need statements is important to them in an ideal job. An individual's results on the MIQ are presented in two sections. On the first page, intraindividual scores on the 21 needs and six values are plotted relative to one another. Thus, an individual is able to see his or her most important needs. Counselors can discuss the client's most important needs, and also which needs are not important to the client. It is critical to explore the client's meaning of the need statements. For example, the need "I could make use of my abilities" may mean very different things to different clients, depending on their preferences and experiences. Clients' awareness of importance of needs often comes from work experiences where they realized they were not able to attain those needs. Thus, older clients with more work experience may have greater awareness of their needs.

The second page consists of comparisons between an individual's need and value profile and reinforcer patterns for various occupations (see Chapter 7). These two pages provide quite different information: On the first page, an individual is compared only with himself or herself, whereas on the second page, an individual's scores are compared with scores derived from normative occupational groups. An additional type of information is the logically consistent triads (LCT) score, which indicates the degree to which the individual responded in a consistent manner across the inventory.

Work Importance Profiler

Similar to the Interest Profiler, the Work Importance Profiler (WIP; McCloy et al., 1999) is part of the O*Net career exploration tools available for free at the O*Net website: http://www.onetcenter.org/WIP.html?p=3. However, the WIP is not currently available for clients to take directly online. Counselors can download the software from the O*Net website or direct clients to another site that has already downloaded the WIP and made it available to the public. The WIP was developed to be very similar to the MIQ. Indeed, Rene Dawis, one of the developers of the MIQ, was a senior advisor to the Department of Labor in the development of the WIP. Just as in the MIQ rank order format, individuals are given several sets of five need statements. Test takers are asked to drag the statements into their order of preference. At the end, also similar to the MIQ, individuals indicate whether each statement is important to them in an ideal job. However, rather than identifying 21 needs, the profile summarizes the relative importance of six values: Achievement, Independence, Recognition, Relationships, Support and Working Conditions. Results are provided in order of importance to the individual, who is then invited to view occupations that are consistent with those needs and level of preferred preparation.

Abilities and Skills

Identification of a client's abilities and skills is an important aspect of career counseling, yet these constructs are less likely to be assessed via formal means than are other constructs such as interests and values. Objective assessment of abilities is available through measures such as the ASVAB and the O*NET Ability Profiler (Metz & Jones, 2013; Ryan Krane & Tirre, 2005). However, in the context of career counseling, self-estimates of abilities, such as the Skills Confidence Inventory (SCI), Kuder Skills Assessment, and ACT's Inventory of Work-Relevant Abilities, are more likely to be used than objective measures. We discuss the SCI below.

Skills Confidence Inventory

The Skills Confidence Inventory was designed to accompany the Strong Interest Inventory (Betz, Borgen, & Harmon, 1996) and is shown in Appendix A, Figure 2. Similar to the SII, the SCI is available from Consulting Psychologists Press. The 60-item SCI assesses the level of confidence an individual has in completing tasks associated with the six General Occupational Themes. The overall objective of the instrument is to identify areas for a client to explore. Each scale consists of 10 items, averaged to produce a score between 1 and 5, with 5 indicating very high level of confidence in that area. The SCI profile is designed to coordinate with the SII, so the levels of confidence and interest are plotted for each General Occupational Theme. Three scenarios are of particular interest in counseling: Confidence and interest are both high, confidence is higher than interest, or interest is higher than confidence. High confidence and interest in a theme are good areas for further exploration.

Personality

The assessment of personality could fit into either of the two broad categories described at the beginning of the chapter; it is an important individual difference related to the choice of a career and is included in theories of career development, yet it also influences how a career decision is made or how career counseling might progress (Swanson & D'Achiardi, 2005). While personality certainly is important to both the process and outcome of career counseling, it is less frequently assessed than other constructs. This may be due to the fact that most objective measures of personality focus on psychopathology or deviance, whereas fewer measures focus on "normal" personality so as to be of value in career counseling. The latter measures include the Myers-Briggs Type Indicator and the NEO Personality Inventory.

Assessment of Other Constructs

As noted earlier, the second broad category of career assessment focuses on the client's status in the career choice process and includes constructs such as decision making, self-efficacy, and career maturity. These constructs often have emerged from specific theories of career development and, thus, are discussed in greater depth in later chapters. In contrast to measures of interests, values, abilities, and personality, measures of the career development process tend to be more informal—that is, not published commercially. Rather, they have been developed initially as research instruments and later have become available for use with clients. For example, the Career Decision-Making Self-Efficacy Scale emerged from social cognitive career theory (see Chapter 10) and was developed to examine the effects of an intervention on self-efficacy. Similarly, measures of career maturity or adaptability emerged from Super's life span, life space theory (see Chapter 8) and attempted to quantify an important construct in the theory. Because these measures are more informal, they tend to have fewer norms or groups available for comparison, and fewer interpretive materials are available to guide the counselor and client. We focus on one assessment here, the Adult Career Concerns Inventory, which we used with the main case of Leslie (Chapter 4).

Adult Career Concerns Inventory

The ACCI was developed by Super and his colleagues (Super, Thompson, & Lindeman, 1988) to assess issues related to developmental career tasks and stages. The ACCI provides scores on Super's four adult career stages (exploration, establishment, maintenance, and disengagement; see Chapter 8 for more detail), as well as scores for three substages within each stage. The ACCI is available from the Vocopher website (http://www.vocopher.com/). Counselors must register for the site, providing their credentials and educational information.

The ACCI asks clients to answer 61 questions about their concerns relative to career stages. Scores reflect the amount of concern that a client expresses about various tasks within the stages and substages. The ACCI can be useful in identifying minicycles within maxicycles of Super's theory. A client's scores can be interpreted relative to one another (intraindividually) or by using norms as a point of reference.

Other Types of Assessment

Several other methods of assessment are available for the counselor to use in career counseling. The first type, card sorts, may be used to assess any of the previously discussed constructs; for example, card sorts have been developed for interests, skills, and values. As noted earlier, card sorts are used in session with the client and are considered a type of qualitative assessment, since the goal is not to arrive at scores or to compare the client's scores to a norm group; rather, the process of completing a card sort reveals information to both the client and the counselor that helps clarify the client's interests, values, or skills.

Another method of qualitative assessment is through a genogram. Genograms are visual representations of some set of connections in a client's life. For example, the personal reflection in Chapter 2 on family work choices is a type of genogram. Genograms were originally developed within the context of family systems (Bowen, 1978) to chart a client's family history and current relations, but they have been adapted to other settings. As with other types of qualitative assessment, the process of completing a genogram may be at least as useful as the product or outcome of the genogram. That is, the discussion that ensues between client and counselor as they work on the genogram may be very fruitful. As Gysbers, Heppner, and Johnston (2009) note, a genogram has "substantial face validity for clients because it provides them with an opportunity to tell their story within the career counseling context" (p. 194). Moreover, it encourages trust and helps build the working alliance between counselor and client and may be adapted creatively to fit a variety of needs (Miller, Dillon, & Swanson, 2007; Okiishi, 1987).

INTERPRETING CAREER ASSESSMENT

Ethical and professional use of assessment in career counseling requires that counselors are planful and thoughtful at each step, including decisions about whether or not to use assessment and which specific assessment(s) to use, how to prepare for interpretation of assessment results, and how to actually interpret and integrate assessment information in session. In this section, we offer some counselor cognitions as suggestions for how to make these decisions explicit: What specific considerations might counselors keep in mind as they approach the use of assessment in career counseling?

Counselor Cognitions About Assessment

Prior to choosing assessment

Careful consideration about assessment in career counseling begins with initial decisions about whether or not to use assessment at all. As we noted earlier, counselors vary in their opinions of the role of formal assessment, with some counselors using assessment routinely with the majority of their clients and other counselors not using assessment at all. These opinions and practices may be influenced by the setting in which the counselor works (i.e., are assessment materials and services available in the agency? Do clients have financial resources to cover the cost of assessment?), as well as by their training and comfort with assessment tools. The decision to use assessment is then followed by a series of decisions about what to assess (interests, values, self-efficacy, etc.) and how to assess it (the specific assessment instrument). Counselors could ask themselves the questions in Box 3.1 as they contemplate using assessment and as they choose specific types of assessment.

BOX 3.1 Counselor Cognitions Before Assessment

- Is assessment a good use of time and money with this client?
- What do I hope that the client will gain from assessment? What new information or perspective might it provide for the client?
- What information do I hope to gain through assessment that will add to helping the client?
- Why did I choose this specific assessment? How does it compare to the alternatives?
- How does this assessment fit with the theoretical approach(es) guiding my work with this client?

Reviewing assessment results prior to session

Using a formal assessment instrument, such as the Strong Interest Inventory or the Minnesota Importance Questionnaire, requires that counselors have specialized knowledge and skills. These instruments frequently result in profiles containing a considerable amount of information, which counselors need to be prepared to explain to clients. To prepare for interpretation, counselors should review clients' results with the questions in Box 3.2 in mind.

BOX 3.2 Preparing for Assessment Interpretation

- Is the assessment profile valid?
- What additional information do I need to locate in the test manual or other sources?
- How might I present results to the client?
- Where are there consistencies and inconsistencies within and across assessment results? How does this information fit with what I already know about the client?
- In how much depth can I go with this specific client?
- What hypotheses are suggested by the assessment results?

Presenting and discussing results with the client

Good preparation prior to interpreting assessment results will make the actual interpretation go smoothly. Guidelines about interpretation are obviously dependent on the specific instrument, but the counselor cognitions in Box 3.3 are applicable across different types of assessment in career counseling:

BOX 3.3 Presenting Assessment Information

- What was the client's frame of mind when taking the assessment?
- What questions might the client have before presenting results?
- What is the client hoping to learn from his or her results? Does he or she have specific expectations, such as confirming a tentative career direction?
- What does the client get out of discussing the results?
- What are the highlights of the assessment results?
- What might be potential concerns raised by the results?
- How does the client process the information?
- How do the assessment results confirm or disconfirm hypotheses, or development of new hypotheses?
- What did the client learn about himself or herself in discussing the results? What did I learn about the client?

General Guidelines for Interpreting Career Assessment

As noted in the previous section, each specific assessment instrument requires that counselors have knowledge relevant to that instrument, and we assume that readers will gain that knowledge through other courses and practicum experiences. However, there are also some general guidelines for interpreting results of career assessment that we discuss here.

- In career counseling, assessment is done for the benefit of *the client* (compared to assessment in other clinical contexts, which may be primarily for the therapist), and the client will be an active participant in the process (Duckworth, 1990)
- Test interpretations should be based on "documented bridges between scores and their real-world implications" and supported by empirical research (Krieshok & Black, 2009, p. 67).
- Prior to presenting the actual results, take sufficient time to review the purpose of the assessment and to create a broader context for the results. Discuss what information the results might provide and set realistic expectations.
- Be prepared to discuss the statistical underpinnings of the instrument in terms that the client will understand.
- Frame assessment results as hypotheses to be checked against the client's experiences, whether in the past, present, or future (Krieshok & Black, 2009).

- Consider the degree to which a client's awareness about themselves and the world of work may have influenced their results. Use the results of assessment to determine whether clients need more occupational information (see Chapter 13).

- Use your counseling skills! Think of the interpretation as an opportunity to engage the client in discussion, and attend to "client first and results second" (Krieshok & Black, 2009, p. 68). Encourage the client to reflect on their experience in taking the assessment and their reactions to the results.

ETHICAL PRINCIPLES AND RESPONSIBLE USE OF ASSESSMENT

The National Career Development Association (NCDA, 2007; see also Appendix B), the American Counseling Association (ACA, 2005), and the American Psychological Association (APA, 2010) all include a section in their ethics codes that focuses on ethical mandates for appropriate assessment. These organizations also collaborated with educational professional associations to form the Joint Committee on Testing Practices (JCTP). This group developed the *Code of Fair Testing Practices in Education* (JCTP, 2004), which outlines the obligations for test users: Test users should administer and score tests correctly and fairly; should report and interpret test results accurately and clearly; and should provide clients with information about the instrument, the use of scores, and where to find more information about the instrument and results.

Counseling and psychological ethical codes address the appropriate use of assessment, in large part because unethical assessment practices may lead to significant client harm. Consider, for example, a client who makes a career decision to be a teacher based, in part, on the results of an assessment of her interests and needs. Imagine that she quits her current job to go back to school for a degree in education. If, however, the test results are invalid or unreliable or were poorly chosen or interpreted, she may suffer a significant loss in terms of time, money, and emotional investment in an unwise decision.

Professional ethical codes emphasize that client welfare is paramount in the assessment process and that counselors need to be competent in the tools that they use. For example, the NCDA *Code of Ethics* (2007; see Appendix B) notes:

> Career professionals do not misuse assessment results and interpretations, and they take reasonable steps to prevent others from misusing the information these tools provide. They respect the client's right to know the results, the interpretations made, and the bases for professionals' conclusions and recommendations. (§ E.1.b)

All ethical codes encourage counselors to inform their clients appropriately of the use of tests and receive their clients' consent to be assessed. All codes emphasize the need to interpret accurately the results of assessment tools and to note the context within which assessment takes place. Finally, all ethical codes address the special issues that arise when career counselors are asked to release assessment results to other professionals. Clients must provide explicit permission to release the assessment results, and information should only be released to qualified professionals. Ethical decision making is discussed more fully in Chapter 12.

BOX 3.4 Personal Reflection

- Have I ever taken an interest inventory? What do I remember of the results?
- Have assessment results affected my career decision making?
- Take the Interest Profile at www.mynextmove.org/explore/ip. What are my reactions to the results?
- Take a values card sort (available online or in many career centers). What are my reactions to my top values? How have my work experiences clarified my work values?

Chapter 4

The Case of Leslie

PRESENTING ISSUE

Leslie is a 35-year-old White woman with a bachelor's degree in secondary education. She is seeking career counseling because she is considering quitting her current job as a math teacher in a large suburban high school. Leslie lives in a midsize metropolitan area in the Midwest; she is married, with a 10-year-old stepson.

Leslie reports a considerable amount of dissatisfaction with her current job, particularly related to the stress of many responsibilities and long working hours, as well as the impersonal nature of the school. Leslie reports that her dissatisfaction has been accumulating for several years but that recent events have brought it to the forefront. First, a newly hired principal has instituted administrative tasks to demonstrate teacher effectiveness that Leslie finds insulting to experienced teachers, such as requiring teachers to keep a weekly log of their activities, submit lesson plans for review, and file quarterly reports on teaching goals. She reports that these activities are "oppressive" and feels quite angry toward the principal. She also is frustrated by the increasing use of student performance on standardized achievement tests as a basis for teacher evaluation. Second, Leslie has had several interactions with parents this year that discouraged her greatly: On one hand, she has spent a considerable amount of time dealing with parents who closely monitor their children's grades online and contact Leslie frequently to discuss assignments; on the other hand, some parents showed little involvement in their children's school activities yet expected her to go "above and beyond" her responsibilities as a teacher. This is particularly frustrating because Leslie sees students dealing with increasingly difficult problems at home. She also is frustrated by the lack of intellectual challenge in her job.

On the positive side, Leslie reports that she did have an opportunity last year to teach an elective advanced math course, in which her students were more motivated and capable, and that she continues to enjoy the one-on-one aspects of teaching. She feels she is a good teacher, and she values the relationships that she develops with students. She displays considerable enthusiasm when discussing what she likes about teaching.

Leslie is unclear at this point whether or not she will quit her current job and, if so, whether she will look for another teaching position or a new career. She wants to explore options to remain in education, whether in a traditional classroom or in some other venue. She also wants to explore new career options outside of teaching. She has thought about a wide range of possible career shifts, such as financial planning, social work, technical writing, and engineering. She is willing to consider pursuing further education if necessary for the career direction that she chooses.

CAREER AND WORK HISTORY

Leslie grew up in a predominantly White suburban area, where she attended public schools. Leslie excelled in a number of subjects in middle school and high school, including math, science, and social studies. She was a member of the French club, was a math tutor for middle school children, and won first place in the high school science fair during her senior year. She did not actively seek out any positions of leadership within the school but was often viewed as a leader by others, in part because she assumed many organizational responsibilities.

Although her family expected her to go to college, she received little direction from them or her high school guidance counselor in choosing a college or selecting a field of study. She delayed making a decision about attending college until the summer after high school graduation and then decided to enroll at a local community college. She chose the community college because many of her friends were going there, it was close to home, and she was unsure about her motivation to pursue a college education and whether she would be successful.

During her first semester at the community college, she enrolled in general English, math, chemistry, and psychology courses. During this time, she ended a relationship with her high school boyfriend and began dating a college student who was home for Christmas vacation. The relationship flourished during her second semester, and he encouraged her to join him at the state university 90 miles from home. She finished her first year at the community college and decided to transfer to the state university, in part to join her boyfriend but also because she was disappointed by the lack of challenge in the math and science classes at her community college.

She entered her sophomore year at the university with a number of possible majors in mind but declared herself as "undecided." She enjoyed taking a variety of classes while in college, and she contemplated a number of diverse options—mathematics, engineering, creative writing, psychology, and premedicine—prior to choosing her major. She enjoyed the challenge of her math classes but did not do well in mechanical drawing. She did not enjoy being one of the few women in her advanced math classes, particularly because she had some negative experiences with professors who singled out her mistakes. A number of factors detracted from her serious consideration of a degree in mathematics, including lack of encouragement from professors and not wanting to commit to pursuing a graduate degree. Her lack of motivation to pursue postbaccalaureate training also precluded her from declaring a major in psychology or premedicine, and she decided not to major in engineering because two professors told her she would have a difficult time combining that career with a family. Leslie finally decided to major in secondary education, with an emphasis in mathematics education, because she could easily combine teaching with raising a family, she could still use her math skills, and teaching would not require schooling beyond a bachelor's degree. In addition, she remembered enjoying her experiences as a math tutor in high school in which she had feelings of accomplishment when her students understood difficult concepts for the first time.

Leslie had a satisfying student teaching experience in a medium-sized high school in her hometown, and she received positive feedback and excellent evaluations from her supervising teacher. This experience led her to feel excited and confident about her decision to become a teacher.

After graduating from college, Leslie took a teaching position in a small town about 2 hours from the city in which her family lived. Her first year in the position was very stressful, but she also loved being a teacher. As the only math teacher in the school, she taught a diverse range of classes and students, and she enjoyed the challenge of taking sole responsibility for her classes. She also enjoyed being a part of the community. However, she worked every night and weekend to keep up with lesson preparation and grading. She was the youngest teacher in the school and found it difficult to meet people with whom she could socialize outside of work. She also missed being close to her family, and her workload made it difficult for her to see them on weekends. Her relationship with her boyfriend suffered, and they ended the relationship during her second year of teaching.

After 3 years, Leslie found a teaching position in a large school district in the city in which her family lived and looked forward to being closer to them. She soon discovered that her new teaching position, although slightly less stressful, offered fewer rewards than her previous position. Because she was teaching in a larger school system, she was assigned five sections of freshman algebra, the least desirable teaching assignment. She found her students to be disinterested in the subject, and because they came from a wide geographic area, she no longer felt part of a community. She was also frustrated by the large bureaucratic structure of the school system. She was, however, able to find a greater degree of social support outside of work, including her family and high school friends. She has been in this position for 10 years.

Leslie has a number of interests outside her job, although she does not have much time to pursue any of these interests during the school year because of the time demands of her job. She enjoys several hobbies during the summer, including gardening and other outdoor activities, and teaches swimming lessons at the local YMCA. She also volunteers at the science center, where she maintains the membership records, and she teaches meditation classes.

FAMILY INFORMATION

Leslie is the second of three children, with an older brother (age 38) and a younger sister (age 30). Her brother has a bachelor's degree in electrical engineering and works for a company that designs computer equipment. He was recently promoted to vice president of one of the company's product divisions in which he coordinates all aspects of a particular product line, from research and development to marketing and sales. He is married to a woman who is a personnel manager for a retail chain; they have two children. Leslie's sister has a bachelor's degree in nursing and has worked at a number of hospitals and home health agencies. She is currently out of the workforce while she cares for two young children; her husband is the district sales manager for a pharmaceutical company.

Leslie's parents are in their early 60s. Her father is a corporate attorney for a midsize manufacturing firm, specializing in product liability and patents. His bachelor's degree was in chemistry, and he worked as a research and development chemist for 10 years before pursuing a law degree. Her mother attended several years of college but left school when she married Leslie's father. She has been involved in community arts organizations by, for example, volunteering as a docent at the art museum and serving on the board of the symphony orchestra. She did not work outside the home until Leslie's younger sister was in high school. At that time, she found a position with a small business specializing in office interior design, where she continues to work part-time as an administrative assistant.

During college, Leslie's parents stated their support for whatever she chose as a major and provided the financial resources for her college education. Her father strongly encouraged her to major in business, but Leslie found that these classes were her least favorite. Her mother felt that the specific major was not critical as long as Leslie received a good education; she expected that Leslie would not remain in the workforce after marrying and having children. Leslie's family expressed some impatience when it was difficult for her to choose a major; Leslie's brother teased her for "changing her mind so often."

Leslie and her siblings all live within the same metropolitan area as her parents, and they see one another frequently. Leslie has discussed her job dissatisfaction with her family, and they have given her conflicting advice: Her father has renewed his encouragement of Leslie's pursuing a business career, her mother and sister have suggested that now would be a good time for Leslie to have children, and her brother has advised her to quit complaining about such inconsequential aspects of her job.

MARITAL INFORMATION

Leslie has been married to Joe (age 39) for 5 years. Joe has an associate's degree from a local community college and is currently a finish carpenter for a residential contractor. He enjoys his work and takes a great deal of pride in his reputation as a highly skilled craftsman; however, he has been thinking about finding a different line of work because of the job's physical demands and the seasonal fluctuations in available work.

Joe is the older of two sons from a middle-class Latino family; both his father and mother are of Mexican descent. Joe's father is a midlevel manager in a hardware store chain. Joe's mother worked as a housekeeper while Joe and his brother were young, but she quit working outside of the home when Joe's father was promoted into management. She has strong connections with the Latino community through her involvement in church and neighborhood activities. Joe's brother works as a youth services coordinator, organizing programs at a city-funded community center.

Joe grew up trying to be "American" like the other kids in school. He did not want to acknowledge his Mexican heritage. He refused to speak Spanish at home, he and his parents had great conflicts during his adolescence when he refused to go to church, and he did not include the other adolescents from his Latino neighborhood in his circle of friends. His parents were particularly upset when he did not show respect for his grandmother, who came to live with them when he was 15.

Joe graduated from high school with a C average. He did not consider going to college, because he did not enjoy high school and wanted to be working and earning money rather than going to school. The only class he liked in high school was his woodworking class, and he became an apprentice carpenter after graduation. He worked his way up to finish carpenter over 10 years. He has worked for the same contractor for the past 7 years.

After the conflicts with his family during and right after high school, Joe increasingly began to appreciate his Mexican heritage. He began to attend community and neighborhood events, although he chose not to live in the same community as his parents. He identifies himself as a Mexican American but has some resistance to the label "Latino." He endorses many traditional Latino values: a strong emphasis on family, a preference for smooth interpersonal relationships, and respect owed to elders. He is more ambivalent about appropriate roles for men and women in the family. On the one hand, his mother's highest goal was to stay home to care for her family; on the other hand, he realizes that some women want to work and to be more independent.

Joe's first marriage was to a young Latino woman who grew up in the same neighborhood. They married at age 22, and his family was very happy that he would stay within their community. His wife, Maria Pilar, worked as a clerk in a small business. The conflicts in their marriage stemmed from her pressuring him to find ways to earn more money. Like his mother, her goal was to have a family and to be a homemaker. Maria was deeply involved in the Latino community and the church, and another source of conflict was his resistance to this level of involvement. Their marriage ended 2 years after their son was born. His first wife has since remarried and moved to another Latino community.

Leslie and Joe met through a common friend and dated for 6 months before marrying. Leslie's family was not wholly supportive of her decision to marry Joe, although they did not express their feelings directly to Leslie. Joe's family also had concerns about Joe and Leslie's marriage; his mother was concerned that Leslie was too American. Their marriage has been relatively stable: Leslie describes herself as being happy in her marriage. She does, however, express some dissatisfaction with their relationship, primarily because of what she characterizes as their "lack of communication about important issues." Leslie reports that Joe is supportive of her considering a career change, but she feels that he does not understand why she is unhappy with her job and that he seems hesitant about her returning to school. She speculates that some of Joe's hesitation is due to questions about their ability to get by on only one income and forfeiting their access to health insurance through Leslie's job.

Joe's 10-year-old son from his first marriage now lives 300 miles from Leslie and Joe and spends school vacations with them, as well as an occasional long weekend. Leslie wants to have a child, and although Joe has expressed some ambivalence since before they were married, he has been supportive of Leslie's desire. He expects that Leslie would postpone any career decisions if they were to have a child so that she could stay at home full-time until the child was in school.

This expectation is consistent with the division of labor that they have assumed, although Leslie is increasingly frustrated that Joe does not contribute more to household responsibilities. Leslie and Joe have had some difficulty related to pregnancy; Leslie had two miscarriages last year. The miscarriages were followed by marital tension and depression, for which Leslie sought individual therapy with a psychologist. Leslie reported that her previous experience with therapy was quite beneficial, although she now wishes that Joe had joined her in therapy.

LESLIE'S EXPECTATIONS FOR CAREER COUNSELING

Leslie was referred to career counseling by a coworker who had heard about the availability of career services. She is enthusiastic about career counseling, she is hopeful that the career counselor will help her define her career direction, and she expects to receive information and perhaps advice from the counselor about her "best" career option. She is eager to take the tests that the counselor recommends, stating that she is waiting to hear what the tests will tell her to do.

Leslie feels that she is at a crossroads in her life and is ready to explore her options for her next step. She is evaluating many aspects of her career, family relationships, and marriage. She is looking forward to beginning counseling.

INITIAL IMPRESSIONS OF LESLIE

Before reading the subsequent section with Leslie's assessment results, use the following questions to formulate your impressions of her:

1. What have you learned about Leslie from the information presented thus far?

2. What general impressions do you have of Leslie? What impressions do you have of her as an employee? As a spouse? As a member of her family of origin?

3. What role do you think Leslie's gender has played in her life and career decisions? What role do you think her culture and socioeconomic status have played? What role do you think her husband's culture and socioeconomic status have played?

4. What more would you like to know about Leslie?

5. What observations or hypotheses do you have about Leslie that the assessment data might clarify? What specifically will you look for in the assessment results?

6. How would you describe her primary career issue(s)? How might you prioritize the direction of counseling? Where would you like to begin in working with Leslie?

ASSESSMENT INFORMATION

Leslie completed four inventories at the beginning of counseling: the Strong Interest Inventory (SII), the Skills Confidence Inventory (SCI), the Minnesota Importance Questionnaire (MIQ), and the Adult Career Concerns Inventory (ACCI). These four inventories were chosen to assess a diversity of components typically considered in career counseling—namely, factors related to career choice *content* (interests, values, and personality) and factors related to career choice *process* (self-efficacy, beliefs, and life span career issues). Typically, clients would take one or two inventories; in Leslie's case, all four were included to illustrate the types of information that might be assessed as part of career counseling.

Strong Interest Inventory (SII)

Leslie's SII profile is shown in sections in Appendix A, Figure 1. Compared with other women, Leslie's SII indicates that she has very high interest in the investigative theme (science and analysis), with high interest in the social theme (helping others) and moderate interest in the conventional theme (organization and structure). She has little interest in the realistic area (working with things) and very little interest in the enterprising theme (business oriented, selling) and artistic theme (creative self-expression). Leslie's primary General Occupational Theme code, then, would be investigative-social-conventional, or ISC.

In the second section, six of Leslie's Basic Interest Scales are in the "very high" range: research, mathematics, and science in the investigative theme; teaching/education and religion/spirituality in the social theme; and taxes/accounting in the conventional theme. She also has a high level of interest in computer hardware/electronics (realistic theme). Her lowest Basic Interest Scales are military (realistic theme) and performing arts, visual arts/design, writing/mass communication, and culinary arts (all artistic theme). All these scores indicate very little interest. The codes for her highest Basic Interest Scales are all investigative, social, or conventional, and the codes for her lowest Basic Interest Scales are artistic, enterprising, or realistic, consistent with the pattern of General Occupational Themes.

Leslie's interests on the Occupational Scales are most similar to those of women who are actuaries, mathematicians, software developers, financial analysts, mathematics teachers, university professors, medical technologists, biologists, bookkeepers, and financial managers; these occupational scales are the top 10 in terms of scores, and all are scores of 59 or higher. Her interests are also similar (scores of 50 or higher) to those of physicists, geologists, chemists, computer scientists, optometrists, science teachers, accountants, credit managers, production managers, technical support specialists, foresters, network administrators, and engineers. There are an additional 12 occupational scales on which Leslie scored between 40 and 50 (see the SII profile for more information). Leslie's interests are least similar (scores of 0 or below) to those of women who are public relations directors, graphic designers, medical illustrators, art teachers, advertising account managers, reporters, English teachers, interior designers, and chefs.

The codes associated with Leslie's highest Occupational Scales are primarily investigative or conventional, and the codes associated with her lowest Occupational Scales are primarily artistic and enterprising. Again, the codes for these scales are consistent with the General Occupational Themes and Basic Interest Scales, with the exception of the social theme. Leslie's interests are moderately similar to only one occupation primarily coded in the social area: special education teachers.

Leslie's score on the Work Style Scale is 54, indicating that she has no marked preference for either working with people or working alone. Leslie scored 56 on the Learning Environment Scale, which indicates a slight preference for a traditional academic environment over practical learning. Leslie scored 45 on the Leadership Style Scale, showing some interest in working alone rather than assuming a high profile as a leader. Leslie's score is 34 on the Risk Taking Scale, indicating that she does not like risk-taking activities and prefers to be careful and play it safe. Finally, Leslie's score of 60 on the Team Orientation Scale suggests that she may enjoy collaborating with others in a team.

Leslie omitted one of the SII items (TR index of 317), and she did not respond in an unusual way. She indicated more dislikes than likes, particularly for items regarding occupations, leisure activities, and types of people. She seemed to be fairly sure about her likes and dislikes, as indicated by very few "indifferent" responses.

Skills Confidence Inventory (SCI)

In addition to the SII, Leslie also completed the SCI (Betz, Borgen, & Harmon, 1996), shown in Appendix A, Figure 2. The 60-item SCI assesses the level of confidence an individual has in completing tasks associated with the six General Occupational Themes. The overall objective of the instrument is to identify areas for a client to explore. Each scale consists of 10 items, averaged to produce a score between 1 and 5, with 5 indicating very high level of confidence in that area. Leslie has the most confidence in the investigative area, followed by social and conventional (see Appendix A, Figure 2). She has very little confidence in her artistic and realistic skills.

The SCI profile is designed to coordinate with the SII, so the levels of confidence and interest are plotted for each General Occupational Theme. Three scenarios are of particular interest in counseling: Confidence and interest are both high, confidence is higher than interest, or interest is higher than confidence. High confidence and interest in a theme are good areas for further exploration. These conditions apply for Leslie in the investigative, social, and conventional areas. Leslie has two themes (investigative and social) in which both her interests and confidence are equally high and one theme (conventional) in which her interests are lower than her confidence. All three areas are avenues of potential career exploration with Leslie, inquiring whether her interests and confidence could be further developed in these areas. A fourth scenario is represented by Leslie's enterprising, artistic, and realistic areas in which both her interests and skills confidence are low, suggesting that these areas are "low priority" for further exploration.

Minnesota Importance Questionnaire (MIQ)

The LCT score for Leslie's MIQ profile is 92%, suggesting that her responses were highly consistent across the items. Leslie's highest needs on the MIQ are moral values ("I could do the work without feeling that it is morally wrong"), ability utilization ("I could do something that makes use of my abilities"), achievement ("The job could give me a feeling of accomplishment"), and social service ("I could do things for other people"). Her lowest needs are authority ("I could tell people what to do"), independence ("I could work alone on the job"), and company policies ("The company would administer its policies fairly"). Her highest value categories are achievement and altruism, and her lowest value is status.

Examining the clusters on the second page reveals that first, four of the six clusters have C index values in the satisfied range (Clusters A, B, C, and F). Leslie's highest C index is for Cluster A (0.68), which is characterized by the values of achievement and autonomy and the need of altruism. Cluster C (0.60), with the next highest C index, is characterized by the value of achievement and the needs of autonomy and compensation. Cluster A has a large number of occupations that correspond to Leslie's pattern of values and needs: 13 of the 15 occupations have C index values in the satisfied range.

The occupations in Cluster A include counseling psychologist, occupational therapist, speech pathologist, secondary and elementary school teacher, interior designer, architect, and recreation leader. Additional occupations found in Cluster C include real estate sales agent, beauty operator, and caseworker. Occupations with high C indexes are also found in other clusters, including librarian and medical technologist in Cluster F. The lowest C index is for Cluster E, characterized by the value comfort; none of the 15 occupations has a C index value in the satisfied range. The lowest indexes are for occupations such as production assembler, meat cutter, and solderer.

Adult Career Concerns Inventory (ACCI)

The ACCI was developed by Super and his colleagues (Super, Thompson, & Lindeman, 1988) to assess issues related to developmental career tasks and stages. The ACCI provides scores on Super's four adult career stages (exploration, establishment, maintenance, and disengagement; see Chapter 8 for more detail), as well as scores for three substages within each stage. A client's scores can be interpreted relative to one another (intraindividually) or by using norms as a point of reference. Scores reflect the amount of concern that a client expresses about various tasks within the stages and substages. The ACCI can be useful in identifying minicycles within maxicycles of Super's theory, which is of particular interest with a client such as Leslie.

Leslie's ACCI profile (see Appendix A, Figure 4) reveals that her highest stage score is in exploration and that her scores decrease with each subsequent developmental stage (that is, establishment is the second highest score, maintenance is the third highest, and disengagement is her lowest stage score). Thus, her primary career concerns are tasks that are typical of the exploration stage of career development.

Moreover, the substage scales within exploration suggest that she is most concerned about the tasks related to specification, closely followed by crystallization, with lesser concern for implementation. Crystallization includes identifying and developing potential career directions, whereas specification emphasizes choosing a specific occupational direction; these two types of concerns are typical for individuals undergoing career transitions (Super, Savickas, & Super, 1996).

An interesting feature of Leslie's ACCI profile is that, although her maintenance score is relatively low, one substage score is markedly higher than the other two within the stage. The maintenance stage is focused on continuation or further development within one's chosen occupation and position. Leslie expressed concerns related to the innovation substage, which indicates a desire to "do something different or at least to do it differently" within one's established occupation (Super et al., 1996). The innovation substage could be viewed as an "exploration and establishment" minicycle within the maintenance stage.

Summary of Leslie's Assessment Information

Leslie has clear interests in the social area, such as teaching, social services, and religious activities, and it is important for her to do things for others and to feel good about what she does. She also has considerable confidence in her ability to do these types of activities, although her interest exceeds her confidence. She enjoys working with people but also values working independently. She is comfortable working alone and frequently prefers doing so to being with other people. Her favorite part of teaching is the one-on-one interactions with students versus lecturing in front of the entire class. Her interest in working with people does not include leadership activities, such as managing, persuading, or directing others. She has neither interest nor confidence in enterprising activities.

Leslie appears very comfortable with structure and organization and demonstrates much attention to detail. She is less comfortable when situations are vague or ambiguous and may work to impose structure when none is forthcoming from the situation at hand. She likes developing systems to make her job more efficient.

Leslie also has strong interests in investigative-type activities. She is unfailingly curious and enjoys learning new things. It is important for her to feel that she is accomplishing something, and she enjoys being intellectually challenged. She is confident of her skills as a learner and problem solver. Although she does not have any interest or confidence in artistic activities, she enjoys the creativity involved in solving new problems or figuring out a new way to do a task.

Leslie would appear to be a good candidate for career counseling with many issues that could be profitably addressed in counseling. She is inquisitive and motivated to address her career concerns at this point. Presently, she seems particularly concerned with defining a new direction for herself or creating new opportunities within her original chosen career field. She has some external constraints to her career choices, most notably, difficulty undertaking a geographic relocation because of family obligations. She also has some internal constraints that the counselor might address, such as the power or influence that she gives to others regarding her career and the way in which she undervalues her own ability and performance. In addition, there might be conflicts due to culture that could benefit from exploration with a counselor.

WORKING WITH LESLIE'S CASE AND ASSESSMENT INFORMATION

In Chapters 1 and 2, we discussed ways in which counselors might use background information and assessment results to develop hypotheses and form a "working model" of the client. Each hypothesis then may be tested by searching for evidence that either confirms or disconfirms the hypothesis, and the working model can be changed to reflect this new evidence. New hypotheses then emerge from the altered model, and the counselor's view of the client is continually refined.

The information presented in this chapter now may be used to develop hypotheses about Leslie. We will present some broad observations about her, followed by specific hypotheses for further investigation.

Observation 1

There seem to be some discrepancies about social-type activities, values, and personality style. For example, her social General Occupational Theme score is high, as are several social Basic Interest Scales, yet no social Occupational Scales are in the "similar" range. She also appears to be somewhat introverted, indicating that she has equal preferences for working alone or working with people but also a slight preference for working in teams.

Hypotheses

- Leslie is likely to enjoy social-type activities, particularly those in which she is helping people, but may also find them tiring and stressful. She may need to withdraw from people to rejuvenate and regain her energy.
- Her interests are dissimilar to those of other women in social-type occupations (e.g., minister, physical education teacher, parks and recreation coordinator). Members of these occupations are likely to be fairly extroverted, and Leslie's lower scores may reflect her relatively introverted nature.
- Leslie's interest in social activities could reflect gender stereotyping; she may feel that she "should" like these activities because of gender-role socialization. The General Occupational Theme and Basic Interest Scales, in particular, may be more readily affected by these influences than are the Occupational Scales because of the transparency of the items.
- Leslie is probably most comfortable when she is in a defined or prescribed role in dealing with others, as is true when she interacts with students as a teacher. She may be less comfortable in less structured interactions.
- Her interest in social-type activities and in working with people might be limited to specific types of people; she indicated "strongly dislike" to over 60% of the items on the Types of People section of the SII.
- Leslie's interest in the social-type activity of teaching also seems to be fairly circumscribed to mathematics. Mathematics teacher is her highest Occupational Scale directly related to teaching and indicates that she has interests very similar to those of other math teachers. In contrast, she has low scores on the elementary teacher, foreign language teacher, and social science teacher Occupational Scales.

Observation 2

Leslie's low artistic interests are matched by her lack of confidence in these areas, and she has not directly pursued any artistic activities. On the other hand, she does like the creativity that comes with solving problems and designing new methods.

Hypotheses

- Leslie may enjoy artistic activities such as going to concerts or attending museums, but her lack of confidence in her ability to perform artistic activities may have influenced her responses to items on the SII. Alternatively, she may be truly averse to artistic activities.
- Leslie may feel uncomfortable in artistic environments—those characterized by flexibility, creativity, and self-expression—because they are not as structured as she prefers.
- Her mother's involvement in artistic organizations and activities is quite different from Leslie's. Leslie may compare herself with her mother and feel that she is not as capable in artistic endeavors.
- Leslie seems to enjoy creativity as a means to an end—to solve problems or create new ways of doing things—rather than as an end itself.

Observation 3

Leslie also has low interest and confidence in enterprising activities. Moreover, she ranked as low the MIQ authority item ("telling others what to do"), and her score on the Leadership Style Scale of the SII suggests that she is not comfortable with taking charge or directing others in activities. She has been viewed by others as a leader but has not herself sought out leadership positions. Leslie seems to avoid (as opposed to merely being indifferent to) activities related to leadership or assumption of power or influence. Yet she has taken on administrative duties in her job and volunteer work.

Hypotheses

- Leslie seems to dislike and avoid enterprising-type activities or those that involve active pursuit of leadership roles. Her introverted nature may be antithetical to enterprising activities.
- Her father, with his interests in law and business, may be an enterprising type. Leslie may be disinterested in these activities to set herself apart from her father or because she feels that she cannot match his accomplishments in this area.
- Leslie has been successful in the administrative responsibilities that she has undertaken. These responsibilities may reflect her conventional interests in structuring and organizing details. Moreover, her administrative duties, such as her enjoyment of creativity, may be a means to an end.
- Leslie's dissatisfaction with the new principal in her school may be due to her aversion to, or even distrust of, enterprising types. She may feel that he

discounts her because she is not like him nor does she value the same things. Leslie may also interpret the new procedures that he has instituted as a sign that he does not respect her ability and experience as a teacher.

Observation 4

Leslie dislikes taking risks and prefers to "play it safe." Yet she has entered career counseling because she is thinking about changing her career direction, and she seems willing to try new activities and work hard toward goals that are important to her.

Hypotheses

- Leslie's dislike of taking risks may be related to her concern about receiving the approval of others. She may be uncomfortable with trying something if there is a possibility that she will fail or will be judged as deficient by someone else.
- Her willingness to consider a radical career change, in light of her preference to avoid risk, seems to reflect the amount of dissatisfaction she is currently feeling. She may be more willing to take risks than is apparent from her inventory results.
- Leslie seems to have a clear sense of what she likes. Equally important, she seems to know what she dislikes. This fact may reduce the perceived risk of exploring a career change.

QUESTIONS FOR DISCUSSION

Review all the material related to Leslie that has been presented in this chapter, remembering that there are multiple sources of information, including the background and career history, family information, and the results of the four inventories. The questions listed below will guide your review.

1. What other observations do you make from a review of Leslie's background information? From the results of her assessments?

2. What consistent patterns occur within each separate source of information? Across all the information?

3. What discrepancies do you observe within each source of information? Across all the information?

4. List specific hypotheses that you have about Leslie.

5. How would you test these hypotheses? How will evidence that you gather confirm or change your working model of Leslie?

6. How is your working model of Leslie shaped by your sex, culture, and socioeconomic background? How is it shaped by her sex, culture, and socioeconomic background?

CONCEPTUALIZING LESLIE FROM VARIOUS THEORETICAL APPROACHES

The material in this chapter provides sufficiently rich information to begin forming hypotheses about Leslie's career concerns. We now turn to specific theoretical perspectives on working with Leslie. In each chapter, we add supplementary information about Leslie as appropriate to the specific theory or approach. This additional information is particularly relevant to the "working model" of Leslie that a counselor using a particular theory would be likely to develop.

Chapter 5

The Delivery of Culturally Responsive Career Counseling

COUNSELOR ROLES AND SETTINGS

Who uses career counseling? Our premise in this book is that *all* counselors need to understand how work and career decisions are conceptualized. Individuals may seek counseling for a variety of concerns, and an understanding of how those concerns may be affected by work or career is critical to a holistic understanding of the client. We return later, in Chapter 14, to a discussion of integrating career-related content into work with clients whose primary presenting concerns are not related to work or career. Having said this, though, in some settings, career or work counseling is the primary focus of the counselor. Some career counselors have private practices in which all their clients are seeking help with voluntary career transitions, such as leaving a job to retire or seek another position, or involuntary transitions, such as a layoff or having to return to the workforce following a divorce.

Amundson, Harris-Bowlsbey, and Niles (2009) note that career counseling has evolved from helping an adolescent choose a college and major, to counseling individuals at all stages of development with work-related choices and decisions. They highlight seven myths about career counseling that are important for students, professionals, and clients to recognize as myths:

1. Career counselors can give clients tests that tell them what to do.

2. Work decisions are made separately from other life decisions.

3. Career counseling does not address personal concerns.

4. Career counselors do not need training or expertise.

5. Career counseling is the same for everyone, regardless of cultural context.

6. Career counseling is needed only when a decision must be made.

7. Career counseling ends when a decision is made.

We address many of these myths in this chapter and throughout the rest of the book. Career counselors at all levels need to be aware that some or all these myths may shape the expectations that clients or students have when they seek career counseling. It is thus important to help clients understand the ways that career counseling may help them, that a single assessment tool cannot predict the success of a future career choice, and that the scope of career counseling is, in fact, often life and work counseling. It is also critical that individuals seek career counseling from trained professionals. Figler (2007) notes that hundreds of millions of individuals "would say they need help with their careers. Yet only a tiny fraction seek and pay for the services of a career counselor" (p. 98). Figler advocates an annual career checkup, in which individuals seek the help of a career counselor in much the same way individuals make an appointment with a health care provider as a preventative measure. He suggests an annual checkup could consist of one or more of several activities, including a review of skills, career exploration, identification of new competencies needed, career redirection, and job search activities.

CONDUCTING CAREER COUNSELING

Career counseling occurs in many settings, including high schools, universities, private practices, or work organizations. It may be useful to think about the different modalities or methods of delivering career services, of which "career counseling" is one option. Savickas (1994a) described the activities of guidance, advising, education, placement, coaching, and mentoring—all of which are designed to promote individuals' career development and may overlap with the activity of career counseling. Moreover, *career counseling* may be considered within the broader set of *career interventions*. These services or activities may share common elements, including using assessment, basing the intervention on career theory, and emphasizing self-awareness and optimal decision making. In this chapter, we discuss career counseling and focus on the broader area of career interventions in Chapter 12.

Individual career counseling is an "ongoing, face-to-face interaction between counselor and client" (Swanson, 1995, p. 245) in which the focus is on work- or career-related concerns. Career counseling is also defined as "the process of assisting individuals in the development of a life-career with focus on the definition of the worker role and how that role interacts with other life roles" (National Career Development Association, 2009, p. 1), highlighting the importance of placing career issues within the broader context of individuals' lives. Career services may also be delivered to groups, such as in classes or workshops, and career interventions often include activities that do not require a counselor's presence, such as computer-assisted guidance packages. In this chapter, we focus on individually delivered career counseling in which there is a relationship between counselor and client. Individual career counseling has been shown to be effective across a large number of studies (Brown & Ryan Krane, 2000; Whiston, Brecheisen, & Stephens, 2003). Brown and Ryan Krane also found that career counseling optimally consists of written exercises, interpretation of assessment tools (e.g., interest inventories), occupational information, role modeling, and helping clients build social support.

Several authors have developed models of career counseling. To return to our earlier discussion of terminology in Chapter 1, these are truly theories of career counseling rather than theories of career development, because their purpose is to outline how counseling might proceed. We cannot provide an exhaustive review of each model but will present one model here, the Culturally Appropriate Career Counseling Model (Fouad & Bingham, 1995) that may be applied to all clients. In general, career counseling models are structured around a phase of introduction and relationship building, a phase devoted to exploration of the client's work-related problem, and a phase devoted to helping the client move toward resolution of the problem. Whiston and Rahardja (2008) further recommend that counselors need to help clients develop insight and facilitate exploration of options and potential barriers to achievement of goals.

Culturally Appropriate Career Counseling Model

We argued the importance of integrating clients' context into career counseling in Chapter 2. In the present chapter, we discuss a model that helps career counselors explicitly incorporate culture in counseling. The culturally appropriate career counseling model (CACCM) specifically assesses the impact of cultural variables in each step of career counseling (Figure 5.1). The CACCM is an extension of models originally proposed by Ward and Bingham (1993; Bingham & Ward, 1994).

Figure 5.1 Culturally Appropriate Career Counseling Model

SOURCE: Fouad and Bingham (1995).

As shown in Figure 5.1, the CACCM has seven steps:

Step 1: The counselor and client establish a culturally appropriate relationship. In this critical first step, the counselor must work to establish a trusting relationship with the client to develop a working consensus. Culturally appropriate relationships will, of necessity, differ from clients' cultural norms and expectations of counseling and of the counseling relationship. It is important for the counselor to be knowledgeable of general cultural expectations but also to be flexible and to suspend judgment.

Step 2: The counselor identifies career issues that the client brings to counseling. This step is conceptualized as a broad examination of the client's concerns that may be related to vocational issues; these are examined within the client's cultural context. Fouad and Bingham (1995) identify five categories of career issues: cognitive, social/emotional, behavioral, environmental, and external. Clients may, of course, bring more than one of these issues to career counseling. Cognitive issues may include faulty information processing or irrational beliefs about working or career decision making. Emotional issues may include anxiety at work, or a client may be managing anger related to racism that prevents him or her from taking advantage of a work-related opportunity. Behavioral concerns may include being referred to career counseling because of a poor interpersonal style or work habits. Environmental issues are those related to the work environment; these include working conditions, coworkers, and supervisors. Fouad and Bingham distinguish environmental concerns from external barriers, which include racial discrimination, oppression, and sexual harassment. External barriers are explicitly defined, because racism and oppression influence career choices for many racial/ethnic group clients. These may operate implicitly, as part of restricting options that clients may consider, or explicitly, as clients are eliminated from positions because of race or gender.

Step 3: The counselor works with the client to assess the impact of cultural variables on the client's career issues.

Fouad and Bingham (1995) conceptualize a series of five concentric circles forming a sphere to help identify the way that culture influences vocational behavior (see Figure 5.2). We discussed the three separate contextual dimensions that may influence individuals' work related choices and decisions in Chapter 2. The sphere in Figure 5.2 is another way to conceptualize the various influences on a single individual.

1. The first, innermost circle represents the core, which comprises the unique aspects of the individual, such as their interests, values and abilities.

2. The next circle, influencing the self most directly, is gender. As we noted in Chapter 2, gender influences the types of careers that individuals will consider and the way that they implement their career choices. The interaction of gender and culture also affects career choices, as some cultures have more clearly defined expectations of men and women, particularly in relation to gender-appropriate occupations.

3. The next circle influencing vocational behavior represents individuals' families. Familial expectations, as well as familial norms and values, play an important role in forming individuals' views of work and their work-related decisions. As noted earlier, for some individuals, the family will be a strong influence; for others, the influence of the family will not be as strong.

Figure 5.2 Spheres of Influence of Cultural Variables

Structural Factors
Perceptions
Barriers (sexism, racism)
Definitions
Expectations

Role
Expectations

Dominant (Majority) Group
Racial or Ethnic Group
Family
Gender
Core

Cultural Factors
Racial Identity
Development
Worldview

Definitions
Expectations
Values

Interests
Values
Abilities

SOURCE: Fouad and Bingham (1995).

4. The fourth layer from the center is the individual's racial/ethnic group, including cultural factors such as cultural values, racial identity, and acculturation level.

5. Finally, Fouad and Bingham (1995) conceptualize the dominant culture as the outermost layer of influence on individuals' career decision making.

These spheres are intended to be dynamic rather than static. Thus, at a particular point in one individual's life, the family sphere may be predominant, with strong influence also from the dominant culture. Then, as individuals gain a greater sense of identification with a racial/ethnic culture, the fourth sphere may increase in influence while the dominant culture sphere reduces in influence on their vocational choices.

Step 4: Once the counselor and client have determined the career issues and the influence of culture on those career issues, they set culturally appropriate processes and goals. The counseling process must be culturally appropriate, and the goals of counseling must fit within the client's cultural framework. An example of an inappropriate process is the use of insight-oriented counseling for clients whose culture places little emphasis on individual introspection (e.g., traditional Asian cultures) or an insistence on addressing solely the individual rather than his or her family. Inappropriate goals for the client may include encouraging career choices based on dominant culture values, such as choosing occupations based on prestigious occupations or nontraditional careers for women.

Step 5: Once the goals and processes have been determined, the counselor and client determine and implement a culturally appropriate intervention. Bowman (1993) recommends that group interventions might be particularly effective with racial/ethnic clients. She also recommends including the family in career counseling and encouraging clients to seek same-gender/ethnic group role models. Career interventions often include assessment, which has unique issues when applied across cultures. Subich (2005) and Flores and Heppner (2002) recommend that counselors be aware of the way that culture may influence traditional vocational assessment; they suggest that counselors seek additional ways to help clients clarify and identify the variables important in their career decision making.

Step 6: The counselor helps the client make a culturally appropriate decision. For clients who feel they straddle several cultural contexts, counselors may help clients understand the cultural consequences of each choice. For example, a traditional Latina may be expected by her family to live close to home, and she may have a conflict between embracing the value placed on family and wanting to pursue a college education far away. A counselor may help her understand the consequences of each decision and help her choose the right decision for her.

Step 7: This step involves implementing the client's plans and following up. Although no studies have examined the effectiveness of the CACCM, per se, Ihle et al. (2005) reviewed empirical studies related to each of the steps. They concluded that racial/ethnic match between counselor and client was important to clients of color and that the client's perception of the counselor's cultural competence was almost as important. They also concluded that much more research is needed to understand if, and how, a culture-centered approach is effective. Heppner and Heppner (2003) also note the importance of investigating the role of culture in career counseling. More information is needed to understand how the culture of the client and the counselor interact and how that influences the career counseling process.

MULTICULTURAL CAREER COUNSELING TENETS

Gysbers, Heppner, and Johnston (2009), working with Lisa Flores, outline six central tenets that are hallmarks of traditional career counseling against which counselors must guard as they work from a multicultural perspective. The first is the tenet of universality; that all theories may be applied to everyone and help explain the career behavior of all. We noted in Chapter 1 that career theories explain only parts of career behavior. We also highlighted the importance of context in Chapter 2, arguing that context helps shape career and work decisions. No single theory discussed in this book helps explain all contextual influences on career and work behavior. The second tenet is individualism and autonomy. As noted earlier, most traditional career counselors focus on the individual as the primary decision maker. In fact, the family unit is the decision maker for many clients, particularly those from cultural minority groups.

The third tenet is an assumption of a certain level of affluence. In other words, most career theories assume that clients can afford to spend time exploring their interests, values, and abilities and then to seek additional training prior to implementing a career choice. However, as discussed earlier, many individuals do not have the economic luxury to do anything other than find a job that pays for necessities, and in fact, for many working poor, their wages do not even cover basic needs. This is particularly the case for racial/ethnic minorities, who are disproportionately overrepresented in lower socioeconomic levels.

A fourth tenet of traditional career counseling is that opportunities are available to all individuals who work hard. In reality, the American dream of success based on hard work is the American nightmare for individuals who are restricted in their career choices due to racial and sexual discrimination, as well as discrimination based on sexual orientation or social class.

A fifth tenet is that work is central in people's lives. But work may not be central for some individuals because of their experiences of institutional racism or because their cultures place higher value on other aspects of life. The final tenet is that of linearity in the career counseling process. Traditional career counseling, consisting of knowledge of self, knowledge of the world of work, and finding a match between the two, is the epitome of the White cultural focus on linear, rational, and objective thinking. But for some racial/ethnic group clients, a more intuitive approach may be more beneficial than a linear one.

BOX 5.1 Personal Reflections

- Considering my own career decisions how would I apply the six tenets described above?
- Think of two friends or family members who are different from me and from each other in some context (e.g., gender, race, sexual orientation). How might I consider their context in career counseling? How would career counseling be different for each of them?

APPLYING A MULTICULTURAL PERSPECTIVE TO THE CASE OF LESLIE

Counselors applying a multicultural perspective would consider the questions in Box 5.2. Counselors actively bring their cultural frameworks, values, and worldviews into their thinking. These factors shape the way that they develop hypotheses about a client and inform specific steps or strategies of career interventions. Counselors examine their own cultural competence with their clients, how cultural context is influencing their clients and the counseling sessions, and how they are being effective with their clients.

BOX 5.2 Counselor Cognitions

- What is my plan for working with this client?
- What are the gaps in my knowledge about the client's context?
- How is my cultural context framing the way I view the client?
- How am I interpreting the client's information?
- What are my strengths and areas of challenge in working with this client?
- How is the client's cultural context shaping his or her perception of work?
- How have the client's multiple contexts influenced his or her work decisions?
- What are the client's external and internal challenges?

Conceptualizing Leslie's Career History

Leslie grew up as the middle child of a relatively affluent White, middle-class family in a large metropolitan area in the midwestern United States. Her ethnicity is not specified, other than to note that she is Caucasian. She is, however, a product of one or more cultures that transmitted values and messages about being a Caucasian woman in the United States. Giordano and McGoldrick (1996) note that "all people are ethnic. . . . It is a fact of our identities, one over which we have no choice" (p. 428). Whites often conceptualize themselves as not having a culture, as being "regular" Americans. However, their cultural backgrounds, whether their ancestors came from the Mediterranean, Eastern Europe, or Western Europe, have shaped the way they view the world, their relationship with nature, the way they define family, the way they define work, and their view of time. To understand fully Leslie's career history, it is critical to understand the cultural messages she received growing up as a White woman.

Katz (1985) discusses several aspects of the White culture. She notes that "Whites share similar cultural dimensions that constitute a separate, unique culture" (p. 616). She explicitly identifies several components of White cultural values and beliefs. These include a focus on individualism, with its emphasis on autonomy and independence; a focus on competition; and a value placed on winning. There is a strong pragmatic orientation, with an emphasis on doing something about a situation or problem. Future planning is stressed, and progress and growth are valued. The scientific method is the favored mode, with preference given to rational and linear thinking and to decision making based on objective as opposed to subjective information. Status and power are based on position and title, and value is placed on economic possessions. The world is viewed as a place to master rather than as a place to tolerate or in which to coexist with nature. Family is primarily viewed as the nuclear family rather than as an extended family including many generations. The Protestant work ethic predominates: Hard work is good, and working hard brings success. Time is viewed as a saleable entity that is apportioned out according to set schedules; deviations from time schedules are not tolerated.

Leslie received messages from her family consistent with White cultural expectations. She was taught to work hard, as evidenced by her excellent academic work in high school. Her family expected her to plan for the future in anticipating that she would go to college. However, they also clearly conveyed a value on individualism and autonomy in not giving her much direction or guidance in choosing a career or a major. Her father communicated a value placed on pragmatic gain in recommending that she enter a business field, although this did not coincide with her interests. Her family also may have transmitted several values in showing their impatience with her decision-making process. They may have indicated that she ought to be more rational and linear in her decision making, taking the information she had and simply making a decision with it. This also is consistent with a preference for doing something about a situation perceived as problematic rather than living with it. Leslie's family also appears to have conveyed messages about appropriate careers for their children that allowed them to gain positions of power and status.

Leslie also received messages of appropriate behavior as a White woman; some of these messages are in direct conflict with appropriate behavior as a White individual. White women are expected to be nurturing and to put others' needs before their own. They are expected to be caring and to be kind and helpful to others, particularly other White people. They also are perceived as being emotional, weak, illogical, and needing security from others. Thus, the culture tells White women to be independent *and* dependent, logical *and* emotional. White women are expected to be passive *and* to take control of a situation. They are to be nurturing *and* autonomous. Leslie seems to have received these mixed messages. She was to be autonomous in making a career decision, but her mother communicated that she should not pursue that career at the same time she was taking care of a family. Her parents may have communicated that the occupation of teacher is a more appropriate occupation for a woman than going into a math or science career, since she would be taking care of others as a teacher. She may also have received messages that it is more appropriate to rely on others to help make decisions rather than being emotionally independent. She may have received messages to avoid positions of leadership and power.

It is not clear what Leslie's perceptions of other races were while she was growing up. She grew up in a suburb of a large midwestern city; she may have grown up in a racially segregated environment. If so, then she had little contact with individuals of other races while she was growing up, thus having little opportunity to develop a consciousness of herself as a member of a racial/ethnic group or to develop a knowledge or understanding of other groups. On the other hand, Leslie may have grown up in a racially integrated neighborhood and may have had significant interpersonal relationships with children from many cultural groups. She may have developed a strong sense of herself as a member of a racial group and an appreciation of and understanding for other cultures. She may, in fact, have spent a great deal of time exploring her own cultural heritage(s) and may have gained an appreciation of the role of White privilege in the United States. Whichever the case, her early upbringing and the messages her family, neighborhood, and school gave her about her own race and about other races helped form her later racial perceptions and attitudes.

Leslie moved to her first job in a small town in the Midwest, which was most probably homogeneously White. Her frustrations with the job appeared to have little to do with the culture of the town but rather with the workload in her job and with the lack of a social support network. She had ended her relationship with her boyfriend, whose ethnicity is not given. She met her husband, Joe, when she was nearly 30. He is second-generation Mexican American. Joe appears to have had some ambivalence about identifying with his Mexican American heritage. He wanted to conform to the dominant culture's behavioral expectations when he was an adolescent, refusing to speak Spanish or to attend church with his family, but his first marriage was to a Latina woman from his neighborhood. He appears to have become more involved in his community and to have developed a greater appreciation for the traditions and values of his heritage. After his marriage dissolved, he appears to have retained his sense of identity as a Mexican American. Although he eventually married a White woman, Leslie, and no longer lives in his family's neighborhood, he still self-identifies as a Mexican American and has embraced many traditional values.

Joe and Leslie's marriage appears to be problematic for both sets of in-laws. Leslie's marriage to a member of another ethnic group may have been an issue for her parents. There are indications that they accepted him as a member of the family, since Leslie and Joe spend a fair amount of time with her family. Leslie's family's initial concerns for her marriage to Joe may have been due less to his ethnicity than to her marriage to a divorced father of one son; they also may have reacted because of their own prejudices and lack of racial awareness. Social class may be another factor that influenced Leslie's family's reaction to Joe, since Joe's educational and occupational level are quite different from those of the rest of her family. Joe's mother has said she thinks Leslie is too American. This may have caused conflicts for Leslie with her mother-in-law; it may also cause conflict between Joe and Leslie if Joe feels torn between his family and his wife.

Conceptualizing Leslie's Present Situation

Conceptualizing Leslie's current situation from a multicultural perspective includes examining Leslie's behaviors and values from the multiple cultural contexts in which she lives. She is a close member of her White family and continues to be influenced by their expectations and values. She is married to a Mexican American man, who has expectations for her behavior that may stem from his own cultural background and values. She works in a high school setting that may have a racially diverse faculty and students.

Leslie's family has conveyed to her that she should be pursuing a career that will give her position and economic benefits and have also suggested that she should start a family; the latter connotes that she cannot both work and raise a family. They again show some impatience with what they perceive as her slow decision making. Her father is still advocating a business career, her mother and sister still suggesting that she stop working to have children. Her brother communicates that she is perhaps making an emotional decision in examining her career choices; he has labeled her dissatisfaction as complaints about inconsequential aspects of her job.

Leslie's husband, Joe, also expects that she would stay home if they have children. She feels that though he is supportive of her changing careers, he is less supportive of her returning to school. The role of women in the traditional Latino family is one of being subservient to their husbands and of caring and nurturing children, a role to which his mother conformed. A woman is expected to be passive and dependent on her husband. Caretaker of the family is her predominant purpose in life. On the other hand, Joe indicates that he knows that women should be able to be independent. Leslie may be violating some of his expectations in her interest in pursuing a career change. Though she and Joe want to have a family together, she may be reluctant to assume the role that he wants her to play in that family. It is not clear whether Joe expects her to play a particular role with his son. Leslie and Joe's lack of communication may be due to differences in cultural values; she may be focusing on discussing all her concerns with him, thereby creating conflict, while he may be motivated by the Latino value of smoothing over conflicts and having harmonious relationships.

Finally, Leslie works in a high school that may or may not be racially diverse in the students she is serving and the faculty with whom she works. Whichever the case, race may be playing a role in Leslie's decisions. Her perceptions that parents are uninvolved in their children's education may actually be due to a cultural difference in attitudes and behaviors. What she is interpreting as lack of involvement may be a cultural respect for authority and viewing the teacher as the expert. Similarly, her perceptions that students are having more difficulties at home may be due to her own racial assumptions about problems. In other words, Leslie may be interpreting her students' behavior from a cultural deficit model, thus concluding that they are dealing with many problems at home.

QUESTIONS FOR DISCUSSION

1. What specific hypotheses would you develop about Leslie from culturally appropriate counseling approaches? How does using these approaches help you understand Leslie? How might it help Leslie understand herself?

2. What role may Leslie's worldview have played in her career development and choices?

3. How could you balance increasing awareness of race and ethnicity as possible influences in Leslie's decision making with an appreciation of her racial consciousness? Where might this be problematic?

4. How could you empower Leslie to make different types of decisions?

5. How may culture have interacted with Leslie's family of origin and her familial obligations to shape her behavior?

6. What role may sexism and racism have played in Leslie's decisions and in the outcomes of those decisions?

7. How might cultural issues influence the relationship between Leslie and Joe?

The Case of Norman

Norman is a 17-year-old African American male who is referred to a counselor to help him "adjust his attitude." He is a junior in high school and needs to find a job. Norman is the youngest son of three children. His father is a cook for a large catering company, and his mother is a nurse; they have been divorced for 10 years. His oldest brother is in college, majoring in business, and his older sister is currently working as a receptionist and hopes to return to school to become a paralegal assistant. Norman has lived primarily with his mother, though she has asked him to live with his father twice during his high school years, when she felt she was not able to "manage" him.

Norman currently has a C average and has taken elective courses in manufacturing and in computers. Norman entered high school with a B average. However, he did not do well in his eighth-grade math and science classes, and his eighth-grade counselor encouraged him to take classes that would prepare him for a vocational technical school, such as applied math courses and business writing. His mother initially expressed some concern about this plan of study, hoping that Norman would enter a college-preparatory curriculum, but Norman did not want to go back and ask his counselor to change his schedule. In addition, his friends were signing up for the same courses, and he thought he'd be able to change once he was in high school. Unfortunately, the curriculum has been less flexible than he thought, and he has been unable to shift to a college-preparatory track.

The course that Norman enjoyed the most during his first year in high school was manufacturing. He enjoyed the material, he enjoyed working on the class projects, and he enjoyed the practical nature of the course. He was less enthusiastic about his other classes; he thought they were either irrelevant or boring. His mother became concerned during his sophomore year that he was not doing well in school. They began to have conflicts at home about his grades and about his friendships with several boys at school. This was the first instance in which he lived with his father, who helped him refocus on school, and his grades improved. He returned to live with his mother during the summer after his sophomore year, since her schedule permitted her to be home more than his father. He lived with his father once more during his junior year for 2 months, returning to his mother's home when he and his father disagreed about the time spent with his friends.

Norman's freshman year manufacturing teacher encouraged him to continue in this track and to apply for an apprenticeship with a manufacturing company. While he did not secure a formal apprenticeship, he did join a cooperative program during his junior year that enabled him to work part-time during the afternoon and take classes in the morning. He enjoyed the work, although he also felt bored at times with the relatively mundane tasks he felt he had to do. He was learning about cell manufacturing and quality improvement techniques in his manufacturing classes at school but was not seeing those policies implemented in the manufacturing company. He began to question his supervisor about the discrepancy between what he was doing and what he had learned in class. The supervisor complained to the teacher, and the teacher referred Norman to the school counselor. The teacher was primarily concerned that Norman learns to adjust his attitude, since questioning supervisors may lead Norman into problematic situations on the job.

Norman was angry that he was referred to his school counselor. He did not think he had a "problem" or that his attitude needed to change. He was resistant at first and did not trust what the counselor would eventually tell his teacher. His counselor, a White woman, reassured him that their sessions would remain confidential and that they would talk together about what she would say to his teacher. She encouraged him to think about how they could work together. They talked a great deal about Norman's feelings and thoughts about working in a factory, and Norman acknowledged his boredom and how uncertain he was about another career choice. They also talked about whether Norman should have conveyed his opinions about his internship to the supervisor and if so, how he could do that. Norman decided he would like to explore his interests and the possibility of going to college instead of entering an apprenticeship.

The counselor found that Norman's vocational interests were primarily in the Realistic and Investigative areas. Norman also scored high on the Mechanics & Construction, Mathematics, and Science Basic Interest Scales, as well as Management, Law, and Politics & Public Speaking Basic Interest Scales. Norman was most similar to men who are engineers, farmers or ranchers, research and development managers, computer systems analysts, and auto mechanics.

QUESTIONS FOR DISCUSSION

1. What cultural values did his family transmit to Norman?

2. What role may racism have played in Norman's school and career history?

3. What role may Norman's parents and siblings have played in Norman's decisions?

4. What cultural variables would you want to incorporate in career counseling?

5. What are some possible career interventions you could use?

6. What cultural strengths could you emphasize in working with Norman?

7. How should you work to "adjust Norman's attitude"? Is that an appropriate request on the part of the instructor?

DIRECTIONS AND IMPLICATIONS FOR CAREER COUNSELING

Goals of Counseling

The goal of counseling from a multicultural perspective is for counselors to deliver culturally appropriate interventions for clients, recognizing that clients come from unique sets of environments and contexts. Before this can happen, however, counselors must have knowledge of their own culture and the way their values, biases, and behaviors reflect that culture. They must have knowledge of and understanding of other groups' worldviews and how individuals' worldviews affect their values and behaviors. In other words, counselors must be multiculturally competent. The goal of multiculturally competent career counseling is to help clients make the most culturally appropriate career decisions that fit within the context of their lives. Readers are referred to Sue and Sue (2013) for further delineation and explanation of multicultural counseling competencies.

Some of the tenets discussed earlier may be important for their counselors to keep in mind when examining Leslie's and Norman's career histories. Leslie has consulted with her family and her husband; her husband, in particular, appears to play an influential role in Leslie's career decisions. The counselor should be aware that Leslie may choose to incorporate her husband in her decision making. Leslie also may have perceived that opportunities were not available to her because she is a woman. The counselor could help her explore some of those assumptions.

Norman's counselor needs to be aware of her own biases and assumptions about African Americans and be open to Norman's perceptions of his experiences. She will need to be aware of the role that racism and discrimination may have played in Norman's schooling and work opportunities. She will also want to be open to the role that racial differences may play in the relationship between her and Norman and work to feel comfortable in discussing this openly with him. Finally, she should be aware of ways that she can advocate for him within the school system to enable him to have more options.

Culturally Appropriate Career Counseling Model

Step 1: Establishing a culturally appropriate relationship

In the first step, the counselor sets the context for a working consensus (Bingham & Ward, 1994). This includes exhibiting empathy, warmth, and positive regard. The counselor and Leslie would discuss Leslie's expectations for counseling, which are shaped by her cultural background. The counselor might ask Leslie, "What do you expect of counseling and of me as your counselor?" Leslie most likely expects that the relationship would be a fairly egalitarian one and that the counselor has some information to share with her. She may also expect that the assessment tools will help her clarify her interests and needs and point her in a particular direction.

Norman's counselor in the case above sets the context for a working consensus by addressing Norman's anger at the referral for counseling and reassuring him that she was working to help him rather than his teacher. Norman felt that he was being "sent to be fixed," and the counselor discussed her role as a school counselor, telling him that what he said would be kept confidential. She also encouraged him to set goals for his time with her and explored with him what had made him unhappy and bored at the factory.

Step 2: Identification of career issues

The counselor then helps the client identify his or her career issues. Counselors also help clients explore additional environmental issues, such as the role that race and ethnicity may be playing in their current environment, external barriers such as possible sexism or racism operating in the work environment, and how gender-role expectations may have influenced their prior decisions. Leslie's career concerns may include her dissatisfaction with her job, her desire to explore other career possibilities, and her desire to make a career decision of which her husband can be supportive as initial issues for counseling. Norman's career issues include uncertainty about how to make a career decision, how to change the educational track he is on, how to handle his supervisor and teacher, and what other options he could choose.

Step 3: Assessing the impact of cultural variables on career issues

In the third step, the counselor helps explore how behavior has been a product of the client's culture and whether these are behaviors the client wants to continue or to change. For example, the counselor may state, "Leslie, you have been dissatisfied with not being able to teach advanced classes but have not said anything when those were assigned to others. You indicated that your mother taught you to play along and that women don't make a fuss. You could choose to be more assertive, which may change the assignments you get. Is this something you would like to change?" The counselor may also explore how Joe's Latino background and values have contributed to the role he expects his wife to play. The counselor could help Leslie examine how her culture and her husband's culture have interacted to help create the conflicts she has experienced in her marriage.

Using the spheres diagram (Figure 5.2), the counselor could help Leslie examine how her gender has influenced her own and others' expectations of her and the roles that she has been taught she should play. The counselor may then help her examine how her family and the values that they have conveyed have influenced her career decisions. The counselor could ask Leslie to identify her cultural heritage and help her understand how her culture has influenced her behavior. The counselor may say, "Leslie, you indicated that you are White. Tell me what ethnic group your family identifies most with. Let's look at how that culture may have influenced you." Finally, the counselor may help Leslie examine how the majority culture has affected her, both in giving her privileges as a White woman and in restricting her options because of sexism.

Norman's counselor might also use Figure 5.2 to help Norman think about the role that racism may have played in his options to this point. She might ask him to consider the messages his family has given him about being an African American man in the United States and how racial differences may have influenced the interactions with his teacher and supervisor. She would also explore the messages he received from his family about working and about how he feels about working in a predominantly White environment.

Step 4: Setting culturally appropriate processes and goals

The counselor works with the client to establish the goals that the client wants to achieve in counseling. Leslie may choose to decide whether to leave teaching or not. In addition, she may want to gain further clarity on how she has accepted messages from her family about being indecisive and overly emotional and how cultural values have influenced her marriage. Norman might decide to switch to a college track in high school or continue to seek an apprenticeship. His goal may also include how to negotiate differences with his supervisor and teacher.

Step 5: Implementing culturally appropriate interventions

In Step 5, the counselor incorporates the assessments that clients have taken, as well as implementing additional interventions that appear appropriate for the goals that clients have set for counseling. For example, Leslie's first goal is to make a decision about whether to stay in the teaching profession or choose another career. Norman's is whether to stay on a vocational track or change his high school classes to prepare to go to college.

The counselor first incorporates the results of the Strong Interest Inventory in counseling. In Norman's case, the counselor wants him to consider a wide variety of occupations, including those that may require more education. She wants to ensure he does not prematurely foreclose options because of racism. Norman's counselor also may advocate within the school system to help him switch to a more college-preparatory program and help him build the skills to do well in these classes.

Clients often restrict their options to gender-stereotypic occupations; Leslie's counselor may help her examine her interest areas other than the female-traditional ones. For example, Leslie's counselor could help her explore interests in the Investigative and Conventional areas, examining the General Occupational Themes and Basic Interest Scales. Thus, the counselor asks her to discuss her interests in Math and Science, as well as in data management and processing. The counselor could also ask Leslie to discuss the occupations in the Investigative and Conventional areas. Leslie may, however, prefer to accommodate her husband's wish that she not seek further schooling; this will limit her options to those careers that she could enter with a bachelor's degree in secondary math education. Interestingly, her Skills Confidence Inventory indicates that she is quite confident about her skills in the nontraditional Investigative areas; her counselor may want to explore this further with her.

Leslie's Minnesota Importance Questionnaire indicates that her highest values are consistent with her cultural expectations: Achievement, Ability Utilization, Moral Values, and Social Service are her highest needs. The counselor could help Leslie examine which of those values are important for her to feel rewarded in an occupation and how she interprets those needs. For example, the counselor may say, "Your highest need is Achievement. Tell me what that means for you, when you feel that you have accomplished something."

Hartung et al. (1998) suggested that many of the assessment tools that Leslie completed may be used within a cultural framework, advocating the use of a qualitative approach. For example, the counselor may examine the items or scales in the Adult Career Concerns Inventory from a cultural perspective within the interview. Thus, the counselor may ask Leslie to discuss her concerns on implementing a career within the context of the cultural differences in her marriage.

Additional interventions that the counselor may employ include the 42-item Career Checklist (Ward & Bingham, 1993). Leslie identifies the issues that influence her career decision making, such as familial obligations; understanding of her abilities, interests, and needs; confidence; knowledge of the world of work; personal or sociopolitical obstacles; decision-making confidence; view of the relationship between education and work; ability to dream; and belief that personal parameters affect career choice. The Career Checklist may help Leslie clarify barriers and obstacles to achieving her goals.

If Leslie's counseling goals include examining the role that culture plays in her decision making and in her marriage, the counselor may invite Joe to be part of career counseling. The counselor may use fantasy exercises to help Leslie identify how she would like to shape her career. The counselor could ask Leslie to find role models who are women in nontraditional occupations to help her explore how such an option would fit in her life. Additional strategies include the use of genograms to help Leslie examine how her family has defined appropriate careers for men and women. Finally, the counselor may ask Leslie to examine the role that culture may play in her decision to leave teaching: "How comfortable are you with teaching a racially diverse student group? Could your decision be related to the different races of your students or of other faculty? Could your decision to leave be due to sexist policies or behavior on the part of your principal?" If so, these issues may be a result of a lack of racial understanding or lack of knowledge of various racial/ethnic groups' cultural values and behavior, and they could be addressed in counseling.

Step 6: Decision making and Step 7: Implementation

Following the interventions, the counselor helps clients make a decision relative to their goals and then helps them formulate a plan to implement it. For example, Leslie may decide to confront Joe and her family about their expectations that she behave in sex-appropriate ways. Leslie's counselor could help her formulate specific steps to implement her decision; the counselor might help Leslie work on assertiveness skills, role-playing a confrontation. Her counselor would help her identify some specific goals she wants as a result of the confrontation, such as more equitable sharing of household tasks or support for a decision to go to graduate school. Norman's counselor may help him make a decision to talk to the teacher and decide to pursue a different educational track.

ADDITIONAL CASES

Case 1: Brenda

Brenda is a 47-year-old Latina who is a police officer in New York City. She entered the police academy in her early 20s because her uncle was a cop and she thought it would be "cool" to be a uniformed officer; her uncle encouraged her by telling her she was "tough" and could handle the work. Brenda recently retired from the force after 25 years on the job but now needs to return because her benefits are being reduced. She has taken some community college courses over the years but hasn't pursued a degree. Without a college degree, she feels that she cannot do much other than work for the police department, although she's has grown a little weary of the physical aspect of the work as she's gotten older. At her age, she still has many working years ahead of her, yet she's not sure what direction to take.

QUESTIONS FOR DISCUSSION

1. In what way have gender-role expectations influenced Brenda?

2. How might you help Brenda deal with the changes that have occurred through retirement and now her return to work?

3. What does the occupational role mean to Brenda? How does it fit with her image of herself as a woman?

4. How have Brenda's experiences in a gender-nontraditional occupation affected her? How do these experiences influence her future work?

5. What contextual influences are salient to her at this point in time?

Case 2: Justino

Justino is a 37-year-old single man from Puerto Rico. He has lived in Atlanta, Georgia, for the past 6 years, while he was a pilot for a major commercial airline. He is seeking career counseling because he has just learned his job was eliminated when his company merged with another airline. Justino graduated from a college in Puerto Rico with a bachelor's degree in airway sciences and received his commercial pilot's license after graduation. He worked for a small commuter airline in Florida for several years after college and then felt very fortunate to get a position with a major airline. His primary routes were in the United States, though he occasionally was able to fly to Europe and Puerto Rico. He loved his work, loved the prestige of being a pilot, and enjoyed the considerable salary he earned. He states several times that his family is very proud of him because of the prestige associated with being a pilot.

Justino is the oldest son of four children. His father worked as an engineer for the government in Puerto Rico. His mother is a real estate agent. His family lives in San Juan, near many of Justino's aunts and uncles and cousins and grandparents. Several of Justino's cousins work in the United States, as does one brother and sister. The family accepts that there are more opportunities for their children in the United States, but they expect weekly communication and frequent visits. Justino has gone home often, since his airline flew to San Juan. He was expected to be at his parents' for every major holiday and family event, and he enjoyed his ability to travel and his position in the family as the eldest son.

The news that he would be laid off is devastating to him. He knew that the merger of the two airlines would result in some job losses but thought he had enough seniority to remain employed. The job outlook for pilots in commercial airlines is not very good, and he does not want to take the pay cut to go back to work for a commuter airline. He has wanted to be a pilot since he was a small child and has never thought of doing something else. He is ashamed of losing his job, worried that his family will see him as a failure and that he will bring disgrace to them.

QUESTIONS FOR DISCUSSION

1. What is the first thing you would focus on as the counselor?

2. What role may Justino's ethnic identity play in his decisions?

3. What cultural values may his family have transmitted to Justino?

4. What cultural variables would you want to incorporate in career counseling?

5. What are some possible career interventions you could use?

6. What cultural strengths could you emphasize in working with Justino?

Case 3: Monica

Monica is a 27-year-old woman who is of Native American and African American descent. She is seeking career counseling because she has lost her government subsidy and must enter the workforce. Monica is the mother of three children, ages 10, 8, and 6. The oldest child is the daughter of a White man; the younger two are children of a relationship Monica had with an African American man who also accepted her first child as his own. The latter relationship has ended. Though the children continue to see their father, his contribution to the household income must be supplemented to support Monica and her three children.

Monica's parents are both biracial. Her mother is half Cherokee and half African American and identifies primarily with her Cherokee heritage. She volunteers at a local museum devoted to Native American history and culture. Her father is half Sioux and half African American; his primary identification is with the African American community, where he is a community police officer. Monica grew up in a middle-class, racially mixed neighborhood, the younger of two children. Her sister, who is 5 years older, is employed as a day care worker, which enables her also to care for her own children. Monica's sister is married to an African American man, who owns his own plumbing company.

Monica did not finish high school, since she dropped out when she was pregnant with her first child. Although her high school had day care available and her counselor encouraged her to complete her high school degree, Monica wanted to concentrate on her baby and on her boyfriend. However, shortly after the child was born, the baby's father left town, and Monica has not seen him since. She went on public aid after he left. She was too depressed to find a job and then began her relationship with Rick. Her government subsidy continued. Rick helped support her and her daughter, and the two additional children that they had together, until their relationship ended. Monica's primary support system consists of her family and friends in her apartment building, most of whom are African American, though feels no particular identification with either the Native American or African American community.

Monica learned last fall that her government subsidy was going to be eliminated this month. She did not know what to do, since she had no skills, no degree, and no job history. Her family encouraged her to seek career counseling some time ago, but she was embarrassed at her lack of skills and did nothing until she learned her last check would come next week.

QUESTIONS FOR DISCUSSION

1. What is the first thing you would focus on as the counselor?

2. What role may Monica's biracial status and her ethnic identity play in her decisions?

3. What cultural values may her family have transmitted to Monica?

4. What cultural variables would you want to incorporate in career counseling?

5. What are some possible career interventions you could use?

6. What cultural strengths could you emphasize in working with Monica?

PART II: THEORIES

Holland's Theory of Vocational Personalities and Work Environments

INTRODUCTORY REVIEW

Theories of person-environment fit, such as Holland's theory (Holland, 1997; Nauta, 2013) and the theory of work adjustment (Dawis, 2005; Dawis & Lofquist, 1984; Swanson & Schneider, 2013), are considered evolutionary extensions of earlier trait-and-factor counseling (Chartrand, 1991; Rounds & Tracey, 1990), which, in turn, had its roots in a social reform movement at the turn of the 20th century (Parsons, 1909/1989). Person-environment psychology is grounded in the basic assumption that a reciprocal relationship exists between people and their environments; that is, people influence their environments, and environments influence people (Walsh, Price, & Craik, 1992). Perhaps nowhere has this fundamental idea been more thoroughly implemented than in the realm of vocational psychology; in fact, the history of vocational psychology as a scholarly field is intimately intertwined with the evolution of person-environment models applied to career behavior (Swanson & Chu, 2000).

Holland's theory of person-environment fit has been an influential force in vocational psychology since its introduction over five decades ago. Part of the theory's appeal is due to the simple and intuitively meaningful premises on which it is based. Holland (1997) described his theory as answering three fundamental questions. First, what characteristics of persons and environments lead to positive vocational outcomes (such as satisfying career decisions), and what characteristics of persons and environments lead to negative vocational outcomes (such as indecision or dissatisfying decisions)? Second, what characteristics of persons and environments lead to career stability or change over the life span? Third, what are the most effective ways of providing assistance to people with career concerns?

Holland's theory is based on the underlying premise that career choice is an expression of one's personality and, thus, that members of an occupation have similar personalities and similar histories. He described four working assumptions of his theory. First, most individuals can be described in terms of their resemblance to six personality types—realistic, investigative, artistic, social, enterprising, or conventional. These types are perhaps best considered as model or theoretical types that describe an individual or with which an individual may be compared. Each personality type has a characteristic set of attitudes and skills to use in response to problems encountered in the environment, and each encompasses preferences for vocational and leisure activities, life goals and values, beliefs about oneself, and problem-solving style (see Table 6.1). An individual is rarely a single "pure" type; rather, individuals are more likely to be a combination of several types, with one type that is dominant and other types that are secondary.

Table 6.1 Characteristics of Holland's Personality and Environmental Types

Type	Self-Concept and Values	Potential Competencies	Typical Work Activities and Environments
Realistic	Emotionally stable, reliable Practical, thrifty, persistent Shy, modest Uncomfortable talking about self Traditional values	Mechanical ability and ingenuity Problem solving with tools, machines Psychomotor skills Physical strength	Job with tangible results Operating heavy equipment Using tools Physical demands Fixing, building, repairing
Investigative	Independent, self-motivated Reserved, introspective Analytical, curious Task oriented Original, creative, nonconforming	Scientific ability Analytical skills Mathematical skills Writing skills Perseverance	Ambiguous or abstract tasks Solving problems through thinking Working independently Scientific or laboratory settings Collecting and organizing data

Type	Self-Concept and Values	Potential Competencies	Typical Work Activities and Environments
Artistic	Independent, nonconforming Self-expressive Intuitive, sensitive, emotional Impulsive Drawn to aesthetic qualities	Creativity, imagination Verbal-linguistic skills Musical ability Artistic ability	Creating artwork or performing Working independently Unstructured, flexible environments that allow self-expression
Social	Humanistic, idealistic, ethical Concerned for welfare of others Tactful, cooperative, generous Kind, friendly, cheerful Understanding, insightful	Social and interpersonal skills Verbal ability Teaching skills Ability to empathize with and understand others	Teaching, explaining, guiding Solving problems, leading discussions Educational, social service, and mental health organizations
Enterprising	Status conscious Ambitious, competitive Sociable, talkative Optimistic, energetic, popular Aggressive, adventuresome	Verbal skills related to speaking, persuading, selling Leadership skills Resilience, high energy, optimism Social and interpersonal skills	Selling, purchasing, leading Managing people and projects Giving speeches and presentations Financial, government, and political organizations
Conventional	Conscientious, persevering Practical, conservative Orderly, systematic, precise, accurate Careful, controlled	Efficiency, organization Management of systems and data Mathematical skills Attention to detail, perfectionism Operation of office machines	Organizing office procedures Keeping records and filing systems Writing reports, making charts Structured organizations with well-ordered chains of command

SOURCE: Adapted from Harmon, Hansen, Borgen, and Hammer (2005); Holland (1997); Sharf (1997).

Types develop as a "product of a characteristic interaction among a variety of cultural and personal forces including peers, biological heredity, parents, social class, culture, and the physical environment" (Holland, 1997, p. 2). These experiences lead to an individual's preference for some activities over others; the preferences then develop into strong interests, which lead to related competencies. An individual's interests in conjunction with his or her competencies form a specific "disposition" that allows the individual to "think, perceive, and act in special ways" (p. 2).

The second assumption in Holland's theory is that environments can be categorized as one of six model types—again realistic, investigative, artistic, social, enterprising, or conventional. The environment's type is determined by the dominant type of the individuals who compose that environment. Because different types of people have varying constellations of skills, abilities, and so on, they prefer to surround themselves with other people who are similar to them: "Where people congregate, they create an environment that reflects the types they most resemble" (Holland, 1997, p. 3). Each environment has a characteristic set of problems and opportunities, as well as requiring differing activities and competencies and offering different rewards (see Table 6.1).

The third assumption of Holland's theory is the heart of the person-environment fit theories—namely, that "people search for environments that will let them exercise their skills and abilities, express their attitudes and values, and take on agreeable problems and roles" (Holland, 1997, p. 4). In a reciprocal manner, environments also search for people, through activities such as social interactions and recruitment and selection practices.

Fourth, personality and environment interact to produce behavior. Knowing an individual's personality type and the type of his or her environment allows us to make predictions about a range of possible outcomes, such as vocational choice, job tenure and turnover, achievement, and satisfaction. Theories of person-environment fit require some mechanism to describe the degree of fit. The mechanism in Holland's theory is the six types, which can be used to describe either persons or environments, thus allowing a description of how individuals match with their environments.

In addition to the four working assumptions, Holland proposed secondary assumptions outline specific and predictable ways in which the types are interrelated. The first is usually referred to as *calculus:* The six types are arranged in a hexagonal structure, with the distance between types inversely proportional to their theoretical interrelations (see Figure 6.1). That is, types adjacent to one another share more in common than the types that are opposing in the hexagon; for example, realistic types are more like investigative types than they are like social types.

Furthermore, Holland postulated four constructs to describe the relationships between types within people or environments and between people and environments: congruence, differentiation, consistency, and identity. The concept of *congruence* occupies a central role in Holland's theory. Congruence refers to the match between a person and his or her environment in terms of the six types

Figure 6.1 Holland's Hexagonal Structure

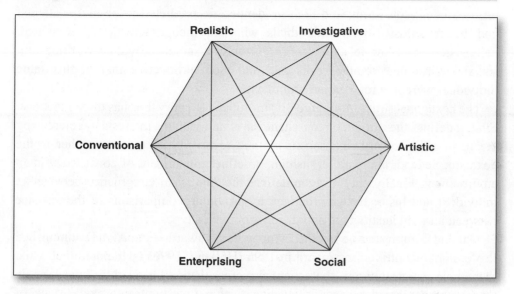

specified by the theory. An enterprising individual working in an enterprising environment is considered highly congruent compared with the same individual working within an investigative environment. Congruence is hypothesized to be related to important outcomes, such as job satisfaction and job tenure. As Holland (1997) described it, "Persons in congruent environments are encouraged to express their favorite behavior repertoires in familiar and congenial settings. In contrast, persons in incongruent environments find that they have behavior repertoires that are out of place and unappreciated" (p. 56).

Differentiation pertains to the degree of definition of an individual's interests; interests are considered well differentiated when there is a clear distinction between what an individual likes and dislikes. *Consistency* is a reflection of the "internal coherence" (Spokane, 1996) of an individual's interests in terms of the hexagonal arrangement; an individual with artistic and investigative interests would be considered to be more consistent than an individual with artistic and conventional interests. *Identity* provides "an estimate of the clarity and stability" (Holland, 1997, p. 5) of a person's identity or goals, interests, and talents. Like other constructs in Holland's theory, differentiation, consistency, and identity are used to describe both individuals and environments. Thus, environments as well as people may be characterized by their level of differentiation, consistency, and identity.

These four additional constructs are useful for making predictions about vocational outcomes. More specifically, individuals who are congruent, differentiated, consistent, and high in identity are predicted to be more satisfied and better adjusted than individuals who are incongruent, undifferentiated, inconsistent, and low in identity. For example, a social individual working in a social environment would be happier and more productive than if this same individual were in a realistic environment.

The hexagonal structure (Figure 6.1) in Holland's theory thus has three functions. First, it defines the amount of consistency in an individual's interests by referencing the relationship of primary, secondary, and tertiary types to one another in the hexagon. Second, in a parallel fashion, it defines the amount of consistency in an environment. Finally, the hexagon defines the amount of congruence between an individual and his or her environment by providing comparisons of the distance between an individual's type and the environment's type.

Holland commented on his theory upon being awarded the APA Distinguished Professional Contributions Award in 1996 (Holland, 1996a). He noted that while there were many strengths, there were also areas that still needed further research. One area that he identified as needing further investigation was the lack of explanatory power of the construct of congruence. As noted earlier, the greater the fit between work personality and environment, the greater the job satisfaction. However, research has shown the relationship to be relatively small (Spokane & Cruza-Guet, 2005). Nauta (2010, 2013) has also noted the need for more research to understand the limited power of congruence to explain expected outcomes (including job satisfaction). Juntunen and Even (2012) and Fouad and Kantamneni (2009) point out another area of concern, the need to examine the contextual factors that influence individuals' choices and the nature of person-environment fit. Fouad and Kantamneni note that some evidence points to the applicability of Holland's theory across cultures, but that much more research is needed, including whether the same six personality types capture vocational personalities across cultural groups and if they do, whether they are in the same RIASEC order.

Nonetheless, as Nauta (2010) and Juntunen and Even (2012) conclude, the theory's longevity and clear applications to practice have helped place this theory among the most successful in vocational psychology. Indeed, Nauta notes that the "theory is unsurpassed in vocational psychology and has been resoundingly successful in terms of the broader realm of counseling psychology" (p. 17). Gottfredson (1999) points out the strengths of Holland's career and theory include the practical utility of the theory for counselors. Betz (2008) comments that Holland's theory was among the most widely researched and supported in vocational psychology and has been incorporated in many career assessment instruments, programs, and interventions, including the major governmental occupational information system (O*Net).

APPLYING HOLLAND'S THEORY

Conceptualizing Leslie's Career History

Leslie's history suggests a stable personality type of investigative and social; she pursued activities in these domains even in childhood. For example, as a child she "played school" with her sister, and in high school she enjoyed her math and science courses and became a math tutor. She has enjoyed working with others through these early activities, as well as through her current hobbies of teaching swimming and teaching meditation classes. Her conventional tertiary code is reflected in her enjoyment of tasks that require attention to detail and developing systems for managing information. For example, she particularly enjoys organizing her lesson plans and keeping track of her students' progress in her current teaching job, and she chose to be membership coordinator in her volunteer work at the local science center.

It is useful to consider whether Leslie's lack of interest in realistic, enterprising, and artistic activities is because she avoided these areas or because she did not have the opportunities to develop interests in these areas. Holland (1997) suggests that "to some degree, types produce types" (p. 17), primarily because parents engage in activities related to their own types, creating circumstances through which children may develop interests. Leslie's father is a corporate attorney, suggesting that he is an enterprising type, which may have led to his encouraging Leslie to pursue a business career. Her father also may have some interest in investigative activities, as evidenced by his bachelor's degree in chemistry and his work in patents and product liability. Leslie's father, then, ostensibly served as a role model of both enterprising and investigative interests, yet she developed interest in the latter but not the former.

Leslie's mother is an administrative assistant at a small business, which would typically be considered a conventional- or enterprising-type occupation. However, this occupation may not be an accurate reflection of her type, because it may have been a choice of convenience rather than an expression of her personality. Moreover, since her job is at an interior design firm, the environment actually may have strong artistic elements, which would be consistent with her involvement in artistic volunteer activities, such as being an art museum docent and being active on the symphony board. As with her father, Leslie's mother may have served as a role model for artistic and conventional interests, and Leslie developed interests in one area (conventional) yet not the other (artistic). It would seem, then, that Leslie grew up in an environment in which she was exposed to artistic, enterprising, investigative, and conventional activities. Her brother also developed investigative interests, expressed in his choice of engineering as an occupation, and her sister pursued social and investigative interests in becoming a nurse.

Leslie entered the university still undecided about her major. She knew that she enjoyed taking advanced math classes and that she had been frustrated by the lack of challenge in those investigative areas in the community college she first attended. Her strategy when she first went to college seemed to be to explore many areas, although most of the options she explored were in the investigative area: engineering, medicine, psychology, and mathematics. There is little information about her social interests in college, either in the coursework she enjoyed or in any outside activities in which she engaged during those years. These two sets of interests—social and investigative—are not wholly consistent in that they are not adjacent to one another on Holland's hexagon. As is true of many individuals with inconsistent interests, Leslie's difficulty with career decision making may have been due to the apparent incompatibility of her investigative and social interests. Leslie's solution was to choose math education, which reflected both types of interests.

The other focal point of Leslie's history from Holland's perspective is evaluation of the environments in which she has been. While she was growing up, her primary environments were her family and various educational settings. Her family represented a heterogeneous environment, with artistic and enterprising elements, as well as investigative and conventional characteristics. Her educational environments were most likely characterized as investigative, particularly in her choice of the more specialized environment that a college math major represented.

Conceptualizing Leslie's Present Situation

Using Holland's theory to understand Leslie's current career dilemma focuses attention on both her characteristics and the features of her environment. First, Leslie's personality type of investigative-social-conventional (ISC) can be further examined in terms of the constructs of Holland's theory. Her Strong Interest Inventory (SII) profile is well differentiated, with the investigative interests representing a high peak in her profile and the artistic interests representing a clear low point. Leslie's three highest scores (I, S, and C) are also differentiated from each other, with I clearly higher than S or C. In terms of Holland's hexagonal arrangement of types, Leslie's investigative, social, and conventional interests represent an inconsistent pattern—that is, interests that are not adjacent to one another on the hexagon. Finally, Leslie's vocational identity is fairly clear and stable: She knows where her interests lie, even though they may feel contradictory, and she has maintained these fundamental interests since high school.

An analysis of Leslie's current work environment reveals some important information. In general, high school teachers are likely to be predominantly social types; however, as indicated on SII, math teachers (conventional-investigative-realistic) and science teachers (investigative-realistic-social) are the colleagues with whom Leslie spends most of her workday. Moreover, her principal is likely to be characterized by social and enterprising interests. From the perspective of person-environment fit, math and science teachers may generally perceive some incongruence in their work environment within a typical high school setting. High schools, in general, and the particular school in which Leslie works, may be characterized as fairly heterogeneous and undifferentiated, because nearly all Holland personality types are represented to varying degrees.

An important question from the perspective of Holland's theory is how much congruence exists between Leslie and her work environment. Leslie's type of ISC would seem to be congruent with the social nature of the high school environment, yet the more immediate environment of her math teacher colleagues presents a more incongruent environment. Furthermore, Leslie may feel somewhere in between the math teachers and the other teachers: She has more social interests than the math teachers yet more investigative interests than the other teachers, and she may feel that she does not really fit with either group. Thus, she may feel unappreciated in her environment.

An additional issue is whether Leslie's current dissatisfaction is related to a shift in her interests in terms of either absolute or relative strength. That is, she may have increased her interest in social activities relative to her investigative activities, or she may simply want more expression of long-standing social interests.

QUESTIONS FOR DISCUSSION

1. What specific hypotheses would you develop about Leslie from Holland's theoretical perspective? How does using Holland's theory help you understand Leslie? How might it help Leslie understand herself?

2. How might the inconsistency in Leslie's typology have had an influence on her career decision making in the past? How might it be affecting her current career decision making?

3. What possible reasons might there be for Leslie's having similar areas of interest to some areas of her mother's and father's interests but not others? What type of influence or encouragement might they have provided her in these areas?

4. How could Leslie find expression for her diverse interests?

5. How might it be helpful for Leslie to conceptualize her current work environment in terms of person-environment congruence? From what does her dissatisfaction stem?

6. What other factors in Leslie's work situation, in addition to congruence, might be related to her dissatisfaction?

7. Leslie can be viewed as existing within multiple environments, such as with her husband, family of origin, and social and leisure activities. To what extent is she congruent with each of these environments? How might this congruence contribute to her overall satisfaction?

8. What types of occupations might offer a more congruent environment for Leslie?

9. What factors in Leslie's life are encouraging her to change occupational directions? What factors are discouraging her from doing so?

The Case of Judy

Judy (a 38-year-old White woman) was a successful attorney who recently became a partner in a medium-sized firm in Denver. Without warning, she tendered her resignation. She sought counseling for depression. She had quit because she was not enjoying her work; she resented the demands made by other partners, as well as the inordinately long hours. Her therapist suggested she also seek career counseling.

Judy finished her baccalaureate degree in psychology at a small midwestern liberal arts college. She had decided on psychology based on her interest in working with people, particularly children, and because her friends told her she was a good listener. She enjoyed her classes in psychology and volunteered at a crisis line during her sophomore year. She became a resident assistant her junior year and worked in the dorms for two years. She did well in college, and her adviser strongly encouraged her to apply to graduate programs in psychology. She considered doing so but was engaged to a young man who did not want her to pursue her doctorate.

She decided to become an attorney because her fiancé was in law school. She thought this would be a good way for them to be in the same geographic location, and she had some interest in the field of law. She was accepted into the same school and excelled. She was particularly interested in litigation, while her fiancé was interested in corporate law. She passed the bar exam on the first try, while her fiancé failed three times and finally chose another career. Their relationship ended. She was quite depressed about the termination of her engagement but decided to move to another city to work and, hopefully, to meet a new man.

Judy joined a law firm after law school and impressed the attorneys with her diligence and willingness to work extra hours. She soon became the associate that partners vied to have assigned to them. She worked hard and enjoyed some of the work she was assigned, though she also found some of it boring. The partners voted to make her partner a year earlier than she had expected. After Judy became a partner, she began to question her activities and values and, in general, became depressed. Although she had dated occasionally, she did not really have any time to devote to a relationship. She also did not have much time to make friends outside of the law firm, and she felt that her life was quite narrowly focused.

QUESTIONS FOR DISCUSSION

1. How would you explain Judy's behavior from the perspective of Holland's theory? What specific hypotheses would you develop about Judy from Holland's theoretical perspective? How does using Holland's theory help you understand Judy? How might it help Judy understand herself?

2. What are Judy's interest themes?

3. How would you incorporate Judy's depression into career counseling through the perspective of Holland's theory?

4. How congruent has Judy been in her work as an attorney?

5. How would you evaluate Judy's person-environment fit in terms of her interests?

6. How do Judy's gender and race/ethnicity enter into her career decisions?

DIRECTIONS AND IMPLICATIONS FOR CAREER COUNSELING

Holland's model has been extensively applied in career counseling, most notably in using the six-category typology to categorize individuals in the interpretation of interest inventories such as the Self-Directed Search (SDS) (Holland, Powell, & Fritzsche, 1994) or the SII (Harmon, Hansen, Borgen, & Hammer, 2005). In addition, Holland's typology has been used to classify occupational information, college majors, and so on in an attempt to facilitate the matching of individuals and environments.

Holland (1996b) attributed the enduring prominence of person-environment fit theories to their focus on two major questions in people's lives: At what kind of work will I be happy? Will I be able to perform the job well? These two questions are relevant to consider in working with both cases.

BOX 6.2 Counselor Cognitions

- What is the client's interest type or combinations of types?
- What is the client's pattern of congruence in his or her vocational environments?
- How consistent are the client's interests?
- How well differentiated are the client's interests?
- How congruent are the client's occupational aspirations?

Goals of Counseling

From the perspective of Holland's theory, career interventions include using the typology to identify a client's typical mode of interacting with the world of work and using the constructs of differentiation, consistency, and congruence to predict the difficulty of the decision-making process. The typology provides a framework for clients to conceptualize their own vocational personalities and see how they may best fit with the world of work. Counseling is intended to "create self-understanding and stimulate more insightful and constructive planning" (Holland, 1997, p. 199).

Nauta (2013) pointed out that Holland's theory is primarily used to help individuals make career choices, but it can also be used to help individuals be more satisfied in their career, as well as help them implement their career choices. However, she also noted some caveats in using the theory to help individuals make career choices. First, although an outcome of counseling is to help increase congruence between vocational personality and the environment, it is important to note that congruence is only moderately predictive and that many other factors go into job satisfaction. Second, it is important to assess external constraints and the role that may have played in accurate representation of interests. In other words, it is important to help clients consider interest areas that may be nonstereotypical for their gender or culture. Finally, Holland's theory assumes freedom of choice, and it is important to understand the limitations and constraints on choices but also to help identify and remove barriers when possible.

As an initial step, the counselor would listen carefully to Leslie's or Judy's concerns to clarify how the client sees her current situation and why she sought counseling. Leslie is unhappy with how she is being treated by her principal, whose behavior might be due to a number of factors, such as poor job performance on her part or poor management style on his part. A goal of counseling with either Leslie or Judy might be to examine the degree to which her current environment is congruent with her characteristics and to examine other careers or jobs that might provide a better match. In addition, counseling with Leslie may focus on the inconsistency of her investigative and social interests and the possible shifting of her primary interests in the social and investigative areas. Counseling with Judy may focus on whether law is a congruent choice for her and whether other options might be more congruent.

Interventions

Knowing a client's type, in terms of Holland's theory, allows the counselor to make predictions about the manner in which counseling will proceed, such as the amount of interaction the client will have with the counselor and the attitude with which the client will approach counseling. How will Leslie behave in counseling as an ISC type? As an investigative type, Leslie will likely be quite invested in the exploratory activities of career counseling. She will enjoy researching occupations, will ask many questions about the details of her assessment results (including how scores are derived), and will engage in "making sense" of her career history and current dissatisfaction. She is likely to be quite comfortable with following through with assignments between sessions and bringing back new information to discuss with the counselor in the next session. Her secondary social type suggests that Leslie is likely to be verbally and socially skilled, and she is likely to be engaged during counseling sessions. Her tertiary conventional type suggests that she will appreciate and work well within structure and will enjoy organizing information about careers. She may prefer the counselor to provide structure and direction within counseling and may feel frustrated if she perceives an insufficient amount of direction. The counselor can thus view Leslie's interest profile and typology as a predictor of her in-session behavior.

Typically, a primary intervention is assessment, both of the client and of his or her environment. A counselor working within Holland's framework would use some assessment tool to determine Judy's primary, secondary, and tertiary types. Identification of type then would guide further interventions. A counselor working within Holland's theory may have used some of the assessments to those provided in Chapter 3, such as the SII or the O*Net Interest Profiler (Armstrong, Allison, & Rounds, 2008). The counselor may also use assessments developed by Holland, himself, such as the SDS (Holland et al., 1994). One unique feature of the SDS is that it elicits a client's vocational daydreams, which then would be classified and coded according to Holland's theory and examined to determine the coherence of her career aspirations. Eliciting Judy's early vocational daydreams and aspirations may provide a rich source of information, particularly given the decisions around work and family she has made over the past several years. These aspirations could also be elicited in session and used in conjunction with the SII results.

Second, the counselor may use the Career Attitudes and Strategies Inventory (CASI) (Holland & Gottfredson, 1994) to evaluate a range of factors related to the client's current career. The CASI was designed to address adult career issues and includes scales measuring job satisfaction, work involvement, and family commitment. For example, the counselor may use the CASI to explore Judy's career situation and her reasons for quitting her position.

Third, the counselor would examine the pattern of types on the assessment tool. As evidenced by the General Occupational Themes of the SII, Leslie's primary type is clearly investigative. Leslie exhibits intellectual curiosity and likes scientific activities, and she tends to use abstract reasoning to solve problems. Her secondary type is social. She is interested in helping others, particularly through teaching, and she values her relationships with others. She uses interpersonal skills to solve problems, such as through discussion with others. Conventional types like structured environments and attend well to detail. She may perceive herself as conforming and preferring to follow established rules.

Interpretation of Leslie's SII profile focuses on determining her three-letter Holland code. Her General Occupational Themes indicate a code of ISC, which also is reflected in the Basic Interest Scales. However, examination of the SII Occupational Scales shows that most of her high scores are for investigative occupations, followed by occupations in the conventional area; she has relatively few high scores on social occupations. The three-letter code resulting from the Occupational Scales portion, determined by the frequency of scales in the "similar" range, is ICS. Following interpretation of the SII, Leslie may consult the *Occupations Finder* (Holland, 1994) or the *Dictionary of Holland Occupational Codes* (Gottfredson & Holland, 1996) to explore occupations with various combinations of her three-letter Holland code, beginning with ISC and ICS.

Leslie's primary code of investigative is less common for women, while social and conventional are frequent types for women. One avenue to explore with Leslie is the gender traditionality of her interests. How did her family's expectations shape her interests? How do her husband's expectations shape her interests? What effect did discouragement during college have on her nontraditional (investigative) interests? Would she describe her interests, and her Holland type, as accurately reflecting her authentic self? These questions introduce a gendered context to interpretation of Leslie's SII profile.

Examination of Leslie's Skills Confidence Inventory supports her three-letter code as evidenced on the SII. Leslie indicates a high degree of confidence and a correspondingly high degree of interest in the three areas of investigative, social, and conventional.

Another important focus of counseling is the degree of incongruence that Leslie may experience with her current work environment. The counselor helps her conceptualize her feeling that she "doesn't fit" in terms of the discrepancy in Holland's typology. This provides Leslie with a framework with which to think about her dissatisfaction that may provide some new clarification and insight.

Holland (1997) recommended using all six themes as part of an analysis of congruence, comparing the relative ordering of types for the individual to the time spent in job tasks or activities related to the six areas. Investigative activities are reflected in the content matter that she teaches, particularly the higher level math courses where she engages students in abstract problem solving. Leslie engages in many social activities at work, primarily through teaching and through using her interpersonal problem-solving skills in interactions with students and teachers. She also incorporates conventional activities throughout her work day and frequently devises new ways of structuring or organizing her tasks. The remaining three types—artistic, enterprising, and realistic—all are infrequently occurring tasks in her current job.

Another issue to explore with Leslie in counseling relates to the potential change in her vocational aspirations—in particular, whether her expressed desire to consider other occupations is a by-product of the dissatisfaction she feels with the specific job she currently holds. Holland (1997) noted the reasons underlying stability of aspirations: "People trying to change themselves or their careers receive little environmental support and must overcome the cumulative learning associated with a particular job or self-concept" (p. 12). Individuals may remain in their initial vocational choices because their exploration of alternatives occurs within a circumscribed range and because environmental influences (employers and significant others) discourage change. These issues also could be addressed in counseling with Leslie.

ADDITIONAL CASES

Case 1: Johnny

Johnny is a 44-year-old Asian American man from a traditional Hmong family. Johnny has lived in the United States since the age of 10, growing up in a primarily White suburb of Atlanta. His parents came to the United States in the 1980s, and his father was able to find work as a teacher, but they maintained traditional Hmong values, including a strong value of family. Johnny is the oldest of seven children, three of whom were born in the United States after his

(Continued)

(Continued)

family immigrated. His parents were in a refugee camp in Laos and endured a number of hardships to come to the United States. He has a strong feeling of family obligation to succeed in his career. His family very much wanted him to be a doctor.

Johnny did well in high school and attended a large university where he majored in biology. He was admitted to a medical school, completed his residency in ophthalmology, and is now practicing in a town close to his parents. He is married to a White woman, Janelle, and they are expecting their first child. His wife is also a physician and plans to take 6 weeks off when the baby is born. Johnny's parents are pressuring Janelle to stay home longer with the baby. Johnny is feeling caught between his desire to please his parents and his wife's commitment to her career and her expectations that they have an egalitarian balance of work and family responsibilities. He is also realizing that his work is not very satisfying, and this might be an opportunity to stay home with the baby and begin considering a new career. He has not enjoyed the patient contact he has had and is impatient with the marketing efforts he must do to attract new patients to the clinic. He is considering taking a position in a research laboratory, using his skills to investigate eye diseases, but he would need more schooling for this career. Janelle is supportive of his thinking about a new career, but his parents are very upset about it. His career as a doctor has brought great honor to them. They also think he should be the primary breadwinner in the family and are disappointed that he is thinking of staying home.

QUESTIONS FOR DISCUSSION

1. What role has congruence played in Johnny's career decisions?

2. Examine Johnny's occupational environment from the perspective of Holland's theory. What would you predict about Johnny given this information?

3. Investigative and realistic interests are stereotypic of Asian males, and these also correspond to Johnny's initial career choice of medicine. How might you help Johnny determine if these are "true" interests, and if not, would it be appropriate for you to help him choose a more congruent environment?

4. How might you help Johnny sort out the expectations he feels from his parents? From Janelle? For himself?

5. What unique strengths and assets may Johnny have that were unappreciated in his various work environments? How might you help identify the environment that would be most congruent?

Case 2: Susan

Susan is a 17-year-old African American high school junior. She has a 2.5 grade point average, and her favorite classes are drafting and woodworking. Susan is in a co-op program in which she attends school in the morning and works in the afternoon, which she enjoys because "it's more fun than sitting in class all day." Her father is a building contractor, and her mother is an administrative assistant in a small business.

Susan enjoys athletics and fixing and repairing things. She has no interest in going to college but is not sure what else she might do. She has been talking with her friends and parents about what she might do after graduating from high school. She doesn't know much about the range of job possibilities but thinks she would like to work with her hands. In her co-op program, she's seen the work of welders, tool-and-die makers, mechanics, and assembly line workers. Susan's brother is an electrician, and her older sister stays home with two young children. She also is familiar with the building trades by observing her father's work. Last summer, she asked her father if she could work with him, but he said she was too young. She has asked him again for the upcoming summer and is awaiting his answer.

Susan's parents have given her little guidance about work but do expect her to finish high school and, beyond that, "be happy." She really would like to try something related to building and construction but wonders how difficult it would be as a girl. Although her father has not overtly discouraged her interest in construction, he believes it is an inappropriate choice for her. He is concerned about her physical safety on the job site as well as whether she might be harassed by her coworkers.

Susan doesn't know what to do after high school and feels confused about how to even start choosing a direction. She secretly hopes that her father will hire her after graduation but is afraid to ask him directly about it.

QUESTIONS FOR DISCUSSION

1. What is Susan's type likely to be, and in what type of environment might she be congruent?

2. How would you use Holland's framework to encourage Susan's exploration? How does Holland's theory assist you in understanding Susan's career dilemma? How might it help you in working with Susan?

3. What interventions might be effective to increase her career exploration and decision making?

4. How might you help Susan address her relationship with her parents, particularly with her father?

5. How would you address Susan's concerns about being a female in the building and construction trades?

Case 3: Cynthia

Cynthia is a 42-year-old White mother of three who is seeking career counseling because she is unhappy in her present job as a purchasing agent for a large furniture company. She took the job a year ago when her own interior design business failed. She started the business 10 years ago when her youngest child started first grade; it had been a dream of hers to own an interior design studio because her friends often told her how nicely decorated her house was. She did quite well in the business for a number of years; however, she developed multiple sclerosis 3 years ago and was increasingly unable to visit clients' homes and engage in the physical activity necessary to keep her business viable.

Cynthia's educational history includes 2 years of college immediately after high school and completion of a certificate program in design. She has taken a few adult education courses at a local community college, primarily to develop new computer skills.

Cynthia's husband died in a car accident 2 years ago. She has managed to save the bulk of an insurance settlement that she received and hopes to keep that money set aside for her inevitable medical expenses. She has been fortunate to have adequate health insurance, but she is concerned about what the future might hold. In addition, her oldest daughter is a sophomore at a state university, and her two younger daughters are planning to attend college if they are financially able to do so. She therefore has a number of practical concerns related to her career, such as maintaining her health insurance, providing for her children, and planning for retirement.

Cynthia took her current job because purchasing for a furniture company was in a similar area as being an interior designer and she believed that she would be able to continue to use her design skills. Unfortunately, in her year on the job, her activities have primarily entailed maintenance of purchasing and client records on the computer, making delivery arrangements, and occasionally dealing with customer complaints. The anticipated promotion to designer does not appear likely in the near future, and although her physical functioning is stabilized, she feels that she should make changes now before her condition deteriorates.

QUESTIONS FOR DISCUSSION

1. Describe Cynthia's past and current work environments in terms of Holland's theory. In what ways do these environments allow her to express her type?

2. What are some alternate occupations that would allow Cynthia to be in a congruent environment and accommodate her disability?

3. What have been (and are) the factors involved in Cynthia's original career decision making? How does she balance her practical financial concerns with her dissatisfaction with her current job?

4. How would you incorporate a consideration of her health status into career counseling?

BOX 6.3 Summary of Key Constructs

Construct	Definition
Congruence	Fit between interests and work environment; the greater the congruence, the greater the predicted job satisfaction.
Consistency	How similar top interests are on the hexagon; consistent interests predict more stable occupational choices.
RIASEC interest types	Realistic, Investigative, Artistic, Social, Enterprising, and Conventional interest types.
Hexagon	RIASEC types arranged in a hexagonal pattern.
Calculus	Interest types are arranged equidistantly around the hexagon; opposing types are least similar and adjacent types most similar.
Differentiation	The difference between the highest and lowest interest types; well-differentiated interests predict more stable occupational choices.

Chapter 7

The Theory of Work Adjustment

INTRODUCTORY REVIEW

The theory of work adjustment (TWA) (Dawis, 2005; Dawis & Lofquist, 1984), like Holland's theory, is considered a theory of "person-environment fit." Although these two theories are quite similar in many respects, Holland's theory places greater emphasis on vocational choice, whereas TWA emphasizes vocational adjustment (Dawis, 1994), thus providing complementary rather than competing views. TWA might be particularly helpful to use with clients who are not satisfied with their jobs, because they may be considering choosing an entirely new career or wondering whether to adjust to a current job (Juntunen & Even, 2012).

TWA consists of a number of formal propositions and their corollaries that address the process of adjustment to work (Dawis, 2005; Dawis & Lofquist, 1984; Swanson & Schneider, 2013). These propositions identify aspects of the individual (e.g., abilities) as well as of the work environment (e.g., rewards) that predict job satisfaction and tenure. In other words, the constructs in TWA suggest whether an individual would be satisfied on the job and how long he or she might remain in the job. According to TWA, the fit between the individual and the environment predicts the individual's satisfaction as well as his or her satisfactoriness as an employee.

As with Holland's theory, the concept of fit, or correspondence, in TWA rests on using a set of parallel dimensions to describe both people and environments. Holland postulates six types of persons or environments; TWA takes a different approach. Dawis (2005) describes two sets of common dimensions—namely, an individual's abilities in relation to those required by his or her job and an individual's needs and work values in relation to the rewards available on the job. Both of these are thought to reciprocally interact; in other words, the environment has requirements of the individual (his or her ability to do the job), and the individual has requirements of the environment (the environment's ability to satisfy his or her needs). For example, among the requirements of the occupation of truck driver are that employees be able to drive a truck, load the truck, and keep to a set schedule. Requirements of people who are truck drivers include that the job provide them with rewards such as secure employment, independence, and good working conditions.

TWA stresses the importance of describing the individual's level of *satisfactoriness,* or how well his or her abilities and skills meet what the job or organization requires—literally how satisfactory an employee the individual is. In the preceding example, how well an individual can function as a truck driver is an indication of satisfactoriness. TWA also stresses the individual's level of *satisfaction,* or how well his or her needs are met by the job. An individual with high security, autonomy, and good working condition needs would be predicted to be satisfied as a truck driver. Satisfactoriness and satisfaction are depicted in Figure 7.1.

Figure 7.1 Prediction of Work Adjustment

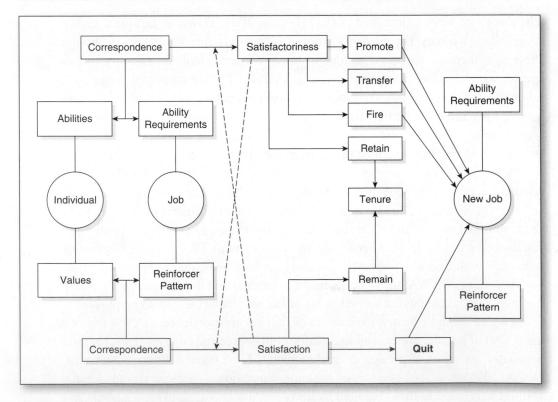

SOURCE: Dawis and Lofquist (1984).

As shown on the left of Figure 7.1, an individual has abilities, and the work environment has ability requirements. If abilities and ability requirements correspond, the individual is satisfactory. For example, if a woman has good interpersonal skills, can take measurements, report, and analyze results of medical tests, then she might meet the ability requirements of a medical sonographer. Once in the position, she may be promoted, transferred, or fired on the basis of her degree of satisfactoriness. The result of promotion, transfer, or termination may be a new job.

The path to satisfaction is portrayed at the bottom of Figure 7.1. An individual has values and needs, and the job has a reinforcer pattern, or pattern of rewards. If needs and reinforcers correspond, an individual is satisfied. The medical sonographer described above may require security and compensation in her work; she would be satisfied if her position in a hospital provides these. If she is not satisfied, she may quit, leading her to seek a new job. The middle of Figure 7.1 shows that if she is both satisfied and satisfactory she is predicted to be retained in the job. A central feature of TWA is that both satisfaction and satisfactoriness are equally important components in the prediction of work adjustment.

Despite the dual focus on person and environment, TWA clearly emphasizes what the person experiences and uses the word *satisfaction* for an individual's satisfaction with his or her job; the word *satisfactoriness* is used for the individual with whom the work environment is satisfied. Therefore, tenure occurs when an individual is both satisfied and has the abilities to do the job (Dawis, 2005). A further extension of these ideas, which is particularly important for career planning, is that length of time in a job depends on an individual's level of satisfaction and ability to do the job.

TWA emphasizes the measurement of abilities and values to facilitate the match of an individual to a work environment. Abilities are viewed as "reference dimensions of skills" (Dawis, 2005, p. 13); that is, abilities are seen as general dimensions that underlie groupings of acquired skills. Similarly, values are viewed as representing a grouping of needs. Dawis defines six crucial values: achievement, comfort, status, altruism, safety, and autonomy. In terms of environment, research underlying TWA has identified occupational ability patterns and occupational reward patterns to describe a wide variety of occupations. In other words, what abilities does an occupation require of an individual, and what needs or values of the individual can the occupation fulfill? In predicting career choice, abilities are compared with ability patterns required, and values are compared with value patterns supported. Occupations are compared according to how they predict satisfaction and satisfactoriness, and a cost-benefit analysis is conducted to predict the optimal choice for an individual.

TWA proposes that satisfaction is predicted from the correspondence between an individual's values and the rewards available in the environment (Dawis, 2005). Satisfaction is predicted to be negatively related to the probability of an individual's quitting a job. An individual's ability to carry out the duties of a job is predicted from the correspondence between his or her abilities and what the environment requires and is negatively related to an individual's being fired from a job. In other words, in a stable economy, people are least likely to lose their jobs if they are able to do those jobs successfully. Adjusting to the job and staying in the job for some length of time (job tenure) results from both an individual's level of satisfaction and his or her ability to do the job at a specific time. Moreover, satisfaction and ability to do the job (satisfactoriness) influence the prediction of each other; that an individual is satisfied in a job helps predict that she or he is able to do the job and vice versa.

TWA postulates that four personality style variables are important in characterizing how an individual interacts with the environment: celerity, pace, rhythm, and endurance. *Celerity* refers to the speed with which an individual initiates interaction with his or her environment. An individual may have a high celerity—quickly, or perhaps impulsively, acting on the environment—or may have a very low celerity—moving slowly to action.

Pace indicates the intensity or activity level of one's interaction with the environment. Once the individual acts on the environment, pace indicates the rate of interaction. Individuals may, for example, be viewed as having very high energy; this is an indication of the pace of their interaction with the environment. A high-energy person, however, may have that high energy only when in front of a group of people or may be able to sustain it for only a short period of time. These are indications of his or her rhythm and endurance.

Rhythm is the pattern of the pace of interaction with the environment (steady, cyclical, or erratic), and *endurance* refers to the sustaining of interaction with the environment. These variables help explain why individuals with similar abilities and values may behave in different ways within a given work environment. Moreover, these constructs can be used to describe environments as well as people, and environments differ from one another in terms of celerity, pace, rhythm, and endurance.

In TWA terms, dissatisfaction serves a central motivational role. Dissatisfaction on the part of either the person or the environment represents disequilibrium in the system and is the impetus for adjustment to occur to restore equilibrium. "Satisfaction motivates 'maintenance' behavior; dissatisfaction motivates adjustment behavior" (Dawis, 1996, p. 87). Figure 7.2 depicts the postulated process of adjustment that occurs when there is discorrespondence between an individual's needs and values and the rewards provided by the job.

Figure 7.2 Relationships Between Adjustment-Style Dimensions

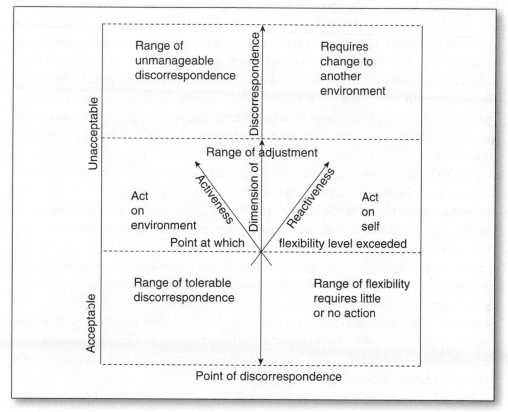

SOURCE: Lofquist and Dawis (1991).

TWA hypothesizes that the stylistic variables of flexibility and perseverance moderate the prediction of satisfaction, satisfactoriness, and work adjustment. The bottom point of the axis in Figure 7.2 indicates zero discorrespondence. *Flexibility* is the ability to tolerate a mismatch (discorrespondence) between needs and rewards offered by the environment before doing something to make an adjustment. However, at some point, the lack of correspondence between an individual's needs and the environmental rewards is too great, and the individual will move into an adjustment mode. This is shown as the lower horizontal line in Figure 7.2. The individual may strive to adjust himself or herself (reduce level of needs) or may try to adjust the environment (increase rewards). These are depicted as the vectors in Figure 7.2; *activeness* is acting on the environment, and *reactiveness* is adjusting self.

Perseverance is continuing in the job after a mismatch is noted and the individual works to bring it into adjustment, shown as the upper horizontal line.

For example, a man who needs autonomy will exhibit flexibility if he is able to tolerate some close supervision. There may be a point, however, when he no longer can tolerate the discrepancy between his need for autonomy and the supervision, and he will try to make an adjustment that reduces the discorrespondence. He will exhibit perseverance if he continues in the environment while he is in adjustment mode. At some point, of course, if he cannot successfully adjust the discorrespondence, he would then be predicted to terminate employment. Flexibility and perseverance are conceptualized as fluctuating constructs; an individual may be flexible and able to tolerate discorrespondence one day, then unable to tolerate it the next, at which point he or she moves into an adjustment mode.

As shown in Figure 7.2, adjustment can occur in two different modes. In the *active mode,* the individual attempts to change the work environment to reduce the amount of discorrespondence by changing the requirements of the environment or the rewards available in the environment. For example, in response to feeling overworked, an employee could ask for a reduction in job assignments or ask for a raise or promotion. In the *reactive mode,* the individual attempts to change himself or herself to reduce discorrespondence by changing his or her work skills or the importance attached to needs. In the previous example, an employee could learn time management skills to increase efficiency or shift priorities so that less focus is placed on work. Thus, adjustment behavior can be aimed at one of four targets: the individual's skills or need requirements and the environment's available ability requirements and rewards.

The concepts of active and reactive modes and of flexibility and perseverance are, thus, important predictors of what individuals are likely to do if they are dissatisfied (or if the environment is dissatisfied with their behavior). These concepts are also important considerations from a broader perspective: An individual develops a characteristic *adjustment style* over time, which is useful information in career counseling.

TWA is heavily based on an individual differences premise—that is, that individuals differ in their abilities, needs, values, and interests, among other variables (Dawis, 1992). This tradition views people as complex individuals who differ on a number of dimensions and believes that counseling needs to be individualized to allow for the expression of those differences (Dawis, 2005). The individual differences approach suggests that individuals' sex, national origin, sexual orientation, or ethnic background, as broad demographic categories, are not reliable bases for determining their abilities and needs.

However, Dawis (2005) notes that an individual's current situation is a product of the opportunities he or she has had to develop work skills and needs. Individuals who have experienced discrimination because of their race, sex, or sexual orientation have been restricted in their opportunities for development (Degges-White & Shoffner, 2002; Lyons, Brenner, & Fassinger, 2005; Lyons & O'Brien, 2006; Velez & Moradi, 2012). The individual differences tradition acknowledges that one's sex or racial or cultural background does not necessarily restrict opportunities, for individuals of all groups and both sexes exist in all occupations. But Dawis (1996) notes that gender and racial and ethnic background "become important when they influence level, ranges, and patterns of work skills and work needs that are or are not developed . . . and when these person characteristics adversely affect employability" (pp. 95–96).

TWA evolved from Dawis and Lofquist's research on how to help vocational rehabilitation clients adjust to work after a disability. Dawis (2005) notes that their team had collected a large amount of data and realized that a theoretical framework was needed to help organize the information. Thus, the foundation of the theory was a framework for research, and its evolution over the past 50 years has been empirically guided. Strongest support has been found for the aspects of the theory outlined in Figure 7.1 (Dawis, 2005). In other words, research has supported the TWA prediction of satisfaction, satisfactoriness, and tenure. There has been less examination and, therefore, less support for the personality style variables and their relationship to adjustment. There has also been limited support for the application of the theory to non-White populations (Betz, 2008; Juntunen & Even, 2012).

BOX 7.1 Personal Reflection

- Have I ever been in a job that was very dissatisfying?
- What needs were not met in this job?
- How did I adjust?
- Did I try to change myself or my job?

APPLYING THE THEORY OF WORK ADJUSTMENT

A counselor who uses the TWA approach would ask the sorts of questions that are outlined in Box 7.2. The counselor would wonder what the client's history might indicate about his or her abilities and needs/values, as well as what information may be gathered from the times the client has been dissatisfied.

> ### BOX 7.2 Counselor Cognitions
>
> - What are the client's needs?
> - What is the client's adjustment style?
> - What are the client's abilities?
> - Is there discorrespondence between the client's actual abilities and the job requirements?
> - Is the client accurately perceiving his or her abilities?
> - Is the client adequately doing the tasks on the job?

Conceptualizing Leslie's Career History

Leslie has high abilities in math and science and the ability to teach children. She did well in other subjects as well, indicating that her overall pattern of abilities was high. Leslie places a high value on achievement, as indicated by her frustration at the lack of challenge in her math classes. She also places a high value on helping others, such as by working as a middle school tutor, and on making decisions on her own rather than having others make them for her.

In her first teaching position, Leslie appeared to be both satisfied and satisfactory. Clearly, the job met some of her needs. Teaching challenged her; it met her achievement needs. She also was able to meet her responsibility needs, because she was able to make decisions in her own classroom. She felt she was able to help others and felt part of the larger community. However, many of her social needs were not met in the smaller town. Although the specific occupation of teaching was a good choice for Leslie, who was both satisfactory and satisfied in the occupation, the overall setting did not provide rewards for her.

Conceptualizing Leslie's Present Situation

Leslie has been a satisfactory employee in her current job in that she has been in the same school for 10 years. However, she reported some dissatisfaction even before a new principal began to change the rewards in the job. Leslie enjoyed the interaction that teaching allowed her with the students, providing social service rewards. However, she reported that the long hours and the stress of the position frustrated her. The stress she reports may be a result of the lack of correspondence with her environment. This has been exacerbated by the new policies implemented by the principal, which have influenced her ability to get her autonomy and responsibility needs met. In addition, interactions with parents have left her feeling that she is not receiving adequate recognition for her work.

QUESTIONS FOR DISCUSSION

1. What specific hypotheses would you develop about Leslie from TWA? How does using TWA help you understand Leslie? How might it help Leslie understand herself?

2. How would you incorporate the other assessment information that Leslie completed?

3. Leslie did not complete an ability assessment; the counselor inferred abilities from past achievements. Is it important for adults to have their abilities tested?

4. The counselor estimated Leslie's satisfactoriness from the length of her tenure in the same position. However, this information is from a single source—the client herself, who may have underestimated or overestimated her satisfactoriness. What are other ways you could assess satisfactoriness?

5. How might it be helpful for Leslie to conceptualize her current work environment in terms of person-environment correspondence or discorrespondence?

6. How would you incorporate other life issues into counseling? What is the degree of Leslie's correspondence with the other multiple environments in her life? How might these multiple environments interact with one another?

7. Working from the perspective of a TWA counselor, how would you incorporate Leslie's gender and cultural background into counseling?

The Case of Charles

Charles is a White man in his early 40s. He has a bachelor's degree in biology and has been employed as a biological technician for a pathology laboratory for 3 years. He seeks career counseling because he is not very satisfied with his work; he is not sure if he wants to find a new job in this field or if he wants to change careers.

Charles grew up as the youngest child of middle-class parents. His sisters are considerably older than he is and had left for college before he had finished grade school. His mother stayed home until he started school and then went to work as a secretary. His father worked as an insurance salesperson and traveled a five-state region during Charles's childhood. His father has just retired after working for the same company his entire career.

Charles was a good student during high school and played a number of sports. He had a large circle of acquaintances but few close friends, because he was viewed as moody and temperamental. His parents had very high expectations of his achievements in school and in athletics and relatively rigid standards for his behavior. He did particularly well in math and science, and they thought he should be a physician. His father offered to pay for his college expenses if he pursued that degree but would not contribute if he went into another field.

Charles went to a state college and majored in biology. He enjoyed his time in college. He formed a close circle of friends and became engaged to a woman during his last year in college. He graduated with a 3.3 grade point average and scored about average on the Medical College Admissions Test (MCAT). However, Charles did not succeed in his application to medical school. He decided to graduate with a major in biology, seek a job in a laboratory as a biological technician, and apply to medical school the following year.

Charles ultimately unsuccessfully applied to medical school three times. The feedback he received on his lack of success varied from lack of distinguishing characteristics to mediocre MCAT scores to a poor interview. While he pursued this goal, he continued to work as a biological technician. He and his wife put off having children, hoping that he would be able to enter medical school.

Charles started his career as a biological technician in a hospital close to the college where he graduated so his wife could pursue an advanced degree. He moved from that hospital to a hospital lab when he and his wife moved for her first postgraduate position. He left that hospital after 3 years because of a personality conflict with his supervisor. He took a position with a local clinic and was there for several years.

Charles had major life changes in his mid-30s. He decided to give up his goal of medical school, he and his wife divorced, and he moved to another city. He took a position in a pathology laboratory, where he began to conduct tests to diagnose cancer. He changed positions again about 3 years ago to a pathology laboratory that serves as a regional center for the diagnosis of cancer, particularly prostate cancer. He reports that he left that position because of personality clashes with his supervisor.

Currently, Charles is unhappy with his pay at the laboratory, dissatisfied with the lack of challenges in his work, and having interpersonal conflicts with his supervisor. He does, however, feel that he is doing work that is important and helping others. He is married again, to a woman about 15 years younger than he is, and they hope to have children soon. He expects that she will stay home when they do have children.

QUESTIONS FOR DISCUSSION

1. What specific hypotheses would you develop about Charles from TWA? How does using TWA help you understand Charles?

2. What information about abilities do you infer from Charles's unsuccessful application to medical school?

3. Does Charles accurately perceive his abilities?

4. What role might Charles's temperament play in his work history? How might this relate to his adjustment style?

5. What are your hypotheses about Charles's dissatisfaction with work? Is it related to other areas of his life?

DIRECTIONS AND IMPLICATIONS FOR CAREER COUNSELING

Career counseling from the perspective of TWA addresses both the client's satisfaction with the occupation and his or her satisfactoriness. TWA counselors assess a client's abilities and needs and evaluate them against the abilities required of and rewards provided by an occupation. As the name implies, however, TWA is particularly well suited to counseling related to job adjustment. In helping clients with career concerns related to adjustment, counselors evaluate where they are in terms of their threshold of flexibility and evaluate their skills in reactive and active adjustment modes.

Goals of Counseling

Career counseling can serve many purposes, including identifying a career choice, clarifying decision making, helping a client identify opportunities for adjustment, and helping a client decide on various ways to change an environment. Fundamentally, person-environment correspondence counseling focuses on the discorrespondence clients experience in the environment. Counseling goals may include career choice, as well as examination of the possibility that the work environment will be adjusted or how likely it is that the client is able to engage in active adjustment.

Interventions

A counselor who uses the TWA approach would first identify the needs and abilities of the client. Often, this is done through the use of assessment tools. Lofquist and Dawis (1991) outline several hypotheses that counselors may entertain as they help clients identify the discorrespondence they are experiencing. These hypotheses, or the way that a counselor might conceptualize the client's concerns, are outlined in Box 7.2.

The first hypothesis concerns the match between abilities and the job requirements. Are the client's abilities too high or too low for the position? For example, a nurse may have more abilities than the job requires, or a secretary may not have sufficient database management skills required by the job.

The second hypothesis focuses on the client's subjective evaluation of his or her abilities and discorrespondence with the environmental ability requirements. The client may perceive his or her abilities as higher or lower than they are in reality, or the environmental requirements may be perceived as more or less difficult than they actually are. Or perhaps the client is seeking counseling because the abilities and requirements correspond to each other but he or she is not performing well.

The counselor might also wonder about the correspondence in needs. Are the client's needs met by the job environment? Another question the counselor might have is whether the rewards are higher or lower than the needs. In the latter situation, a client's needs are not met by the job environment. Finally, the counselor may test the hypothesis that the client is both satisfactory and satisfied and is coping with problems in other domains. In this case, the client's concerns are less with the work environment than with possible dissatisfaction in other areas of life, such as in a marital relationship.

Assessment is critical to career counseling from the TWA perspective. Thus, TWA counselors set expectations that clients will participate in the assessment process and will complete all homework assignments: "The career counseling process that we will go through will include taking a variety of assessment tools to find out more about your abilities and needs. We will spend time talking about the results in here and which occupations best correspond to your needs and abilities. It will also be important for you to do some work outside of the session."

Counselors often explore the environments in which clients have experienced the most problems. This exploration helps the counselor identify situations and environments in which needs have not been met. For example, in the case of Leslie, the counselor may say, "Leslie, you have talked about teaching in a smaller school and teaching at your current school. Tell me about some of the problems you have encountered in these situations." Leslie's problems as a teacher in her first position included the stress of not feeling competent and of feeling isolated in the community; in her current position, she is frustrated with new policies imposed by the principal, not having the opportunity to teach advanced classes, discouraging interactions with parents, and student problems. The counselor could identify Leslie's needs for achievement and recognitions from her work history.

In the case of Charles, the counselor might hypothesize that Charles's work history includes a number of situations in which he has had conflicts with supervisors. Are these conflicts due to Charles's interpersonal style or his reaction to discorrespondence, or is Charles an unsatisfactory employee? Charles identified dissatisfaction with compensation, achievement, and his supervisor. The counselor would work with Charles to determine which of these are the most pressing of his concerns. The counselor would also help Charles to identify if he wants to adjust to his current position or find a new career. Perhaps Charles continues to be disappointed with a career as a biological technician because he was not able to pursue his goal to be a physician. Charles's history also indicates that he has changed positions frequently, in 2- or 3-year intervals. Some of these changes might have been prompted by other life changes, but the counselor might also hypothesize that Charles does not adjust well to discorrespondence and does not persevere in the face of discorrespondence. Thus, the counselor's goals might include exploring his pattern of adjustment in other areas of his life. The counselor will also assess the likely motivation to engage in adjustment and could ask Charles to take an environmental satisfaction questionnaire for his current work environment as homework.

A TWA counselor will also evaluate clients' needs and abilities. For example, Leslie's Minnesota Importance Questionnaire (MIQ) indicated that her highest values are achievement, altruism, and autonomy. Her most important rewards are moral values (doing the work without feeling it is morally wrong), ability utilization (doing something that makes use of her abilities), achievement (the job's giving her a feeling of accomplishment), and social service (doing things for others). She also indicated that coworkers (making friends with coworkers), autonomy (planning her work with little supervision), and responsibility (making decisions on her own) are important. Leslie did not take an ability assessment; therefore, she is inferred to be high in general cognitive ability and verbal ability because she successfully completed her college degree, and, from her math background, high in numerical ability. No information is available on her perceptual or motor abilities. However, it should be noted that a TWA counselor would have asked Leslie to take an ability assessment in addition to the other instruments.

The TWA counselor would also assess Charles's work abilities and needs, as well as the abilities required and rewards provided by his environment. This is done through the use of expert ratings, previous research, or interpretation of the information Charles has provided. The occupational aptitude patterns indicate that Charles's work environment of biological technician has ability requirements of cognitive ability, verbal ability, and scientific reasoning. It appears that he has been a satisfactory employee able to do this work for nearly 20 years, although he has changed the specific environment in which he works. Rewards available in the job of biological technician have been found, through previous research, to be altruism, security, working conditions, and supervision. The work of technicians is relatively closely supervised and monitored. Other occupations that reward those needs are nurse, dietician, physical therapist, and firefighter.

Both Leslie and Charles indicate discorrespondence between the rewards in the environment and their needs. Leslie identified the discorrespondence between the environment and her needs for achievement, ability utilization, and autonomy. Although Charles noted that while his altruism needs are met, there is discorrespondence in his needs for achievement, compensation, and autonomy needs. It is possible that the close supervision he has had over the years did not correspond with his autonomy and achievement needs, leading to the clash with his supervisors.

It is critical to understand what a client means in responding to each MIQ statement. Thus, the counselor might ask Leslie, "Tell me what you mean by not doing work that you feel is morally wrong? What might be some examples of times that have occurred?" The counselor asks similar probes about feeling that the job would give Leslie a feeling of accomplishment, make use of her abilities, or allow her to help others. Leslie gives examples of times she felt that she was using her abilities, accomplishing things on the job, and helping others. Leslie also discusses how her needs for responsibility and autonomy are not being met with the new bureaucratic policies implemented by the principal. She acknowledges that the most important priority is to create more correspondence between the environment and her need for achievement and ability utilization.

The counselor would also identify actions to reduce the discorrespondence between the client and the environment, discussing this in terms of personality and adjustment styles. Charles's personality style appears to be characterized by a relatively steady rhythm but a low level of endurance; both of these inferred from his job changes every 3 years. It is more difficult to infer his celerity or pace from his employment history. The counselor uses a personality style checklist to aid in this discussion. In assessing Charles's adjustment style, the counselor finds that Charles has not adjusted reactively (changing himself), nor is there evidence that he has taken steps to change the environment. It appears that when he feels too discorrespondent with the environment, he leaves. The counselor identifies actions that Charles might take to adjust to his current position before leaving, also discussing the consequences of those actions. These actions may include identifying ways that he might change his environment to increase his feelings of accomplishment, autonomy, and ability utilization or ways that he might find other environments to meet those needs. For example, the counselor might want to know if Charles has ever talked to his supervisor about the level of autonomy he could build. He might also choose to reprioritize to increase the importance of rewards available in the environment, such as security or altruism.

ADDITIONAL CASES

Case 1: Phil

Phil is a 48-year-old Latino man who is a foreperson in charge of shipping in a small manufacturing company. He sought career counseling at the urging of his wife, who is concerned that he is underemployed; she feels that he could be earning more money than in his current job. Phil had attended college briefly but did not complete a degree. He had planned to major in accounting, primarily because of his father's encouragement rather than as a reflection of his real interests. He was much more interested in fixing things and was particularly interested in anything related to cars.

Phil has worked at a variety of unskilled jobs. He did not want to go back to college or work at a career, primarily because he did not want to climb a corporate ladder. Phil began working as an assembly line worker for a manufacturing company to support his family. He described this first job as "checking his brain at the door," but in reality, he was not overly concerned that the work did not engage him intellectually. He was able to use his abilities in a number of ways outside of work; he was active in chess clubs and was an avid reader of *Science* and *Scientific American* magazines.

Phil also enjoys building and repairing model trains and has an extensive model train collection that he inherited from his father. Both his father and grandfather had been railroad executives, and his only brother is a civil engineer who designs railroad bridges. Phil's family has a love of railroads in general and of the Burlington Northern railroads in particular. Phil's model railroad collection includes several antique engines; he has developed a small following on Internet hobby websites as an antique model train expert.

Phil's first marriage ended in divorce, and he was left with financial obligations to his first wife and their daughter. He subsequently married again, and he and his second wife have two sons and are expecting a third child. Phil eventually worked his way from entry-level loading dock to foreperson of shipping. This advancement was primarily because his supervisors recognized his abilities. His tested abilities are uniformly high in all areas, and he places high value on security, compensation, and achievement. Phil is quite bright and capable of learning, but his lack of formal education has limited his options. His supervisor has told him he cannot expect any more promotions in the company because he would need a baccalaureate degree to be eligible.

Phil is not averse to returning to school to finish his degree, but his credits will not transfer, and he would have to start over. Meanwhile, he will soon have four children, and his wife is not currently working outside the home. He cannot afford to quit his job to go to school, and he is very unsure what he would major in if he did go back. Overall, Phil is satisfied with his job. He likes feeling that he can do the work without a lot of stress, likes the men and one woman he works with, likes the security of belonging to a union, and likes the benefits the company provides. He is dissatisfied with the amount of money he is making, however, and has a vague feeling that he could be doing more.

QUESTIONS FOR DISCUSSION

1. Given the financial pressures that Phil feels, how does he balance his high need for achievement with his equally high need for security?

2. What are other possible environments that could provide achievement rewards for Phil?

3. How would you evaluate Phil's adjustment style?

4. Phil entered counseling at the urging of his wife. How would you handle this? How would you incorporate Phil's other life roles into counseling?

5. How would you incorporate Phil's avocational interests into counseling?

6. How do Phil's gender and race influence his career decisions?

Case 2: Melissa

Melissa is a 32-year-old White woman who is a midlevel executive working for a large firm that conducts marketing research. She holds a bachelor's degree in economics and an MBA in marketing. She is married to Kevin (a 42-year-old White man) who works for a similar company in another town; they met while they were attending a professional meeting. They have been married for 7 years and have two small children, ages 2 and 4. The children live primarily with Melissa; Kevin comes home each weekend. Melissa, then, has primary responsibility for the household and child rearing during the week, but she and Kevin share the tasks on the weekend.

Melissa sought career counseling because she was feeling anxious and resentful of the demands she was juggling at work and at home. She feels that she and Kevin are able to communicate very well; they talk and e-mail each other several times a day, and they maintain time for themselves on the weekends. She also feels that they both make time for their children. But she is frustrated that they live so far apart and that her job is not as rewarding as she hoped. She enjoys some aspects of her work, primarily the opportunity to create new research surveys, and she enjoys working with clients and with her colleagues in the company. Melissa does not feel, however, that she is able to use her skills most effectively and also feels that she does not receive adequate recognition for her work. She has been passed over for promotions, and she is not certain if this was due to her performance or her status as a working mother or because she is a woman. The last time she was passed over for a promotion, she seriously considered talking to her manager about it but decided against it because she did not want to "rock the boat."

She and Kevin have talked about opening their own marketing research firm; that is one option that she is considering. Kevin's company has no openings at her level, so it is not possible for her to move to join him at his firm. There is no real reason they need to stay in this geographic area, because they have no family obligations or ties other than their current jobs.

QUESTIONS FOR DISCUSSION

1. What are the rewards in Melissa's environments?

2. How would TWA characterize Melissa's satisfactoriness? How would you incorporate this into counseling?

3. What is Melissa's adjustment style, and how would you work with her to increase the correspondence with her environment?

4. How would you incorporate the personal issues that Melissa is facing into career counseling?

5. How would you incorporate Melissa and Kevin's work-family interface into counseling?

6. How do Melissa's gender and race influence her career decisions?

Case 3: Linda

Linda is an 18-year-old college freshman. Both of her parents are Korean and immigrated to the United States when Linda and her sisters were small children. Linda was 10 when they arrived in the United States; her sisters were 8, 5, and 2. She grew up in a primarily Korean community in Los Angeles, living with her parents, three sisters, and her paternal grandmother. Linda's parents both completed college degrees in Korea prior to the immigration. Linda's father was in business in Korea, and her mother was a teacher. However, when they came to the United States, neither was able to find work commensurate with their education and work experience. Her father worked for another Korean family in a grocery store, and her mother took in sewing and took care of the children. When Linda was 15, her parents were able to buy the grocery store. Since then, her mother has worked in the store with her father.

(Continued)

(Continued)

Linda's parents learned to speak English, though her grandmother refused to learn and only spoke Korean at home. Linda's parents spoke Korean at home as well, out of respect for her grandmother. Thus, Linda grew up speaking Korean and English. Her parents came in contact with individuals from many cultures in the grocery store, but their primary social network consisted of the Korean American community; much of this community was focused on involvement with the Korean Church. Linda and her sisters were expected to be very involved with the Korean community as well, participating in activities in the church and forming friendships with other Korean children.

Linda attended an elementary school that was predominantly Korean and African American. Her parents placed a very high emphasis on education, making sure that she and her sisters worked hard at their studies each evening. She made some friends at school but was discouraged from participating in afterschool activities, since those might interfere with her studies. She also was discouraged from making friends outside her parents' social circle. Eventually, she did not want to bring friends home, since she was embarrassed at her grandmother's inability to communicate with anyone who could not speak Korean.

Linda did well in school and was chosen to attend a high school known for its science and math instruction and college-preparatory curriculum. Linda's parents were very pleased at their daughter's accomplishment and wanted to ensure that she would do well enough to enter a very good university; they increased their expectations of the time she spent studying. The high school was a racially diverse school with many gifted students. Linda became friends with students from a wide geographic region and began to want to participate in more school and off-campus activities. Linda and her parents entered into many conflicts during her high school years: They expected her to be home working on her schoolwork, but she wanted to have the same freedoms as her new friends. She was particularly interested in participating in theater and received much verbal encouragement to pursue her interest in acting from her teachers and drama coach.

Her grandmother was highly critical of her mother during this time, blaming her mother for what she perceived as Linda's disobedience and disrespect. Her mother expected her father to support her against his mother, but he also felt that Linda was disrespectful and selfish in her desire to be "more American." This led to increased conflict between her parents as well. They were very concerned that her sisters not learn "bad lessons" from Linda, wanting them to find their primary social relationships within their Korean community.

Linda finished high school with a 4.0 grade point average and won an academic scholarship to a prestigious university in the Los Angeles area. She enrolled as a biology major and did well in her classes during the first semester. The second semester, however, her grades began to slip. Linda was suddenly unsure of her decision to pursue a biology major and began to reconsider her interests in acting. She sought the help of a career counselor on campus to decide whether to change majors.

QUESTIONS FOR DISCUSSION

1. How would you explain Linda's behavior from the perspective of a TWA counselor?

2. What is the correspondence between Linda's abilities and the requirements of her environment? Between her values and the reinforcers?

3. How would you incorporate Linda's feelings about her decisions into counseling through the perspective of TWA?

4. What is Linda's adjustment style?

5. How would you evaluate Linda's person-environment fit in terms of true needs?

6. How do Linda's gender and race/ethnicity influence her decisions?

BOX 7.3 Summary of Key Constructs

Construct	Definition
Values	Grouping of needs
Abilities	General dimensions that underlie groupings of acquired skills
Satisfaction	How well an individual's needs are met by the job
Satisfactoriness	How well an individual's abilities and skills meet what the job or organization requires
Reinforcer pattern	Pattern of rewards
Tenure	Length of time in a job
Celerity	Speed with which an individual initiates interaction with his or her environment
Pace	Intensity or activity level of one's interaction with the environment
Rhythm	Pattern of the pace of interaction with the environment
Endurance	Sustaining of interaction with the environment
Flexibility	Ability to tolerate a mismatch (discorrespondence) between needs and rewards
Perseverance	Continuing in the environment while in adjustment mode
Active adjustment	Acting on the environment
Reactive adjustment	Acting on self

Chapter 8

Super's Developmental Theory

INTRODUCTORY REVIEW

Developmental theories include Super's life span, life space approach and Gottfredson's theory of circumscription and compromise, which is discussed in the next chapter. Compared to the person-environment fit theories described in Chapters 6 and 7, Super's and Gottfredson's theories are characterized by viewing career choice as a process rather than an event and by incorporating developmental concepts into this process.

The developmental theory of Donald Super has been one of the most influential vocational theories of the 20th century (Borgen, 1991). Super died in 1994, and his last chapter outlining 14 theoretical propositions was published posthumously (Super, Savickas, & Super, 1996). Savickas (2002, 2005) updated Super's theory but has gone on to incorporate the central constructs of the theory with a constructionist perspective (Savickas, 2013), explained more fully in Chapter 11.

Super (1953) introduced the propositions outlining his theory in his 1952 presidential address to the Division of Counseling Psychology of the American Psychological Association. Super continued to develop and refine his theory until his death in 1994 and was remarkable for his active scientific investigation of real-life phenomena, their eventual theoretical implications, and the application of his work in counseling (Hartung, 2013; Herr, 1997; Savickas, 1997). Savickas (2005) modified some of the original propositions and added others.

One of the hallmarks of Super's theory is that vocational development is a process of making several decisions, which culminate in vocational choices that represent an implementation of the self-concept. Vocational choices are viewed as successive approximations of a good match between the vocational self and the world of work.

Among the basic assumptions underlying the propositions is that development is a process (Super et al., 1996; Savickas, 2005). Three propositions focus on developmental contextualism, which is the process of developing a work identity that occurs within the individual's social context. This social context helps create both opportunities and constraints. Five propositions indicate an underlying belief in the differences among people and among occupations. People differ in terms of their abilities, personalities, and values, as well as other variables. Occupations have distinctive combinations of required abilities and personality traits. Differences among individuals translate into suitability for a number of different occupations. Individuals may have characteristics appropriate for multiple occupations. Thus, no one occupation is the only possible fit for an individual, nor does only one individual fit a particular occupation. Work satisfaction is predicted to increase proportionately with self-concept implementation and is dependent on the importance of and satisfaction with other life roles. Super suggested that individuals hold various roles in their lives that vary in importance across the life span. Individuals may, in fact, find little satisfaction with the worker role but may be fully satisfied with another life role.

Eight additional propositions discuss development of the self-concept and its implementation in vocational choices, stages, and work roles. Embedded in these propositions are the notions that self-concepts are formed by vocational preferences and competencies, that these change and evolve over time in interaction with situations, that they are products of social learning, and that they are increasingly stable over the life span. Super proposed five distinct life stages, noting that each has unique developmental tasks. He also suggested that career patterns (the sequence of jobs or occupations held by individuals) are determined by a variety of personal and environmental characteristics. One proposition discusses the concept of career adaptability, which is the readiness of the individual to cope with the demands of the environment; another proposition focuses on career maturity, or the readiness and resources to cope with developmental tasks.

The five life stages, or "maxicycles," are Growth (ages 4 to 13), Exploration (ages 14 to 24), Establishment (ages 25 to 44), Maintenance or Management (ages 45 to 65), and Disengagement (over age 65) (Hartung, 2013). Super characterized the stages as linear and predictable but not invariant. In other words, he described a series of stages that individuals typically go through but was careful to note that not everyone progresses through these stages in the same manner or at fixed ages. Each transition between stages is characterized by a "minicycle," or a recycling through the stages of growth, reexploration, and reestablishment. The age ranges are the approximate ages at which most individuals encounter each stage.

Within each stage, Super proposed characteristic developmental tasks (Hartung, 2013. Successful mastery of these tasks allows individuals to function effectively in their life roles within that stage and prepares them for the next task. Successful coping with the requirements of each stage is dependent on an individual's career maturity. Career maturity—or readiness to master the developmental tasks of each stage effectively—involves both attitudinal factors and cognitive factors. Osipow and Fitzgerald (1996) note that "vocational maturity allows the observer to assess the rate and level of an individual's development with respect to career matters" (p. 114). In adults, however, the concept of maturation is less appropriate, and Super et al. (1996) and Savickas (1994a) discuss *career adaptability,* defined as "readiness to cope with changing work and work conditions" (Savickas, 1994a, p. 58).

Super considered the development of vocational choices within the context of other life roles: "While making a living, people live a life" (Super et al., 1996). He delineated six roles that individuals hold, sometimes concurrently: child, student, homemaker, worker, citizen, and leisurite. Individuals hold multiple roles, and those roles interact. The life-career rainbow schema in Figure 8.1 is a pictorial representation of the intersection of stages and roles and may be used to clarify the various roles for a particular client (Super, 1980). *Life space* corresponds to the roles that one fulfills at various times in life, and *life span* denotes the stages described earlier. An individual "lives in the intersection of the two dimensions" (Super et al., 1996, p. 128).

Figure 8.1 Super's Life-Career Rainbow

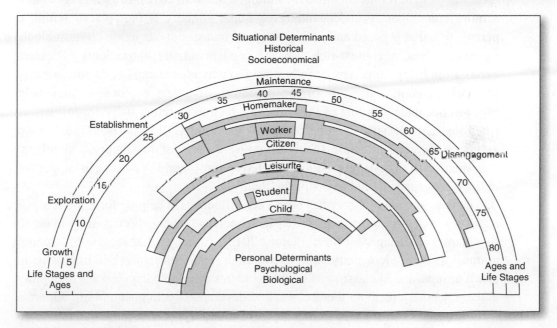

SOURCE: Super (1980).

A fundamental aspect of Super's theory is that vocational choice is an implementation of the self-concept (Hartung, 2013). The self-concept includes the objective and subjective views of the self. Individuals construct their careers in a continuing self-evaluation within their social context. Individuals begin to consider work roles that fit their self-concepts. Their self-concepts are shaped by feedback from the external world (e.g., parents, teachers, employers), and in turn, the evolving self-concept begins to be implemented in different work roles. The implication for career counselors is that in addition to providing clients with objective information about the self (i.e., interests, values, abilities), counselors also need to integrate clients' subjective views of who they are and the role that they want work to play in their lives.

Salomone (1996) traced the development of Super's theory over 40 years and concluded that the theory did not change substantially over the years but that many of the propositions still needed to be empirically tested. Blustein (1997) and Herr (1997) both noted that Super's theory was a framework flexible enough to be revised and refined as the context of working changed. One example of this is Richardson's (2013) call to attend to the private and public spheres in which individuals work, encouraging the field to attend to both market work and personal care work. Herr highlighted the need for Super's theory to incorporate the impact of economic changes on careers, as well as the role of barriers due to gender and culture in career development, and indeed that continues to be a criticism of the theory (Fouad & Kantamneni, 2013; Juntunen & Even, 2012). Blustein argues that a more contemporary understanding of Super's theory is best placed within a perspective that is broad and inclusive of the many contexts in which individuals function. Thus, a context-rich way of conceptualizing antecedents of career exploration helps explain more fully how and why clients explore various aspects of work. A contextual view of the outcomes of career exploration may help broaden our understanding of the ways in which exploratory behavior influences life roles and decisions. Nonetheless, as Hartung (2013) notes, Super's own approach rigorous attention to investigating aspects of the theory and others' examination of various propositions has led to considerable evidence in support of many of the fundamental tenets of the theory.

The developmental theory has been very influential in helping form the basis of activities related to career exploration in schools, which we discuss more in depth in Chapter 12 (Lapan, Turner Pierce, 2012; Turner & Lapan, 2005). School counselors at the elementary, middle, and high school levels work individually, in small groups, and in classrooms to help students develop competencies to explore careers, learn more about themselves, and develop skills to plan and implement a future career. School-based career interventions focus on helping students learn more about themselves (e.g., exploring vocational interests and values), about the world of work (e.g., knowing about different types of engineering careers), and how to make career decisions. Lapan (2004) describes a number of different types of interventions that promote career development. Turner and Lapan (2005) reviewed research on school-based career counseling, concluding that "overall, analyses of such group-based interventions have shown that they are related to positive changes in . . . vocational identity, career maturity, reduced career indecision, and greater psychological development" (p. 429).

BOX 8.1 Personal Reflection

- What role does work play in my life now?
- What balance do I want among the roles in my life?
- How have I constructed the work role over my life span?

APPLYING DEVELOPMENTAL THEORY

Counselors who use the developmental approach would ask the sorts of questions that are outlined in Box 8.2. They would ask about the client's life roles and assess which roles are more important than others and how those life roles have evolved over the client's work history. They would ask questions to assess the client's life themes, and they would listen to the client's narrative story and assess how the client attaches meaning to the various events in his or her development. They would listen to how the client has constructed his or her career, including how the self-concept has been implemented in career decisions over time.

BOX 8.2 Counselor Cognitions

- What are the client's life themes?
- What is the client's life structure?
- What are the client's adaptive coping strategies?
- What are the client's individual style characteristics, such as abilities, interests, and personality?
- What are the client's narrative stories?
- What is the relative importance of a client's life roles?
- How does the client's context affect his or her decisions and developmental process?
- How does the client's self-concept influence his or her vocational choices?

Conceptualizing Leslie's Career History

Developmental theorists would view Leslie's case as a series of decisions from childhood through adulthood. We will discuss Leslie's decisions using Super's stages as a framework. We will then discuss developmental career counseling and possible career interventions.

Childhood

Four tasks are addressed in the Growth stage (ages 4–13): becoming concerned about the future, increasing personal control over one's own life, convincing oneself to achieve in school and at work, and acquiring competent work habits and attitudes (Super et al., 1996).

Leslie consistently enjoyed school throughout her elementary and junior high years. Many subjects intrigued her, and she enjoyed the attention of good teachers who challenged her and sparked her interest in a variety of activities. She began to excel in math and science in elementary school and continued to take these courses in middle school.

Other influences on her developing self-concept included her mother, who was her primary role model during childhood. Her father, however, was her earliest occupational role model. As she progressed through elementary and middle school, additional role models were teachers. School in general played an important role in Leslie's life, and her teachers provided valuable support and encouragement.

Leslie's parents communicated their expectations to her about achievement, emphasizing that she should do her best. On the other hand, while her parents were happy that Leslie enjoyed and excelled in school, they did not expect work-related achievement to be a central focus in Leslie's life. She was not expected to work throughout her adult life but rather work until she married and had children, a pattern that was modeled by Leslie's mother and followed by her sister. Thus, she received messages to continue to achieve but not to place achievement as her top priority. These messages influenced the constructions of her developing sense of career.

Adolescence/early adulthood

During the Exploration stage (ages 14–24), the primary tasks are crystallizing, specifying, and implementing, or actualizing, a career choice (Super et al., 1996). Leslie experimented with a number of different options, and her difficulty in choosing was related to her ability to see many possible selves due to her wide-ranging interests and talents. Moreover, her indecision may have been exacerbated by the expectations that Leslie experienced from others, particularly her parents, about the importance of the work role in her life: It may have been difficult for her to be planful and decisive about something that others believed would not be important in her life. In contrast to Leslie's experience, her older brother was coached and encouraged by their parents to consider his career alternatives carefully, beginning in early adolescence. Leslie, on the other hand, received little guidance and direction about the process of planning for the future; consequently, she did not plan her entrance into college and had difficulty negotiating the tasks of the exploration stage. Within her family, then, Leslie experienced messages about career choice that differed by one's gender. As she moved into high school, her natural interest in math, particularly advanced math, carried her into a time when she enjoyed being recognized for her ability in math. She tutored other students while in high school and later in college. Thus, excelling at math became a central part of Leslie's developing self-concept. Leslie also developed conscientious study habits, and she took pride in her work.

These messages about career issues relative to gender issues were mirrored by other sources throughout Leslie's adolescence. She continued to receive mixed messages about the appropriate role that a career should play in her life, as well as the appropriateness of her interest in math-related activities and her pursuit of these activities as a career.

Leslie's subjective view of herself conformed to traditional gender-role socialization, in that she focused on marriage and family roles as opposed to long-term investment in her work role. She therefore opted out of some career decisions because they were outside of her self-concept. For example, she decided against engineering because of her perceptions of the difficulty of combining work and family in that field, and she decided against math because of her disinterest in pursuing graduate-level education. Math education, on the other hand, represented a compromise between traditional and nontraditional options.

Readiness to make vocational decisions becomes central in Super's Exploration stage. Leslie's difficulty with making a decision about attending college and about her college major may have been related to slightly delayed career maturity; developmentally, she was not as ready to make a decision as she ideally might have been. This delay, in turn, may have been related to the issues just discussed: Leslie had little experience in making career plans prior to entering college because she was not encouraged or expected to do so. The "unreadiness" also led to some discomfort at not having a decision made, and she found herself comparing her progress in making a decision with her college friends, as well as with her brother, who teased her when she had difficulty with decision making. She at times agonized over the "right" choice of college major and career, and the actual decision point stretched over several semesters as she struggled to keep her options open. Her salient life roles during this period included child and student, although she also was preparing for the homemaker role because she anticipated marrying after college.

In spite of the difficulty she experienced in making a decision, Leslie's choice of secondary education seemed to represent a good avenue for implementing her self-concept as it was developed to that point in her life. The salient parts of her self-concept included being good at math and being recognized for her achievements, as well as being responsible, conscientious, and caring. Teaching allowed her to express these elements of her identity.

Conceptualizing Leslie's Present Situation

The Establishment stage (ages 25–40) entails entering and becoming established in one's career and work life, and the tasks of this stage include stabilizing, consolidating, and advancing. *Stabilizing* involves settling in and learning what needs to be done to perform one's job adequately. *Consolidating* occurs when an individual feels comfortable that he or she possesses the skills required by the job and feels secure that he or she is performing well in the eyes of supervisors and coworkers. *Advancing* refers to moving up within one's job, assuming greater responsibility at higher pay. Advancing can occur throughout the Establishment stage but is typically subsequent to stabilizing and consolidating.

Leslie entered teaching with much enthusiasm and experienced the transition into her full-time work role in a manner typical to many young adults; that is, she found it both satisfying and stressful. Despite her success as a teacher, she decided to leave her first position. This decision was primarily based on a discrepancy between her work and nonwork roles. Leslie's feeling that she did not have enough time to spend with her parents and siblings and the termination of the relationship with her boyfriend led her to question her work-nonwork priorities. She hoped that the job change would provide a better balance between roles and, therefore, that she would feel less stressed and more satisfied. In Super's terms, Leslie spent most of the three years in her first job working on the task of stabilizing. Although from an objective perspective, she clearly possessed the necessary skills, her subjective view was that her skills were not sufficient to make her a good teacher. She wondered whether the amount of stress she was experiencing resulted from her being inadequate at her job, and she did not have any other new teachers to whom she could compare her job performance and stress level. In the absence of external feedback, her career construction was that she was a poor teacher.

Upon taking her new (current) job, Leslie was able to get a different perspective on her skills as a teacher, primarily because she noticed that other teachers seemed to experience a similar level of stress. She thus completed the process of stabilizing and moved on to the tasks related to consolidating in her career. Currently, however, Leslie's dissatisfaction with a number of factors in her job suggests that these tasks may need additional attention and exploration within counseling.

Leslie's current dissatisfaction can be viewed as related to career adaptation; namely, that she is struggling to adapt to changes in her work environment. These changes may be simply too extensive for her to address simultaneously, as she expressed dissatisfaction with the principal, her fellow teachers, the students, and their parents. An alternative hypothesis is that her dissatisfaction with one aspect may have spilled over into other areas and colored her view of the entire work situation. Moreover, a view consonant with developmental theory is that Leslie's dissatisfaction has escalated as her self-concept has become more refined and crystallized. Following this line of thought, the counselor might choose to affirm and validate Leslie's feelings of anger and dissatisfaction, as they may indicate an evolving clarity of who she is and who she wants to become.

Leslie has primarily focused on her student and worker roles. In addition, her role as "child" is still active, as her family of origin continues to be an important influence in her current career situation. Moreover, Leslie is considering a shift in the priority of her life roles by having a child. As with many people in early adulthood, Leslie has focused on entering and establishing her career and now is stopping to examine her decisions to date. Leslie could be viewed as experiencing an additional stage of midlife career renewal (Williams & Savickas, 1990).

In summary, Leslie can be conceptualized as being in the midst of the Establishment stage (stabilizing, consolidating, advancing). However, like many individuals who have entered career counseling at this point in their careers, she may be recycling back to a consideration of tasks in the Exploration stage (crystallizing, specifying, implementing).

QUESTIONS FOR DISCUSSION

1. What specific hypotheses would you develop about Leslie from Super's theory? How does using Super's theory help you understand Leslie? How might it help Leslie understand herself?

2. What are the advantages of viewing Leslie as reentering the Exploration stage (minicycle within maxicycle)? What are the disadvantages?

3. How ready is Leslie to make a career decision right now? How does she feel about the prospect of making a decision, particularly of making a job or career change? How might her previous experiences with career decision making influence the process or content of this current decision?

4. Who is likely to influence her decision? How much pressure does she feel now? What types of pressure and from whom?

5. Which life roles seem most salient to Leslie? How can she balance the roles that she desires?

6. How might Leslie describe her self-concept and the narrative of her life? How does she make meaning from the interaction of her various life roles?

The Case of Karen

Karen is a 52-year-old White woman living in the southwest United States. She seeks career counseling because she is struggling to understand how she can continue to advance in her career and still take care of her elderly mother. Karen is divorced, with two grown children who are starting careers of their own. Her mother, Irene, is in her early 80s and lives in an independent living apartment in a midsize town in Iowa. Irene recently fell and broke her hip. In the process of helping her mother, Karen discovered that her mother has several signs of advancing dementia. Karen is not sure that Irene can live on her own any more, but Irene refuses to move from her home or leave her friends.

Karen went to nursing school right after her high school graduation. She wanted to help others and liked her science courses in high school. Her original goal was to have a job that she could easily blend with her strong desire to stay home with children. She also hoped to meet a doctor and not have to work after she had children. She graduated with an RN and began working at a hospital in Iowa, where she met her future husband, a medical intern. They married and had two children in 3 years. Karen did not work after her children were born. She noted that her husband's career took precedence in their family and his hours as an internist were unpredictable. She stayed home with her children until they were in school full-time. She enjoyed being a doctor's wife in their community and was very involved in civic and political organizations. Soon, though, she realized that all her friends were returning to work, and she needed more to occupy her time.

She began to look for work but found that employers preferred nurses with a bachelor's degree rather than an RN. She went back to school to complete her bachelor's of science in nursing (BSN), and in the process of her schoolwork, realized she really enjoyed the role that information played in the work of medical professionals. She began to consider working in health information, but she was not sure if she would need more schooling for that career. As she was finishing her BSN degree, her husband accepted a position with a practice in Phoenix, Arizona, and, though their marriage was beginning to unravel, she moved with him. Her children did not join them; they were already in college and chose to stay with their grandmother during summers.

Karen's life roles shifted in Phoenix. Her children were not actively part of her household, her husband's work hours were long, and her role as a doctor's wife was very different in a big city than in a small town. She started to look for a job and found a position as a nursing supervisor in a hospital. She took the job in part because the hospital would give her an opportunity to work her way into health information systems. In fact, she was offered a position in the health information department within a year and quickly excelled, receiving three promotions within 5 years.

Karen's work became more important to her as she and her husband decided to divorce. She enjoyed the tasks in her work, enjoyed the challenges of solving technology problems, and enjoyed the recognition she was receiving. She liked having her own money and independence. She also felt that she was in the right place at the right time, because the health care industry was booming in Phoenix. She began to be recruited to work for other hospitals and firms and was considering an offer from a software company when her mother fell.

Currently, Karen is very torn about her future. She feels that she should go back to take care of Irene. Moving back to Iowa would also bring her closer to her children, who stayed in the Midwest. But the opportunities to work in health information systems are very limited in her mother's hometown. Karen feels that she has to choose between caring for her mother and her work and independence.

QUESTIONS FOR DISCUSSION

1. What specific hypotheses would you develop about Karen from Super's theory? How does using Super's theory help you understand Karen? How might it help Karen understand herself?

2. What are the advantages of viewing Karen as reentering the Maintenance/Management stage? What are the disadvantages?

3. How ready is Karen to make a career decision right now? What alternatives might Karen consider?

4. Who is likely to influence her decision? How much pressure does she feel now? What types of pressure and from whom?

5. How can Karen balance the roles that she desires?

6. How might Karen describe her self-concept and the narrative of her life? How does she make meaning from the interaction of her various life roles?

DIRECTIONS AND IMPLICATIONS FOR CAREER COUNSELING

Goals of Counseling

From Super's framework, the goals of counseling for clients are as follows:

To (1) develop and accept an integrated and adequate picture of themselves and their life roles, (2) test the concept against reality, and (3) convert it into reality by making choices that implement the self-concept and lead to job success and satisfaction as well as benefit to society. (Super et al., 1996, pp. 158–159)

Super's theory also has been expanded into an explicit model of counseling, named the career development assessment and counseling model (C-DAC) (Hartung, 2013; Osborne, Brown, Niles, & Miner, 1997; Super, 1983; Super, Osborne, Walsh, Brown, & Niles, 1992). The C-DAC model was developed to use concepts from Super's developmental theory to augment trait-and-factor approaches to career counseling. The model incorporates four phases of assessment: (1) life space and work-role salience; (2) career development status and resources, or career adaptability; (3) vocational identity, including values, interests, and abilities; and (4) vocational self-concepts and life themes. In each of these four phases, assessment can be accomplished either in session with the client or by using inventories developed by Super and his colleagues.

The first step, assessment of life space and work-role salience, begins by exploring the importance of the work role to the client, particularly in relation to the other potential roles in a client's life, such as child, student, homemaker, citizen, and leisurite. *Life structure* refers to the constellation of core and peripheral roles that define an individual's life. The degree to which the work role is salient will influence the weight placed on the three subsequent assessments, since these focus specifically on the work role and identity.

The second focus of assessment is career development status and resources, or the client's career adaptability. The counselor needs to determine which developmental tasks are of concern to the client. Identification of the client's concerns is followed by an assessment of the coping resources that he or she possesses to deal with those concerns. Coping resources are typically viewed as the attitudes and competencies that the client holds for dealing with the specific developmental tasks that he or she is facing. Hartung and Taber (2008) describe this as the focus on adaptive coping strategies that the client has, or needs to develop, to resolve career concerns.

Third, the assessment of vocational identity represents the "traditional trait-and-factor" portion of the C-DAC model (Hartung, 2013; Super et al., 1996) and includes values, abilities, and interests. However, rather than the trait-factor view that assessment focuses on uncovering objective traits that a client may possess, career construction theory views this phase as assessing the client's way of coping with the world, or style (Hartung & Taber, 2008). The goal of this step is to develop a description of these aspects of the client's vocational identity, and then explore how this identity might be expressed in the various roles in the client's life.

The fourth and final step in assessment focuses on occupational self-concepts and life themes. Here, the focus shifts from the "objective" assessment during the previous step to an assessment of the client's subjective self-concept. The C-DAC model recommends two methods: a cross-sectional method, which focuses on the client's current self-schema, and a longitudinal method, which focuses on themes that have developed throughout the client's life. Hartung and Taber (2008) describe this as helping the client identify his or her career story. The career style interview (Savickas, 2005) may be used to assess life themes by assessing domains of role models, favorite television shows or magazines, leisure activities, favorite school subjects, early memories, and favorite sayings.

Following these four steps in assessment, the counselor then develops an "integrative interpretation which narrates the client's life story" (Super et al., 1996, p. 157) and serves as a transition from the assessment phase to the counseling phase. Super (1957) described a process of counseling that alternates between directive and nondirective techniques. For example, the counselor may begin with a nondirective exploration of Leslie's career concerns, followed by a directive setting of topics for further discussion, then nondirective clarification of Leslie's self-concept and life structure, directive discussion of assessment results, and nondirective discussion of her reactions to the assessment. This cyclical approach to career counseling offers a way to "balance attention to the objective and subjective dimensions of self and career" (Super et al., 1996, p. 162). Karen's counselor may be less directive than Leslie's counselor, because Karen appears to be more concerned with the salience of different life roles. Thus, her counselor may focus more on her life structure and on her life themes.

Interventions

Consonant with the goals of developmental theory, Leslie's goals include achieving a better view of herself and what is causing her dissatisfaction at work and an understanding of the ways in which she can juggle the multiple roles of child, worker, and parent. She stated that she wants to decide whether to stay at her current job or move to a new field and that she wants to discuss incorporating possible shifts of roles. Karen's goals are to decide how to balance the roles of child, parent, and worker. She also needs to decide whether to move back to Iowa and, if she does not move, to determine how to take care of her mother.

Assessment of life space and work-role salience

The interaction of primary roles has potential for either creating stress or reducing stress: "Multiple roles can enrich life or overburden it" (Super et al., 1996, p. 129). Further, the process of completing a career transition may lead to the evolution of roles and how roles interact in a client's life: roles may be added or deleted, or ongoing roles may be modified.

The counselor begins with a clarification of roles and their relative salience at this point. For example, how might Leslie characterize her current balance of roles? How might she construct an ideal balance of roles? How much discrepancy is there between her current balance of roles and her ideal balance? Moreover, Leslie is contemplating adding the role of "parent" to her life, and the interaction of that role with her work role needs to be examined.

Super's life-career rainbow suggests that Leslie is fulfilling a number of different social roles in her life and that she may be reevaluating the relative priority or salience of these roles. An intervention that may help Leslie clarify her life roles is an "interrole assessment" technique (Brown & Brooks, 1991). This technique can be used to identify and clarify the interaction of work roles with other life roles. First, Leslie lists the life roles in which she currently is involved and estimates the amount of time spent in each role. Next, she ranks her life roles using values as the basis for ranking. Finally, she identifies roles that conflict with one another, roles that are compensatory with one another, and roles that complement one another (Brown & Brooks, 1991).

The life-career rainbow shows that Karen's current primary role is that of worker, but that is now in conflict with her child role. Karen has not often had to balance multiple roles. Early in her marriage, her role as parent was the most salient, with some importance given to the role of citizen. As her children grew and were home less, her primary role was that of student. After she moved and her marriage ended, her primary role was that of worker. Now, with her mother ill and needing her help while her career is advancing with many opportunities, she is struggling with the balance among roles.

Assessment of career adaptability

To determine which developmental tasks are of concern to Leslie, a counselor might use results from the Adult Career Concerns Inventory (ACCI) (Super,

Thompson, & Lindeman, 1988) as a guide. Leslie's highest score of the four stage scales is in Exploration, suggesting that her primary career concerns are tasks related to the Exploration stage (see Appendix A, Figure 4). This is particularly useful to note and to address in counseling, because Leslie may be feeling some discrepancy between her age and her expected career stage. That is, she may feel that she should be further along in her career path. Indeed, she expresses that she "should have figured this out by now." Moreover, Leslie's parents and siblings convey their amusement about her still being "undecided about what she wants to do."

The counselor also would examine the substage scores on the ACCI for further clues about Leslie's concerns. Her highest scores within the Exploration stage are on Specification and Crystallization, with a relatively lower score on Implementation. These scores suggest that Leslie is focused on identifying and choosing a specific occupational direction, confirming what she has expressed to the counselor.

Given the career concerns that Leslie expresses, the counselor then may assess the coping resources available to Leslie. The first type of resource is positive attitudes toward career planning. Leslie is quite enthused about career counseling and feels ready to "make a career choice the right way this time." She is interested in researching different occupations, and her analytical skills would serve her well in this regard.

A second type of coping resource is Leslie's knowledge about herself and about the world of work. Her knowledge about herself appears appropriate to her age and experience, as indicated by her confidence in completing the assessment inventories, her ability to describe the positive and negative aspects of her current job, and her self-description of her strengths and weaknesses. The counselor, however, would remain attentive for areas in which Leslie could benefit from additional self-exploration, as well as areas in which Leslie underestimates her abilities and skills. Leslie's knowledge of occupational information also seems quite appropriate to her situation, and she clearly expresses specific occupations about which she would like additional information. Again, the counselor would be attentive to misinformation that Leslie might hold or areas in which she needs further information.

The final type of coping resource that the counselor assesses is decision-making skills. Because Leslie reports that she has "not made good decisions in the past," the counselor would attempt to make a careful and thorough assessment of her decision-making strategies and skills. The counselor would ask Leslie to describe the process that she uses to make decisions by analyzing several situations in which Leslie has made decisions in the past (e.g., changing jobs, buying a car).

One hypothesis that the counselor may explore is whether Leslie's decision-making skills are truly inadequate or whether she only believes this to be true because her family has told her so.

In Karen's case, the career concern may be related to curiosity about her future self and how to resolve the dilemma of balancing multiple roles, but the counselor would go through very similar processes. The counselor would assess Karen's attitudes toward considering various ways to resolve her concerns. An open attitude to examining options leads to competence in exploring various alternatives. Karen's counselor might encourage her to experiment with a variety of solutions. The counselor would also help Karen identify factors that are inhibiting her from developing confidence in ways that she could blend multiple roles. Finally, the counselor would help Karen identify the resources she has to construct her future career, including her planning and decision-making skills, the strength of her relationship with her mother, and her vocational options as a professional in a growing field.

Assessment of vocational identity

Vocational identity, the focus of the third step, is described by integrating information about the client's interests, values, abilities, and personality. In Leslie's case, these would be seen in the inventories that she took prior to counseling. In Karen's case, this would be assessed in an interview focusing on the tasks and activities she does or does not enjoy at work.

Leslie is interested in working with and helping people, as evidenced by her scores on the SII and the MIQ, yet her confidence in social activities does not match her interest; her lack of confidence may be due to her tendency to be introverted in nature. She also is quite comfortable working alone and may, in fact, be perceived by others as preferring to work alone. Leslie also is interested in mathematical and scientific activities, which is supported by her logical and analytical style and her valuing of achievement and the use of her abilities.

The counselor may explore how Leslie's vocational identity is expressed in her life through her work role and other life roles. One area for exploration is whether Leslie wishes to incorporate more social-type activities into her work role or whether she can express those interests in her leisure pursuits.

Assessment of occupational self-concepts and life themes

In the final step of assessment in the C-DAC model, the client's subjective self-concept is explored. The focus in this step is on clients' self-schemas—how they "make sense" of themselves and their world. For example, Leslie's counselor would assess Leslie's self-concept by listening carefully to how she describes herself, both as she is today and as she has seen herself throughout her life. Leslie seems to view herself as capable and talented, yet she is self-critical and easily discouraged when she compares herself to others. She has internalized her family's perception of her as indecisive as well as their mixed messages about achievement, although she is beginning to examine these beliefs about herself. Leslie feels that she has much to offer, if only she could identify the best outlet for her talents.

Karen's counselor would also listen carefully to her stories and life themes. Karen's career concerns focus more on the balance of her roles as child and parent with her worker role. Her self-concept in early adulthood was shaped by her own expectations of her roles as a mother and doctor's wife, and her self-concept as a worker did not develop until she returned to school and realized she had interests in technology. She began to construct her career as a health information professional as her other roles began to be less demanding or not available to her. Now she is struggling between her self-concept as an independent professional woman and her self-concept as a caring daughter and mother. She does not know how—or even if—she can blend the roles.

Other interventions

The cases of Leslie and Karen suggest the use of interventions related to exploratory behavior. The counselor would thoroughly examine career decisions up to this point in time. How did Leslie and Karen make earlier career decisions? What factors influenced the process and outcome of their decisions? What other career options had they considered and why? Why were the other options discarded?

Leslie's counselor would help her acknowledge explicitly and accept her status in the Exploration stage. She may benefit from "making meaning" for herself about where she is in the career development process. For example, she may decide that she is "starting over" but this time possessing greater wisdom and self-knowledge and having different questions to answer for herself. The counselor would encourage Leslie to see herself as "recycling" through the Exploration stage with a description of the tasks of crystallizing, specifying, and implementing career choice. Super proposed that individuals go through a minicycle during career transitions; Leslie could be conceptualized as being in a career transition, although the extent of the transition is not yet clear.

Super et al. (1996) stated that "individuals eventually complete the task of specifying an occupational choice by translating the privately experienced occupational self-concept into educational/vocational choices" (p. 132). Leslie's self-concept continues to evolve, becoming more clearly defined with age and with experience. The counselor may help Leslie explore how her current self-concept fits with the career choice that she implemented immediately after college and whether her dissatisfaction with her current job may be related to changes in her self-concept. Have her job responsibilities kept up with her evolving self-concept? Are there opportunities where she is now or in a new teaching-related position, or is a career change indicated?

The construct of career maturity (or career adaptability) is particularly relevant in the Exploration stage, and the counselor would examine how ready Leslie is to make vocational decisions. The uncertainty of her future pregnancy plans adds another dimension to Leslie's readiness. How is she feeling about making a career decision? Moreover, Leslie's previous experiences with career decision making were associated with some anxiety related to time pressure, family expectations, and/or the decision-making process itself.

ADDITIONAL CASES

Case 1: Walter

Walter is a 65-year-old White man who is a manufacturing representative for a large tractor company. He has worked for this company for almost 40 years and worked his way up to his current position of regional manager. Walter plans to retire within a year or two.

Walter married his wife, Martha, while he was in his first year of college. He completed two years of college but discontinued his education when their first daughter was born. Walter did not pursue any further formal education and expresses regret that he did not complete his degree.

Walter and Martha have four children, all of whom are married and successfully employed. Walter and Martha have nine grandchildren, seven of whom live within a 30-mile radius. Martha worked part time but also took on the primary role of raising the children and supporting Walter's business activities. She is currently retired, is a very active civic volunteer and maintains a busy schedule.

Walter (and Martha) will be entering retirement with good health and financial security. He is preparing himself for voluntary retirement; he would prefer to continue working indefinitely, but Martha has encouraged him to retire so that they can do more traveling. Also, Walter is feeling some unspoken pressure to retire from the vice president of sales so that another individual can be promoted into Walter's position.

Walter typically worked 80 hours per week and spent a good deal of time on the road. Because of this very busy workload, he has not had time to develop many hobbies other than the golf he played as a business activity. His expressed plans for retirement include traveling, playing golf, and learning French. He also has expressed interest in taking college courses, perhaps to finish his degree. Martha has encouraged Walter to enter counseling because of her worry that he will not have enough to do and will "be underfoot" at home. He recently has experienced several anxiety attacks that were initially believed to be minor heart attacks, and his physician also has encouraged him to pursue counseling.

Another issue facing Walter and Martha is that his 87-year-old mother may need more daily living assistance than she currently is receiving in her apartment.

QUESTIONS FOR DISCUSSION

1. How would you conceptualize the salience of roles in Walter's life? How might he be experiencing the shifting roles in his life with more emphasis on the grandparent, leisurite, student, and/or caretaking roles?

2. What issues would you encourage Walter to consider as he shifts into the Disengagement phase of his career? How might he use the remaining time in his work role to prepare for retirement?

3. In what specific activities could Walter engage to develop alternate roles?

4. Are there any unresolved tasks from earlier life/career stages that might need to be addressed in counseling?

5. How would you assess Walter's career adaptability?

6. What issues might be occurring between Martha and Walter? How might you address these issues?

Case 2: Maria Josefina

Maria Josefina is a 16-year-old girl of Puerto Rican descent living in the Southeast. She is the oldest daughter of six children; her father is a skilled laborer in construction, and her mother is a home health aide. She has one older brother who attended a community college to learn how to be an electrician and is working for the same construction company as their father. Maria Josefina's family moved from Puerto Rico 8 years ago, when she was 8 and her older brother was 10 and her younger sisters and brothers were 6, 4, 2, and 1. Her family lives in a middle-class neighborhood that is ethnically diverse, and they get along well with their neighbors. They primarily socialize with other Puerto Ricans, though, and often spend time with members of their extended family in the area.

(Continued)

(Continued)

Maria Josefina feels that she lives in two worlds: school and home, each characterized by different languages, expectations, and relationships. At school, she speaks English and has many friends with whom she enjoys spending time talking about boys and clothes and the future. At home, she speaks Spanish, spends time with her brothers and sisters, and enjoys the support and warmth of having her aunts, uncles, grandparents, and cousins around her.

Maria Josefina has done well in school and is being encouraged by her high school teachers and guidance counselors to consider college. Her parents, though, do not want her to leave home and are encouraging her to consider attending the same community college that her brother attended. Maria Josefina knows that, as the oldest daughter, she is expected to be home to help her mother, but she would very much like to become a social worker. Her aunt, who is strongly encouraging her to attend one of the universities, has referred her for career counseling.

QUESTIONS FOR DISCUSSION

1. How would you conceptualize Maria Josefina from a developmental framework?

2. What developmental tasks has she accomplished? What tasks does she yet have to accomplish?

3. How would you characterize her objective and subjective self-concepts?

4. What are the role interactions she is encountering?

5. How would you help her make a decision?

6. How do Maria Josefina's gender and race/ethnicity influence her decisions?

Case 3: Deborah and Trish

Deborah (age 33) enters counseling at a community agency specializing in women's issues at the urging of her partner, Trish (age 38); both Deborah and Trish are White. Deborah has been depressed and irritable for the past few months, and Trish is concerned that Deborah is unhappy with their 5-year relationship, although Deborah has denied that this is the case.

Deborah is currently experiencing considerable dissatisfaction in her career. She is a lawyer in the district attorney's office in a medium-sized town in the Southwest. She views her work environment as undesirable for a number of reasons, including the lack of opportunities for advancement and her perception that she cannot disclose her sexual orientation at work. She frequently comes home from work depressed. Deborah recently had an offer from a law firm in San Francisco that was quite attractive; however, she did not accept the position because of the difficulty of relocating.

Trish is an associate professor of biology at a state university. She has successfully established herself and is happy in her profession and work environment. She supported Deborah's application for the San Francisco job, but she also made it clear that moving to another university might be difficult and would disrupt her career. Trish expresses skepticism that Deborah's depression could be the result of work factors and continues to believe that Deborah is dissatisfied with their relationship.

As is typical in their professions, Deborah and Trish both work many hours and frequently work at home in the evenings and weekends. This dedication to their respective careers was one of the aspects that first attracted them to one another, and they support one another's career advancement. However, lately Deborah has begun to wonder if there isn't more to life than work and has wished that she and Trish could spend more time together taking trips and just enjoying the weekends. Trish, however, easily gets absorbed in the work that she brings home and frequently stays up late at night working on projects.

QUESTIONS FOR DISCUSSION

1. How might Deborah be conceptualized from the perspective of developmental theories? How might Trish be conceptualized?

2. With what developmental tasks might Deborah be struggling?

3. How could you help Deborah and Trish understand one another's career perspectives? What, if any, discrepancies exist between their respective career stages and issues?

4. How might you address their relationship issues? How might career and relationship concerns be connected for Deborah? For Trish?

5. How do Deborah's gender and race/ethnicity influence her decisions? How do gender and race/ethnicity influence Trish's decisions?

BOX 8.3 Summary of Key Constructs

Construct	Definition
Career construction	Developing and implementing the self-concept through vocational choices.
Developmental contextualism	Belief that the process of developing a work identity occurs within the individual's social context.
Stages	Series of steps that individuals typically go through in constructing a career, though not everyone progresses through these stages in the same manner or at fixed ages.
Growth	Stage, typically occurring in childhood, whose primary tasks include becoming concerned about the future, learning more about self and the need to make future decisions.
Exploration	Stage, typically occurring in adolescence and early adulthood, whose primary tasks are crystallizing, specifying, and implementing, or actualizing, a career choice.
Establishment	Stage, typically occurring in adulthood, which entails entering and becoming established in one's career and work life. The tasks of this stage include stabilizing, consolidating, and advancing.
Maintenance/ Management	Stage, typically occurring in middle adulthood, in which individuals are maintaining and advancing in their careers. Primary tasks are renewal, holding, updating, and innovating.
Disengagement	Stage, typically occurring in later adulthood, in which an individual retires or disengages from work.
Developmental tasks	Career concerns specific to each stage.
Career maturity	Readiness to master the developmental tasks of each stage effectively.
Career adaptability	Readiness and resources to cope with developmental tasks.
Life roles	Roles individuals have in their lives: child, student, homemaker, worker, citizen, leisurite. Roles may interact and hold different levels of importance throughout life span.
Work role salience	Importance of the work role in relation to the other potential roles in a client's life.
Vocational identity	An individual's work values, interests, and abilities.

Chapter 9

Gottfredson's Theory of Circumscription and Compromise

INTRODUCTORY REVIEW

As noted in the previous chapter, Gottfredson's theory of circumscription and compromise is a developmental theory, characterized by viewing career choice as a process rather than an event and by incorporating developmental concepts into this process. Gottfredson (1996, 2005) developed her theory of circumscription and compromise to explain why individuals' vocational expectations, even when they are children, vary by sex, race, and social class. Gottfredson differs from Super in that she views vocational choice first as an implementation of the social self and only secondarily as an implementation of the psychological self. Inherent in this approach is the circumscription of psychological variables, such as interests or values, by social variables, such as gender or social class. Gottfredson focuses on cognitive development as children grow in awareness of themselves and their social place in the world and begin to eliminate vocational options that are not compatible with their evolving self-image.

In a recent description of her theory, Gottfredson (2005) poses the scenario of 1,000 newborns in their cribs. They are unaware of differences among themselves or among social or occupational options in the world. Yet, within 15 to 20 years, all will have developed similar perceptions of occupations and will have "reproduced most of the class and gender differences of the parent generation"

(p. 72). How does this happen? Gottfredson proposes that four development processes provide an explanation: cognitive growth, self-creation, circumscription, and compromise.

Cognitive Growth

During the normal process of development, children develop increasingly complex cognitive structures. These structures allow the processing of occupational information and determining the quality of matches. As Gottfredson (2005) notes, children begin to narrow their options and make other decisions that directly affect their career choices long before they have developed sufficient cognitive complexity to do so satisfactorily. As children develop their cognitive abilities, they are increasingly able to think abstractly and to consider multiple dimensions when evaluating information. Further, cognitive growth affects two important components of vocational choice: the cognitive map of occupations and the self-concept. As in person-environment fit models, accurate perceptions of occupations and of oneself are crucial features in Gottfredson's model.

Self-Creation

An age-old question in psychology is the relative influence of nature (genetic factors) versus nurture (environmental influences) on human development. A corollary is whether individuals are passive recipients of either (or both) nature and nurture or if they have an active role in their own development. An early critique of Gottfredson's theory was that its use of genetic concepts gave it a deterministic flavor; that it implied individuals have little control over the course of their career lives. In her most recent writing, Gottfredson (2005) explicitly discusses the concept of self-creation, suggesting that although many characteristics of an individual are biologically based, the emergence and further development of these characteristics are shaped by the experiences that one chooses. Repeated experiences consolidate an individual's genetically based characteristics, turning them into "traits" that gain stability across a variety of situations. We come to realize our characteristics and traits through interactions with others, by observing ourselves and others' reactions to us, leading to the self-concept. Thus, a wealth or lack of exposure to a variety of experiences influences the expression of an individual's genetic makeup. Further, adolescents rarely have sufficient experiences to draw on when they are making choices related to education and career.

Gottfredson (1996, 2005) also discusses *niche seeking*, *birth niches*, and *ecological niches*—concepts derived from developmental psychology to explain how individuals find their place in the world. As social beings, we strive to find our place in society, and vocational choice is one way to announce our place.

Circumscription

The importance of our social nature becomes apparent in considering how children view the variety of occupations in their world. Circumscription is the process by which children narrow the "zone of acceptable alternatives" by progressive elimination of unacceptable alternatives, or those that conflict with one's self-concept (see Figure 9.1). Gottfredson's four-stage model of circumscription characterizes children as having an increasing capacity to think abstractly. She also suggests that elimination of alternatives is progressive and irreversible (except under unusual circumstances) and mostly occurs without conscious awareness of the process or of the details of the occupations that are being eliminated.

Gottfredson's four stages are as follows:

Stage 1 (ages 3–5): Children develop an orientation to size and power. They categorize people in simple ways, such as big versus little. Although they do not have firm ideas about sex differences or gender roles, they do recognize observable physical differences between men and women.

Stage 2 (ages 6–8): This recognition increases in Stage 2, when children develop an orientation to sex roles. They tend to use dichotomous thinking, characterize their own sex as superior to the other sex, and use sex-appropriateness to define their vocational aspirations. In this stage, children construct their tolerable-sex-type boundary (see Figure 9.1).

Stage 3 (ages 9–13): This stage entails orientation to social valuation, or sensitivity to prestige and status, whether by their peers or the larger society. Children become aware of status hierarchies among occupational choices and now view the range of occupations along the two dimensions of prestige level and sex type. Children establish their tolerable-level boundary to eliminate occupations that are unacceptably low in prestige and their tolerable-effort boundary to eliminate occupations that are too difficult to attain (see Figure 9.1). By the end of Stage 3, the full range of occupations has been whittled down to those that are of the appropriate sex type, that have high enough prestige, and that are not too difficult. What remains is a child's zone of acceptable alternatives (or social space). As Gottfredson (2005) notes, vocational choice to this point "seems to be mostly a by-product of wanting to belong, be respected, and live a comfortable life as defined by the individual's reference group" (p. 81), and vocational interest or personal fulfillment has not entered the equation.

Stage 4 (ages 14 and older): Adolescents become aware of the need to consider their vocational choices, and they develop their orientation to the internal, unique self. Here, interests, values, and abilities are clarified, and occupational exploration occurs within the zone of acceptable alternatives as circumscribed in earlier stages. Stages 1 through 3 are focused on rejecting unacceptable alternatives, with greater attention to the social self; Stage 4 is focused on identifying which of the acceptable alternatives are most preferred, with greater attention to the psychological self (Gottfredson, 1996). Stage 4 thus begins the process of compromise.

Compromise

As the pressure to make vocationally relevant decisions intensifies, adolescents begin to consider more concrete aspects of different occupations. Vocational aspirations can be viewed as the product of accessibility (choices that are most realistic) and compatibility (person-environment fit), and idealistic aspirations may give way to realistic ones.

Compromise entails the modification of alternatives because of inaccessibility, leading to the acceptance of less attractive alternatives. Gottfredson (1996)

Figure 9.1 Gottfredson's Model of Circumscription and Compromise

SOURCE: Gottfredson (1996).

suggests that sex type, prestige, and field of interest are the three dimensions considered in the process of compromise. She also discusses three factors pertinent to the compromise process (Gottfredson, 2005).

The first factor, "truncated search, limited knowledge," describes how people minimize their required effort by searching for information only for their most-preferred occupations, only when they need to make a decision, and only from sources that they already know. This strategy severely restricts the range of occupational information that adolescents gather, thus limiting their perceived opportunities.

Second, "bigger investment, better accessibility" refers to the important role that an individual's initiative has in exposing him or her to a broad range of opportunities; the more active an individual is in terms of creating his or her own options, the greater number of options that will be accessible.

Third, most individuals will settle for a "good enough or not too bad" choice rather than the best possible choice. People look for compatible career choices within those that seem accessible or those that provide a good match with their three preferred dimensions of sex type, prestige level, and field of interest. However, these three dimensions are compromised in a specific order such that sex type is least likely and field of interest most likely to be compromised. In other words, the dimensions that are established first developmentally, those closest to the core of self-concept, are maintained longer. So individuals will choose an occupation from among those in their zone of acceptable alternatives on the basis of interest first. If none is accessible, they will sacrifice interest but maintain preferred prestige and sex type. Occupations outside the zone of acceptable alternatives will be considered only if those inside the zone are not perceived as accessible, and the zone will be expanded beyond the tolerable-level boundary (prestige) before the tolerable-sex-type boundary.

The order of compromise might also vary depending on the degree of compromise. Based on some initial research evidence, the theory was revised to take into account the discrepancy between one's ideal and realistic choices (Gottfredson, 1996; Gottfredson & Lapan, 1997). If the discrepancy is small, then interests are hypothesized to be the most influential; if the discrepancy is moderate, then prestige is hypothesized to be most influential; and, if the discrepancy is large, interests will be sacrificed before sex type or prestige (Betz, 2008).

Gottfredson's theory explicitly addresses the impact of sex-role socialization and other societal factors that influence the development of occupational aspirations. As such, it offers a complementary perspective to Super's theory. On the other hand, Super's theory was designed to span a much broader scope of career behavior than does Gottfredson's theory and, thus, is a more comprehensive theory of life span career development.

Gottfredson's theory has received relatively little attention from researchers, despite its intuitive appeal to practitioners. One reason for the minimal attention is likely related to the difficulty in assessing perceptions in early childhood and in measuring the important constructs in the theory (Fassinger, 2005; Fouad & Kantamneni, 2013; Swanson & Gore, 2000). Further, the dimensions of sex type, prestige, and interest are difficult to consider separately from one another (Phillips & Jome, 2005). Some support has been shown for the revised theory regarding different degrees of compromise (Blanchard & Lichtenberg, 2003).

BOX 9.1 Personal Reflection

- How were my aspirations constrained by sex type? By prestige?
- Which occupations did I eliminate from my "zone of acceptable alternatives"?
- Have I reconsidered occupations previously outside the zone?

APPLYING GOTTFREDSON'S THEORY

Counselors who use Gottfredson's theory would ask the sorts of questions that are outlined in Box 9.2. They would wonder what occupations clients have rejected earlier in their lives and for what reasons, the extent of information that clients have about themselves, and what level of complexity will best meet clients' current needs.

BOX 9.2 Counselor Cognitions

- How does the client view his or her available alternatives?
- What alternatives has the client eliminated because of sex type or prestige?
- In what ways has the client compromised his or her preferred alternatives?

Conceptualizing Leslie's Career History

As noted in the previous chapter, developmental theorists such as Super and Gottfredson would view Leslie as having made a series of decisions from childhood through adulthood. We will discuss Leslie's decisions using Gottfredson's stages as a framework.

Childhood

Gottfredson's (1996, 2005) theory places greater emphasis on childhood and early adolescence than do other theories. She suggests that children ages 3 to 5 (Stage 1) recognize that there is an adult world and that occupations are part of that adult world. Stage 2 (ages 6 to 8) is characterized by a child's increasing awareness of gender-appropriate roles and by dichotomous thinking. Children are motivated by choices that they believe are socially appropriate, particularly focusing on sex-typed choices. During ages 9 to 13, children begin to incorporate prestige as a factor in consideration of acceptable alternatives (Stage 3).

Leslie's early childhood experiences may not be readily accessible to either the counselor or to Leslie, but she appears to have had a typical and relatively uneventful time as a young child. The period during which she was aged 3 to 5 coincided with her brother starting elementary school, so she was home alone with her mother until her sister was born when Leslie was 5. Leslie reports stories that her mother has told about how much Leslie missed her brother when he went to school; she would wait for him at the bus stop at the end of the day. Leslie also has heard family stories about how excited she was to help with "the new baby" when her sister was born. Leslie looked forward to starting kindergarten but also didn't want to leave her mother and sister. After a brief period of adjustment, she loved going to school.

Leslie's elementary school experience was very positive. As noted in the previous chapter, she enjoyed a variety of subjects and responded to attention and praise from her teachers. Since her brother attended the same school, she frequently was referred to as "Scott's sister." Even though she demonstrated the same level of math ability as her brother, he received more encouragement, even in elementary school, teachers and parents suggested that Scott might pursue engineering, whereas they did not suggest that path for Leslie. Leslie's early interest in teaching continued into elementary school, and she would come home from school and "teach" her younger sister what she had learned that day. It was Leslie who taught her younger sister how to read, and she identified more closely with her sister than with her older brother.

The middle school years correspond to the third stage of Gottfredson's theory, and Leslie became more aware of the status of different occupational choices, partly by observing her older brother. Scott had a passionate childhood interest in trucks and construction equipment, which their parents channeled into the higher prestige occupational fields of engineering and architecture. Leslie also became more aware of the social status of their family and understood that they were better-off financially than some of her friends. She knew that she was expected to choose an occupation that was "important" enough and that would use her abilities.

Adolescence and early adulthood

Gottfredson proposes that the occupational alternatives adolescents consider are circumscribed by options considered appropriate for their sex and within the range acceptable for their social class and self-perceived abilities. The fourth stage in Gottfredson's theory begins around age 14, which corresponds to transition from middle school to high school. As Gottfredson (2005) notes, this is a time when "vocational development erupts into conscious awareness" (p. 81).

In this stage, Leslie began to pay more attention to who she was and what she liked to do—and how she was different from her brother and from other adolescents. She had heard clear statements from her parents to Scott about how he needed to be able to support a family in the future and to her about how she could rely on a husband's financial support. These messages were mirrored by what she heard from her friends and at school. Leslie took a mandatory career exploration class during high school and learned more about her interests and skills and the range of occupational options. In retrospect, she doesn't remember much detail from the class other than feeling a bit lost. At the same time, her parents worked closely with Scott to plan his choices about college and career, and Leslie both envied the attention and was happy not to feel the pressure.

Completion of the last stage of circumscription ushers in the process of compromise, which entails relinquishing one's most preferred alternatives for ones that are more realistic. Leslie continued to excel at math throughout high school, but the career options that built on her strengths were already circumscribed in accordance with acceptable levels of sex type and prestige. She occasionally considered a number of other occupations, such as physician, engineer, computer programmer, and math professor; however, these seemed less accessible to her than being a high school math teacher.

Conceptualizing Leslie's Present Situation

Unlike Super's theory, Gottfredson's theory does not contain stages that extend into adulthood, although compromise is a process that may continue throughout one's career. Leslie's current feelings about her job and/or career could present an opportunity for her to investigate the choices made earlier in her life, most of which were not in her conscious awareness at the time. Although some of her current dissatisfaction is likely due to changes in the work environment, it also may be related to the way in which she circumscribed her options earlier in her life. Her choice of teaching rather than engineering or other occupations that would utilize her math abilities has its roots in early childhood and in the subsequent decisions later in her life.

QUESTIONS FOR DISCUSSION

1. What specific hypotheses would you develop about Leslie from Gottfredson's theory? How does using Gottfredson's theory help you understand Leslie? How might it help Leslie understand herself?

2. What are the advantages of viewing Leslie as being in her current occupation as a result of the processes of circumscription? Of compromise?

3. How ready is Leslie to make a career decision right now? How does she feel about the prospect of making a decision, particularly of making a job or career change? How might her previous experiences with career decision making influence the process or content of this current decision?

4. Who is likely to influence her decision? How much pressure does she feel now? What types of pressure and from whom?

5. What kind of career life does Leslie seem to be envisioning? How can she optimize her chance of achieving that career life?

6. How might Leslie describe her social self-concept? How does she see her occupational social space?

7. How has Leslie circumscribed and compromised her occupational aspirations?

The Case of Gary

Gary is a 16-year-old White high school sophomore in a small town in rural Georgia. Both of his parents worked in a furniture mill in a nearby town until its closure last year; Gary's father now works at a hardware store, and his mother works part-time in a nursing home after a brief stint at an administrative aide in a local real estate office. Gary's 20-year-old brother went to work at the furniture mill right after high school and, after the mill's closure, now spends much of his time working on cars in the family's yard; he also does some part-time work as an auto mechanic. Gary's 14-year-old sister is very active in drama and choir activities in her school, and she is thinking about a career in nursing.

The closing of the furniture mill has had a subtle but pervasive impact on Gary's family. Although his parents were able to find other employment, the pay and benefits are far below what they had received at the mill, and they have had to cut back substantially on their spending. His mom's first job after the mill closed, at the real estate office, did not last long because of cutbacks in the office due to slowing sales. The economic climate of the entire community has been affected. In addition to these tangible changes, Gary's family also has experienced other consequences: His parents are worried about money and anxious about the future, and there is more tension in the household.

Gary doesn't see many employment options in his community, particularly given his parents' recent experience in losing their jobs. He perceives an increasingly strong message to pursue some type of postsecondary training or education from his family, as well as from his high school teachers. His father has encouraged him to consider joining the military, and his mother has suggested some health care occupations. Gary spends much of his free time playing video games and would like to be a video software designer. The community college in his area offers courses in Web design, animation, and digital media technology. He has little motivation to explore career options and, other than hearing radio commercials about the community college offerings, has not received much information about possible careers or educational choices. His contact with the high school guidance counselor has been mostly to schedule classes, in which he has been getting Bs and Cs without too much effort or interest. His science teacher has encouraged Gary to go to a summer camp sponsored by the community college, but Gary isn't sure he wants to break his summer video game routine, and his parents are pushing him to look for a job at a fast-food restaurant.

QUESTIONS FOR DISCUSSION

1. What specific hypotheses would you develop about Gary from Gottfredson's theory? How does using Gottfredson's theory help you understand Gary? How might it help Gary understand himself?

2. What is Gary's status in terms of the processes of circumscription? Of compromise?

3. How ready is Gary to make a career decision right now? How could you engage him in the process?

4. Who is likely to influence Gary's decision? How much pressure does he feel now? What types of pressure and from whom?

5. What kind of career life does Gary seem to be envisioning? What kinds of messages is he receiving from his parents and community?

6. How would you describe Gary's "zone of acceptable alternatives"?

DIRECTIONS AND IMPLICATIONS FOR CAREER COUNSELING

Goals of Counseling

Gottfredson (2005) describes the traditional goal of career counseling as helping individuals "clarify and implement their visions of a satisfying career life, even if parents or social engineers might prefer something different" (p. 85). She suggests that the similarity of assumptions among theories leads to similar strategies for counseling but that her theoretical perspective may require some rethinking of how to assist clients. For example, she cites several issues that present challenges to counselors, such as helping adolescents reexamine their childhood choices without undermining these choices, encouraging realism of choice without placing limits on clients' dreams, and presenting complex information without overwhelming clients (Gottfredson, 2005). All these dilemmas arise from the specific focus within the theory on circumscription and compromise.

Interventions

Meta-analytic evidence produced by Brown and Ryan Krane (2000) suggests that there are five critical components in effective career interventions: (1) written exercises to enhance personal reflection, (2) individualized interpretation and feedback, (3) practical information about the world of work, (4) opportunities to observe role models who are successful in career exploration and decision making, and (5) attention to building social support for choices. Gottfredson (2005) incorporates these five elements into her proposed career guidance and counseling system. Her system addresses each of the four developmental processes outlined in her theory, as described earlier—cognitive growth, self-creation, circumscription, and compromise—and matches them with the counseling strategies aimed at optimizing a set of client behaviors of learning, experience, self-insight, and self-investment, respectively.

Optimize learning

Adolescents may not gain sufficient knowledge to make good career decisions because it is cognitively demanding to do so. But inadequate knowledge then contributes to the processes of circumscription and compromise, limiting occupational alternatives. How can counselors optimize clients' learning? As Gottfredson (2005) notes, vocational psychology has long valued the role of gathering information about oneself and the world of work, yet it is important to not exceed an individual's cognitive capacity at any given time. She suggests two specific counseling strategies: reducing task complexity to meet clients' needs and accommodating cognitive diversity among individuals by tailoring information.

Leslie exhibits substantial cognitive complexity and ability to deal with abstract ideas; she enjoys putting new information together in meaningful ways. For her, the counselor might provide some general direction in terms of useful resources and then encourage Leslie to explore and gather information on her own, assigning homework between sessions to assess how she is progressing.

In Gary's case, most of his exposure to occupational information and to career planning has been in classes at school, in which he has not been very engaged. A counselor working individually with Gary would need to gauge how he is processing occupational information and adjust accordingly. For example, the counselor might explore a website with Gary and ask him to think aloud as he's reading the information. What does he gain from the website's information? Does he seem to be attending to the most important information? How would he summarize what he has read? The counselor, in class or individually, could use some structured worksheets to help Gary gather information. A good place to start might be with something that grabs his attention, even if it might not be Gary's most realistic option, such as video software developer.

Optimize experience

Adolescents may not experience a sufficient variety of activities to understand their own career-related traits, such as interests, values, and skills. How can counselors optimize clients' experience? Gottfredson (2005) suggests two counseling strategies: providing "broad menus of experience" (p. 87) by systematically exposing students to a wide variety of occupations and promoting awareness of the active role that clients may take in shaping their own experience.

Leslie has entered counseling to focus on the pros and cons of staying in her current position, and she appears to be ready and willing to explore a broad range of options. Although she did not have the kind of early broad exposure that Gottfredson promotes, the counselor could help Leslie systematically explore the full range of options now. Further, Leslie and the counselor could identify areas in which she has not had experience, such as administration, leadership, or writing.

Gary clearly could benefit from systematic exposure to "broad menus of experience." His actual experience has been fairly limited, and the vicarious exposure through his parents' experience has not been positive or encouraging. The counselor could address this lack of (or negative) exposure directly and encourage Gary to engage in the available career exploration in his school.

Optimize self-insight

Adolescents may prematurely eliminate occupations that could be good choices if they lack self-knowledge. How can counselors optimize clients' self-insight? Gottfredson (2005) suggests that counselors first encourage clients to "take stock" of what they already know about themselves, then encourage clients to think of making the choice of an occupation within the broader context of other factors (in other words, choosing an occupation entails commitment to a "career life" that encompasses other life roles). Helping clients understand how career options might have been circumscribed and compromised earlier in the choice process might lead to "more authentic choices" (Heppner, 2013, p. 204).

Leslie's entry into counseling signals her readiness to take stock of herself and her situation, and the counselor can help with this process. She also is acutely aware of the impact of the broader context of her choices, given her work and life experience, and is likely to benefit from an extended discussion of these factors in her current career dilemma. Gary, on the other hand, does not currently demonstrate much insight about himself or his future. The counselor may use formal assessment to help Gary learn more about himself and also may walk him through the long-term implications of making an informed career decision.

Optimize self-investment

Adolescents (and other clients) may compromise in implementing a career choice because of perceived inaccessibility or unrealism of the choice. However, such compromise may be unnecessary. How can counselors help clients increase the chances that they will achieve their choice? Gottfredson (2005) suggests the two strategies of assessing the accessibility of clients' choices and promoting awareness of enhancing one's own qualifications, as well as creating one's own opportunities and support.

Leslie is at a crossroads in her career and life, and choosing and implementing a new direction may be difficult. The counselor would support and encourage Leslie's ability to pursue new options and help her determine the next steps and how to overcome challenges she might encounter. A counselor working with Gary would emphasize the importance of his investment in the process of career exploration and in the actions he needs to take to achieve goals that he defines.

ADDITIONAL CASES

Case 1: Dorece

Dorece is a 21-year-old African American woman who is a student at a major urban university on the East Coast. She was referred to career counseling by her academic adviser, because she had not yet declared a major despite accumulating enough credits to be considered a junior. Dorece presents herself as quite self-assured yet seems unnerved by the prospect of making a decision. She comes to counseling each week with a different idea of what she might choose, which she states with considerable enthusiasm. However, she does not complete the tasks assigned by her counselor, such as investigating the requirements of the major or what the job might entail, nor does her enthusiasm carry into the following week.

(Continued)

(Continued)

Dorece is the youngest child of four and grew up in an upper-middle-class home in suburban Washington, DC. Her father is an advertising manager for a radio station, and her mother is a lobbyist. Dorece attended an exclusive all-girls private high school, where she excelled in all her courses and graduated with a 3.8 grade point average. She enjoyed choir, French club, and the sailing club. Her older siblings have successfully completed graduate or professional degrees and are working in the Washington, DC. area.

When she entered college, Dorece was encouraged by her parents not to choose a major too hastily but rather to explore various opportunities before she settled on the "right choice." She initially enrolled in standard freshman year courses and did well in all of them. She particularly enjoyed her English classes and found that she appreciated the challenge of creative writing. Despite this, however, she did not declare English as a major because her father expressed concerns about what she could "do" with a degree in English. After rejecting English as a major, she experienced similar concerns with other majors and soon found herself ruling out most of the possibilities. She has considered becoming a broadcast journalist because many have told her that her good looks and presentation style would serve her well in that field. She has considered nursing because she enjoys caring for others and has considered teaching for the same reason. Her sisters, however, were horrified when she mentioned these possibilities, claiming that she would disgrace the family if she entered such a gender-stereotypic occupation. She continued to search for the "right choice" for a major.

Dorece is in a serious relationship with an African American man who is attending graduate school at the same university. He is completing his doctorate in political science and has some aspirations to a political career; if that is not possible, he would like an academic career. He and Dorece have discussed her lack of decision making; he thinks she should become an English major. He also has expressed concern that it may be detrimental to his future political career if she were to enter broadcast journalism.

QUESTIONS FOR DISCUSSION

1. What specific hypotheses would you develop about Dorece from Gottfredson's theory?

2. How has Dorece circumscribed her career options? How has she compromised her choices?

3. What interventions might be effective in addressing her current career status?

4. What would you do as a counselor from the perspective of Gottfredson's theory to help Dorece make a career decision?

5. Who is likely to influence Dorece's decision? How much pressure does she feel now? What types of pressure and from whom?

Case 2: Steve

Steve is a White man, aged 39, and a divorced father of an 8-year-old son. He is employed as a writer for a greeting card company. He seeks career counseling because he is not satisfied as a greeting card writer but is not sure he wants to continue his original goal of becoming a college professor. Steve majored in English as an undergraduate and pursued a doctorate in American literature. However, he dropped out of his graduate program in the middle of his third year and has not returned to finish his degree.

Steve met his ex-wife, Mariela, while he was an undergraduate. She had already finished her degree and was working as a secretary. She worked while he finished his undergraduate degree and continued supporting him while he was in his first year of graduate school. In his second year, however, she quit working when she became pregnant with their son. He took out loans to support them but realized in the third year of his graduate program that he needed to leave school and work while she stayed home with their child. Their plan was that she would return to work when their son was 3 years old, at which point Steve would return to finish his degree and pursue a career as a college professor.

Their marriage failed, however, and Steve's financial obligations for child support and alimony are significant enough that he feels he cannot quit his job to return to school to finish his degree. He is also questioning his original plans to get a doctorate and become a professor. He is the oldest son of eight children born to lower working class parents; his mother stayed home with the children, and his father worked in a factory. His father often worked two jobs to make ends meet. Steve is the first child in his entire extended family to attend college, much less graduate and enter graduate school. His parents are disappointed that his marriage failed but have been very supportive of his decision to quit school to support his family.

When he took the job as a greeting card writer, he anticipated that he would be with the company only temporarily. However, he has now worked there for over 5 years and has worked his way up to increased levels of responsibility. He enjoys some aspects of the greeting card business, or at least some parts of business decisions. He does not like having to create trite greeting card phrases but does enjoy the marketing meetings that he attends.

QUESTIONS FOR DISCUSSION

1. How does using Gottfredson's theory help you understand Steve? How might it help Steve understand himself?

2. How would you describe Steve's zone of acceptable alternatives?

3. What interventions might be effective in dealing with his decision making?

4. How has Steve's family influenced his decision making?

5. How might you help Steve with his career concerns?

Case 3: Lori

Lori is referred for career counseling by a good friend who is a social worker and is concerned about Lori's lack of energy and possible depression. Lori is a 45-year-old White woman. She is married to John, who is running his family's farm in southeastern Iowa. Lori met John when they were both in college, where John was studying agricultural economics and Lori was studying home economics. They both finished their bachelor's degrees and moved to John's hometown, a small farming community. When they were first married, they lived in town while John's parents lived on the farm. John worked with his father, incorporating more modern agricultural practices into the farm operation, and gradually took over the farm business from his father. John's mother was a very traditional farm wife, raising chickens and helping her husband on the farm when necessary but primarily taking care of her seven children.

Lori and John have two children, both daughters. They moved to the farm when John's father had a stroke; they needed to take care of him and John's mother, who also was in poor health. Lori had worked as a home economist for the local extension office after she and John married, but at the encouragement of her husband and mother-in-law, she quit her job when her first daughter was born. She had enjoyed working, especially the teaching aspects of her work, as well as meeting lots of new people.

Lori's daughters are now in high school, and the older one just received her driver's license. Her daughters have been spending more time away from home than in the past with activities in town and at the consolidated school several miles away. The oldest daughter's newly acquired driver's license means that Lori is not asked to drive the girls to and from their activities as often as she had previously done. Her father-in-law died the previous month, and Lori and John are struggling with decisions about caring for her mother-in-law, who requires daily assistance from Lori because of deteriorating health.

Lori feels quite isolated on the farm. She would like to return to work but does not know what she wants to do or even what options are open to her. Lori and John are not able to relocate, because John is committed to maintaining the family farm for their daughters. She had enjoyed her work as a home economist, but because women are now less often at home, Lori doesn't know if that job even exists anymore.

QUESTIONS FOR DISCUSSION

1. How have Lori's early experiences affected her career decision making, and how have her life circumstances affected her current situation?

2. How would you incorporate the personal issues that Lori is facing into career counseling?

3. How would you incorporate Lori's possible depression into career counseling from Gottfredson's perspective?

4. How has Lori circumscribed her career options? How has she compromised her choices?

5. What would you do as a counselor from the perspective of Gottfredson's theory to help Lori?

BOX 9.3 Summary of Key Constructs

Construct	Definition
Circumscription	Process by which children narrow their occupational alternatives by eliminating those that are not acceptable in prestige or sex type.
Compromise	Process by which preferred alternatives are sacrificed because they are inaccessible.
Cognitive growth	Development of increasingly complex cognitive ability during childhood, which influences the cognitive occupational map and the self-concept.
Self-creation	How the experiences that one chooses build on biologically based characteristics of an individual.
Zone of acceptable alternatives	The occupations remaining after an individual eliminates occupations because of sex type, intolerably low prestige, or intolerably high effort.
Tolerable-effort boundary	The lowest level of prestige considered acceptable among occupational alternatives.
Tolerable-level boundary	The highest level of effort considered acceptable among occupational alternatives.
Sex type	A limiting boundary within one's zone of acceptable alternatives; it emerges as an influence in Stage 2, where children become aware of the sex-appropriateness of different occupations.
Prestige	A limiting floor and ceiling boundary within one's zone of acceptable alternatives; it emerges as a factor in Stage 3, where children become aware of the differential prestige of occupations within society.

Chapter 10

Social Cognitive Career Theory

INTRODUCTORY REVIEW

The theoretical approaches we have examined thus far have been well-established theories that have shaped vocational psychology for several decades. However, the theory we discuss in this chapter was developed about two decades ago. The concepts were first introduced in 1981 (Hackett & Betz, 1981), and a complete description of the theory wasn't published until 1994 (Lent, Brown, & Hackett, 1994). We include this theory because of its utility and because of the impact this theory has had on the field. It differs from the other theories in its focus on the personal constructions that people place on events related to career decision making (Lent, Brown, & Hackett, 2002; Lent, 2013).

Social cognitive theory (Bandura, 1977, 1986, 1997) has been recently applied in vocational psychology to help explain how individuals' career interests develop, how they make career choices, and how they determine their level of performance. Bandura hypothesizes that individuals' conception of their confidence to perform tasks (self-efficacy) mediates between what they know and how they act and that people's beliefs in their ability to accomplish things helps determine the actions they will take. Self-efficacy comes from individuals' previous performance accomplishments, vicariously by observing others, from verbal persuasion, and from physiological states and arousal.

Bandura also postulates that self-efficacy is distinct from outcome expectancies, or the expectations one has of the result of behavior. Bandura (1986) notes that self-efficacy and "outcome expectancies judgments are differentiated because individuals can believe that a particular course of action will produce certain outcomes, but they do not act on that outcome belief because they question whether they can actually execute the necessary activities" (p. 392). The constructs of self-efficacy and outcome expectancies are an individual's perceptions of reality; as such, those perceptions may or may not be realistic. It is important to note that in decision making, individuals' perceptions of reality are hypothesized to be greater determinants of their behavior than objective reality.

Hackett and Betz (1981) were the first to apply Bandura's social cognitive theory, with its emphasis on the role of self-efficacy, to career choices. They focused on self-efficacy theory to explain women's traditional career choices, suggesting that low self-efficacy may explain the restricted range of women's career options. Their work led to investigations of the role self-efficacy may play in a variety of career-related behaviors, and the constructs of self-efficacy and outcome expectancies were then incorporated into a theoretical framework related to career decisions. Lent et al. (1994, 2002) developed a social cognitive framework to explain and predict career behavior. Specifically, their three-part model links interests, choices, and performance based on Bandura's social cognitive model.

Basic to all three of the segments of the model, Lent et al. (1994, 2002; Lent, 2013) propose that performance accomplishments, verbal persuasion, vicarious learning, and physiological states and arousal forge an individual's self-efficacy expectations. For example, a young woman who does well in French class is persuaded by others that she could be mistaken for a native French speaker, observes others speaking French, and is mildly anxious about performing well would be expected to have high self-efficacy beliefs for speaking French. It is important to note that Bandura's conceptualization of self-efficacy is situation-specific. In the example above, the young woman may have high self-efficacy for speaking French but lower self-efficacy beliefs for speaking German or Russian.

Lent et al. (1994, 2002; Lent, 2013) also propose that demographic and individual difference variables (such as sex, race/ethnicity, and socioeconomic status) interact with background and contextual variables to influence learning experiences that play a role in forming self-efficacy beliefs. Those self-efficacy expectations, in turn, are related to outcome expectations that individuals have about the outcomes of behavior. In the earlier example of the young, French-speaking woman, a high socioeconomic status may have provided her with opportunities to learn French and may lead to her outcome expectations of speaking French, such as opportunities to travel or live in France.

In the *interest* segment (see Figure 10.1), outcome expectancies and self-efficacy beliefs both predict interests (Lent, 2013). Interests (together with self-efficacy beliefs and outcome expectancies) predict goals, which in turn lead to behaviors related to choosing and practicing activities, which then lead to performance attainments. For example, a young man may have developed an interest in playing the drums based on his self-efficacy beliefs that he is competent as a drum player.

He also expects positive outcomes out of playing the drums, such as social interaction with friends or enjoying the music, as well as verbal reinforcement from his family. He then is predicted to intend to continue to play the drums and perhaps to form a goal to join a band. This leads to his increased choice to practice the drums and eventually to his skill development in drum playing.

Figure 10.1 Predicting Interest Development in Social Cognitive Career Theory

SOURCE: Lent, Brown, and Hackett (1994).

Lent et al. (2000, 2002, 2013) also propose that background and contextual variables, termed *contextual affordances,* help explain why an individual does not pursue an area in which he or she has strong interest. Background and contextual variables may serve as perceived barriers, or supports, to entry or to outcome expectations. For example, a young man with high interests in helping others and in medical fields may not go into nursing because of his perception that nursing is not an appropriate occupation for a man. He may further perceive weak support from others to enter that occupation, support that might have helped him overcome that barrier. Similarly, a young woman who has strong parental and teacher support to achieve in math courses may choose to major in engineering.

Lent et al. (2000, 2002; Lent, 2013) conceptualize two types of contextual affordances, those that are much earlier (distal) than the choice and those that are closer in time (proximal) to the choice. Examples of distal influences may be factors that either constrict or facilitate the development of self-efficacy and outcome expectations (e.g., gender-role socialization, impoverished learning environments), while proximal barriers and supports affect the implementation of choices (e.g., anxiety about moving, financial support to go to college). Barriers may be objective or subjective; what is important is an individual's perception of the barrier (Kenny, Blustein, Chaves, Grossman, & Gallagher, 2003; McWhirter, 1997; Swanson, Daniels, & Tokar, 1996).

The *choice* model (Lent et al., 2002; Lent, 2013) proposes that person inputs (e.g., gender, race, disability, personality, and predispositions) and background context together influence learning experiences, which influence self-efficacy beliefs and outcome expectancies (see Figure 10.2). As already described, these influence interests, which influence choice goals; goals influence actions, and actions influence performance attainments. For example, a young girl from an affluent background is taken to science museums, encouraged to read and learn about science and famous scientists, and given opportunities to take science classes and to attend summer science camp. These learning experiences, afforded by her socioeconomic status, influence the development of her beliefs in her ability to do well in science. Her performance in science and her knowledge that

Figure 10.2 Predicting Vocational Choice in Social Cognitive Career Theory

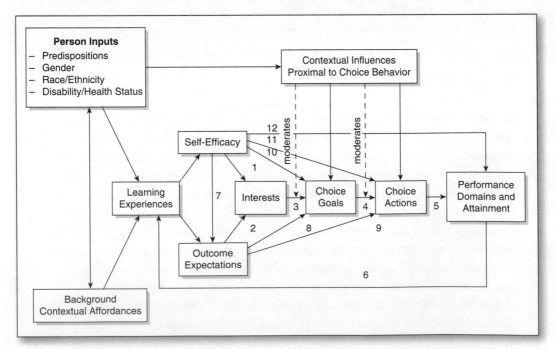

SOURCE: Lent, Brown, and Hackett (1994).

doing well in science will lead to positive outcomes, such as good grades, parental approval, and time spent with friends, lead to the development of her interest in science. She believes she can do well in science in college, she learns that science is a field that is well compensated and one that is not typical for women, and she develops an intention to enter a science major in college. Lent (2013) notes that the process of making a career choice involves choosing a goal (e.g., becoming a scientist), taking action to implement that goal (completing courses in a biology major), and the subsequent consequences of those actions (successful graduation in biology).

The *performance* model predicts the level of performance as well as the persistence an individual has in pursuing goals (Lent et al., 2002; Lent, 2013). This segment (see Figure 10.3) proposes that past performance accomplishments influence self-efficacy and outcome expectancies, which in turn influence performance goals; these lead to performance attainment level. In other words, past performance influences self-efficacy beliefs along with the expectations individuals have about the outcomes of their future behavior. These expectations affect the goals that people set for themselves. These goals then affect the level of performance they may attain. Thus, a woman who did well in basketball while in high school has confidence in her ability to play and decides to try out for the basketball team in college. After making the team, she sets challenging goals for her offensive and

Figure 10.3 Predicting Task Performance in Social Cognitive Career Theory

SOURCE: Lent, Brown, and Hackett (1994).

defensive performance (e.g., averaging at least 12 points a game), based on her past successes and current self-efficacy and outcome beliefs. Lent et al. differentiate their choice and interest models from the performance model. The former involve the content of career choices, such as the field or specific occupation in which one would like to work, while the performance model predicts the level of performance toward which one aspires within one's chosen field.

Bandura (1997) comments that "in making career decisions, people must come to grips with uncertainties about their capabilities, the stability of their interests, . . . the prospects of alternative occupations, . . . and the type of identity they seek to construct for themselves" (p. 422). Individuals' perceptions of their own efficacy in mastering various skills and tasks play an important role in predicting their choices as well as their perseverance to accomplish their goals. Social cognitive theory thus is readily applicable to development of interventions targeted at increasing individuals' self-efficacy in a variety of areas (Betz & Schifano, 2000). Other areas for intervention include promoting aspirations and interests in children and adolescents, expanding career choice options, fostering positive and realistic outcome expectations, setting specific goals, coping with barriers and building supports, and increasing coping self-efficacy and strong performance skills (Lent, 2013). Interventions may be targeted at expanding vocational interests, at increasing decision-making skills and exploratory behavior, at helping clients explore various careers, and at increasing consideration of nontraditional careers.

The social cognitive career model has generated a great deal of interest among researchers in vocational psychology. Roughly 20% of the articles published in vocational psychology in the past 10 years have emphasized some aspect of the social cognitive career theory (SCCT). Research has demonstrated support for the relationship between self-efficacy and interests, between self-efficacy and outcome expectations, and the influence of the model in predicting occupational choices (Betz, 2008; Juntunen & Even, 2012; Lent, 2013; Lent et al., 2002). Donnay and Borgen (1999) demonstrated that self-efficacy helps explain vocational choice over and above vocational interests, and Sheu et al. (2010) found that self-efficacy, interests, and outcome expectations predicted choices across Holland themes. Finally, performance accomplishments have been shown to be the most powerful influence on self-efficacy (Williams & Subich, 2006). Research on SCCT has also supported the model across racial/ethnic groups, across many developmental levels, and for both men and women (Fouad & Kantamneni, 2013). Betz (2008) concludes her review of the research on SCCT by noting that "the theory has relevance for understanding a wide range of vocational behaviors relevant to both career choice and adjustment" (p. 365).

BOX 10.1 Personal Reflection

- Have I ever thought, "I can't do that career!"?
- What factors have influenced my self-efficacy about the career?
- What outcomes did I expect?

APPLYING SOCIAL COGNITIVE CAREER THEORY

Counselors who use a social cognitive theoretical model would wonder about their clients' learning experiences, their self-efficacy to approaching various choice options, their career decision-making self-efficacy, how realistic their outcome expectations are, and the barriers or supports for their career decisions. They would also question which options their clients have foreclosed and how to help them expand their career options (Lent, 2013). Counselors' cognitions from an SCCT perspective are presented in Box 10.2.

Conceptualizing Leslie's Career History

In conceptualizing Leslie's career history, counselors using a social cognitive model (Lent 2013) would focus on the learning experiences Leslie has had. They would examine how those learning experiences may relate to the self-efficacy beliefs and outcome expectations Leslie had as an adolescent, how those may have influenced her interests, and, in turn, how those affected performance and choices as she grew older.

Leslie's family had the resources to expose her to a variety of opportunities when she was a child. Her mother was very involved in the arts in their community,

---

BOX 10.2 Counselor Cognitions

- What is the client's self-efficacy for various career options?
- What are the client's outcome expectations for various career options?
- What are the client's interests?
- What is the client's career decision-making self-efficacy?
- What learning experiences does the client have?
- What choices has the client foreclosed?
- Are the client's outcome expectations realistic?
- How do barriers and supports influence the client's vocational choices?

and thus Leslie visited the art museum with her mother, took art or music classes, and attended symphony concerts with her family. Leslie also had significant learning experiences while in school; her active roles as a math tutor, as a leader in the French club, and her successful participation in her school's science fair were opportunities for her to learn about herself and to gain confidence in her skills. Leslie did well academically, as well as socially, in high school. Others perceived her as a leader, though she did not view herself as a leader, since she did not seek out leadership positions.

Leslie's learning experiences were related to her eventual occupational choice. In other words, the activities in which Leslie was engaged as a child and adolescent, such as becoming a tutor, helped in preparation for a career as a teacher. However, there were barriers to her translation of her learning experiences into a major occupational direction. She knew she was going to attend college, consistent with her parents' expectations, but did not declare a major until well into her sophomore year. She took general courses in the community college she attended after high school and then was "undecided" for several semesters after she transferred to a larger university.

In the performance model proposed by Lent et al. (1994; Lent, 2013), the level of goals toward which Leslie aspired was influenced by her self-efficacy beliefs and the outcomes she expected would result from pursuing her goals. Leslie did very well academically in high school yet chose to attend a community college rather than a university. Leslie set lower goals for herself than were consistent with her level of performance. This may have been due to faulty self-efficacy beliefs about her ability to do well academically; this is evidenced in her uncertainty about being successful in college. Such lowered self-efficacy beliefs may have been due to a lack of role models or verbal encouragement to seek an academically challenging curriculum. Leslie also may not have had a good knowledge of the outcomes associated with attending a community college versus the university, although she did expect that her parents would approve of her decision to pursue some postsecondary education. Once she was enrolled in the community college, however, she was frustrated by the lack of challenge. This may have led to increased self-efficacy beliefs about her ability to do well academically and to her decision to transfer to the university.

Even after she enrolled in the university, Leslie still struggled with making a career decision. She did well in many of her classes, though she did not do well in mechanical drawing, which led her to conclude that she would not do well in engineering. Her overall self-efficacy beliefs in her ability to do well academically were relatively high; however, her self-efficacy beliefs in her ability to do well in the specific areas related to engineering were low. She also appeared to have low self-efficacy beliefs related to advanced training, or she may have had low self-efficacy beliefs in her ability to juggle the multiple roles required of balancing career and family obligations. These beliefs led her to foreclose career options that required postgraduate training.

Leslie did not want to consider options that were nontraditional for a woman. This was influenced by the outcomes she expected of entering a nontraditional career, such as continuing to be among the few women in her area or having difficulty in combining her career with raising a family. Leslie also received little encouragement to consider nontraditional careers; in fact, she was at times actively discouraged by her professors.

Leslie's learning experiences led her to know that she was proficient in math and that she was interested in teaching and in helping others. She had developed self-efficacy beliefs in her ability to teach when she was a math tutor in high school. Leslie's decision to major in secondary math education was influenced by her self-efficacy beliefs in her math and teaching abilities and her lower self-efficacy beliefs about advanced training, since teaching did not require a graduate degree. Her student teaching experience gave her a sense of accomplishment and verbal encouragement, which led to increased self-efficacy beliefs in her teaching ability, which led to greater interest in being a teacher and then to her subsequent implementation of that choice. Her choice also was influenced by the outcomes she expected of a teaching career: She would have a career that she could combine with raising a family, as well as a career in which she would not be singled out as one of the few women. In addition, Leslie expected that the choice of teaching would meet with her family's approval. Leslie's decision, then, was strongly influenced by her pattern of self-efficacy and outcome expectations, which perhaps led to her setting a lower performance goal than she was capable of (Lent et al., 1996). However, her decision to be a math teacher was a choice consonant with her self-efficacy beliefs and with her outcome expectations.

Leslie's early career years were a time of increasing her self-efficacy beliefs in her teaching ability. Lent et al. (1996) note that the social cognitive model "asserts that people form an enduring interest in an activity when they view themselves as competent at it and when they anticipate that performing it will produce valued outcomes" (p. 383). Leslie viewed herself as a good, perhaps even very good, teacher. She also began to anticipate that being a teacher would have outcomes that she enjoyed and appreciated. The outcomes included approval from her family, approval from her students and peers, and feeling competent as a teacher. Leslie also enjoyed the challenge of teaching a variety of math classes and being able to be autonomous and creative in her own classroom.

Lent et al.'s (1996; Lent, 2013) performance model suggests that Leslie's performance accomplishments as a teacher and positive outcome expectations of a teaching career would lead her to set higher accomplishment goals. However,

Leslie made a lateral move to a teaching position in a larger city to be closer to her family. This change of environment brought with it some unwelcome changes in the rewards of her work and, subsequently, her outcome expectations. She did not pursue a graduate degree, even though she took several continuing education classes, thus suggesting that she may have low outcome expectancies about the student role or the rewards that an advanced degree may bring her. She may also have anticipated barriers to pursuing a graduate degree, either from her family or from her husband.

Conceptualizing Leslie's Present Situation

Leslie has been a teacher for over 13 years, suggesting that she has high self-efficacy beliefs in her ability to teach, that she expects positive outcomes from the occupation, and that she has formed long-lasting interest in the occupation. However, Leslie is reporting considerable dissatisfaction with her job. Some of her concerns may be related to changes in outcomes she has come to expect from the job; others may be related to her own changing self-efficacy beliefs regarding certain aspects of her current teaching role. Or, conversely, she may have developed interests in another field in which she has higher self-efficacy beliefs and higher outcome expectancies.

Leslie states that she is a good teacher, suggesting high teaching efficacy overall. She enjoys the outcomes associated with direct interactions with her students. However, she also notes frustration in not reaching some students, and this may be threatening her self-efficacy beliefs about her teaching ability. She has had some difficult interactions with parents as well, which led her to question her teaching efficacy, at least within the context of her current school and teaching assignment.

Some of the outcomes associated with being a teacher, such as approval from parents and students, autonomy in her classroom, and ability to challenge herself through teaching advanced classes, have recently diminished for Leslie. She reports frustration with the principal's new accountability measures. She may perceive this as feedback on her teaching, interpreting that the principal does not trust her ability to teach, which in turn may lead to lower teaching efficacy. She also is distrustful of participating in reporting on her teaching goals and activities. She may fear, for example, that she will be evaluated negatively or that she may lose her ability to set her own goals and activities in the class. Other outcomes that Leslie has expected of teaching have changed, as well. Approval from students and parents is not as frequent as it once was for Leslie. She has had fewer opportunities to teach challenging courses, even though she has been at this high school for 10 years.

One of the outcomes that Leslie expected from her teaching was the ability to combine teaching with raising a family. However, she is having difficulty having children and her stepson does not live with them full time, which may lead her to question the premise on which that expectancy was based. She also reports some dissatisfaction with the division of labor in her marriage, suggesting that she may be questioning the way in which she had intended to combine work and family.

Leslie reports that she is willing to consider graduate school at this point, indicating that her efficacy beliefs in her academic skills have become more congruent with her documented skills in doing well academically and/or that her expectations of the outcomes of attending graduate school have changed. Leslie is considering a wide range of occupational areas, though she continues to have weak self-efficacy beliefs in her ability to make a career decision. Her family has given her little encouragement in her career exploration; her brother has actively discouraged her from changing careers, and her mother and sister feel that she should quit work to concentrate on having a family. It is not known whether Leslie has had any role models of individuals who have changed careers in midlife. It would appear that Leslie is less inclined than earlier in her life to foreclose options that are nontraditional for women; she indicated, for example, that she would consider engineering as a career. Leslie may perceive the relatively traditional division of labor in her marriage as a barrier to choices, however, particularly since she reports that her husband and family expect her to stay home if and when she does have children.

QUESTIONS FOR DISCUSSION

1. What specific hypotheses would you develop about Leslie from SCCT? How does using social cognitive theory help you understand Leslie? How might it help Leslie understand herself?

2. Leslie appears to be struggling to make some midlife career changes. How would you address the issues that Leslie is dealing with regarding her career from a social cognitive career model perspective? How would you address the issues that she is dealing with in her marriage?

3. How may Leslie's efficacy beliefs be influenced by the messages she has received from her husband and family about the role of work in her life?

4. How might you incorporate information from the additional inventories that Leslie completed?

5. What interventions or techniques from social cognitive theory might you use with Leslie?

6. What role did Leslie's gender socialization play in her career decisions as an adolescent? What role is her gender socialization playing in her career decisions as an adult?

7. What additional barriers may Leslie encounter if she decides to stay in her current profession of teaching? What barriers may she encounter if she chooses to become a social worker? Engineer? Minister? Technical writer?

The Case of Ron

Ron, a 57-year-old White male, has been employed as a mechanical assembler for a large manufacturing company for the last 38 years. His company, which has been in business in his hometown for 100 years, has just announced a major restructuring to cut costs. The company says that these changes are necessary to remain competitive in the global market. To achieve its ends, it is offering a buyout for all employees who have been with the company for at least 30 years. Ron needs to decide whether to take the buyout offer and seek a new job or to stay in the position. The buyout offer includes a lump sum of $42,000, health insurance for 2 years, and a guarantee that he will receive the pension he has earned to this point if he begins drawing it when he turns 62. If he stays in the position, his income will continue to go up, and he will contribute more to his pension, but he risks being laid off. He has 45 days to decide whether to take the offer. If he does not take the buyout offer and is laid off later, he will not get the lump sum payout or health insurance. His company has offered career counseling, and he seeks help to make the decision.

Ron grew up in a working-class family, the oldest of five children. His father worked for a company that supplied parts to the company where Ron is currently employed. There were no family expectations of schooling beyond high school. Ron's father had graduated from high school, and his mother had a year of secretarial school but did not work after she had children. Both grandfathers had been farmers, and none of his grandparents finished high school. There was a strong expectation that men were the primary breadwinners while women stayed home to take care of children.

Ron was an average student in high school and had no interest in going to college or to a technical school. He did well in high school shop classes, so he decided to apply to the manufacturing company in his hometown. Two of his uncles worked there and recommended he apply. He felt lucky to be hired right after graduation and has worked there for nearly 40 years. During those years, he has worked on many products. Each time there was a change in production, he was able to adjust to the needs of the new process. Although the company has had tuition reimbursement programs, Ron has never taken any outside coursework. He has, however, learned a number of skills, including running computer-controlled equipment, while he rotated through several tasks. He has enjoyed the security of working for a company that had been in business for over 100 years.

Ron married his high school sweetheart shortly after he began working. They had three children. All are grown; two are married and have children of their own. One grandchild lives in Washington, DC, and the other set of grandchildren live in Oregon. His youngest son has moved back home following a layoff. Ron's wife did not work while their children were young, and although she has an administrative position now, it has been important to Ron to be the provider for his family.

Ron has worked steadily for nearly 40 years. Although he reports that there have been several periods of layoffs over the years, his assembly job has always been safe. He credits the union for this security but acknowledges there have been attempts to reduce the bargaining power of the union. Although his job has been secure, he feels his wages have not kept up with his family's needs. He and his wife recently refinanced their home to add an extra room for the son who moved home. They help support his mother-in-law, who is now in a nursing home. They travel as often as they can to see their grandchildren who live at opposite ends of the country. These expenses have led to a substantial amount of credit card debt. Ron and his wife have no savings set aside for retirement because they had been told, and witnessed through friends, that the company pension was excellent.

Ron was aware that the company had been losing market share, and he had seen several product lines move to Mexico. He felt, though, that his position would not be affected because assemblers had always been needed. He was stunned when the union agreed to the buyout offer. He is angry, scared of his financial obligations, and worried about supporting his family. His pride in this company has shaped his identity for nearly 40 years. He also is very unsure of how to go about making a career decision.

QUESTIONS FOR DISCUSSION

1. What specific hypotheses would you develop about Ron from SCCT? How does using social cognitive theory help you understand Ron? How might it help Ron understand himself?

2. How would you address Ron's dilemma about choosing the buyout option or not from a social cognitive career model perspective?

3. How may Ron's efficacy beliefs be influenced by the messages he has received from his family about his role as a breadwinner?

4. What interventions or techniques from social cognitive theory might you use with Ron?

5. What additional barriers may Ron encounter if he decides to stay in his current job? What barriers may he encounter if he chooses to leave his career as an assembler? What supports does Ron have?

DIRECTIONS AND IMPLICATIONS FOR CAREER COUNSELING

Career counseling within the framework of the social cognitive career model focuses on helping clients identify faulty efficacy beliefs and unrealistic outcome expectations that have led them to make poor career decisions or, as in Ron's case, helping clients expand career options. Brown and Lent (1996) and Lent (2013) suggest three basic tenets inherent in career counseling from a social cognitive framework:

1. Help clients explore options and identify those options that they have foreclosed because they have unrealistic or faulty self-efficacy beliefs or outcome expectancies.

2. Identify and evaluate barriers to, and supports for, various career choices, particularly barriers that may have led clients to eliminate a career possibility prematurely from consideration.

3. Help clients modify and counteract faulty efficacy beliefs and faulty occupational information.

These interventions are not necessarily done in a linear order. For example, it may be necessary to work with clients to identify options that they have eliminated from consideration. It may be important then to help clients modify efficacy beliefs or to correct their occupational information so that they can consider careers that seem to be particularly appropriate choices. It may be important finally to help them identify supports and eliminate barriers to implementing that choice.

Goals of Counseling

The overarching goal of the social cognitive career model is to help clients make a career choice that "correspond[s] reasonably well with important aspects of their work personality" (Lent, 2013, p. 137). In other words, the goal of career counseling within this framework is to help clients find a career that matches their interests, values, and skills. An important part of this process is to help clients explore possibilities that are a good match but were discarded from consideration because of poor self-efficacy perceptions or inaccurate outcome expectations.

Identify foreclosed options

Career counseling begins with helping clients clarify their goals for career counseling. For example, the career counselor works with Leslie to help her identify whether she was seeking counseling to help her choose an entirely new career path or whether she wanted to make some changes to be more satisfied in her current position. Ron's counselor helps him clarify if career counseling will focus on the decision to stay in his position or if he wants to identify new career paths. Initially, the counselor works to help Leslie or Ron clarify goals. The counselor asks the question "When will you know counseling has been successful?" Clarifying the counseling goals helps the client and counselor focus the assessments and interventions toward that goal and helps clients and counselors evaluate the process and result of counseling.

Once the client and counselor have clarified the goals for counseling, the counselor focuses on exploring those paths the client has dropped from consideration and to expand the possibilities that he or she could consider. In Leslie's case, the counselor also encourages Leslie to explore options to become more satisfied with her current career. The counselor might say, "Leslie, I noticed that you were considering the occupations of engineering, psychology, and medicine. Let's examine why you decided those weren't for you. We can also spend some times looking at ways to make teaching a more viable career option for you." In Ron's case, the counselor might begin by asking Ron to consider the outcomes expected of the various options. What outcomes would Ron expect if he stayed in the job? What outcomes might occur if he took the buyout, and what career paths might he consider if he chose this option? The counselor might also ask Ron what career options he has foreclosed by choosing a career so quickly out of high school and by not seeking additional training over the years.

Results from an interest inventory may be used by the counselor, using both high-scoring interests as well as those interest scales on which clients scored lower. In the latter case, the counselor incorporates an analysis of the basis of those areas of less interest. This approach may also include an analysis of the relationship between interest and level of confidence across different Holland themes, such as that provided by the Skills Confidence Inventory (SCI). Obvious areas for exploration include areas in which Ron has both high interest and high self-efficacy, but the counselor could also examine areas of high interest but low self-efficacy, because an intervention could help bolster self-efficacy. Thus, Ron's counselor could suggest that Ron take the Strong Interest Inventory (SII) and the SCI to help identify possible career options.

Leslie's results on the SII indicated high interest in the Investigative, Social, and Conventional General Occupational Themes and the Research, Teaching, Mathematics, Taxes and Accounting, and Science Basic Interest Scales. Leslie had much less interest in the Enterprising and Artistic General Occupational Themes and indicated low interest in the Basic Interest Scales associated with the Artistic General Occupational Theme, such as Performing Arts, Visual Arts, Culinary Arts, and Writing. She also indicated little interest in Military, Healthcare Services, Law, Sales, Management, Politics, Marketing, and Entrepreneurship. The counselor explores these areas to examine the basis for a low level of interest in the areas. For example, as noted earlier, Leslie had a variety of opportunities to be exposed to careers related to the arts through her mother's work in community arts organizations. The basis for her lack of interest in the arts area may be due to a realistic appraisal of her skills in the area. However, Leslie also may have decided early in her adolescence that she did not want to pursue careers in the arts areas for reasons unrelated to her skills. For example, she may have decided that she did not want to pursue a path followed by her mother, she may have negative outcome expectations associated with entering the arts field, or she may have erroneously decided that she did not have the skills to pursue an arts career further. The counselor spends some time exploring this as a possible avenue for further consideration: "Leslie, the Strong Interest Inventory results indicate that, compared to a large group of women, you aren't very interested in the areas represented in the Artistic General Occupational Theme. Can you think back to a time when you may have been interested in this area? Perhaps there are some occupations that you would like to explore for further consideration?"

The counselor also discusses the scales on which Leslie scored high but that she has not pursued in her career, specifically the areas indicated by the Science, Research, Mathematics, and Tax and Accounting Basic Interest Scales, as well as those related to the Religion and Spirituality Basic Interest Scale. Occupations on which Leslie scored high include mathematician, software developer, actuary, financial analyst, biologist, financial manager, university professor, and medical technologist. She also scored high on the Mathematics Teacher Occupational Scale, indicating that she is a good match for her own career. The latter may indicate that career counseling should focus on helping her find a different occupational environment rather than a different career. However, the counselor may also encourage her to explore the occupations on which she scored similarly to women in that occupation: "Leslie, your pattern of likes and dislikes was similar to that of women who are school counselors and special education teachers; these two are in the Social General Occupational Theme area. Tell me what you think of these occupations."

Leslie's Learning Environment Scale score on the SII indicates that she enjoys learning through lectures and books, which may help the counselor explore her reluctance to pursue a graduate degree. Her decision not to seek advanced training may have been related to her negative outcome expectations related to the type of learning required in graduate school rather than to her low self-efficacy beliefs related to graduate training.

Examination of the comparison between Leslie's interests and skills confidence on the SCI lends some support for the counselor to encourage Leslie to explore options in both the Investigative and Social General Occupational Theme areas. Interventions for areas in which a client has lower interest than confidence would target outcome expectancies. Self-efficacy beliefs would be the target of interventions in areas in which confidence is lower than interest. Leslie's results indicate that Leslie has more confidence in her skills than interest in the Conventional area and more interest than skill confidence in the Investigative and Social areas. The lower confidence in the Conventional theme may be due to her lower outcome expectations in this area. The counselor explores this with Leslie: "I notice that the Strong and SCI results indicate that you have more confidence in your ability to do the tasks related to the Conventional area than you have interests in the area. This may be related to the outcomes you would expect from tasks and occupations in this area. Tell me what you would expect if you were to pursue the occupation of financial analyst or actuary." The counselor then helps Leslie determine if this is related to her negative outcome expectations related to further education. The counselor helps her reevaluate those outcome expectations or to determine if other Investigative occupations are more consonant with her educational goals.

The difference in Leslie's confidence and interest in the Social area may be due to lack of learning opportunities available to Leslie in the areas tapped by the Social Skills Confidence scale, such as directly working to help people with their problems or counseling an unhappy couple. The counselor works with Leslie to assess areas that she wants to consider, particularly focusing on those areas that might be fruitful for further investigation but that Leslie is not considering because of poor self-efficacy beliefs or low outcome expectations. If, for example, Leslie indicates that she might be interested in being a social worker but does not feel she could actually help people, social work would be an area the counselor would target for further exploration.

A second approach for identifying foreclosed options is to analyze discrepancies between occupations identified on an interest inventory and those identified on an aptitude inventory or on a needs inventory, such as the Minnesota Importance

Questionnaire (MIQ). The assumption behind the latter analysis is that occupations predicted to be satisfying based on needs would also be predicted to be satisfying based on interests, unless faulty efficacy or outcome perceptions have prevented the development of interest in that area. Identifying those discrepant occupations may help the client expand the possible range of occupations she or he is considering. This should be used only as a guide, however, since the occupations on each inventory do not overlap entirely (i.e., not all occupations on the MIQ are found on the Strong and vice versa). It is important to note that SCCT views needs and values as outcome expectations and would consider the MIQ as providing information related to the outcome expectations (i.e., rewards) a client may have about an occupation.

Occupations on which Leslie had high scores in both the SII and MIQ included secondary teacher, speech pathologist, engineer, and programmer. Occupations in which Leslie was predicted to be satisfied based on her needs results but in which she did not indicate an interest included architect, interior designer, librarian, technical writer, minister, occupational therapist, social worker, real estate agent, and law enforcement officer. These provide additional areas for the counselor to explore with Leslie: "Leslie, I note that several occupations may provide the rewards you would expect from an occupation, but you did not indicate you were interested in that occupation. In particular, I wonder what you think of those occupations in the Social area, such as nurse and occupational therapist, as well as in the Artistic area, such as librarian and architect." Two occupations may deserve further discussion. Leslie's interests in religious activities suggest that the occupation of minister may be an occupation worthy of in-depth consideration, particularly if her lack of efficacy beliefs regarding helping others has caused her to preclude it as an option. The other occupation to discuss is technical writing, since she entered counseling having listed that as an option. She may have low efficacy beliefs in her writing ability that have led to low interests in this area; these merit further investigation to determine the accuracy of those efficacy beliefs.

A third approach to identifying foreclosed options is to use a card sort (Dewey, 1974; Dolliver, 1969). In this strategy, the counselor gives Leslie a set of cards with an occupation listed on each card and asks her to sort them into three piles. The first pile consists of occupations she might choose, the second pile is occupations she would not choose, and the last pile consists of occupations "in question." The counselor then focuses on the occupations in the "in question" and "would not choose" piles. Leslie is asked to further sort these occupations into occupations she might choose if she felt she had the skills to do the job well, those she might choose if she felt the occupation would result in positive outcomes, and occupations she would not ever choose. The counselor then focuses on occupations targeted either for further skill development, if in fact Leslie does not have the skills to accomplish the job, or for modification of efficacy beliefs, if her perceptions of her skills are inaccurate. The latter may be the case if Leslie feels she could not enter engineering because she does not have the skills to take advanced math courses such training would require. The counselor then focuses on the "might choose if result in positive outcomes" pile. The counselor asks Leslie: "Tell me what you would expect from the occupations in this pile. How accurate do you think your perceptions of the outcomes might be?" The counselor also encourages Leslie to obtain more information if her knowledge of outcomes expected of various occupations is incomplete or inaccurate. For example, if Leslie still believed that she would not be able to combine work as an engineer with a family, the counselor refers her for informational interviewing to women engineers who are combining both.

Reevaluate and modify efficacy beliefs

A second tenet of the social cognitive career model is that counselors need to help their clients modify faulty self-efficacy beliefs that are preventing them from considering viable career options. Lent (2013) suggests that counselors working with clients who have evidence of skills but who have weak self-efficacy develop strategies that promote efficacy. These strategies may be designed specifically to encourage performance accomplishments or to rethink previous performance accomplishments such that the client's accomplishments are not discounted. Ron, for example, might have no confidence in his ability to make a career decision and, thus, might believe that he cannot take the buyout option. He might also have low self-efficacy beliefs in pursuing careers other than factory work. The counselor would work to counteract these weak career decision-making self-efficacy beliefs.

Brown and Lent (1996) and Lent (2013) identify several strategies to help clients modify their efficacy beliefs, including helping clients create opportunities to experience successful performance accomplishments. One strategy is to give Leslie additional opportunities to form efficacy beliefs about her ability to do graduate work, for example, encouraging her to talk to current graduate students or to examine syllabi for graduate courses. The counselor also needs to help her attribute her performance correctly as related to her abilities when she performs well, as opposed to attributing it to some other external source, such as ease of the test or mere effort on her part. It is important that Leslie gain a more accurate view of her abilities to raise her efficacy beliefs.

Additionally, the counselor works with Leslie to help her further reanalyze previous experiences that led her to conclude she would not do well in school. For example, the counselor encourages Leslie to identify the faulty efficacy beliefs she had as an adolescent that led her to choose entering a community college instead of a university or that led her to close off a number of options that required graduate training. The counselor helps Leslie analyze which of those efficacy beliefs are still operating and helps her identify methods to change those beliefs. The counselor could, for example, encourage Leslie to gather more information about how she compares with others. Her beliefs in her ability to perform well in graduate school may have been due to inaccurate perceptions of the performance level required of graduate students. Gathering more accurate information of graduate school expectations, as well as gaining a more accurate picture of herself, may help Leslie modify her efficacy beliefs.

Identify barriers and supports

The third tenet in career counseling from a social cognitive model is that counselors need to work with clients to help them identify barriers and supports to implementing career options. Once barriers are identified, counselors need to help clients evaluate whether the perceptions of barriers are based on a realistic appraisal of the environment, to help clients evaluate how likely they are to encounter those barriers, and then to identify ways to cope with those barriers. For example, Ron has financial barriers that influence either option he is considering. His considerable debt affects his decisions. On the one hand, the $42,000 lump sum payout would help his immediate financial burdens, but the buyout option would reduce his company pension. On the other hand, staying at the company could give him more income and a greater contribution to his pension, but he would run the risk of being laid off with no lump sum payout. Ron's supports include strong family ties, his wife's job that provides some income, and his ability to be flexible in the work environment.

Leslie's greatest barriers in making a career decision appear to be related to her focus on others' approval and involvement in her decisions, as well as what appears to be her lack of willingness to take risks. The counselor works to help Leslie identify strategies to overcome the identified barriers. One strategy identified by Brown and Lent (1996) is to ask clients to complete a decisional balance sheet (Janis & Mann, 1977) for each career alternative under consideration. Clients are asked to indicate positive and negative consequences related to each alternative; they identify consequences anticipated for themselves and for others in both the short and long term.

Leslie's counselor asks her to complete a decisional balance sheet for staying in her current occupation and for each alternative career she was considering. Leslie may, for example, identify her husband's and mother's traditional views of women's role in child rearing as a barrier to pursuing a career as an engineer, or she may identify her own discomfort with being in a nontraditional field as a barrier. She may identify her lack of confidence in helping others as a barrier to entering ministry, also perhaps voicing a fear that her family would not support such a choice. She may also identify her anger at the principal and lack of challenge as barriers to continuing in her current position.

Leslie's counselor then helps her identify how realistic each of those barriers may be: "Leslie, you indicated that your family may not approve of your pursuing a degree in engineering. What information have they given you that has led you to this conclusion? What might happen if you discussed the possibilities of further education with your husband or if you talked about engineering as a possible option with your family?" Her fears of their reaction may, in fact, be well grounded, or they may be inaccurate. If her fears were realistic barriers to her pursuing these options, the counselor would encourage her to identify possible ways to manage or prevent those barriers. For example, the counselor may encourage her to talk further with her husband to enlist his help in a more role-sharing model of child rearing. Leslie may, however, also decide that the consequence of losing familial support is too great, and that may help her decide to stay in her current position as a teacher.

If Leslie decides to remain a math teacher, identification of the barriers associated with that position might help her determine specific actions to make her more satisfied in that occupation. For example, she may decide that the barriers include her principal and that she has little power to change his specific actions. This may lead her to seek a position as a math teacher in another school, knowing that she would be happier in a smaller school system in which she could teach a greater variety of classes.

ADDITIONAL CASES

Case 1: Jerry

Jerry is a 32-year-old gay White man who is seeking career counseling because he was diagnosed as HIV-positive several years ago. When he was first diagnosed, he expected his health to deteriorate rapidly, initially thinking he had only 4 years to live, and he decided to continue working as a hair stylist. However, his regimen of treatments has enabled him to be well enough to work, and he is in a position of facing that he never really liked his work as a stylist. He continued to do that work because it paid the bills. Now he is seeking career counseling because he is ready to make a different career choice.

(Continued)

(Continued)

Jerry is a licensed hair stylist working in a suite of hair salons; he shares his leased space with another stylist, Latasha. Jerry initially became a hair stylist because he enjoyed the creativity of working with different styles and liked helping people look better; he also was "sick of school," so he did not want an occupation that entailed a college degree. Jerry had been struggling with his sexual identity through high school and did not do well in his high school classes, precluding options for postsecondary training. He had taken drafting in high school and enjoyed that, as well as a drafting class he took as a senior. Jerry was also on the basketball team during his first two years in high school but dropped out during his junior year. He came out to his parents during his senior year in high school; they were initially unhappy but were eventually supportive of his orientation. His decision to become a stylist was also influenced by his perception that it was an occupation in which others would be supportive of a gay man.

His counselor began to clarify Jerry's goals and found that Jerry also had some interpersonal conflicts in his current work environment with Latasha. Jerry complained that Latasha was stealing his items and was forming alliances with others in the suite against him. Jerry was reluctant to confront her directly, however, suggesting that if he ignored the problems, they would go away. However, Latasha had informed him that she was breaking their agreement and moving to a salon by herself, leaving Jerry solely responsible for the rent on their shared suite. Again, Jerry was reluctant to confront the issue, choosing not to take legal action against her. His career decisions then included whether he should quit being a hair stylist altogether, declare bankruptcy and move back to his parents' home while he considered what to do, expand his services to make more money to cover the rent in the salon, or seek and train another partner.

Jerry indicated that he really "got sick of hearing people talk all day" and did not enjoy the interpersonal conflicts that others seemed to create. He was frustrated at having to be inside a lot, when he would rather be outside. He did enjoy being able to work with his hands and still enjoyed some of the creative aspects of his job. He appreciated some of the flexibility of his work as well, since it enabled him to schedule around days when he was not feeling well.

Jerry's SII indicated that his highest interests were in the Realistic and Social General Occupational Themes, with high Counseling & Helping, Culinary Arts, Mechanics & Construction, Athletics, Teaching, and Mathematics Basic Interest Scales. He was most similar to men who are law enforcement officers, auto mechanics, athletic trainers, and occupational therapists. Jerry's MIQ indicated that it was very important for him to get along well with his coworkers, do things for other people, and do something that made use of his abilities. His scores on the General Aptitude Test Battery indicated that he was at least 1 standard deviation above the mean in all tested areas and had particularly high level of ability in verbal reasoning, numerical reasoning, and general learning ability.

QUESTIONS FOR DISCUSSION

1. How might Jerry's self-efficacy beliefs or outcome expectations have foreclosed his options? What are specific examples of options he may have foreclosed?

2. What barriers is Jerry facing in his career alternatives?

3. What are Jerry's likely outcome expectations about his various career alternatives?

4. How would you incorporate the information presented by Jerry's career history and his assessment results?

5. How might Jerry's learning opportunities have been partly shaped by his sexual orientation?

6. How might you modify Jerry's self-efficacy beliefs?

7. How may Jerry's interpersonal conflicts affect his career decisions? What role might have self-efficacy beliefs and/or outcome expectancies played in his interpersonal conflicts?

8. How do Jerry's gender and race/ethnicity influence his decisions?

Case 2: Kamisha

Kamisha is a 21-year-old African American woman in her third year of college. She is seeking counseling because she is undecided about her college major. She is attending a private liberal arts college and has done very well in all her courses. She originally declared a major in chemistry, then changed to English during her second year, and finally changed to psychology. Although she is getting an A in the class, she does not like the psychology course she is currently taking and has begun to have doubts about her entry into the field. She knows she will need to continue on to graduate school if she wishes to be a psychologist. She is confident she would do well if she would choose to pursue this avenue; she is concerned, however, that psychology may not be the right choice for her.

Kamisha is the daughter of two successful corporate executives; she is the older of two sisters. Her parents, though busy with their careers while she was growing up, were able to provide her with numerous educational opportunities. She attended a prestigious private high school, traveled abroad extensively with her family, and spent her junior year in high school studying in France. Kamisha also attended various summer camps, as well as participating in several

(Continued)

(Continued)

classes provided by the local university specifically targeting African American girls. She particularly enjoyed her classes in science, in English, in math, and in social studies. The latter area included courses in political science, sociology, and psychology.

Kamisha's parents have high expectations for their daughters. They believe that they both should not only finish college but should seek some additional postgraduate training, such as a law degree or a doctorate. They provided them both with many opportunities, and they also feel that their daughters "owe it to their race" to do well. Kamisha's parents have worked hard also to shield their daughters from overt discrimination, sending them to private educational institutions known for their racially egalitarian policies and practices. Kamisha's sister is currently on an athletic scholarship at another private university, where she is excelling as a soccer player and doing well in her premedical studies.

Although Kamisha has done well in all her courses and is interested in most of the material she has studied, she is genuinely confused about which avenue to pursue. She has changed her major so often because she has been pressured by the college to declare a major, but she does not feel that she can determine which one is best for her. Her interest inventory results indicate that she is interested in Artistic, Investigative, and Social areas and that she is similar to women who are psychologists, college professors, mathematicians, biologists, chemists, and English teachers.

QUESTIONS FOR DISCUSSION

1. How may Kamisha have foreclosed her career options? What are specific examples of options she has foreclosed, if any?

2. What barriers is Kamisha encountering, if any?

3. What might be Kamisha's outcome expectations about her college major decision?

4. How may a counselor incorporate Kamisha's assessment results into counseling?

5. What additional information may the counselor seek?

6. How have Kamisha's learning opportunities been shaped by her socioeconomic status and by her cultural background?

7. What social cognitive strategies would you employ to help Kamisha make a career choice?

Case 3: Jim

Jim is a 27-year-old White male who suffered a spinal cord injury in the neck area 4 years ago, which has severely limited his mobility. How his injury occurred is unknown to Jim. He related that he was attending a party in honor of his completion of the Reserve Officer's Training Corp (ROTC), and the last thing he remembers is opening the bathroom door and closing it behind him. The next thing he knew, he was lying on the bathroom floor and could not move. He underwent 6 months of hospitalization and therapy. Jim returned to finish his baccalaureate degree, is currently enrolled in a graduate program, and is seeking counseling because he has begun to have doubts about whether or not he is taking the right career path.

During his high school years, Jim was involved in volunteer work at two schools for children with physical and cognitive disabilities. He enjoyed working with the kids individually and in groups. One of the things that he liked most was seeing the progression that the children made over time. He also enjoyed sports and being active. The aspects of sports he enjoyed the most were the teamwork, motivation, and the sense of achievement he received after successfully accomplishing a goal. He wanted to incorporate both of these factors in choosing a career and chose to pursue physical education with an adaptive emphasis to include children with special needs.

Jim was very active in college, becoming involved in many campus activities, such as student government, intramural sports, and ROTC. He also continued to volunteer working with children. After 4 years in college, he was a year and a half from finishing his degree, a well-respected student leader on campus, and near completion of the ROTC program, when the accident occurred.

Following the accident, Jim knew he could no longer pursue physical education and decided to major in recreation therapy, because it involved actively participating with a client or groups and also might include sporting activities. He completed his degree three and half years later and decided to enroll in graduate school. He hoped one day to pursue a doctorate and decided first to enroll in a master's program. He also hoped to move away from home and establish his independence.

Jim found a few things that were difficult in going to a school out of state. Two roadblocks were a lack of wheelchair-accessible housing accommodations and insurance and medical benefits. After researching the possibility of a move, he found that it would be more difficult than it was worth, and, feeling pressured by the time constraints of the deadlines for applications, he applied to a local graduate program in rehabilitation counseling. He chose rehabilitation counseling as a good complement to his bachelor's degree in recreation therapy. He was admitted and began to take classes.

Although his conflict had been solved, Jim felt rushed by the decision and was not 100% sure this was the right direction for him. He took one class in the summer session to ease himself into attending classes again, to get familiar with the campus, and establish himself in the program. This class was a basic introductory counseling class that exposed him to a few different aspects of counseling he had not considered. He now wants to determine whether to leave rehabilitation counseling and enter a more general counseling curriculum for his master's work or finish his master's and seek a doctorate in clinical or counseling psychology.

QUESTIONS FOR DISCUSSION

1. How may Jim have foreclosed his career options? What are specific examples of options he has foreclosed, if any?

2. What barriers is Jim encountering, if any?

3. What might be Jim's outcome expectations about his decisions about graduate training?

4. How would you incorporate Jim's disability into your approach to counseling?

5. What additional information would you seek?

6. How have Jim's learning opportunities been shaped by his disability and by his cultural background?

7. What social cognitive strategies would you employ to help Jim make a career choice?

BOX 10.3 Summary of Key Constructs

Construct	Definition
Self-efficacy	Confidence in ability to accomplish tasks in a particular domain
Outcome expectations	Outcomes expected of domain-specific actions
Interests	Preference for activities
Distal barriers and supports	Factors that hinder or facilitate the development of learning experiences and self-efficacy
Proximal barriers and supports	Factors that hinder or facilitate implementation of career choices that are close in time to the choice
Contextual affordances	Environmental resources and obstacles that shape career development

Chapter 11

Emerging Theoretical Approaches: 21st-Century Views of Work

In the past decade or more, substantial changes have occurred within the field of vocational psychology, and new theoretical approaches are emerging in an effort to better explain career and work behavior (Fouad, 2007; Juntunen & Even, 2012). Theories of career development (or vocational choice) have shifted from a sole focus on the individual, to an explicit recognition of contextual factors, to a perspective that might be best described as a "person-in-complex-social-and-economic-systems" focus (Swanson, 2013). These newer approaches are characterized by several different primary emphases, including (a) equal valuing of work and relationship, or market and care work, (b) viewing work within a broader context of relational aspects, (c) expanding consideration of the experience of *work* beyond that of *career*, and (d) building on postmodern perspectives of work.

We begin this chapter by discussing assumptions about work and career that have changed over time, because these assumptions relate to the emerging theoretical approaches. We then discuss several emerging approaches and how they may help inform contemporary career or work-related interventions.

Note: Portions of this chapter were drawn from Swanson, J. L. (2013). Traditional and emerging career development theory and the psychology of working. In D. L. Blustein (Ed.), *Handbook of the psychology of working* (pp. 49–67). New York: Oxford University Press.

CHANGING ASSUMPTIONS ABOUT WORK/CAREER

A number of assumptions underlie career theory and practice (Fouad, 2007) and are relevant to how we view the "traditional" theories discussed in Chapters 6–10 and the "emerging" theories discussed in this chapter. These assumptions are in flux, or may even present an outdated view of individuals and work.

Assumption #1: Everyone has the ability to make work choices

Traditional theories of career choice assume that individuals have *volition* in aspects of choice; in fact, the early theories were developed to address the increasingly diverse choices that were available to individuals in an expanding economy and world of work. For example, Parsons' work at the beginning of the 20th century (Zytowski, 2001) and the education and employment of veterans after WWII (Whiteley, 1984) led to practical assistance for individuals sorting through the multitude of options. In particular, the theories that originated up through the late 20th century, including theories proposed by Holland and Super, and the Theory of Work Adjustment (TWA), assumed that individuals had many available choices, and that they were able to make choices relatively freely. In contrast, theories developed in the 1980s or later, such as Gottfredson's theory or Social Cognitive Career Theory, incorporated constructs that acknowledged that there were environmental constraints on an individual's choice. The question of volition is at the forefront of changes within emerging theories of career choice and development.

Assumption #2: Work is a contained part of people's lives

Traditional theories of career choice focused almost exclusively on the world of work and rarely made connections to the other aspects of individuals' lives. In the mid-20th century, the world of work was dominated by men (specifically middle-class and White men), and so work was predominantly a male domain, and family and home were predominantly female domains. When women entered the world of work in greater numbers, and particularly as they pursued *careers*, questions regarding the interface between work and nonwork became more salient. Women's nonwork responsibilities did not change substantially despite their increased involvement in the world of work (Hochschild, 1989), thus, creating the dual roles that led to study of the intersection of the two domains. Conversely, being male required a consideration of work decisions and career choices; being female allowed one to avoid those choices if one so desired. The social revolution brought about by women's entry into the world of work required changes in career theories. Super's acknowledgment of a variety of life roles was the first step, and contemporary discussions of market work and personal work provide a rich development of these ideas (Richardson, 2012).

Assumption #3: The world of work is predictable

The world of work perhaps has never been as predictable as we believe it to be; however, recent economic and social changes have radically altered the landscape locally, nationally, and globally (DeBell, 2001, 2006; Fouad & Bynner, 2008). DeBell (2001) described the "new world economy," characterized by increased globalization, an expanding gulf between the rich and the poor (and a shift in jobs), instability in businesses because of mergers and acquisitions, restructuring of work itself, and rapid and unpredictable technological changes. Theories of vocational choice and development, and how these theories apply to clients, must be sufficiently flexible to account for the unpredictability of the future.

Assumption #4: An individual will make one decision early in life

This assumption is clearly no longer sustainable, particularly given the unpredictability of the world of work and economic factors. Traditional theories have accommodated and are able to explain multiple choice points throughout the lifespan (such as the Theory of Work Adjustment's focus on the process and outcome of work adjustment and Super's notion of recycling of stages). However, the traditional *application* of these theories through career counseling focuses on choice points, such as choosing an academic major in higher education, and so has perpetuated the idea that individuals make a single decision early in life.

Assumption #5: Career counseling is short term and focused on providing information

An increasingly complex and unpredictable world of work, coupled with the importance of considering the intersection of work and nonwork, argues that counselors and clients must consider a broad range of issues beyond gathering information and making a decision. As Savickas et al. (2009) noted, "counselors have to face the fact that information about traditional career paths becomes more and more questionable and hazardous" (p. 242). As we discuss in Chapter 13, information about the world of work is important but should be placed in a broader context.

BOX 11.1 Personal Reflection

- What do I believe about my own ability or volition in making choices about work/career? What do I believe about my clients' ability to make choices?
- How does work connect with the nonwork aspects of my own life?
- How have I experienced instability or unpredictability in the world of work? How has that affected my choices?
- How would I characterize the career decisions that I have made in my life?

BACKGROUND ABOUT EMERGING THEORIES

Emerging theories have been described as paradigm-shifting (Richardson, 2012), in that they represent a radical departure from previous views and an opening up of new perspectives to understanding behavior and events that would previously have not been considered valid. Generally speaking, a major thrust of the paradigm shift in vocational psychology has been from a *positivist epistemology*, in which individuals are defined "objectively" as a set of traits that are discoverable and quantifiable through assessment or other empirical observations, to *postmodern epistemologies* such as constructionism, in which individuals define their own meaning and construct their own stories.

The history of vocational psychology and career counseling is strongly tied to the psychometric movement in the first half of the 20th century (Dawis, 1992), and measures of vocationally-relevant constructs served a central role for researchers and practitioners. These measures were built on and reinforced the positivist epistemology: Interests, values, and abilities were viewed as very real yet unobservable traits that could be revealed through the use of well-constructed scales. Used in career counseling, the scores produced by interest and other inventories often were treated as infallible indicators of something to be uncovered and confirmed by the counselor and client (Reed, Patton, & Gold, 1993).

These newer "emerging" perspectives represent a marked departure from "traditional" theories, yet there also are clear continuities with the earlier theories. For example, Frank Parsons (1909), who is credited with launching the field of vocational guidance, published his landmark work in response to social change occurring at the beginning of the 20th century, and the newly emerging and contemporary perspectives may also be characterized by their responsiveness to social change (Juntunen & Even, 2012).

Contemporary thinking in theories of work/life/career encompass a number of overlapping approaches with distinct contributions, including relational perspectives, narrative approaches, social constructionism epistemologies, and more expansive definitions of "work." These approaches corroborate Fouad's (2007) five assumptions as described earlier and have provided expanded views of the role of work in people's lives.

Writing within traditional vocational psychology has often suffered from a lack of recognition of the impact of economic and labor market factors. Yet these factors have considerable bearing on the progression and experience of work/career. Another factor in the emerging perspectives is explicit recognition of role of economic and market influences. Vocational psychology has had as its primary focus the individual, yet has often neglected the economic and social realities in which individuals engage in work and career.

Three recent conceptualizations represent significant departures from the traditional paradigms: Savickas's (2011, 2013) career construction theory and life design paradigm, Richardson's (2012) model of counseling for work and relationships, and Blustein's psychology of working. A major impetus for these new models is the changing nature, or "new social arrangement," of work (Savickas et al., 2009, p. 239). Recent conceptualizations of "work" have expanded to include unpaid work such as caregiving and volunteer activities, in an attempt to capture the multiple forms that work may take in an individual's life. For example, work has been defined as "an instrumental and purposive activity that produces goods, services, or social relations which have both social and/or personal value" (Richardson, Constantine, & Washburn, 2005, p. 60). Similarly, Blustein (2006, p. 3) defined working as entailing "effort, activity, and human energy in given tasks that contribute to the overall social and economic welfare of a given culture."

All three of these frameworks have been influenced by, and contributed to, postmodern or postpositivist epistemologies. This perspective redirects attention to understanding how people construct meaning about their careers and assisting them in designing meaning (Richardson et al., 2005; Savickas et al., 2009; Young & Collin, 2004).

Career Construction Theory and the Life Design Paradigm (Savickas)

In Chapter 8, we discussed Super's life span, life space theory and some of the additions and revisions made by Savickas and others. Thus, the origins of career construction theory are found in Super's theory, and remnants of Super's theory are evident in Savickas's formulation, yet Savickas has diverged from Super in the development of career construction theory. Career construction theory explains the processes through which "individuals construct themselves, impose direction on their vocational behavior, and make meaning of their careers" (Savickas, 2013, p. 1). The primary concept is *self-construction,* which begins during childhood as individuals are first actors, then become agents, and later authors of their own lives and careers. Career construction theory draws from McAdams and Olson's (2010) view of personality development, which views individuals as driven by adaptation to their environment, versus by "maturation of inner structures" (Savickas, 2013, p. 2).

Savickas argued for a reconceptualization of how careers are constructed given societal changes in the way that work is structured. In the 20th century, "career" as articulated by Super meant a path through one's work life, which could be objectively defined and was evident to others. In contrast, the 21st century view is of boundaryless, protean careers, which require subjective construction by the individual and adaptation to changing conditions. Career construction theory "views career as a story that individuals tell about their working life, not progress down a path or up a ladder" (Savickas, 2013, p. 6). While everyone has an "objective" career, they also construct a subjective career with which to impose meaning and direction on their behavior. This subjective career story carries an individual throughout transitions.

As noted in Chapter 8, the concept of "career maturity" as proposed by Super evolved into "career adaptability" by Savickas. Assessment of career adaptability involves assessing the client's career concern, the developmental tasks the client is encountering, and the skills and resources the individual brings to resolving those tasks. Savickas (2005, 2013) described the "four Cs" or four dimensions of career adaptability as concern, control, curiosity, and confidence. Each task is proposed to have specific attitudes, competencies, and coping behaviors, as well as types of career interventions to address it. *Career concern* refers to a future orientation and recognition of the importance of planning for tomorrow, characterized by planfulness and optimism, versus *career indifference* characterized by apathy and pessimism. *Career control* entails the ability to have control over one's own choices, versus *career indecision*, which is characterized by confusion, procrastination, and impulsivity. *Career curiosity* follows self-control, as an individual becomes inquisitive about his or her interests and occupational alternatives. The important role of curiosity is reflected in the attention paid to exploration in other theories of career development (Savickas, 2013). A lack of curiosity leads to *unrealism* about self and environment. *Career confidence* reflects self-efficacy or anticipating success regarding education and career. Lack of confidence may lead to career *inhibition*. These four processes have some developmental progression, in that it would seem necessary to express concern prior to experiencing control, which would in turn be a necessary condition for curiosity and confidence. Savickas (2013) described these four Cs as dimensions that may progress at different rates, and "disequilibrium between the four developmental lines" could produce problems that would be labeled as indifference, indecision, unrealism, and inhibition.

Savickas (2011, 2012) also proposed a model of career counseling. In discussing the evolution of theories/approaches, Savickas (2011) described distinctions among the three types of interventions of vocational guidance, career education, and career counseling, which he linked to the historical progression of theoretical perspectives in vocational psychology. According to Savickas, *vocational guidance* focuses on scores and traits and is concerned about matching and occupational fit, such as through Holland's theory. *Career education* focuses on stages and tasks and is concerned with readiness and vocational development, such as through Super's theory. Savickas reserved the term *career counseling* for his own life design paradigm, with a focus on stories and themes and with designing work life via career construction theory.

Savickas's (2011) counseling model rests on a narrative approach to career counseling, in which counselors first engage clients in a *career story interview*. The career story interview consists of five questions that elicit clients' stories: The questions focus on a client's (1) role models, (2) favorite magazines or television shows, (3) favorite stories, (4) mottos, and (5) early recollections. Exploring these stories allows the counselor and client to glean information about, respectively, (1) self-concept, (2) preferred work environment, (3) how they might enact the self in the preferred work environment, (4) strategy for moving forward to the next step, and (5) metaphors for their "central preoccupation" or life theme (p. 62). Counselors then distill meaning from the career story interview and relate it to the reasons that clients have entered career counseling, and so helping clients understand and construct their stories and determine solutions.

Counseling for Work and Relationships (Richardson)

The second emerging framework was articulated by Richardson (1993, 1996, 2009, 2012) as a paradigm shift from the study of *career development* to a *study of work in people's lives*. She described how the study of careers became more about occupations than it did about an individual's sense of self and separated the aspect of self that is associated with occupational domain from other aspects of the self. With a focus on occupational alternatives, the aspect of self that is connected to vocation was now located outside of the self, in the structure of the occupational world. As Juntunen (2006) paraphrased Richardson's position, "by focusing on career as an activity that is external to the person (because it is regulated by the occupational structure), we negate the central role of work in human experience" (Juntunen, 2006, p. 345).

Richardson (2012) has addressed the intersections of work and relationships, most recently describing the four major social contexts of market work, personal care work, personal relationships, and market work relationships. *Market work* is akin to the traditional view of work, defined as the work that people do for pay; Richardson's definition also includes work that people do within educational institutions to prepare for paid work. *Personal care work* is work done in one's personal (non-paid work) life to care for oneself and others (including care for dependents, relationships, and communities). *Personal relationships* encompass interpersonal relationships outside of work, with family and friends, whereas *market work relationships* include relationships within the market work context, such as supervisors, colleagues, and teachers.

Richardson discussed the limits of traditional paradigms and perspectives about career choice. For example, the vocational choice paradigm initiated by Parsons and carried into person-environment fit models "masked the ways in which 'choice' was, in fact, very limited or even nonexistent" for some individuals, who did not have the luxury of choosing among jobs or vocational paths (Richardson, 2012, p. 195). A focus on *choice* thus "perpetuates a belief in free will, that the individual is the master of his or her fate, and that any problems or limitations are the fault of that individual" (p. 196). The career development paradigm, such as proposed by Super, kept choice as a central concept and added a "verticality" component by emphasizing the upward progression of careers over time. The concept of "boundaryless" careers (Arthur & Rousseau, 1996) further highlighted the aspect of choice by focusing on individuals' ability to define their own careers regardless of organizational structures. "What is being masked is not only lack of choice but also the deteriorating conditions of market work" (Richardson, 2012, p. 197).

The limits of the extant paradigms are what lead to paradigm shifts; Richardson (2012) argued for a paradigm shift that would reflect and be responsive to changes in the nature of peoples' lives and in the nature of work. Her view that career counseling "has become overidentified with and trapped in the occupational structure" (Richardson, 1996, p. 356) led her to propose that the label of "career counseling" be retired, and to suggest an alternative label of "counseling/ psychotherapy and work, jobs, and careers" (Richardson, 1996) or "counseling for work and relationship" (Richardson, 2009). She described two central shifts in thinking: a shift from "career" to "work," and a shift beyond the occupational domain to a broader consideration of multiple, interrelated social contexts (Richardson, 2009).

The complex intersection of work and nonwork roles in peoples' lives has received considerable research attention, including models of role spillover, role conflict, and role enhancement. However, most of this literature is influenced by the market work or industrial/organizational perspective, which may focus primarily on employers' perspectives and goals and overlook individuals' perspectives (Blustein, Medvide, & Kozan, 2012).

Psychology of Working (Blustein)

The psychology of working perspective, as described by Blustein (2006, 2008, 2011), represents a shift from the study of the psychology of *careers* to a psychology of *working*. "Career" has been defined as "the individually perceived sequence of attitudes and behaviors associated with work-related experiences and activities over the span of the person's life" (Hall, 1976, p. 4). As Blustein (2006, p. 3) noted, however, our concept of "career" is "deeply embedded in a sociocultural framework that is relevant to only a minority of individuals around the globe"—those characterized by status and achievement. A key feature of Blustein's perspective is an explicit recognition that not all individuals have choice or volition related to work and careers; in fact, there is considerable variability in individuals' experiences regarding volition, and poor and working-class individuals may experience little choice regarding their working lives (Blustein & Fouad, 2008; Liu & Ali, 2008). "Working" is thus a more universal and inclusive term than "career."

Blustein's (2006) perspective focused on three fundamental human needs that are potentially fulfilled by working: need for survival, need for relatedness, and need for self-determination. *Need for survival* is attained through work via the power gained through the exchange of work for money or for goods and services. Although this view of work is closely linked to the study of work by economists, Blustein (2006) argued that there are important psychological implications as well. Further, work as a means of fulfilling survival needs may also confer or enhance social status. Prestige, status, and power as functions of work, according to Blustein (2006), have been "woefully neglected in contemporary discussions of careers" (p. 22), although some scholars have included prestige in explaining occupational choice (such as Gottfredson, 2005).

The need for survival becomes increasingly evident in difficult economic times, as access to work becomes even more scarce and the impact of unemployment (and underemployment) on mental health becomes more pervasive (Paul & Moser, 2009; Goldsmith & Diette, 2012; Swanson, 2012). Richardson (2012) commented that the context of market work is one of radical change but also of "deteriorating conditions" (p. 193) such as erosion of wages, health insurance and pension benefits, increased income volatility and wage inequality, and poor labor conditions.

Work also provides a means of social connection that fulfills a *need for relatedness*, both in terms of a link to the "broader social milieu" and in development of interpersonal relationships (Blustein, 2006). Blustein (2011) further described the need-for-relatedness function of work in an expanded "relational theory of working." This model conceptualizes working as "an inherently relational act . . . which underscores that each decision, experience, and interaction with the working world is understood, influenced, and shaped by relationships" (p. 1). Based on this theory, Blustein outlined a series of research directions, including understanding the experiences of relationships and work, the role of relational support in choice and transitions, and the intersection of "care" or personal work and market work (Richardson, 1996, 2009; Schultheiss, 2006). Further, the changes in the structure of work, noted earlier, may change the availability and nature of interpersonal relationships (Juntunen & Even, 2012).

Finally, work provides a mechanism for addressing the *need for self-determination*. Deci and Ryan (Deci & Ryan, 1985; Ryan & Deci, 2000) have focused on self-determination as the process by which activities that are extrinsically motivating are internalized. Blustein (2006) noted that self-determination offers a broader perspective than existing literature on job satisfaction, which may not capture the experience of poor or working class individuals.

Summary of Emerging Theories

The "traditional" or foundational theories of vocational psychology and career development—represented by person-environment fit, developmental, and social cognitive perspectives—continue to provide useful predictions about vocational behavior as well as practical guidance to practitioners working with individuals seeking career assistance. However, it may be time to incorporate other perspectives, given economic and societal changes in the way that work is structured and experienced and growing recognition that there are many individuals for whom these theories are not explanatory. The emerging perspectives of Blustein, Savickas, and Richardson offer great promise and warrant additional consideration. Moreover, an important next step is to explore the extent to which concepts from the foundational theories may be retained and integrated with concepts from the emerging theories.

Future expansion and integration of foundational and emerging theories would benefit from explicit attention to the assumptions noted by Fouad (2007), described at the beginning of this chapter. Identification of these assumptions underlying 20th century notions of career development also leads to consideration of each assumption's converse—namely, the lack of volition in making work choices, the important connections of work to other arenas of individuals' lives, the unpredictability of the world of work, the multiple career- and work-related decisions an individual will make throughout life, and revisioning career counseling as broader and more integrative. These revised assumptions may guide theorists, researchers, and practitioners in adapting to 21st century realities of work.

APPLYING EMERGING APPROACHES

Because the three emerging approaches discussed in this chapter offer perspectives that differ considerably from one another, applying them to Leslie's career history and present situation varies as well. Career construction theory has the most to offer from a developmental and self-concept perspective, given its genesis in Super's theory. Counseling for work and relationships is most directly applicable to understanding the messages that Leslie received about the role of work in her life and her current desire to have children. The psychology of working perspective would help to understand Leslie's central purposes for work, whether, for example, Leslie needs work for survival, relational, and/or self-determination purposes.

Conceptualizing Leslie's Career History

Career construction theory

Career construction theory focuses on the subjective elements of Leslie's career history, through the process of self-construction. As a child and adolescent, Leslie began to build a story about herself as a teacher and helper. She internalized the message from her parents about the importance of achievement but did not develop a strong sense of how that achievement would be expressed in the world through occupational roles. In terms of the four dimensions of career adaptability, as an adolescent and young adult, Leslie seemed to have an appropriate level of *concern* about her career, including understanding the importance of making plans for the future. Regarding the second dimension of *control*, Leslie at times seemed to cede control to others, such as her family and boyfriend, which may have led to her indecision about career choices. Messages from her family may have increased her indecision, since they encouraged the lessened centrality of the occupational role in her life. Despite not totally mastering control, she did demonstrate *curiosity* about her career alternatives, as she developed interests and skills in mathematics. Finally, she demonstrated wavering levels of *confidence*, the fourth dimension, resulting in times when she has seemed stuck about how to move forward and unsure of her abilities.

Counseling for work and relationship

Adopting a framework of work and relationships focuses attention on the intersections of these two domains and provides additional context for Leslie's career history. Leslie's decisions about career were frequently made with clear reference to her current relationships and informed by expectations conveyed by her parents about the relative roles of work and family. Her initial decision to become a high school teacher was an effort to combine work and family. The dissatisfaction that she felt in her first teaching job was related to lack of social support, both in and out of the work environment (market work relationships and personal relationships, respectively, as described by Richardson).

Psychology of working

Leslie grew up in a position of privilege, in terms of her ability to pursue higher education (and the expectation that she would do so) and the level of apparent volition that she enjoyed (whether or not she took advantage of it). Her family has been relatively insulated from the negative effects of changing economic conditions, and so she had the good fortune of making early career decisions without the added layer of financial stress.

Leslie's perception and experience of *work*, then, did not begin with a focus on fulfilling her need for survival because there was always the implied message that her family would take care of her financially and the stated message that she would marry and depend on her spouse for financial support. Leslie's career exploration was influenced by fulfilling her need for relatedness: She wanted to gain others' approval for her choices, and it was important to her to choose a career in which she could help others and also have good work relationships. The need for self-determination may not have been a strong consideration in her early decisions.

Conceptualizing Leslie's Present Situation

Career construction theory

In terms of career construction theory, Leslie is now reconstructing her occupational story by reevaluating her previous choices and whether to continue or change direction. Revisiting the four dimensions of career adaptability, Leslie's decision to pursue career counseling demonstrates her *concern* about planning for the future and taking *control* over her future. She also seems to have a fair amount of *curiosity* and *confidence* about her options.

Counseling for work and relationship

Leslie's concerns about combining work and family are at the forefront given her expressed desire to have a child. Her relationship with Joe is also central to her current career issues, both in terms of his reactions to her career concerns and in terms of his thoughts about changing jobs. Use of this perspective highlights how the relational aspects of Leslie's life intersect with her work and career decisions.

Psychology of working

Shifting to a focus on the experience of *work* rather than *career* provides a different perspective of Leslie's current situation, particularly in relation to the nonwork aspects of her life. As an adult who has been financially self-sufficient for 10 years, Leslie is aware of but not overly concerned with the need for survival. Although some school districts in her city have cut back teaching staff, Leslie has sufficient seniority in her school to not feel threatened. However, need for survival is a concern if she were to quit her job to return to school, or if Joe experiences additional reductions in work hours. Need for relatedness continues to be an important motivating force in her life, through her work role and family roles. Further, need for self-determination may be more salient now than in the past, which could be viewed as an impetus for Leslie to enter career counseling: She is more attuned to who she is and whether or not work is fulfilling her sense of self.

QUESTIONS FOR DISCUSSION

1. What specific hypotheses would you develop about Leslie from the "psychology of working" approach? How does using this approach help you understand Leslie? How might it help Leslie understand herself?

2. What specific hypotheses would you develop about Leslie from the perspective of career construction theory? How does using this approach help you understand Leslie? How might it help Leslie understand herself?

3. What specific hypotheses would you develop about Leslie from a work and relationships approach? How does using this approach help you understand Leslie? How might it help Leslie understand herself?

4. How does Leslie feel about the prospect of making a decision, particularly of making a job or career change? How would she tell the story of her life? How might her previous experiences with career decision making influence the process or content of this current decision?

5. How will the relational component influence her career decisions?

6. What kind of life does Leslie seem to be envisioning, in terms of the integration of work and nonwork roles? How can she optimize her chance of achieving that life?

The Case of Diana and Bill

Diana and Bill, both White, are a dual-career couple in their mid-40s. Diana is a systems analyst within the communications industry; Bill is an actuary, most recently with an insurance company. They moved to a new state 18 months ago so that Diana could accept a major promotion within her company. They have been married 20 years and have two daughters in high school; the oldest daughter is currently in France on a year-long exchange program.

Bill sought counseling because he is having difficulty finding a new job since their move. For the first few months, he looked for a position similar to the one he'd just left, but he expanded his search when he was unable to find such a job. Before moving, Bill had been successful at his job but was beginning to experience some burnout. The vice president in his division was grooming him to take over a supervisory position, yet Bill had been feeling ambivalent about the promotion. He felt pressured by Diana to take the position, because it was accompanied by a hefty raise and more status within the organization. He felt some relief when Diana's company offered her the promotion and transfer to another state, because it took the pressure off of his decision; he also felt that the move might provide him with a new beginning.

Diana and Bill met as sophomores in college and married soon after graduation. They both wanted a family and thought they'd have a "traditional" marriage, where Bill would provide financially for the family and Diana would stay at home to raise the children. She initially worked as a computer programmer for a small company but quit her job after their first child was born.

Diana reentered the workforce 5 years ago after a 10-year hiatus for child rearing, and she has been very successful at her job. The position for which they recently moved represented a major move up the corporate ladder for Diana. Bill has been supportive of Diana's career and felt relieved that he was no longer the primary breadwinner. On the other hand, he is somewhat uncomfortable with her success because of their shifting roles: He was becoming less committed to his job and career as Diana was becoming more committed to hers. He became angry when his former coworkers made comments that Bill was quitting his job so he could be supported by his wife, and the vice president who wanted to promote him wrote him a weak letter of reference, questioning his drive and ability to achieve.

Neither Bill nor Diana were concerned when Bill did not find a job immediately after their move; he had decided not to spend much time looking until they actually moved and were settled into their new home, and he'd heard that it could take up to a year to find a suitable job given his years of experience. However, now that it's been 18 months, both Bill and Diana are becoming concerned about Bill's continued unemployment. Diana has found herself wondering why Bill hasn't found anything yet and is beginning to doubt that he is investing sufficient time and energy into the job search. She experiences occasional resentment about being the sole wage earner and the increasing financial pressure as their daughters get closer to pursuing college education. Bill vacillates between feeling confident that a satisfactory position will come along and feeling worried that his skills and experience are not good enough. The longer he has gone without a job, the more he has taken over household responsibilities, at Diana's urging.

QUESTIONS FOR DISCUSSION

1. How does Richardson's "work and relationship" approach help you understand the current situation that Diana and Bill are experiencing?

2. How might you help Bill deal with the changes that have occurred because of his inability to find a job?

3. What does the occupational role mean to Bill? How does it fit with his image of himself as a man, a husband, and a father?

4. How might you help Diana deal with the changes that have occurred because of Bill's unemployment?

5. What does the occupational role mean to Diana? How does it fit with her image of herself as a woman, a wife, and a mother?

DIRECTIONS AND IMPLICATIONS FOR CAREER COUNSELING

The three emerging approaches discussed in this chapter differ from one another in terms of an explicit focus on working with clients, and because the approaches are so new, suggestions for how a counselor would apply are less well developed. This is particularly true for Richardson's and Blustein's approaches; Savickas's (2012) approach has the most specific types of interventions, and so we will use career construction to discuss Leslie. The case of Diana and Bill will be discussed from the perspective of Richardson's approach.

Goals of Counseling

In career construction counseling, counselors "must help clients find a way to deal with what they feel they must" (p. 49). The counselor may ask "How can I be useful to you as you construct your career?" (Savickas, 2011, p. 49), and use the answer to this question to structure the initial intervention. The overall goal of counseling for work and relationships is to help "people construct lives" (Richardson, 2012, p. 223).

Interventions

The initial question ("How can I be useful as you construct your career?") would then lead to the life story interview, which consists of the five questions noted earlier. The counselor listens carefully to the client's answers to these questions and asks follow-up probes. The counselor then assesses the meaning within the client's answers and prepares to retell the client's story "in a manner that draws a sharp character sketch, highlights the career theme, and envisions scenarios that extend the occupational plot" (Savickas, 2011, p. 67).

Leslie reported that her early role models were her kindergarten teacher and her father. Leslie loved going to school in kindergarten and remembered thinking that her teacher was "magical" because she knew so many things. Her teacher helped Leslie solidify her reading skills, and she immersed herself in books. She perceived her father at that time as a very important person, because he left for work every morning dressed in a suit and carrying a briefcase. She always wondered what he did every day.

Leslie's current favorite television show is *CSI*, which she likes because they use scientific clues such as DNA to solve mysteries, and each case is wrapped up in a single episode. Her favorite stories growing up were about princesses living in castles and looking for princes to carry them away, and she admitted that she still liked the idea of living in a castle and having people wait on her. She couldn't readily come up with a motto but recalled hearing the Golden Rule ("do unto others as you would have them do unto you") frequently as she was growing up and indicated that she tried to follow that in her current life.

She reported several early recollections: (1) being excited when her baby sister came home from the hospital, but then getting annoyed by having a baby in the house; (2) waiting at the bus stop for her brother to come home from school but he didn't get off the bus because he stayed at school, and she ran to tell her mother because she was scared that something happened to him; (3) when she was in first grade, teaching her sister to read using her favorite books.

Using Savickas's approach, the counselor would use Leslie's answers to shape a discussion of her career theme. The counselor might focus on the theme of finding a balance between work and family, as revealed in Leslie's role models and early recollections, and of the degree to which Leslie views work as a way to contribute to others in the world. Leslie's answers also seem to reflect some ambivalence or mixed messages about gender expectations related to work, which are part of her current thinking about the role of career in her life.

Richardson describes a four-step counseling process from her approach that would help clients become more agentic. The first step is helping clients become more comfortable with their subjectivity. The counselor in this step would help Bill construct the stories of his life and help him become comfortable with those narratives. The counselor might also ask Bill to include Diana in the counseling process. The first step might then include helping them understand that each has a narrative of his or her own life, a narrative of the other's life, and then a narrative of their lives together. The counselor would help them clarify their subjective experiences about the role of work in their lives and in their marriage, also helping them uncover the differences in those perceptions.

The second step is to help them participate in reflexive processing, thinking back on those narratives and uncover the thoughts and feelings in actions they took. For example, how do Diana and Bill remember the decision to have a "traditional" marriage? How did Bill feel about having market work play such a prominent role in his life, while Diana was home focusing more on personal care work? Conversely, how did Diana feel about those times? And how are they feeling now as roles have reversed with Diana more focused on market work and Bill on personal care work?

The third step the counselor would take is to help Diana and Bill look at the actions they are taking, and see if these actions are in line with how they want to move forward. Diana is frustrated that Bill is not finding work and suspicious of his drive to move back into market work. Bill is taking on more personal care work but still trying to find market work. Is this the way they want to live their lives, both individually and together? What balance does each want between market and personal care work? What role do they want market work to play in their marriage?

Finally, the fourth step the counselor would take is to help challenge any social constraints that are limiting consideration of various options. Both Diana and Bill may be operating under embedded cultural expectations that men should be engaged full time in market work. The counselor might challenge them to critically examine these assumptions. Are Diana and Bill accepting Bill's former supervisor's evaluation of a weak drive to work? And if he is, how has that affected his subjective experience and subsequent actions? Does Bill value the opportunity to spend more time in personal care work, or is he feeling that this is not an appropriate role for men? The counselor would help both Diana and Bill evaluate these assumptions to determine which, if any, they want to discard, and which they want to keep. The counselor will encourage them to consider how they want to move forward, both in determining how they want to balance their market work and personal care work and how they want to balance those roles in their marriage.

ADDITIONAL CASES

Case 1: Lian

Lian is a 27-year-old woman from Taiwan. She has come to the United States for graduate school in psychology in the southern part of the United States. She graduated from National Taiwan University, one of the most prestigious, and most competitive, universities in Taiwan. She did very well in her undergraduate work and was strongly encouraged by her mentors to come to the United States for graduate work. She is nearing completion of her PhD in psychology and is seeking career counseling because she does not know if she should return to Taiwan or seek a university position in the United States.

Lian is the middle of three children. Her father is an accountant, and her mother helps take care of Lian's grandmother. Lian's older brother, Tai, is also studying in the United States and is nearing completion of a medical degree. He has at least 3 more years of medical training before he finishes. Her younger brother, Wei, will start an engineering graduate program in California in the fall. Lian's parents are very proud of their children, but they feel that it is time for their daughter to come home. Her mother needs help taking care of Lian's grandmother; her father has been recently diagnosed with diabetes and also needs more care.

Lian has done very well in her graduate work in experimental social psychology. She has been part of a very productive research team and has published several articles with her major professor. This past year, she helped him write a federal grant, and it included a postdoctoral fellowship. He has just offered it to her, providing her an opportunity to stay in the United States at least another year. The fellowship would also provide her the opportunity to conduct a systematic search for a university position. Lian is struggling with whether to take the fellowship or return home. She knows her mother needs her help, and it is her obligation as a daughter to go back to Taiwan. However, she enjoys her work very much, believes she is on the track to pursue an academic career in the United States, and knows she would not have the same opportunities in Taiwan. She also does not want to disappoint her adviser, who has helped her a lot. She has not talked to him about her dilemma, feeling guilty for not accepting the fellowship immediately.

QUESTIONS FOR DISCUSSION

1. What is the first thing you would focus on as the counselor?

2. What role may Lian's ethnic identity play in her decisions?

3. What cultural values may her family have transmitted to Lian?

4. What cultural variables would you want to incorporate in career counseling?

5. What additional work-nonwork concerns would you want to address?

6. What cultural strengths could you emphasize in working with Lian?

Case 2: Ellen

Ellen is a 50-year-old White woman who entered counseling at a women's center in her community. Her husband, Tim, recently filed for divorce after 27 years of marriage, and Ellen is feeling bewildered. They have three children—two sons aged 21 and 19, who are both in college, and a daughter aged 16.

Ellen and Tim met and married while in college—Ellen as a sophomore and Tim as a senior. Ellen quit school to take a secretarial job to support them while Tim went to graduate school in anthropology. He finished his PhD in 5 years and obtained a faculty position at a prestigious state university. Their oldest child was born during the first year of Tim's new job, and Ellen did not look for work outside of the home. When the youngest child went to elementary school, Ellen contemplated getting a job, but Tim's career was so demanding that she felt it was more important for her to focus her attention on the children and household responsibilities.

Ellen knew that Tim had seemed dissatisfied for the last few years, but his decision to ask for a divorce came as a shock to her. He told her that he wanted to leave the marriage because he was disappointed in how "traditional" their relationship was and that he wished she could be more like the professional women he dealt with daily at the university. Ellen reports feeling "betrayed," because he never expressed these concerns at any time earlier in their 27 years together. She feels that they had an unspoken arrangement in which she would take most of the responsibility for raising their children, entertaining his colleagues, and generally doing whatever was necessary to support Tim's career advancement. Yet now she feels that he is changing the rules and criticizing her for what she felt he wanted her to do.

In addition to her emotional distress about Tim's announcement, Ellen is also thinking about many practical details resulting from the divorce. Tim seems amenable to a fair financial settlement and is committed to providing for a college education for all three children. However, he has told Ellen that he doesn't intend to provide her with any financial support after their youngest daughter leaves home, and Ellen is feeling quite concerned about her future. Ellen will no longer be able to anticipate financial security at retirement, so at age 50, she would like to plan how she will use the next 15 years to prepare for her own retirement. Because she hasn't been in the workforce for 20 years, however, Ellen feels very unsure of what she could do to support herself. Ellen is thus entering counseling with a variety of pressing issues.

QUESTIONS FOR DISCUSSION

1. How would you conceptualize Ellen's current situation from each of the three perspectives discussed in this chapter?

2. Ellen may be feeling as if she has little control or choice about her options for the future. How might you help her understand this lack of choice? How might you help her regain a sense of control?

3. How might you work with Ellen regarding career planning? How could she identify work-related skills?

4. How might Ellen describe her own life story?

5. What specific interventions or techniques would you like to use with Ellen?

Case 3: Tony

Tony is a 19-year-old African American sophomore who came to the university counseling center because he is undecided about a major. He has considered physical education or restaurant management, although he does not know much about either of these majors or occupational fields. He states that he wants to make a lot of money and also wants a job where he is his own boss. What he'd really like to do is own and manage a nightclub, and he has thought about many of the details, such as the name and format of the club, the kind of manager he would be, and so on.

Tony is a first-generation college student, and he feels pressure from his parents to complete his bachelor's degree. College was not entirely what he expected, however, and he wishes he could quit and find a job in a nightclub. He wonders if getting a degree will help him anyway. Tony is engaged to a woman who is a junior majoring in marketing, and she is encouraging him to stay in school. They plan to get married after she graduates next year.

During counseling, you ask him about how he envisions his job or career fitting with the rest of his roles in life and use a guided imagery exercise to help Tony think about his lifestyle and his daily activities. When you ask him how working in a nightclub will fit with other aspects of his life, he talks about how it won't affect other aspects of his life because his friends will probably "hang out" with him at the nightclub. You then specifically ask about whether he wants to have children; Tony responds by saying that "Why does that matter? It will be my wife's job to take care of any kids."

QUESTIONS FOR DISCUSSION

1. How would you deal with your feelings and reactions to Tony's statements?

2. What is the first thing you would focus on as the counselor?

3. What techniques might you use to help Tony explore the various roles in his life? How might you convince Tony of the value of doing so?

4. What gender-role expectations might Tony be experiencing from his parents, particularly as an African American man?

5. What factors might be occurring between Tony and his fiancée? How might their careers and their relationship be conceptualized from each of the emerging theories in this chapter?

PART III: APPLICATIONS

Chapter 12

Ethics and Professional Issues Integrating Career Development in Different Settings

The previous chapters have focused on individual career counseling and the importance of a counselor's theoretical perspective in developing hypotheses. But career interventions are the focus of counselors' work in a number of settings other than individual counseling. And, as Whiston and Blustein (2013) have summarized, we know that career interventions are effective in helping individuals make career and work-related decisions, optimally starting in elementary school.

We noted in Chapter 1 that the growth in school counseling programs was fueled in large part by the 1958 National Defense Education Act's mandate for school professionals to help students develop an academic and career plan. This is still a core part of the work of schools counselors at all levels of education. At the K–12 level, the American School Counseling Association identified career development as one of three key areas for student development. Career counseling and career services are a large part of student services on college and university campuses as students need help deciding on a college major and choosing a career path. Communities, often with financial support from federal and state governments, have developed career centers to help dislocated or unemployed workers, to help veterans transition out of the military, or to help people with disabilities find meaningful work. In short, knowledge of career development and career exploration is critical for effective and ethical practice in a number of settings in addition to individual or group counseling.

It is useful to consider that some career interventions will focus on career exploration, helping clients gain an awareness of their interests, values and skills and explore various occupations that might be a good fit. Other career interventions will focus on helping individuals prepare for various transitions involving work, such as preparing for a job, finding a job, or managing career transitions. Because these interventions tend to differ across the lifespan, in this chapter we discuss ideal career interventions across the lifespan as identified by the National Career Development Association's (2011) policy on career development. The NCDA outlined career development relevant to six life stages: preschool, elementary school, grades 7–9, high school (grades 10–12), adults, and retired individuals. The policy is grounded in assumptions of the importance of work in people's lives, the belief that career development assistance is best delivered as a partnership among home, family, schools, and communities, that freedom of choice is a U.S. birthright (including to choose multiple jobs/occupations across the lifespan), that accurate information is vital, that helping individuals understand their own abilities is important, and that interests and values are a critical foundation of career development. The interventions outlined by NCDA represent the ideal delivery of career development interventions across a lifespan. However, circumstances rarely allow counselors the ability to deliver ideal career services. Thus, we also discuss challenges across a variety of professional settings. Finally, because professional challenges often become ethical dilemmas, we discuss ethical decision making and present ethical vignettes for career interventions in different settings.

CAREER INTERVENTIONS IN SCHOOLS

In school settings, career exploration is most often done by school counselors. The American School Counseling Association (2004) identified three key areas of student standards: academic development, career development, and personal/social

---

BOX 12.1 Personal Reflection

- What career guidance did I receive in high school? What did I learn about occupations and career decision making? Who provided that information and how effectively was it conveyed as a developmental process?
- What career assistance did I receive in college? Did I attend a career decision-making workshop or seek assistance from a career counselor?
- If I were designing an ideal career services center for a 4-year college, what would be included?

development. These key areas intersect considerably. For example, academic development includes being prepared academically for post-graduate transitions and career development includes identifying and implementing career goals. School counselors focus on career development activities, particularly at the high school level. High school counselors help adolescents manage the anxiety of an uncertain future after high school, navigate the process of choosing a major and college or postsecondary work setting, and understand the relationship between high school activities and grades and future opportunities. The American School Counselor Association's *National Standards for Students* includes three major career development standards:

1. Students will acquire the skills to investigate the world of work in relation to knowledge of self and to make informed career decisions.

   A. Develop career awareness (help learn more about oneself, about the world of work, and the importance of planning)
   B. Develop employment readiness (acquire employability skills, learn how to be an employee, understand changing work force)

2. Students will employ strategies to achieve future career goals with success and satisfaction.

   A. Acquire career information (acquire and apply decision making skills, understanding classification systems of career, learn how to explore occupations)
   B. Identify career goals (demonstrate awareness of preparation needed to achieve goals)

3. Students will understand the relationship between personal qualities, education, training, and the world of work.

   A. Acquire knowledge to achieve career goals (understand the relationship between educational preparation and success)
   B. Apply skills to achieve career goals (demonstrate how interests, values and skills relate to goals, learn to work with others)

The ASCA career development standards are intended to be the final outcome of a K–12 guidance curriculum, with many activities designed to build on one another as students progress through their education. As we noted in Chapter 1, career development interventions in schools are based on the developmental models outlined in Chapters 8 and 9. We discuss the recommended interventions at different educational levels, and it will become clear how interventions at the elementary level (exploring options), the middle school level (relating self to the world of work) and high school level (helping students make decisions) lead to the first ASCA student standard (Students will acquire the skills to investigate the world of work in relation to knowledge of self and to make informed career decisions). Readers are encouraged to visit the website for the American School Counselor Association for a variety of resources to help deliver age-appropriate career interventions.

Preschool and Elementary School Years

Children form initial ideas about occupations during the preschool years. The NCDA recommendations (2011) highlight the importance of home and family in helping children develop a wide view of occupations, especially the role of families in helping children develop nonstereotypic views of occupations. For example, parents can help counter the perceptions that only men can do some jobs by deliberately pointing out women who do the same work (or vice versa). School counselors in elementary schools, working with kindergarten teachers, can help reinforce this by designing activities to counter stereotyped views of occupations. An example might be to display posters of men and women working in nontraditional occupational roles, such as women police officers or male nurses.

During the elementary years, the critical developmental tasks related to career development are to help students begin to gain a sense of self (what do I like?) and to help them continue to explore career options. School counselors can work with teachers to help infuse career exploration into the curriculum, helping students, for example, to understand what biologists do as part of a science lesson. In addition to helping students understand the application of classroom lessons to career areas, the NCDA policy statement includes five types of activities that teachers, counselors and parents can help develop and deliver. The first is to make the classroom a workplace, to help students develop work values. Some teachers ask students to interview a parent or other adult to ask about workplace rules, and then lead a discussion for the class about how to adopt those rules for the class (a popular rule is being on time). The second type of activity is to teach and reinforce productive work habits, such as on-task behavior or respectful listening. While these are often classroom management goals, explicitly linking them to the workplace helps students develop good work habits. The third type of activity is to use community resource individuals (including parents) to present many types of occupations to students. This may, for example, be part of a panel or a career day. It is important, though, that students are accountable for the information in some way (e.g., developing a brief report on questions raised in the panel or career day). Finally, the fifth and sixth types of activities are to ensure general career awareness rather than expecting students to choose specific occupations and to continue countering occupational biases and stereotypes.

Middle and High School Years

NCDA (2011) recommends that, moving into the middle school years, career development interventions increasingly focus on self-understanding and on helping students realize the relationship between self and the world of work. Career exploration tools can be very useful if they are used for broad exploration because, again, the policy statement strongly advises against pushing students to make a specific occupational choice. Rather, school counselors and teachers can help students find volunteer activities that help students develop good work habits and gain a better understanding of their work values. The policy statement also recommends that activities promote readiness for high school activities. This might include asking students to complete an online self-guided career exploration tool, such as the O*Net Interest Profiler, and to seek shadowing opportunities with current high school students or find out about volunteer activities in a related field.

At the high school level, NCDA (2011) recommends that school counselors help students make good decisions about preparation for post-secondary plans. This includes helping students make decisions that will prevent prematurely foreclosing on options. A prime example of helping students to prevent foreclosing on options is encouraging them to take math classes, because math is a filter for many higher education majors. NCDA also encourages school counselors to engage in specific activities for students transitioning immediately into the workforce after high school, for those transitioning to a technical or community college, and for those transitioning to a college or university.

School counselors are encouraged to work with those seeking to enter the workforce after high school to help them develop strong work habits and to help them identify job preparation programs. School counselors are encouraged to work with community and business partners to provide work study, cooperative education programs or other industry apprenticeships. NCDA policy also encourages school counselors to provide assistance to students so they know their many options and know how to make work-related decisions, under the assumption that they may make many work changes in their lives. It is a strong NCDA policy that students have multiple occupational choices rather than just one choice: "No person should be faced with only one available route, and thus, no real freedom of choice" (p. 4). For example, if a student is determined to enter an apprenticeship program after high school, it is important for that student to also be aware of additional educational alternatives to the apprenticeship program.

School counselors working with students seeking vocational or technical education are encouraged to work with employers to help students acquire employability skills and technical training (NCDA, 2011). These may include apprenticeships, tech-prep programs, technical training in community colleges or vocational training institutions. It is important for counselors to be knowledgeable about these institutions so they can help students make informed decisions. Counselors should help students consider all possible options to help them meet their goals (not just one type of schooling). This requires counselors to develop extensive knowledge of educational and training opportunities in their region, but the NCDA policy statement also recommends that colleges and training institutions reach out and inform school counselors about their programming.

NCDA (2011) recommends that career counseling be provided for all students considering a 4-year college or university. They note that many students are anxious about making a college major choice, yet many will change that choice once they enter college. Thus it is important for them to learn *how* to make a decision, not just make a one-time choice. It is important for counselors to help students learn how to apply for college and financial aid and to help them consider factors in choosing a college, particularly those students whose parents have not gone to college. Counselors should discuss work values as a critical part of decision making. Finally, career counselors working with college-bound youth are encouraged to help them view college, itself, as helping them develop employability skills.

CAREER INTERVENTIONS IN HIGHER EDUCATION

Career interventions in higher education can range from dedicated career counseling services (either in a career development center or in a university counseling center), to career interventions provided by advisors, faculty, and student services personnel. In general, college students may need help making decisions (What should I major in? What should I do after college? Should I work or go to law school first?), managing the anxiety of indecision or indecisiveness, and planning their next steps. Depending on the specific institution, college career counselors help students who enter college as "undecided" about their major or wish to change their major and assist students in exploring various options and building decision-making skills. College career counselors also help students transition to settings after college, such as work, internships, or further schooling. In some institutions, these concerns are addressed by the college or university counseling center and a separate career center helps students with job placement skills.

The National Association of Colleges and Employers (2013) has developed a set of professional competencies required for career services practitioners. The eight competencies are very comprehensive and range from counseling to management and teaching. Not every career service center will expect that each practitioner will be competent in all areas, but a review of the areas may help illustrate the breadth of career interventions on a college or university campus.

1. Counseling, including the types of competencies we have addressed in the chapters in this book: counseling, assessment, use of occupational information, and delivering individual and group interventions.

2. "Brokering, connecting and linking," encompassing the many facets of consulting with constituent groups interested in career services. This includes reaching out to students, alumni, faculty, employers, the community, parents and advisory boards. This competency dovetails with the NCDA (2011) recommendations that college and university counselors help students identify and secure job and experiential learning opportunities.

3. Information management, helping manage the wealth of information on occupations and career exploration, as well as job placement web services.

4. Marketing and promoting the career services office, including raising funds, public speaking, and sales skills, but also helping identify needs and setting goals for marketing purposes.

5. Program and event planning and administration (including budgeting and time management).

6. Research and evaluation of effective programs.

7. Teaching and training.

8. Management.

Clearly, the role of the college or university career counselor will depend on the individual mission of the institution. Some universities or colleges place a special emphasis on the placement rates of their students, others focus on ensuring all students have a major before they start college, others make an explicit goal to link career services to retention efforts. Still others have a particular concern about first-generation college students or students of color. The institution's specific mission will help define the range of services in a college or university. Regardless of where it occurs, though, it is critical that universities and colleges have two sorts of services. First, they need some unit on campus designated to help students with career concerns. These can range from help with choosing a major to anxieties related to indecision. And, as we note in Chapter 14, often career issues are related to other issues. Second, because it is impractical to provide individual services to each student in the institution, a unit on campus needs to develop classes and workshops to help larger groups of students learn about career decision making. Students may also need to identify job preparation opportunities, may need help with job seeking skills, and may need help with employability skills related to transitioning after college.

CAREER INTERVENTIONS IN COMMUNITY SETTINGS

Finally, the NCDA (2011) recommendations on career interventions for adults lay out a very bold vision for a Community Career Development Center, funded by both public and private sectors, as well as with fees paid by clients. The Center could provide career assessments, have career and occupational information available, with an emphasis on local information, and provide career counseling, career training, job search assistance, and job placement. In short, NCDA's vision is an updated version of what Parsons provided to adolescent boys in Boston in the early part of the 20th century.

The NCDA (2011) recommendations identify five specific types of clients particularly in need of Career Development Center services: recent high school leavers in need of help find immediate employment, adults who have lost a job involuntarily, couples seeking dual careers or employment, individuals who have been discriminated against, and those in career transitions.

Specific career interventions are identified for each of the five groups. Counselors working with high school leavers are encouraged to provide information to help young adults find meaning through volunteer and leisure work and to encourage them to rethink continuing with their education. Displaced adults are viewed as needing comprehensive career services, including career awareness, exploration, planning, decision making and job placement (and career adjustment if need be). The comprehensiveness of the needs of displaced workers, who have involuntarily lost a job, led NCDA to advocate for highly qualified career counselors to do this work.

The NCDA described three different types of dual earner couples, each with different needs. Dual career couples, with both partners placing high priority on their careers, need career counseling with both partners attending to paid and unpaid work. Dual earner couples, where neither partner has a high value on work, can be helped to find greater meaning in work for both partners as well as meaning found in volunteer work. Finally, for the one career/one earner couples, counselors are encouraged to help the career partner find meaningful work and the earner to find meaningful activities outside of work.

NCDA recommends that career interventions target activities "aimed at providing full equity of career development opportunities to ALL persons at ALL age levels" (2011, p. 6). They suggest that this occur not only during K–12 schooling but that efforts toward helping individuals find meaningful work and helping counter biases and stereotyping are also community efforts. NCDA also recommends that Career Development Centers provide services to support individuals seeking to advance in their careers or who want to change occupations. The recommendation of comprehensive services for dislocated workers applies to all adults who could benefit from career counseling.

The NCDA recommendations (2011) also extend to retired persons, targeting services to those who need to continue to work (or to seek work again) as a result of financial need, as well as those who find they are most happy when they work. This could include helping retirees find part-time work, or even short-term work, for the former and volunteer activities or unpaid work for the latter.

The Career Development Center proposed by the NCDA (2011) policy statement could also serve as a source of career interventions for a number of other clients. There has been a growing advocacy for career services for offenders who have recently been released from prison, with proponents arguing that good career planning can help prevent recidivism (Varghese, 2013). Scholars have also encouraged communities to provide career interventions in domestic violence centers, viewing this as a way for women to have the economic freedom to leave a violent partner (Chronister, Harley, Aranda, Barr, & Luginbuhl, 2012; Davidson, Nitzel, Duke, Baker, & Bovaird, 2012). The center could also be a site for work exploration and job training for individuals preparing to move from welfare support to work (Juntunen et al., 2006). Finally, the Career Development Center could serve as a source of support for military veterans returning to civilian life. There have been considerable efforts on the part of the federal government to provide information to help veterans learn about civilian jobs, but researchers have found that career counseling can help veterans deal with the myriad issues related to returning from one or more military deployments (Robertson, 2013).

Two additional community settings provide career services. The first is rehabilitation services, which may be publicly funded (through the Division of Vocational Rehabilitation) or may be part of private rehabilitation counseling. Appropriate job placement is often the outcome of rehabilitation counselors, and career counseling is part of that process. The Theory of Work Adjustment, described in Chapter 7, was developed as result of Dawis and Lofquist's work with the Minnesota Division of Vocational Rehabilitation, and their focus was to help identify additional satisfying occupations for individuals who, because of a disability, could no longer continue with their previous work. The second community setting is represented by the private practitioner, who specializes in career counseling, for a wide array of clients. He or she may work with adolescents making initial career choices or increasingly, with individuals in mid-career who are facing a transition and want help with that process.

Finally, many organizations have counselors to help individuals make career decisions within the organization. Large companies may help individuals choose various options, such as ways to advance within the company or how to be involved in other areas of the company (e.g., choosing to work overseas or on another product line).

PROFESSIONAL CHALLENGES

Individuals may thus provide career counseling as part of their work in a K–12 school, in a college career center, in private practice, or as part of an organization. Although each setting has unique professional and ethical challenges there are a number of similarities in professional challenges for counselors providing career services. These include finding enough resources to provide effective services (Schenck, Anctil, Smith, & Dahir, 2012), highlighting the importance of career interventions to help individuals' well-being (Whiston, Fouad, & Juntunen, 2013), multiple demands on career counselors within schools and colleges (Schenck et al., 2012), reimbursement policies only for certain diagnosable disorders (Fouad & Jackson, 2013), federal educational policies and legislation that influence priorities in schools (Schenck et al., 2012), and the perception that anyone who wants to help can become a career coach (Fouad & Jackson, 2013).

We noted at the beginning of the chapter that the practices we would outline were "best practices" and that often, practitioners have to cope with circumstances that do not allow them the time, resources, or support to provide those best practices. Schenck et al. (2012), writing about the role of career guidance and counseling in school settings, eloquently describe the frustrations that counselors face in implementing the ASCA standards. Career development is one of the three ASCA standards, along with academic achievement and personal/social development. The three are intended to be equal in importance, and indeed, they are intertwined: Students who have a good sense of a career plan and trajectory are more likely to achieve and feel better about themselves. But recent federal legislation of the No Child Left Behind Act and the movement toward evaluating teachers (and entire schools) on student performance has shifted much of the focus and resources to academic achievement, reducing time and energy for career exploration and development. Teachers are also less willing to give up class time for nonacademic activities, reducing the collaborative nature of career exploration linked to curricular activities. This brings into conflict what counselors know about effective practice, the focus on the well-being of the student, their own competent practice and their ethical obligations to be part of an interdisciplinary team.

Resource limitations also are a concern for college and university career counselors. Some universities are turning to employers for help funding career centers, which at times may create a conflict of interest. Universities that emphasize the placement rates of their students may put more resources into placement activities, reducing time and support for career interventions (such as classes and workshops) and career counseling. Technology and increased sources of Internet-based information can be a wonderful adjunct to career counselors in universities and colleges, but do not replace counseling (Niles & Harris-Bowlsbey, 2009). Yet, in times of restricted funding for universities, many universities are cutting student support services, including career offices. Career counselors in university and college settings have a primary obligation for the well-being of their clients and more broadly the career development of the overall student body. But they also have obligations to their employers and an obligation to inform their employers when they are aware of negative conditions.

A related professional challenge is the need to emphasize (and sometimes convince others) of the importance of work in people's lives. In an economic downturn and reduced funding for educational services, career counselors have to be advocates for the important preventive role that career counseling plays. But, often, career services are not as valued as other types of counseling services. As we point out in Chapter 14, part of the perception that there are different types of counseling has grown from different historical evolutions. And certainly, policy statements such as the Guidelines to Integrate Work into Psychotherapeutic Practices (Whiston, Fouad, & Juntunen, 2013) and the NCDA policy statement on career development help bolster the importance of career counseling. But arguments from the field notwithstanding, it continues to be a professional challenge to demonstrate and document that work is a very important part of people's lives.

This challenge is demonstrated when third-party insurers often will not reimburse practitioners for career counseling services because they do not stem from a diagnosable mental disorder, perpetuating the perception that work concerns are not related to mental health. Ironically, though, the field is also challenged by the perception that anyone can be a career coach with limited training. Fouad and Jackson (2013) point out, "If we do not do it, others will and are, but without good knowledge and training" (p. 314), arguing for vocational psychologists and career counselors to do a better job of marketing their specialized skills and training. The challenge is to ethically treat clients, provide informed consent, and explain the potential limits of reimbursement policies to clients at the beginning of counseling services.

We have talked a great deal about the competencies needed to be an effective career counselor or career services professional. Another professional challenge is to continue to maintain high levels of competence in a very fast changing field. We have highlighted the many changes in the world of work, and the challenge for career professionals is to understand the changes enough to help people make decisions in a world that is rapidly changing. This means keeping up with technological changes, globalization, shifting job and occupational roles and responsibilities, as well as local and national labor projections. It also means understanding the changes within organizations and the workplace. And those technological changes bring challenges of their own to career counselors, who increasingly may be providing counseling via the Internet.

A final set of professional challenges affect career counselors in private practice and college and university settings. In many cases, a client will be referred to a career counselor for help with career issues by another therapist. Thus, the client is seeing two counselors. The NCDA Ethics Code B.3 (2007) notes that it is critical that each counselor discuss the limits of their work with the client, ask the client for a release to talk with each other, if appropriate, and make sure the client is not confused or subject to conflict. This becomes more a different sort of challenge if both counselors are in a university setting, where each office has different structural limits, such as different number of sessions a client may be seen or different methods of processing paperwork for clients. Again, the important concern is to ensure the needs of the client are met and to eliminate confusion or conflict.

ETHICAL DECISION MAKING

Many of the professional challenges above point out that career counselors often are challenged by competing ethical mandates, leading them to engage in ethical decision making. Ethical decision making occurs when a counselor is faced with an ethical dilemma, defined as a situation in which there may be conflicting ethical mandates (i.e., professional codes differ), conflicting moral values, or standards may not easily be applied (Cottone & Tarvydas, 2007). Career counselors face ethical dilemmas inherent to all mental health professionals. For example, counselors are responsible for safeguarding clients' welfare and for ensuring that information shared by the client is kept confidential. But sometimes, guarding the welfare of the client means that someone else may be harmed. In that situation, the counselor faces an ethical dilemma and must decide how to act to resolve the dilemma. At other times, career counselors need to become advocates for their clients, putting their clients' welfare in direct contradiction to the interests of their own employers. Consider how to resolve a situation in a college career center where a student majoring in French is being sexually harassed by her professor and wants to change majors. Ethically, the counselor cannot tell the professor to stop harassing the student without revealing her name, but it is equally important to stop the professor from harassing other students and allowing the client to continue as a French major. The counselor needs to make a decision safeguarding all interests as much as possible.

There are many ethical decision-making models, but we highlight Welfel's (2013) 10-step model. Step 1 is becoming sensitive to potential ethical conflicts and the moral aspects of professional practice. Welfel argues that counselors have many demands on their time, and that "a shift in one's mental set about ethics is needed . . . [and] practitioners need to recognize the commonness, complexities and subtleties of ethical dilemmas" (p. 33). In the above example, a busy counselor could view the client's decision as a request to change majors and automatically approve it without delving further. Welfel argues that counselors need to be attuned to ethical concerns. Step 2 is examining relevant external facts, including the cultural context. How does the student's culture influence her perception and reaction to sexual harassment? Has she taken other steps to address the problem with the professor or university? Step 3 is defining the central issues in the dilemma and available options. In the situation above, the dilemma is protecting the confidentiality of the student versus ensuring other students are not harmed. It may also be ensuring that the student herself is not prevented from her goal by the act of the professor. Step 4 is consulting professional standards and ethical codes, such as the NCDA *Code of Ethics* (2007) in Appendix B. Section B of the *Code* focuses on confidentiality, privileged communication, and privacy, noting that career professionals respect clients rights and "do not share confidential information without client consent or without sound legal or ethical justification" (§ B.1.c.). However, section B.2 concerns exceptions: B.2.a., Danger and Legal Requirements, indicates that confidentiality "does not apply when disclosure is required to protect clients or identified others from serious and foreseeable harm." In this case, what is serious and foreseeable harm? Welfel's (2013) next step (Step 5) includes examining relevant literature (e.g., Cottone & Tarvydas, 2007; Welfel, 2013) and laws. In this example, the counselor needs to be aware of state laws governing confidentiality and the university's policies around sexual harassment.

Step 6 involves considering which of the five principles of moral behavior are involved. Counselors' decisions on how to resolve ethical dilemmas revolve around their professional and moral judgment of ethical behavior and their balance of ethical principles. The ACA, the NCDA, and the APA focus on five major ethical principles. The first is respect for autonomy and individuals' freedom to make their own decisions regarding their welfare. The second is nonmaleficence—that is, not to take any actions that would harm clients. The third is to do beneficence, meaning to do good by helping clients or the greater society. The fourth principle is justice and fairness. And the fifth is fidelity and honesty, or to keep promises made. The counselor in the dilemma above faces a conflict between fidelity to the client by keeping the promise of confidentiality and not doing harm to the client versus doing good for the greater society. In Step 7, counselors consult with colleagues and supervisors, and in Step 8, they decide what actions to take. In Step 9, counselors inform others, including the client, and in Step 10, counselors reflect on the experience.

As is clear from this example, ethical decision making is most difficult when ethical mandates compete or counselors need to decide on an action when major principles may conflict. Consider the vignettes in Box 12.2, which demonstrate the ethical challenges that may occur for career counselors in various settings. Readers are encouraged to consult the NCDA *Code of Ethics* (2007) in Appendix B as they consider each vignette.

Ethical Vignette #1, in a high school setting, may be a conflict between the welfare of many students versus two specific students. It may also be considered a conflict involving the informed consent for two students, the consideration of the validity of the instrument for two students, or multicultural issues in assessment. Counselors may feel that justice conflicts with doing no harm in this situation.

Ethical Vignette #2 takes place in a college setting. The ethical dilemma also involves cultural sensitivity to the client's relationship with her father, but this vignette involves an adult who has the right to refuse to release the information, including to her father. This vignette also highlights the importance of client welfare and the appropriate use of assessment tools. Counselors may feel a conflict between a client's right to autonomy and helping the client (doing good).

Ethical Vignette #3 occurs in an organizational setting, calling into question identification of the client. This case also highlights ethical concerns with confidentiality, informed consent, and the multiple relationships between the counselor and colleagues, as well as between the supervisor and employee. Counselors may feel a conflict between a promise made to the supervisor, doing good for the company, and doing no harm to society (via the patients' tissue analyses).

Finally, the fourth vignette takes place in a private practice. Ethical conflicts in this vignette also include the appropriate use of assessment and release of information, but in this case, assessment may be very helpful to provide some information to the client. However, the counselor appears to have urged the client to take an assessment tool, calling into question whose needs are met by the assessment: Is it the client's need for information or the counselor's need for guidance on how to move the client forward? The counselor may be dealing with the conflicts between principles of doing good and fidelity to promises made to the referring therapist.

In summary, while it is critical to consider the purposes of testing, the characteristics of tests, and the settings and conditions of testing, as well as to be competent to administer and interpret tests (AAC, 2003a), it is even more critical to consider the responsible use of tests in career counseling.

BOX 12.2 Ethical Vignettes

VIGNETTE #1

You are a career counselor in a large public high school. You are asked to conduct a week-long unit on career decision making for students in the AP English classes. Your plan is to have two classes on self-exploration, giving students an interest inventory and an ability checklist. Two classes will focus on world-of-work information and college exploration, and the final class will be on decision making. Two African American students refuse to take the interest inventory because they will base their future choices on how to be a credit to their race, not on their interests.

1. What would you do in this situation?
2. On which ethical codes and professional standards would you base your decision
3. Are you obligated to ensure that all students receive the same curriculum in the class, or can you release the two students from taking the interest inventory?
4. What is a multiculturally appropriate response to the two African American students? What is a multiculturally appropriate response to the rest of the class?

VIGNETTE #2

You are a career counselor in a community college. A 35-year-old Latina woman comes to you for counseling because she is considering returning to school. She had been taking care of her mother for several years, but her mother passed away three months ago. Her father is encouraging her to become a nurse. Her father is very supportive of her seeking counseling and brings her to each session. He is encouraging you to "give her the test that tells her what to do." He sits outside the door of the counseling session, waiting for her. He says he is there to protect her. He would like to see the results of the assessment tools to ensure she is making the right decision.

1. What would you do in this situation?
2. On which ethical codes and professional standards would you base your decision?

(Continued)

(Continued)

3. Would interacting with the father violate your client's confidentiality?

4. Would you consider inviting the father into the career counseling with his daughter? What steps would you need to take if you were to do that?

5. Your client feels a very strong obligation to family. Do you have an obligation to include her father in career counseling?

VIGNETTE #3

You are a career counselor in a large company. You are asked by a supervisor at a pathology laboratory to see an employee who works in the lab. Helen, the supervisor, is concerned that the employee has very good skills and is able to provide some guidance to the pathologists. However, she has been very frustrated that he does not follow her rules about the chain of command and continues to believe he can provide diagnoses on his own. She notes that he does not have a medical degree; he is a bachelor's-trained biological technician. She is not only frustrated but deeply worried that his independent work will lead to an erroneous diagnosis, with concomitant legal and ethical issues. She wants you to support her perceptions.

1. What would you do in this situation?

2. On which ethical codes and professional standards would you base your decision?

3. Who is your client—the supervisor or the employee?

4. You have information that the employee is less than satisfactory. Would you inform him of this?

5. Do you have any ethical obligations to the patients whose tissues are being analyzed by the technician?

VIGNETTE #4

You are a career counselor in private practice. A 25-year-old client is referred by her therapist because she is very indecisive about her career, and her indecision is impeding the other aspects of her therapy. She tells you she is just waiting for God to tell her what to do. She is resistant to taking any assessment tools but finally agrees to take an interest inventory if she can pray beforehand to discern what her interests are.

1. What would you do in this situation?

2. On which ethical codes and professional standards would you base your decision?

3. Would you help the client discern what she is called to do?

4. At what point would you decide that her indecision is dysfunctional?

5. What are your ethical obligations to the referring therapist?

Chapter 13

Information About the World of Work

The basis for Parsons's (1909) original tripartite model of career counseling, which we discussed in Chapter 1, was knowledge of self, knowledge of the world of work, and what he called "true reasoning on the relations of these two groups of facts'" (p. 5). Much of the previous chapters in this book have focused on different theoretical approaches to helping clients gain knowledge of self and understanding the ways they can use that knowledge to make decisions. We turn now to the second part of Parsons's model, world-of-work information, including where to find such information: how it is organized, how to evaluate world-of-work information, and most critically how to use that information in career counseling.

Parsons (1909) delineated world-of-work information as "knowledge of the requirements and conditions of success, advantages and disadvantages, compensation, opportunities and prospects in different lines of work" (p. 5). Parsons created a table of 200 occupations that employed men and 200 occupations that employed women in the Boston area, which he distributed to clients. One of his recommendations for counselors was to know the industries and employers in the area. Fortunately, today's counselors are able to rely on a number of national databases and sources that have compiled a large amount of information about occupations across the country as well as in other countries.

Clients clearly need information to make good decisions, and they need to know what various occupations entail, their compensation and opportunities for advancement. Consider the following vignettes:

- Isabella is a 16-year-old high school student who has no idea what major she wants to declare in college.
- Anh is a college senior who is majoring in English and French but does not know what to do with those majors.
- Matthew is a 28-year-old military veteran, returning from Afghanistan, who is not sure what civilian options would match his military training as a tank crew specialist.

All these individuals would benefit from learning more about occupations and the world of work. And, as Gore, Leuwerke, and Kelly (2013) point out, occupational information is widely available on the Internet with the result that sometimes there is too much information to digest and use effectively. Clients may be overwhelmed with the amount of information available, uncertain how to use that information, and more problematic, sometimes the information is inaccurate. Counselors can help clients make sense of the information available. They can also use occupational information sources to help clients explore possible occupational choices. Gore et al. (2013) provide an in-depth examination of the structure and sources of occupational information, and interested readers are referred to their chapter. We use their framework in this chapter and first discuss the various ways occupations are classified, sources of occupational information and how to use occupational information in counseling.

CLASSIFICATION SYSTEMS

Occupational classification systems are used for two purposes: to organize occupations into meaningful categories and to help promote career exploration. We have already discussed the basis for a classification system that uses Holland's theory in Chapter 6. For example, the Strong Interest Inventory (Appendix A) profile is organized by Holland themes. The organization of the occupational scales by Holland themes also allows users to examine related occupations. A student who is interested in chemistry (Investigative-Realistic) as an occupation might also consider work as a physicist, biologist, geologist, or software developer. Gottfredson and Holland (1996) developed the *Dictionary of Holland Occupational Codes*, categorizing thousands of occupations by Holland codes and level of complexity, which is the level of preparation and skill needed to do the occupation. Thus, the student with Investigative and Realistic interests could explore some 300 IR options and over 1000 RI options, narrowing the options further by using a higher complexity cutoff (e.g., only considering jobs with complexity above 65). In this narrower group of occupations, the student might also consider engineering (RI, complexity code 76) as well as veterinarian (IR, complexity code 73).

The most recent classification used by the Department of Labor is the Standard Occupational Classification System (SOC). The SOC was revised in 2010 (Emmel & Cosca, 2010) to have a unified classification system for all federal agencies. The SOC classifies all paid occupations using a six-digit code. The first two digits are the major group, next two are the minor group, the fifth digit is the broad occupation and the last digit is the detailed occupation. There are 23 major groups, 97 minor groups and 461 broad occupations. The SOC code for career counselors is 21–1012.00, indicating it is in the Community and Social Services Occupations major group, in the minor group of educational, guidance, school, and vocational counselors minor group.

Classification systems of occupations can be helpful to counselors wanting to encourage clients to explore options. The structure provided by one of the classification systems discussed above is helpful to clients who are overwhelmed by the wealth of information available on various occupations. It can be very useful to help clients who are stuck in considering just a few options. Guiding them through an O*Net search may help them see there are a number of additional occupations for them to consider. Finally, the classification system helps provide additional similar options for clients who may, for some reason, not be able to implement their first choice. This latter situation may include a client with a disability that does not allow them to continue in their previous employment, or someone who is unable to complete the educational requirements of their first occupational choice.

SOURCES OF OCCUPATIONAL INFORMATION

In the past, career counselors had a thick bound copy of the *Dictionary of Occupational Titles* on their bookshelf, because it was a source of occupational information for clients to learn more about the specifics of an occupation. Now counselors help clients find that information online. Several websites help clients and counselors learn more about various occupations, as well as how to prepare to enter an occupation and related occupations.

The Bureau of Labor Statistics publishes a yearly updated *Occupational Outlook Handbook* (OOH), available at www.bls.gov/ooh/home.htm. The OOH is also available in Spanish on the website. The Bureau of Labor Statistics also publishes projections of occupations (the current projections are through 2020).

The OOH has 25 categories of occupations (slightly different than the 23 in the SOC). Each category includes a number of occupations, with a summary chart of the median pay, entry level education, required work experience, required on-the-job training, job outlook, and employment projections. In addition, similar occupations are provided and additional resources are available. Users are also able to delve more deeply into each occupation, learning more about the duties, work environment, preparation, job outlook and similar occupations.

The OOH also provides a link to O*Net, which provides a number of additional characteristics about occupations, including abilities, interests and values of the workers in that occupations. It also identifies requirements needed for an occupation, such as education, knowledge and skills, training and licensure, and provides a listing of the tasks and duties of the job. An additional advantage to O*Net is all the labor market information embedded in the occupational profile, including current and projected employment, educational requirements, compensation and work context. In fact, O*Net includes all the types of information Parsons recommended in 1909. In addition, as we noted in Chapter 3, the O*Net also includes free career exploration tools such as the Interest Profiler and the Work Importance Profiler.

O*Net may be entered in a variety of ways via the main website: http://www.onetonline.org/. Users may explore occupations using certain criteria, such as occupations that are fast growing, that are in sectors of the economy labeled "green" (or environmentally focused), or by Science, Technology, Engineering or Math (STEM) discipline. Searches could also focus on more traditional categories, such as job family (e.g., healthcare, architecture and engineering), level of preparation needed (from none to extensive), or by career cluster (e.g., architecture, finance, helping professions). Users may also probe more deeply to search by specific skills, abilities, interests, or values. Finally, users may connect to additional databases, such as apprenticeships, military branches or instructional program codes.

BOX 13.1 Personal Reflection

- Answer the question: What two (or more) occupations have I considered? Enter these occupations into O*Net (www.onetonline.org). What are the similarities between the two occupations in terms of interests or work requirements? What are the employment projections for the two occupations?
- Did I consider information about employment projections or compensation in my decision to enter my current occupation?

A review of the Summary Report reprinted in Appendix C shows the wealth of occupational information available on O*Net. This summary report for mental health counselors shows that in 2012, the job outlook is bright, a master's degree is needed, it is projected to grow as an occupation, and the Holland code for the occupation is SIA. The summary report also shows that adaptability and self-control are needed, and that work values of relationships, achievement, and independence are rewarded in this job. Readers are encouraged to visit the O*Net website to see the most up-to-date information for their occupational choice.

The Summary Report also allows users to go directly to the Career One Stop website to get more local information by state and compares that local information with the national trends. Career One Stop (www.careeronestop.org) is sponsored by the Department of Labor (which also houses the Bureau of Labor Statistics) and is essentially an online career exploration and job service website. The assessment section of this website is linked to the O*Net database.

O*Net can be accessed directly online through the O*Net website, but O*Net is also a database of occupational information used in a number of other websites. A more user-friendly federal website is available at www.mynextmove.org. Additionally, several states have developed their own websites using the O*Net database.

HOW TO USE OCCUPATIONAL INFORMATION IN COUNSELING

Evaluation of Information

It is clear from Appendix C that a wealth of occupational information is available, and the Department of Labor has spent considerable time and effort to ensure that the data are accurate and comprehensive. And, indeed, the first key concern in using occupational information is to ensure it is accurate. However, many clients will find occupational information on a variety of different websites, and counselors need to know how to evaluate that information.

The National Career Development Association has developed a set of guidelines to help counselors evaluate career and occupational information (NCDA, 2013). One critical recommendation is that the information must be current, accurate and "free from distortion caused by self-serving bias, sex-stereotyping, or dated resources" (p. 2). They recommend that the intended audience be clearly identified, and that the vocabulary be appropriate for the audience. They also recommend that occupational information be as comprehensive as possible, including the types of information provided by O*Net.

Finally, clients will have occupational information from friends, family, and the media that may or may not be accurate. It is hard to overestimate the powerful role of the media in portraying various occupations. At times the portrayal is not very accurate, and at other times, the type of preparation for the occupation is not very clear. For example, the number of majors in forensic science increased dramatically with the advent of the television show *CSI*, but many students were unaware of the amount of science coursework needed and subsequently changed majors. Counselors may need to assess the accuracy of the occupational information that clients bring to counseling.

Information in Career Counseling

Once counselors determine the accuracy and completeness of occupational information, the role of information in counseling necessitates a number of counselor cognitions and decisions. Many of the interventions we discussed in Chapter 12 included providing career information, helping students consider more options by having them explore websites, and using information to help clients learn what is needed to pursue various options. But, just as it is critical to present assessment results as part of the counseling process, so is it critical to carefully consider how occupational information can be part of the counseling process.

We encourage counselors to consider the questions in Box 13.2 when incorporating occupational information into career counseling. Several questions should be considered prior to the session in which the information is to be discussed or shared, including what information the counselor should seek to be most helpful to the client. We cannot emphasize enough that there is a wealth of information available, and while helping a client navigate the Internet sites is useful, it is more useful if the counselor has done some preparation to determine the best sites to navigate.

The next set of questions concern the use of occupational information during the counseling session. There is a delicate balance between providing too much information and not enough information. And the client who does not know they need the information is different from the client who has too much information (Gysbers, Heppner, & Johnston, 2009). Again, counseling skills are needed to help match the type and amount of information to the client's needs.

It may be helpful to illustrate the use of occupational information in counseling through the vignettes at the beginning of this chapter. Asking Isabella, the 16-year-old, to explore options on a website would be of little help until considerable discussion and assessment has helped her narrow her search. It is important to

BOX 13.2 Counselor Cognitions

Prior to the Session

- What information might be most helpful to the client?
- What occupational information should I retrieve to be most helpful to my client?
- When is the best time to introduce occupational information?
- What is the best match between occupational information and the client's concerns?

During the Session

- How much information is appropriate to share?
- How much information should the client seek outside of the session?
- How much information exploration should be part of the counseling session?
- If the client brings in occupational information on his or her own, how accurate is the information?
- How is the client processing the information? Is the client able to take in the information? Is the information too much for the client or too little to help him or her make a decision?

clarify if Isabella wants to learn how to narrow down some options or is feeling pressure and anxiety to choose a major. In other words, what are the counseling goals and how does occupational information fit into the overall goals for counseling? Career counseling could help her explore her interests and values and assess her self-efficacy to explore potential occupational options. Helping her gain an understanding of an overall structure of the world of work, such as the one in the Holland classification system, may help her narrow down her focus into a few areas. Those options could then be explored. In this way, her anxiety about having to choose may be alleviated by helping her understand the various ingredients in making a career decision. Her counselor could help her see the possible occupations during a session, and ask her to bring back five additional occupations she had explored.

Occupational information and exploration could help Anh, the English and French major, as well. Just as we emphasized with Isabella, it is important to assess the overall counseling goals and in what manner occupational information could fit. Options for both majors include continuing on to graduate school or using her French skills as a translator. Is Anh considering a doctorate, and is she interested in learning about prospects for that occupation? The O*Net could provide projected growth in the field. But if she is not considering postgraduate education or becoming a translator, the O*Net could also help her see some additional occupational options by exploring specific knowledge areas in the Advanced Search option. For example, a number of knowledge areas may be of interest to her, such as communications and media, education and training, or telecommunications. Clicking on any one of those knowledge areas provides a number of occupations that use that knowledge (e.g., Communications and Media includes Public Relations Specialist). Again, it is important to understand Anh's counseling goals and to determine the right time to introduce occupational information. It may be that Anh just wanted to know how she could find different options and once she understands the tool, her goal has been met. But counselors need to also be alert that the expressed need for information is a "presenting problem" and there may be other concerns that are behind the request for information. Perhaps Anh is also struggling with emotional reactions to not knowing what to do after graduation or perhaps there are relationship concerns. It is important to help clarify the client's goals and the appropriate point to introduce occupational information.

Matthew, the military veteran, can benefit from the section of O*Net that allows veterans to directly enter their military occupation and see the variety of civilian options that match that training. Matthew was a tank crewman. If he enjoyed the work he did as a tank crewman for the Marines and wants to find ways to do similar work, then the occupational information in the O*Net search for veterans is an ideal way. Entering his military occupation into the O*Net search engine, he can see that this is most similar to Bus and Truck Mechanics, which also has a registered apprenticeship program. He can view available apprenticeships within his state that will help him prepare to transfer his skills in taking care of tanks in Afghanistan to taking care of buses and trucks in the United States. However, just as with the other vignettes, it is critical to find out his overall concerns and counseling goals. For example, perhaps he did not enjoy the work he did or is no longer able to perform essential aspects of the work. He may not know how to find other work, how to integrate back to the United States, or he may be dealing with a variety of additional transition issues. Counselors may want to be alert to additional concerns for Matthew, either to help him explore those concerns or to refer him to appropriate additional services for veterans.

Counselors are encouraged to consider the purposes listed in Box 13.3 to consider incorporating occupational information into their career counseling and interventions.

**BOX 13.3 Purposes of Occupational Information
in Career Counseling**

- Learn more about occupations to expand a search
- Provide a framework of related occupations to explore
- Learn more about projections for occupations
- Learn about new job areas
- Confirm information about a particular occupation

ADDITIONAL CASES

Case 1: Elon

Elon is a 35-year-old African American man who has worked in his family's printing business since graduating from college. His father just sold the business for a significant profit and retired because neither of his sons wanted to own the business. Elon and his brother have the option of continuing to work for the new owner or to look for another line of work. His father has offered to pay for any additional training or schooling they want.

Elon graduated from college with a 3.5 GPA, majoring in graphic design, knowing he would enter the family business and there was an increasing need for digital printing and design knowledge. He enjoyed working with his father and brother, enjoyed the flexibility of the environment, and liked knowing he did not have to worry about where to find a job after college. However, he does not have an interest in continuing to be a graphic designer and so would rather leave the business and find additional work.

He seeks career counseling because he has no idea how to make a career choice based on his own interests and values. He does not know if he should look for work in another field, or if there is other work he could do that uses his graphic design background.

QUESTIONS FOR DISCUSSION

1. What would you focus on as a counselor?

2. How might occupational information help Elon?

3. When would you consider introducing occupational information?

4. What concerns would you have about providing occupational information to Elon?

5. What additional contextual influences would you want to consider in working with Elon?

6. What additional occupational information do *you* need to know to help Elon?

Case 2: Katherine

Katherine is a 28-year-old Native American school psychologist. She has worked in a school setting for three years and is very dissatisfied. She seeks career counseling for help choosing another career. She is very disappointed that this career did not work out. She thought she had made an informed decision. She did very well in high school and in her undergraduate psychology major. She took every opportunity to study about children and worked in a day care center during college. She loved working with children and enjoyed psychology, so thought school psychology would be a good fit for her career choice.

Katherine had high scores on the Graduate Record Exam and was accepted into a very competitive Educational Specialist program in School Psychology. She enjoyed the coursework that focused on therapy and consultation but disliked the assessment coursework. She did her practicum and internship in two small school districts. Each had one school psychologist across the entire district and she had considerable freedom to do the tasks she enjoyed, including developing individual therapeutic relationships with children.

Katherine graduated with high honors and had very good letters of recommendation from her professors and received two job offers within weeks of graduation. She accepted one in a medium sized suburban district, where she was one of two school psychologists. She was responsible for all the assessment and special services placement for two elementary schools and the middle school in the district. She was also responsible for evaluating the effectiveness of a variety of school programs. She had almost no time for individual therapy with students. She ended the school year considerably depressed and realized she could not go back to being a school psychologist the following year.

QUESTIONS FOR DISCUSSION

1. What would you focus on as a counselor?

2. How might occupational information help Katherine?

3. When would you consider introducing occupational information?

4. What concerns would you have about providing occupational information to Katherine?

5. What additional contextual influences would you want to consider in working with Katherine?

6. What additional occupational information do *you* need to know to help Katherine?

Case 3: Daniel

Daniel is a 43-year-old Asian American man. He considers himself to be highly acculturated and does not want to focus on his ethnicity. His employer encouraged him to seek career counseling for help in choosing the next position in his company. He is a computer engineer for a large company in the defense industry. His project team is being disbanded due to the budget cuts in the Department of Defense. His supervisor is committed to keeping all the employees on the team, moving them to other projects. The Human Resources Department of the company has also offered each employee on the team the option of taking early retirement or taking a limited educational package to prepare for another position within the company.

Daniel feels that he is too young to consider retirement and has a strong identification as an employee of this company. He would like to stay employed in this company but does not know which path to take, whether to seek additional training or another position as an engineer. He is married, with three school-aged children. His wife is also an engineer, although is employed in another industry. She is supportive of his seeking career counseling to help him sort through his options.

Daniel arrives for career counseling having already done considerable search on O*Net. He has downloaded information on several options for occupations he could pursue within his company, has a number of videos he wants his counselor to watch with him, and has already searched for other jobs in the company.

QUESTIONS FOR DISCUSSION

1. What would you focus on as a counselor?

2. How might the occupational information exploration Daniel has already done help the counseling process?

3. What concerns would you have about discussing occupational information with Daniel?

4. What additional contextual influences would you want to consider in working with Daniel?

5. What additional occupational information do *you* need to know to help Daniel?

Chapter 14

The Intersection of Career and Noncareer Issues

How much should career counselors focus on noncareer (personal) issues in counseling? When clients enter therapy to work on personal issues, how and when should work- or career-related issues be addressed? What are the similarities and differences between career counseling and personal counseling? How do work-related problems affect mental health and adjustment? How do chronic mental health issues influence work and career? These questions are vital to good therapeutic practice—whether primarily career or noncareer in focus—and we address them in this chapter.

Because career counseling and personal-emotional counseling developed from different historical traditions and within different professional specialties, they are often viewed as independent activities. Haverkamp and Moore (1993) discussed the perceptual dichotomy in which career counseling and personal counseling appear to function as distinct cognitive schemas. They argued that the implicit definition of personal counseling is too broad, consisting of anything not directly related to career; the implicit definition of career counseling, on the other hand, is too narrow, consisting primarily of initial career choices of young adults and neglecting adult work adjustment.

However, research suggests that it is unwise to view clients with career issues as substantially different from those with personal issues, and that they may experience similar levels of psychological distress (Gold & Scanlon, 1993; Lucas, 1992). Moreover, clients might be less well served or less satisfied with career counseling when personal issues are evident but are not addressed (Juntunen,

2006; Phillips, Friedlander, Kost, Specterman, & Robbins, 1988). As Hackett (1993) noted, "We are undoubtedly doing our clients a disservice by any attempt to neatly compartmentalize their lives" (p. 110).

A related area of research highlights the connections between career counseling and mental health outcomes. There is increasing recognition that work and mental health are interwoven and that adult vocational needs are complex (Blustein, 2008; Fouad, 2007; Hackett, 1993; Haverkamp & Moore, 1993; Herr, Cramer, & Niles, 2004; Swanson, 2012). Brown and Brooks (1985) argued that career counseling with adults may be a viable alternative to stress management and even to personal counseling. Furthermore, they argued that mental health practitioners have overlooked the potential of career counseling, and they encourage practitioners to recognize that the source of psychological symptoms may be in the work situation.

Another crucial point made by Brown and Brooks (1985) is that, although all practitioners cannot be skilled career counselors, all should become skilled in recognizing situations in which career counseling is an appropriate intervention. Whiston, Fouad, and Juntunen (2013) make the same argument in outlining six guiding principles that all practitioners should know when incorporating work into counseling practice. These principles encourage practitioners to (1) be aware of the impact of work on quality of life; (2) be aware of the influence that work has on health (behavioral, emotional, and physical), as well as the influence of health on work; (3) understand the implications of work transitions; (4) understand how sociocultural factors (such as gender, ethnicity, socioeconomic status, sexual orientation, disability status, and urban/rural residence) may influence the career development and experience of work; (5) understand how individuals negotiate multiple life roles, including that of "worker"; and (6) understand how economic and social factors (such as labor market, access to education, and globalization) impact access to employment (Whiston et al., 2013).

In terms of structure and process, career counseling can be very similar to personal counseling, but it can also be very different. Career counseling requires the counselor to use many of the same skills that personal counseling requires; therefore, the process, at least at times, can be quite similar. Perhaps most importantly, counselors need to be aware of how career and personal factors are intertwined in their clients' lives and to explicitly address the spectrum of issues that clients experience.

Several of the career development theories that we discussed in earlier chapters opened the door to consideration of roles and activities outside of career and work *per se*. For example, Super's theory explicitly acknowledged multiple roles in people's lives and how those roles might fluctuate in importance and intersect with one another throughout the lifespan. The "emerging" perspectives described by

Richardson and by Blustein acknowledged the important role of relational factors in the experience of work and career.

There are a number of ways to approach the connection between career counseling and noncareer (personal) counseling, or between career issues and noncareer (personal) issues. We begin by considering how problems that arise in the career or work domain create or worsen problems in the personal domain and, conversely, how personal or mental health issues create or worsen problems in the work or career domain. We then focus on career counseling as the primary venue, using the case of Leslie, and discuss how and when it is appropriate to address noncareer issues. A second case, Julie, will be used to focus on personal counseling as the entry point, to discuss how and when it is appropriate to address issues pertaining to work or career.

CAREER AND NONCAREER ISSUES

How Work Affects Mental Health

The experience of work itself may influence an individual's mental health and may be the identified reason an individual enters counseling, or the underlying reason for other concerns (such as physical or health issues). Common issues are job stress, work-nonwork conflict, dissatisfaction with work, unemployment, and underemployment.

Work-related stress

Experiencing stress in the workplace may be an instigating factor for a person seeking counseling—either in the "personal" or "career" realm. Job-related stress may be considered a characteristic of specific jobs or of the workplace environment and also as resulting from the intersection of work and nonwork roles. Potential stressors present in the work environment include task demands, role ambiguities and conflicts, ethical dilemmas, interpersonal conflicts, and demands of the physical setting (Schermerhorn, Hunt, & Osborn, 2008). These work stressors may interact or spill over with other personal life stressors such as family events and economic conditions.

Stress is often classified as constructive stress (or eustress), which occurs at moderate levels of stress and motivates effort, or destructive stress (or distress). Chronic stress may lead to burnout, demonstrated by a loss of interest and satisfaction (Shirom, 2003). Chronic and ongoing stress affects psychological and physical health, including hypertension, strokes, heart attacks, migraines, ulcers, substance abuse, and depression (Schermerhorn et al., 2008). Moreover, stress is likely to affect job and life satisfaction.

Job loss, unemployment, and underemployment

Previous research has demonstrated that unemployment—as well as underemployment—may result in symptoms of depression, anxiety, lowered self-esteem, and other negative affect or mood. These symptoms also may precede work events and may spill over into work roles. For example, if depressive episodes are characterized by loss of interest, lack of motivation, poor concentration, and so forth, then work behavior is likely to be affected as well. Specific events at work also may trigger the onset of or worsen depression.

Mental health problems that result from job loss and unemployment may have long-lasting effects even after the period of unemployment ends (Swanson, 2012). Frequently those who are reemployed are underemployed (Feldman, 1996), as indicated by decreases in pay, status, and responsibilities compared to the pre-unemployment period. Being underemployed also may contribute to mental health problems, such as depression, and decreased well-being and life satisfaction. Feldman (1996) estimated that 25% of the workforce is underemployed, a proportion that may have increased during recent economic fluctuations and structural changes. Underemployment may be particularly evident for (1) contingent (part-time or temporary) employees, who represent an increasingly large part of the workforce; (2) laid-off workers who have been reemployed with lower wages, benefits, and status; and (3) recent high school and college graduates (Feldman, Leana, & Bolino, 2002).

How Mental Health Issues Affect Work

Although psychological disorders are pervasive (Zunker, 2008), we focus in this chapter on situations that are most likely to be encountered in "typical" career counseling settings (such as colleges or universities), or for clients in mental health settings who are functioning at a high level, including depression/mood disorders, generalized and social anxiety, and personality disorders. Mental health concerns may be acute or chronic.

Individuals with acute mental health concerns

Individuals may seek counseling when they are dealing with difficulties that are acute in nature, such as grief following the death of a spouse or depression or anxiety because of job loss or financial setback. The concern that brings them to therapy is not career in nature, yet depending on the severity of the concern in terms of daily functioning, there could be consequences for work or career. For example, depression or grief following a loss could easily influence daily work activities and productivity, and mental health professionals should be alert to these effects (Juntunen, 2006). Further, experiencing a personal loss or transition may lead the client to reconsider their current career direction. Consider Annette, who was in a serious car accident that did not leave her with lasting injuries but led to an existential crisis about the direction of her life, which resulted in a decision to retire early so that she could focus on other interests and pursuits.

When clients are not pursuing career counseling per se, it might be easy for counselors to overlook any career- and work-related issues, yet it is important to consider the "whole-person" perspective (Zunker, 2008). Juntunen (2006) encouraged mental health professionals to routinely focus on clients' current functioning in the work and career domains, regardless of the nature of their presenting concerns. She suggested including questions related to work on intake forms, beyond occupational title or employer, such as satisfaction with work and concerns about work. She also suggested that therapists explicitly discuss the interaction of work and life roles with clients and explore the meaning of work for clients. Guindon and Giordano (2012) warned that counselors often miss cues that clients need career counseling as well as mental health counseling, as suggested by evidence that personal concerns can "overshadow" vocational or career concerns (Magee & Whiston, 2010; Spengler, Blustein, & Strohmer, 1990). Practitioners can minimize the likelihood that this will occur by systematically addressing work or career concerns in intake and throughout therapy with *all* clients.

Individuals with chronic mental health concerns

It is beyond the scope of this chapter to address chronic mental health concerns in depth, yet it is important to acknowledge their impact on, and interaction with, career issues. Practitioners will encounter chronic mental health concerns, whether mild or severe, and whether clients are seeking career or noncareer counseling. Individuals with moderate to severe mental illnesses must cope with stigma associated with their illnesses, as well as other barriers and misconceptions (Caporoso & Kinselica, 2004). As noted earlier, mental health issues also may increase the likelihood of job loss, unemployment, or underemployment but not be recognized as a contributing factor.

The common mental health issues noted in the previous section as acute concerns also may be chronic in nature, such as depression and other mood disorders and generalized and social anxiety. Another type of chronic mental health issue is personality disorders. Although little has been written about the impact of personality disorders on career counseling, it seems clear that there would be career implications. As Kjos (1995) noted, features of such disorders affect career decision making, on-the-job performance, occupational success, and occupational functioning, including reaction to job loss, on-the-job pressure, management style, and coworker relationships. Characteristics of personality disorders also are likely to affect clients' behavior in counseling and their relationship with the counselor. Depending on the specific diagnosis as outlined in the DSM-5 (American Psychiatric Association, 2013), individuals may be viewed by others as odd, eccentric, dramatic, emotional, erratic, anxious or fearful (Kjos, 1995; Zunker, 2008), which would be important to discuss in career counseling.

IMPLICATIONS FOR CAREER COUNSELING

Guindon and Giordano (2012) discussed career counseling as a primary, secondary, or tertiary intervention, defining career counseling as a primary intervention when it may *prevent* threats to mental health, as a secondary intervention when it may *moderate* effects of existing mental health concerns by identifying and treating work-life issues, and as a tertiary intervention when it may be suitable *in conjunction with* mental health counseling. For example, they identified career counseling as a primary intervention for depressive and anxiety disorders, job loss issues and reactions to work stress. Career counseling was viewed as a secondary intervention for the additional presenting concerns of severe mental disorders, personality disorders, and substance abuse.

For clients in a mental health or private practice setting, this is a useful way to think about how career counseling as a distinct type of intervention may be integrated or interwoven with counseling that focuses more specifically on the presenting concern.

A similar framework was offered by Robitschek and DeBell (2002), who proposed that vocational or career issues be considered as either *primary issues* or as *contextual factors* in counseling. They argued for a new perspective on counseling, in which vocational issues would "provide another facet to understanding the multiple life roles and complex contexts in which we live" (Robitschek & DeBell, 2002, p. 801–802). Thus, instead of defining counseling per se as either "career" or "personal," clients would bring primary issues and contextual factors to counseling; some clients would have primary issues that are vocational or career in nature, and the counselor would explore other contextual factors relevant to those issues; for other clients, career or work issues would be among a variety of contextual issues surrounding a nonvocational primary issue.

A third approach is a "domain-sensitive approach" to counseling (Blustein, 2006; Blustein & Spengler, 1995), with the goals of improving adjustment and functioning within both the career and noncareer realms. Counselors make decisions about where to intervene based on their judgments about the origin of clients' presenting concerns, as well as determining the most accessible place to intervene.

In addition, a number of authors have offered conceptual and practical suggestions regarding the integration of work and personal issues within counseling. Robitschek and DeBell (2002) offered several suggestions regarding how counseling practitioners might implement their new paradigm. To reduce the artificial distinction between the two domains, a counselor could: (1) assess functioning in the work domain with every client, regardless of presenting issue, particularly how work functioning interacts with presenting concerns; (2) assess the importance of work with every client, regardless of presenting issue, given that the salience of the work role may intersect with other presenting concerns; and (3) "work broadly" with clients who present career or work issues as primary concerns, to fully explore the range of nonvocational factors that provide context.

These perspectives require a broader view of "career counseling," a view that may differ according to constraints within practice settings (see Chapter 12). For example, in a university counseling center that incorporates career and academic concerns as part of its mission, career and noncareer issues might be naturally combined on a conceptual level: If a student comes to the center with depression as a primary concern, it is likely (and warranted) that the counselor addresses how the client's depression affects her academic work and career plans, and vice versa. However, in a community mental health setting with time limits on therapy, career or work issues may need to take a back seat to directly dealing with disruptions in daily functioning because of the depression; while counselor and client might acknowledge the interaction of the depression with work-related functioning, there simply may not be time or resources to address the work/career component.

APPLYING CAREER-NONCAREER FRAMEWORKS

A Review of Leslie's Presenting Concern and Noncareer Issues

Leslie is seeking career counseling because she is considering quitting her current job; she is dissatisfied primarily because of the stress of many responsibilities and long working hours. She reports that her dissatisfaction has been accumulating for several years but has increased in salience because of several recent work events. She does continue to enjoy aspects of teaching and feels that she is a good teacher. Leslie is unclear at this point whether or not she will quit her current job and, if so, whether she will look for another teaching position or a new career. Leslie feels that she is at a crossroads in her life and is ready to explore her options for her next step. She is evaluating many aspects of her career, family relationships, and marriage. She is looking forward to beginning counseling.

Conceptualizing Leslie's work and nonwork concerns

There are a number of aspects of Leslie's life story that could be characterized as "noncareer," some of which are directly and naturally related to her presenting concern, and others that may influence her decisions in more indirect ways. These issues include:

1. *Desire to have children.* Leslie clearly wants to have a child, which is becoming more pressing in terms of time. This issue seems closely connected to any career decisions under consideration. Leslie was steered away from some career paths because of messages about combining work and family, and now it is a highly salient factor. Several other factors include Joe's expectation that she will delay any career decisions and will stay home to care for a child, her recent miscarriages that may include unresolved grief, and her mother's and sister's messages about her work and family roles.

2. *Marital relationship.* Leslie reported that she is happy with her marriage but also that there is some dissatisfaction about communication, division of labor, and career decisions and family plans. There seem to be mixed messages about Joe's support of Leslie's career change. Joe is also thinking about changing jobs, and his decisions and Leslie's decisions will interact; it might be helpful for them to engage in career counseling as a couple (Evans, 2012).

3. *Her role in her family of origin.* Leslie's reported relationships with her siblings and parents reveal some clues about how they view her and perhaps how she views herself. She seems to be perceived as indecisive, uncertain, and floundering, and her brother and sister have each accomplished things that she has not, including having children and achieving financially successful careers. Her family also conveys messages about Joe not having a "professional" job.

4. *Role of others in her career decisions.* Some of Leslie's career and educational decisions have been influenced by her relationships with others, both familial and romantic relationships. Although these decisions may have led her in productive and satisfying directions, it might be valuable to discuss this pattern in context of her current decisions.

5. *How she copes with job stress.* Leslie described her first job after college as very stressful and lonely; she broke up with her boyfriend, and after three years moved to be near her family. Her current job is less stressful but offers fewer rewards. There are aspects of her current job structure that are related to stress, and her coping mechanisms for dealing with this stress could be explored in counseling, particularly whether there is spillover of stress

between work and home. Also, it might be important to discuss coping with stress in any future career direction that she chooses.

The Case of Julie

Julie is a 29-year-old White woman who seeks therapy from a counselor in private practice to deal with depression. The counselor learns during intake that Julie has had some struggles with mild depression throughout her life, but these symptoms have worsened in the past year. Julie traces the beginning of her current depression to her brother's death from cancer eight months ago, a disease that he fought for two years prior to his death. His death has led Julie to question many things, including existential questions about meaning and purpose in her own life, the role of faith, and the importance of family relationships.

1. Where would you start with Julie? What would you want to know?

2. There are times when Julie feels her depression is incapacitating and other times when it is manageable. How would you help her deal with these fluctuations?

3. What work- or career-related issues do you think Julie is experiencing? How might you work with these issues?

4. She expressed concerns with finding meaning and purpose in her own life. How would you approach this with Julie?

DIRECTIONS AND IMPLICATIONS FOR CAREER COUNSELING

Goals of Counseling

The primary goal is to systematically explore work and nonwork domains in counseling, regardless of the client's presenting issue or the setting in which counseling occurs. A second goal is to explore the intersection of work and nonwork domains in clients' lives and to integrate the work and nonwork domains as appropriate in counseling. On a practical level, this entails ensuring that when clients seek career counseling, nonwork or noncareer issues also receive attention; conversely, when clients seek personal counseling, work or career issues receive attention.

Interventions

Interventions to integrate career and noncareer issues begin at the very outset of counseling, when the client first defines the presenting issue and the counselor conducts an intake interview. Following Juntunen's (2006) suggestions noted earlier, Leslie and Julie would be asked about their level of satisfaction with work and any concerns about work. The counselor also might explicitly ask Leslie about how her dissatisfaction with her current job affects other aspects of her life and what impact any career decisions that she might make would have on other people or situations. Leslie is already aware of some of the spillover of her job dissatisfaction and stress; Joe has commented that she takes her job too seriously and that if she "lightened up," she wouldn't be so unhappy. Leslie agrees with this somewhat but also feels that Joe doesn't fully understand why she is dissatisfied. She knows that if she changes jobs or goes back to school, then there will be implications for Joe in terms of how their days are structured and the distribution of workload in their household. Their plan to have children also is closely linked to her career decisions.

With Julie, the counselor could ask her to describe the effect that her depression has had on her daily work as well as on her overall career satisfaction. There have been some days that Julie calls in sick because she just doesn't want to get out of bed and other days that she has gone to work but knows that she is not very effective. The counselor may try to separate short term or acute effects of the depression, as a normal part of Julie grieving her brother's death, from long term or chronic effects of the depression that Julie has experienced throughout her life. The counselor also may spend some focused time on Julie's statements about finding meaning and whether she is considering making a career change to pursue something that holds more meaning; however, the counselor may also discourage Julie from making any quick decisions until she's had more time to cope with her grief and depression.

ADDITIONAL CASES

Case 1: Jason

Jason is a 26-year-old multiracial (Native American/African American) Marine Corps veteran who served two tours of duty in Iraq. He is in his third semester at the local university but has only successfully completed 20 credits (mostly Fs but some INCs). He gets stuck about halfway through each semester and struggles with episodes of depression and PTSD.

Jason comes from a lower middle class family in a small town in the Southwest. He and his family are very proud of his making it into the Marine Corps. He identifies strongly with being a Marine, such as using a picture of himself in dress uniform on his social media profile. After his discharge, he returned to his hometown but then moved to an apartment to be closer to the university. His PTSD is "typical" of other veterans of the Iraq or Afghanistan wars, in that he has physiological and emotional reactions to noisy or crowded environments. Jason also has a specific memory that haunts him—that of killing a 9-year-old boy while he was patrolling a neighborhood—which recurs as a visual flashback that interferes with his ability to function, particularly when he is under other types of stress such as related to his academic demands.

Jason is currently seeing a therapist at a regional VA hospital, as well as working with a social worker and a peer counselor in the VA support network. He is taking antidepressant and antianxiety medications, although he has been trying to reduce the dosage because he does not like being dependent on the medications for daily functioning. However, he recently had a bout of severe depression in which he stayed in bed for days, but increasing his medications then resulted in him being unable to sleep for days at a time. This episode significantly affected his academic work because he did not attend classes for several weeks in the middle of the semester. He is now trying to get caught up on assignments and has sought career counseling. He is pursuing a degree in psychology and wants to work with veterans like himself, but his spotty academic record is making it less likely that he'll be admitted to a graduate program. He has sought career counseling to look at his options.

QUESTIONS FOR DISCUSSION

1. What is the first thing you would focus on as the counselor?

2. How do you see your role as a counselor with Jason, given the other mental health professionals in his life?

3. How do you envision the connection between the career and noncareer aspects of Jason's life? How do you see working with these aspects?

4. What are some possible career interventions you could use?

Case 2: Beth

Beth is a 20-year-old White student at a community college; she recently has been diagnosed as having bipolar disorder. Beth excelled in high school and received a full scholarship at a prestigious university on the East coast, 500 miles from home. In her freshman year, Beth had her first manic episode. One night Beth's roommate told her about the experiences she had in a summer internship, and so Beth decided to immediately drive to Montreal to check it out. After going without much sleep for several days, she "crashed" at a hostel, where few people spoke English regularly and she did not understand their French, and she called her parents for help. She had several other episodes of manic activity followed by depressive periods throughout the rest of her freshman year, and her parents encouraged her to return home where she could receive more support (and monitoring). She is now enrolled in the local community college and wants to decide what to do next.

Because her diagnosis is recent, Beth is not sure what impact it will have on her life. When she feels "up," she tends to discuss grandiose plans for her career—such as traveling around the world as the public relations person for a famous movie star, writing articles about luxurious hotels for travel magazines, or moving to Paris to study fashion design. When she feels "down," it is difficult for her to imagine working 40 hours per week in any job. She is just beginning to try medications to stabilize her mood.

QUESTIONS FOR DISCUSSION

1. What is the first thing you would focus on as the counselor?

2. How would you address career planning with Beth, given her recent diagnosis and uncertainty about its effects?

3. How do you envision the connection between the career and noncareer aspects of Beth's life? How do you see working with these aspects?

4. How does Beth imagine coping and managing her bipolar disorder within a work environment?

5. What are some possible career interventions you could use?

Case 3: Alex

Alex is a 34-year-old African American who entered therapy because he has had several minor panic attacks while on duty as a firefighter. He has been able to work through it and continue without interruption, and he believes that the rest of his crew has been unaware of what Alex was experiencing. However, he is worried that it will happen again, and that he will endanger others on his crew if he cannot fully function. He also is worried that he will lose his job if others become aware of his experiences.

Alex wanted to be a firefighter since he was a young child. His father and uncle both were firefighters; Alex's father plans to retire in a few years, and his uncle died while fighting a fire in an industrial plant five years ago. Although Alex is experiencing anxiety while on the job, it is very difficult for him to talk about the possibility of no longer being a firefighter; his anxiety in session is apparent when the topic of leaving is raised. He is determined to stick it out but also not sure if he is able to do so.

QUESTIONS FOR DISCUSSION

1. What is the first thing you would focus on as the counselor?

2. How would you integrate the work and mental health aspects of Alex's presenting concerns?

3. How might Alex's family history be connected to his current difficulties? In what way would you approach this with him?

4. How would you approach Alex's difficulty in thinking about other careers? His anxiety in session?

Chapter 15

Summary and Integration

We wrote this book to give students an understanding of how theories of career development could be applied in career counseling, how to practice culturally responsive career counseling, and how work and mental health intersect. Our intent in the theories chapters in Section 2 was to give a brief overview of the theory, apply it to a client (Leslie) as well as to another case, and then discuss how a career counselor with that theoretical perspective would work with these two clients. We also used additional case studies at the end of each chapter to encourage readers to develop hypotheses about a wide variety of clients and to practice applying each theory to realistic cases.

In the process of writing the book, we ourselves were frequently reminded how focusing on one theoretical perspective very much influenced the course of counseling. It determined the questions we asked about Leslie, it determined the behavior that was examined and brought into counseling, and it determined the goals we imagined Leslie would set for herself. We realized that in our own career counseling, neither of us uses a single theory. Although we were both trained initially in the theory of work adjustment at the University of Minnesota, our approaches stem from a combination of theoretical perspectives and interventions.

At this point, many readers may ask: How do these theories compare? What are the strengths and weaknesses of each? How well do they apply to clients with whom I work (or will work in the future)? Is there any empirical support for these theories? How can I combine the theories in my own work? These are the questions we hope to begin to answer in this chapter. We will first summarize and compare each of the major theoretical approaches we examined in the book. As we did in Chapter 1, we then ask readers to stop and think about how each perspective applies to their own lives. Theories were designed to represent reality and help us understand and predict behavior, and it is helpful to think of how each has contributed to a greater understanding of our own career history and decision making.

Consistent with the format in Section 2, we examine how each theory or approach contributes to our understanding of Leslie. We explicate the contributions of each theory to career counseling with Leslie and examine what may be the unique contributions of each theory to conceptualizing the case. Then, just as we have used cases throughout the book to exemplify the application of theories and approaches, we will present two cases to illustrate the integration of theoretical perspectives. We ask readers to consider thoroughly how each theoretical perspective would approach the new cases.

In the first case, George, we discuss our view of what a counselor from each perspective would do. We summarize by outlining what we would do as counselors and identifying the theoretical approaches on which we are drawing. We hope, in doing so, that we are modeling the integrative perspective that we discussed in Chapter 1. In the second case, Tom, we present the case and follow-up stimulus questions and then leave it to readers to consider how each theoretical perspective would approach Tom.

We then turn our attention to the questions readers may have about support for these theories. As strong proponents of the scientist-practitioner model, we believe it is important to evaluate the research foundation underlying each theory. We briefly examine the empirical support available for the constructs delineated in each theory and the empirical support for the application of the theory to a broad range of populations, regardless of sex, racial and ethnic background, socioeconomic level, disability, or sexual orientation. Because no theory has been empirically supported for every construct and every population, we also identify some areas we would encourage researchers to examine in the future. Finally, we finish by suggesting areas for further training and skill development.

SUMMARY AND COMPARISON OF THE THEORIES

Recall from Chapter 1 that it is useful to think of theories as GPS maps. We use maps to plan a trip, considering alternate routes to a final destination and locating interesting sights to visit along the road. Maps prevent us from arriving at the wrong destination (or not arriving at all) and from taking circuitous routes when more direct ones are available. Likewise, theories offer us alternate views of reality, of explaining human behavior, and of conducting counseling to assist clients with their concerns. Each of the theories discussed in this book has many areas in which it overlaps with other theories. For example, each attempts to predict optimal situations for clients, whether good career or work-related choices or satisfying work environments. Each uses a variety of ways to help clients learn more about themselves, and although each theory uses different language to describe it, each assumes that individuals interact with their environment in some way. However, a review of the major constructs reveals that each theory does more than use different labels for the same behavior; rather, each focuses on a unique perspective of work-related behavior.

We summarize the major constructs for each established theory (Chapters 6–10) in Table 15.1, along with the outcomes that each theory predicts. We do not include the emerging theories in Chapter 11 in this table, since they have yet to be empirically examined. This information will aid readers in keeping track of which construct is used by which theory and which theoretical perspective is most likely to be used in helping clients make career choices or adjustments. We will discuss the last two columns of Table 15.1 in later sections.

Holland's theory describes vocational personalities and work environments and how they fit together. Individuals differ in their vocational personalities and seek out the environments that fit with their personality types. Outcomes predicted by Holland's theory include vocational choice as well as vocational adjustment; both of these are predicted by congruence with the environment. The theory of work adjustment (TWA) also describes individual differences, although this theory highlights individuals' abilities and needs. The environmental focus is on ability requirements and rewards rather than on vocational personality. The TWA delineates processes postulated to occur as an individual tries to decrease job dissatisfaction. Similar to Holland's theory, outcomes predicted by the TWA also include vocational choice and adjustment, although the focus is much more on adjustment and behavior within a work setting.

The developmental theories of Super and Gottfredson describe the development of an individual's career over the life span. Super's theory puts more emphasis on later life stages, ranging from implementing a career choice to retirement, than does Gottfredson's, which places more emphasis on childhood and adolescence. Developmental models explain how choices are made and implemented more than the other theories discussed in this book. Both theories predict vocational choice and development; Super's outcomes also include implementation of the self-concept and delineation of work as one of many life roles.

Social cognitive career theory also focuses on how individuals learn from others, but this model emphasizes the personal construction that individuals place on what they have learned. This model also highlights how interests develop and how choices develop, with an emphasis on an individual's beliefs about his or her competence in the related abilities and the outcomes expected of pursuing that field. The social cognitive model is the most explicit in its consideration of environmental conditions and events. In addition to the theories in Table 15.1, the three emerging theories described in Chapter 11 encourage an expanded view of the integration of work and nonwork domains, as well as introducing a consideration of the role of volition and choice in work and individuals' construction of their career stories.

As we noted in Chapter 1, the counselor's theoretical perspective helps determine the way clients and their concerns are conceptualized, the most appropriate tools to use with clients, and the overall goals of counseling. Choosing which theory to incorporate into your own map of your client's career behavior will depend on your own experiences as well as on the client's presenting problem. Osipow's (1996) description of the focus of theoretical perspectives may be helpful as readers evaluate which of these theories they will use in their own counseling, for which theory you use will depend on what you want to emphasize. Osipow summarizes the theories by noting that Holland's theory identifies *what happens,* developmental theories describe *how it happens,* and the TWA depicts *how it happens and the outcome.* He did not include social cognitive career theory (or any of the emerging theories) in his discussion, but the social cognitive career model describes how an individual's perceptions of reality help make career outcomes happen. Savickas's career construction theory focuses on how the individual makes meaning out of his or her career and work, and Blustein's and Richardson's approaches emphasize the work-nonwork integration of a person's life.

Table 15.1 Comparison of Theories

Theories	Constructs	Outcome	Understanding Leslie	Support
Holland	Personality types (RIASEC) Environmental type (RIASEC) Congruence Consistency Differentiation Identity	Congruence Satisfaction	Congruence between her personality type and current work environment	Well researched Empirically supported Evidence of support for women and racial/ethnic minority groups

Theories	Constructs	Outcome	Understanding Leslie	Support
Theory of Work Adjustment	Abilities Ability requirements Needs Rewards (need reinforcers) Satisfaction Satisfactoriness Reactive adjustment Active adjustment Person-environment correspondence Flexibility Perseverance	Satisfaction Tenure Work adjustment	Dissatisfaction because of discorrespondence between her needs and environmental rewards	Well researched Well supported for some constructs, less supported for personality style variables Some evidence of support for women and racial/ethnic minority groups
Developmental (Super)	Life stages Career adaptability Developmental tasks Career maturity Implementation of the self-concept Career construction Life roles Salience	Vocational choice Life role balance	Recycling through exploration tasks Balancing roles in her life	Well researched Well supported for some constructs, less supported for newer constructs Some evidence of support for women and racial/ethnic minority groups
Gottfredson	Circumscription Compromise Vocational aspirations Life stages	Vocational choice	Circumscription of investigative aspirations	Not fully empirically examined Limited evidence of support for women and racial/ethnic minority groups
Social Cognitive Career Theory	Self-efficacy beliefs Outcome expectations Choice model Performance model Interest model Identifying barriers Foreclosure of options	Interests Vocational choice Level of performance	Self-efficacy beliefs for math and teaching Changing outcome expectations	Well researched Substantial empirical support for constructs and model Substantial evidence of support for women and racial/ethnic minority groups

Applying Theories to Your Own Career Development

Before reading the subsequent section on applying theoretical perspectives, use the personal reflections throughout the book and the following questions to evaluate how each theory may contribute to a greater understanding of your own career history.

1. What insights have you gained about your own career history from each of the theories?

2. Is one theory more applicable to your own career decision making than others?

3. How might a combination of two or more theories be more applicable than just one? Which parts of the theories would be more applicable?

4. How can you use the major concepts from each theory to explain your career history?

5. What aspects of your career history and decision making are not explained by the theories?

6. What role has your culture and gender played in your own career decisions?

INTEGRATING THEORETICAL PERSPECTIVES

We have summarized the major constructs of each theory and discussed how they may shape a counselor's perspective in conducting career counseling. The manner in which that can happen is what we have tried to illustrate throughout the book as we have applied each theory to Leslie's situation (presented in Chapter 4). We have conceptualized her career history and present situation from each perspective and conducted career counseling with her from each theoretical viewpoint. In this section, we connect these pieces to examine what we believe has been each theory's contribution to a fuller understanding of Leslie's history, her expectations, and her career goals. This understanding is summarized in the fourth column of Table 15.1. We then apply each theoretical focus to a new case, George. Following our discussion of each theory's perspective on George, we share how we would integrate theoretical approaches in career counseling with him.

Contributions of Different Theories to Understanding Leslie

The model of culturally appropriate counseling reminds us to consider the multiple contextual factors that exert influence in Leslie's life. Her educational and career experiences have been shaped by societal expectations for her as a White, middle-class, heterosexual woman, regardless of her level of awareness of these expectations. Exploring these contextual factors will help Leslie realize the influence that they have had on her choices and help her make future decisions with a clearer sense of who she is and who she wants to be. Moreover, the counselor's own contextual experiences might influence his or her interaction with Leslie in counseling.

The two theories of person-environment fit help us understand the sources of satisfaction and dissatisfaction that Leslie perceives in her current job and in her career. Holland's theory does so by suggesting that her type (investigative-social-conventional) is relatively congruent with her occupation as a math teacher (coded on the Strong Interest Inventory [SII] profile as CIR for women). Furthermore, many other types of high school teachers are primarily social types, so the individuals in her environment are likely to be social types. Her dissatisfaction, therefore, is probably not due to being in an occupation that is incongruent with her type. This understanding helps the counselor look at other factors that might contribute to her dissatisfaction, such as people and policies in her specific job environment.

The TWA also offers a perspective on how Leslie corresponds to her environment, this time in terms of her satisfaction and her satisfactoriness. Here, her dissatisfaction is conceptualized as related to whether her values and needs are being met by the reward structure available in her work environment. We know that part of her dissatisfaction is likely due to her frustrated needs for autonomy, even as her other needs continue to be met on the job. An important feature that the TWA adds to our understanding is the explicit attention to determining if she has been a satisfactory employee. We have some information that she has performed well on the job, but the TWA helps us focus more specifically on her job performance.

Both of these theories also suggest other alternatives, should Leslie decide that she wants to change jobs or occupations. In the case of Holland's theory, Leslie's type of investigative, social, and conventional can be used as a guide for identifying other occupations with which she might be congruent. In the TWA, her identified values and needs, as well as her identified dissatisfactions with her current job, provide the avenue for exploring new occupational choices. Her needs to achieve and to use her talents, as well as her need to help others, are important to consider in occupational exploration.

Developmental theories provide a life span perspective in understanding Leslie. Her career concerns are not atypical for someone of her age and career stage, as she is trying to determine the role of work in her life, particularly in relation to her other current (and desired) life roles. She has established herself as a teacher, yet she is still struggling with Super's developmental tasks of consolidating and advancing in her career, and she is questioning whether she wants to continue in this occupation or move into a new career. Considering the totality of Leslie's life space allows the counselor to incorporate an explicit discussion of her various life roles and their relation to one another. Leslie's other life roles undoubtedly interact with how she experiences her work role; for example, her dissatisfaction with her job may influence or be influenced by her desire to have children. Super's focus on career choice as an implementation of the self-concept thus helps us understand Leslie's life in context.

Furthermore, Gottfredson's theory adds hypotheses about how Leslie may have circumscribed her occupational aspirations as a child and adolescent and then compromised her choices from those remaining acceptable alternatives. Leslie's compromises corresponded to those predicted by Gottfredson, in that she chose an occupation that appeared to preserve her sex-typed aspirations (teaching), perhaps at the expense of her interests (engineering, math, and science).

Social cognitive career theory also uses learning experiences in understanding Leslie, with a particular focus on her self-efficacy for specific activities and the expected outcomes she anticipates from performing these activities. Leslie has considerable self-efficacy about mathematics and about teaching, and she also values the outcomes provided by doing well in math and teaching. Social cognitive career theory also suggests that her job dissatisfaction might be due to changing self-efficacy or outcome expectations, particularly as related to her desire to have children.

Finally, the emerging theories and integration of work and mental health help provide a holistic perspective on Leslie. These included her concerns about her marriage, her family of origin and how her desire to have children influences her career and work decisions.

THE CASE OF GEORGE

We will use the case of George to demonstrate the way in which different theoretical perspectives inform how career counseling might proceed with another client. Assume that the following information was gathered during an intake interview with George; as you read, think about each of the theoretical approaches described in this book.

George is a 54-year-old White male of German and English descent. He is seeking counseling because he is becoming increasingly dissatisfied with his career as a financial planner. George lives in a semirural area in the northeastern United States. He is married with two college-aged children, and his wife is a special education teacher.

George has a bachelor's degree in industrial engineering. He had been accepted at several major universities after high school graduation and chose the one he attended because of its reputation for engineering and because it was his father's alma mater (who also received a degree in industrial engineering). George knew at that time that math and science were his "strong suits" and that he had interest and skills in working with people. However, he states now that he "never felt engineering was the right fit" but that industrial engineering was the best fit of the possible specialties within engineering.

After college graduation, he sought a position in engineering sales; after interviewing with several firms, he was hired by a company that manufactured french fryers to sell to fast food restaurants. George reported that he enjoyed this job and was very good at it. After 5 years, however, he tired of the constant travel, and he did not like some of the company's policies or some of the customers with whom he had to deal routinely. He quit the job with no plans for what he might do next and despite the company's efforts to retain him.

While on a vacation shortly after he quit his job, George bought a large quantity of Oriental rugs and returned home to open a retail store in a historic district of his small town that was undergoing redevelopment. The business flourished for several years, until an economic recession dried up the market. A friend asked for his assistance in setting up a food business in another town, and when George visited him to help, he decided to close his own business and join with his friend. This business grew rapidly, and George and his friend split into two independent operations so that George was managing a restaurant on his own.

George thoroughly enjoyed managing the restaurant. He handled all catering sales, hired and trained personnel, and managed the orders and accounts. The restaurant was very successful for several years until a highway was rerouted, which caused the traffic into the restaurant to drop off precipitously. George then found himself somewhat stranded, and he worried that he would need to move elsewhere to find a sales job with a corporation. However, one of his customers at the restaurant had been recruiting him to join his life insurance office as a financial planner, and George decided to give it a try.

George felt out of place with the other agents and planners at first but quickly "learned the ropes." He felt that it was the first time in his life that he was doing something to help other people. He has been working in life insurance and financial planning for 11 years; as he stated, "I took the job because I had to, and I've continued because I'm good at it." However, lately he's been feeling like "it's not fun anymore." He enjoys meeting with clients, but he finds it harder to make the phone calls necessary to set up the meetings and to solicit new sales prospects. He also finds himself more consciously aware that he benefits from each sale and wonders whether that awareness affects how he works with clients. He's worried that he is not doing as good a job for his clients as he would like.

When asked what he would do if he could change careers, he answered without hesitation: "Teach." He has had some experience teaching basic insurance courses to new agents, which he enjoyed. He is interested in teaching math but is unsure about the practicality of doing so at his age.

Seven years ago, George took the SII as part of a continuing education workshop sponsored by his office. His highest General Occupational Theme scores were social (very high), enterprising (high), and artistic (high), and his investigative score was moderately high. Other notable features of his SII profile are high Basic Interest Scale scores in Athletics, Military, Medical Science, Teaching and Education, Counseling and Helping, Religion and Spirituality, Politics and Public Speaking, Law, Marketing and Advertising, and Sales, and he had a very high score on the Risk-Taking Personal Style Scale. High Occupational Scale scores include law enforcement officer, dentist, optometrist, registered nurse, parks and recreation manager, community service director, school administrator, life insurance agent, purchasing agent, nursing home administrator, real estate agent, and credit manager.

Working With George

Before we turn to a consideration of George from the various theoretical perspectives, consider the following questions:

1. What are your impressions of George?

2. What more would you like to know about him?

3. What hypotheses would you develop about George from the perspective of each approach, including gender-aware and culturally appropriate career counseling?

4. How will you gather information to test your hypotheses?

5. How does each of these theoretical approaches influence the next step in counseling? What direction would you take from the perspective of each, including gender-aware and culturally appropriate career counseling?

Considering George From Various Theoretical Perspectives

We will begin with a contextual analysis and work through the theories (Chapters 6–11). We will consider George from each approach or theoretical perspective, highlighting the unique contributions of each perspective.

Contextual analysis

George is a White, middle-class, heterosexual male, possibly belonging to the upper middle class. He is of German and English descent. It is not indicated to what ethnic group his wife belongs, nor is his religious background noted. One more aspect of his context is given in the case study; he is from the Northeast and lives in a small town. Several aspects of George's career history seem pertinent to a gender analysis. First, George clearly identified with his father early in his career: His decision of university and major were both influenced by his father's choices, and although engineering did not seem like a good fit at the time, he pursued it anyway. More information about George's father would be helpful, particularly related to how George perceived his father's expectations for him generally and for his career success specifically.

Second, there is a theme in George's career history of working hard at building businesses but also having an underlying interest in and concern for people. The latter interest seems to be increasing in strength, as evidenced by George's expressed desire to teach. The interest in people may be an area that he did not feel encouraged to express earlier in his life.

The culturally appropriate approach would assume that as a heterosexual White male, George had a great deal of privilege in his life. His options appear not to have been restricted by racism or sexism. He was able twice to open a new business impulsively and was successful at it, apparently without a barrier because of his race or sex. He was affected when the highway was rerouted, but there is no indication that he construed that as anything other than a neutral environmental event. However, George may have felt restricted because of the cultural messages he received about appropriate behavior for men.

The culturally appropriate approach would examine what George's multiple cultural contexts have conveyed to him. For example, George attended his father's alma mater, following his father's footsteps into a career that was not necessarily a good fit for him. Did his family expect him to carry on a family tradition? If so, are there other similar expectations? What expectations did George have in terms of being a financial provider for his family? George's ethnic background was German and English; how were those different ethnic backgrounds integrated into his upbringing? How may they affect him now?

Holland's theory

A counselor working from the perspective of Holland's theory would examine George's aspirations from early in his life and the relation between George's personality type and the environments in which he has worked. Clearly, George has had entrepreneurial aspirations and has always excelled at occupations that require persuasive abilities and sales skills—enterprising-type occupations. According to the General Occupational Themes of the SII, George is an SEA type, and the work environments in which he has thrived have been predominantly enterprising and social in nature.

George's decisions to change jobs relatively frequently may not be viewed as an unstable pattern, because he remained in occupations with the same environmental type. In fact, he probably has moved into more congruent occupations, incorporating increasingly more of his social interests.

The Theory of Work Adjustment

George has indicated that he is not satisfied in his occupation. The TWA would conceptualize George as a satisfactory employee whose abilities have matched the job requirements for the past 11 years. However, George's needs have not been met by the job. He would appear to have high compensation and social service needs as well as achievement needs. It would also seem that his social service needs at times interfere with his compensation needs, and when they do, the social service needs are stronger. George's adjustment style would appear to have a relatively high level of flexibility but a low level of perseverance (he stayed in a job he did not like for 5 years, then quit with no other plans in place). He seems to have a high level of pace.

His counselor would begin by examining whether George can increase the correspondence with his environment, either by changing his needs or by changing the environment. George may, for example, work to resolve the conflict between his social service needs and his compensation needs, perhaps finding ways to meet his social service needs by volunteering for a local youth group. Alternatively, he may work to change the environment, perhaps by taking on different aspects of financial planning within the organization or by encouraging his firm to offer more free seminars and workshops so that he can feel he is helping others.

If George decides that he would rather explore new occupations than make his current occupation a better fit, the counselor would give George additional assessments, particularly the Minnesota Importance Questionnaire (MIQ) to help identify occupations in which he would be predicted to fit. He would be assumed to have high abilities in a variety of areas, including math, reasoning, and interpersonal communication. Occupations that dovetail between the SII and the MIQ would be good options for more exploration.

Developmental theories

Developmental theories add explicit attention to how George's self-concept has evolved throughout his life. He seems to have longstanding interests both in entrepreneurial and social service activities, but perhaps the relative importance of these two areas has shifted with time. George's self-concept thus has remained stable throughout his life, with a clear sense of what he is good at doing and what is important to him.

In Super's formulation, George is in the age range corresponding to Maintenance stage career tasks; however, he has made enough career shifts that he could be conceptualized as being in the Establishment stage. In fact, his current career dissatisfaction seems to be related to his transition into Maintenance: He seems to be asking, "Should I do something new or continue with this until retirement?"

Gottfredson's theory

George's current interest in teaching may be an example of an occupation eliminated during the process of circumscription earlier in his life. When George was a child, being a teacher may have fallen outside of his tolerable sex-type boundary; being a teacher also may have not been prestigious enough, given his family background and expectations, therefore falling below his tolerable-level boundary. Engineering, on the other hand, clearly was within the zone of acceptable alternatives that he developed during childhood and adolescence.

Social cognitive career theory

The social cognitive theoretical perspective would focus on George's self-efficacy beliefs and his outcome expectations. He has been in an occupation for several years that he feels he is good at but that he does not want to continue doing. George would appear to have high self-efficacy beliefs about his abilities as a financial planner, but the outcomes he is expecting from his occupation are not as positive as perhaps they once were. He does not like cold sales calls and would like to feel that he is of more help to people than he may be. He expects better outcomes from being a teacher.

George appears to have high self-efficacy beliefs related to change, including changing careers. He has changed careers several times and been successful at it. He has a large number of diverse interests, indicating a variety of areas that may be options for him to examine. A career counselor working from a social cognitive perspective would help George examine the option of becoming a teacher, identifying possible barriers he may have. The counselor would also examine whether George has prematurely foreclosed other options, many of which may be identified by the SII results.

Emerging perspectives

George's career decisions may be characterized as volitional in nature; he has always perceived that he had control over his choices and directions, and he has acted accordingly. His family of origin instilled beliefs about living the democratic American dream and the importance of bettering one's position in society, and he has been able to operate from a position of privilege in society. These may be important beliefs to explore, particularly as George considers another career change, this time during a more economically challenging period.

George grew up in a traditional family structure, with clearly defined gender roles about work and family life, although he has broadened his definition of these roles as an adult. He may want to more explicitly consider the market and relational aspects of his life, and their interaction, as he moves forward with a career decision. Further, his experience of work and the needs met by work, may have evolved through his previous career decisions to his current position: His earlier choices were influenced by a pressing need for survival, whereas his current decision may be tapping needs for relatedness and self-determination.

Our own approach to conceptualizing George

We blend a variety of approaches when we do career counseling, based on our own experiences of using different career counseling approaches with diverse clients. We have tried to show how that may be done in this section. However, it is important to note that this is just an example and certainly not a prescription for working with all clients. There are many ways to blend and integrate various theoretical approaches, and these will vary both with the counselor and the concern brought by the client.

George may be seeking career counseling for help adjusting to his current occupation or for help choosing a new career. He has an idea of an area that he might like to explore—teaching—but is not certain that it is a viable option for him. George has a large number of strengths: He appears to have high abilities in a variety of areas, including general intellectual ability and strong interpersonal skills; he has been successful in a number of ventures; he has the skills and confidence to initiate and adapt to change; and he has interests in diverse areas.

We would use a combination of person-environment fit theories (Holland's and the TWA), as well as Super's developmental theory, to begin to conceptualize hypotheses about George's current career concerns. We would use a combination of social cognitive theory and Super's developmental theory to conceptualize his career history.

His career history would appear to include increasing knowledge in high school about his abilities but perhaps not about his interests. For example, he notes that he knew he excelled in math and science and chose to enter an engineering curriculum, but he does not say why he chose engineering; he does not indicate whether this was based on an examination of his interests and abilities. Nonetheless, by the end of high school, he had crystallized an occupation (engineering), and by the time he had graduated from college, he had specified an occupation (industrial engineering). When he implemented that choice, however, he did not decide to pursue a traditional industrial engineering job; rather, he implemented his choice in engineering sales. It would seem that George was implementing a self-concept that combined engineering knowledge with greater use of interpersonal skills than a traditional engineering position would involve.

Developmental theory does not entirely explain some of George's decisions, however. Why did he choose industrial engineering, even though he felt engineering was not a good fit for him? Why did he continue in it, and how did he decide to go into engineering sales? Examining George's decisions from a social cognitive perspective may be useful in formulating hypotheses about his early choices. George reported that he knew he was good in math and science, thus indicating that he had high self-efficacy beliefs about his abilities in these areas. He attended his father's alma mater, majoring in the same field as his father. It may be that George expected very positive outcomes from pursuing this avenue, such as strong approval from his father or other family members. What other occupations did George consider, and what were the barriers to pursuing those occupations?

Social cognitive theory may help explain George's decisions when he quit his first job in engineering sales. He had high self-efficacy beliefs in his ability to find another job, and his outcome expectancies for leaving the position and finding a new job were more positive than the outcomes expected of staying. The TWA would explicate this further.

His correspondence with the first job was very poor; he may have tried to adjust himself or his environment, but despite being a satisfactory employee, his needs were not met and he chose to leave the environment. What may have been his adjustment style in that job? Has that been consistent in other jobs?

The TWA would suggest that George's subsequent jobs of owning an Oriental rug store and managing a restaurant were more correspondent occupations for him. Both of those jobs ended for reasons outside his control; there is no indication that he was dissatisfied in either position. In fact, he notes that he enjoyed them very much. It would appear that managing a restaurant met his compensation, social service, and achievement needs and that he was well able to do it, because the restaurant was quite successful. George is less correspondent with the occupation of financial planner. He complains that it is "no longer any fun," connoting that his needs are not being met. We would hypothesize that his social service needs, in particular, are not being met, as well as, perhaps, his achievement needs.

George's current dilemma is what to do about his dissatisfaction with his job. Should he change jobs? The first approach we would take would be to talk with

George about the context of this decision. What other factors does George need to consider? He has two college-aged children; what responsibilities does he have for their education? How would a change in jobs or in life circumstances affect George's wife, and are there concomitant dual career concerns? Does he have aging parents for whom he is responsible? In other words, does this decision affect others? What about the context of his decision within the other roles George plays in his life? What role does he want work to have at this point? Are there other roles (e.g., leisurite, student, citizen) that may be just as salient for George or that he would like to make more salient? How do his decisions about market work and market relationships affect aspects of his life related to personal care work and personal relationships? What cultural messages does George have about the role of work in a man's life? Which of those messages would he like to include in the way he lives his life? He may, for example, decide that he likes to be the major breadwinner and provider in the family. On the other hand, he may choose to share this role with his wife if he returns to school.

We would incorporate the developmental perspective in examining George's life roles and the context of the decision. Another aspect of the developmental perspective we would include is encouraging George to talk about the development of his career as a financial planner. He has worked as a financial planner for 11 years; he may be moving out of the establishment stage into the maintenance stage and using this transition point to stop and examine his options.

One of the questions we would want to explore with George is whether he is dissatisfied with the occupation of financial planner or if he is feeling dissatisfaction with the specific job environment. This question is from the TWA approach. He is a satisfactory employee, but his needs and the rewards provided by the job do not correspond. Three options or combinations of options are possible. First, counseling may focus on either adjusting himself or his environment. Is it very important to him that his social service needs are met in the work environment, or can he meet those needs in other domains of his life? How amenable is the work environment to being adjusted? Is it possible to increase the social service activities he does as part of his job and reduce the activities he finds aversive? If this is not possible in this job, the second option is to determine if he would be more satisfied as a financial planner in another firm or agency.

The third option is that the activities he finds aversive are integral to the occupation of financial planner and he will have to change his occupation to find a better fit. We would turn to Holland's theory to help George find a new occupational area. His General Occupational Theme code is SEA, with some moderate interest in Investigative. This code illuminates the lack of fit for George as an engineer, an environment characterized as realistic and investigative. It also may illuminate why he has enjoyed a variety of enterprising types of occupations over the course of his career that capitalized on his experience in sales and his enterprising interests, such as owning a store and managing a restaurant. Financial planner is not an occupation included on the SII, nor is it included in the *Dictionary of Holland Occupational Codes* (Gottfredson & Holland, 1996). However, George is in an office that combines life insurance agents and financial planners, and life insurance agents have a Holland code of E on the SII. This would indicate that George has some interests that are congruent with his work environment but that he may be seeking an environment more congruent with his social interests. We would encourage George to begin to examine the occupations with a strong social component from the SII, such as nurse, parks and recreation leader, community service organization director, and special education teacher.

We would return to the questions raised earlier about context and life roles as George moves toward making a decision first about whether he would like to adjust to the occupation, move to another company, or choose a new career. Are these options that George would like to pursue, how do they fit in his life right now, and what would he need to do differently to fit them into his life in the future? How does this fit with the developmental stage he is in right now and how he feels about the role of work in his life? How does he feel about taking on the role of student if he decides to go back to school for a teaching degree? How can George find out more information about the occupations he is considering?

Summary

Each of the theoretical perspectives offers a different perspective about George's career history and his current career concerns. The theories also suggest different hypotheses and directions for counseling. As we just demonstrated, the theories are not necessarily incompatible or mutually exclusive, and there are benefits to using multiple approaches to conceptualize a single client. This is particularly true when the client has had considerable life and career experience. Now consider the case of Tom, who is a traditional college-aged student.

THE CASE OF TOM

Tom is a 21-year-old White man of Irish descent and the younger of two brothers from a medium-sized town in the southern United States. He grew up in a lower-middle-class neighborhood; his mother works as a postal clerk, and his father is an airplane mechanic. They live near many relatives, and much of the family's social life revolves around family celebrations and events.

Tom enjoyed high school. He was an average student. He enjoyed the material he learned in school, but his main goal in high school was to be with his friends.

He was very social, and he participated in as many activities as he could while still playing football and basketball. He was an average athlete in high school, and he knew he could not compete athletically at the college level, but he had fun being a part of the team and playing when he could.

In contrast to Tom, his older brother, Jeff, was an outstanding student. He graduated from high school with a 4.0 grade point average, took several advanced placement courses, and received scholarships to many universities. He ended up attending a prestigious school about 70 miles away from his parents. Jeff is able to come home frequently and still participates in the family activities.

Tom and Jeff are three and a half years apart in age but are very close emotionally. Jeff was eager to give Tom advice about attending college and was very disappointed when Tom's grades were not high enough to enable him to attend the same university. Tom was unsure of whether to go to college or not. His parents, aunts, and uncles had not graduated from college, and he thought they were successful and happy. He is happy at home, enjoys his family, and enjoys his friends. Tom feels no particular need to leave his hometown or to move far away from his family. But his brother told him that increasingly, more jobs require college degrees and he would be severely hampered in the future if he did not go to college.

Tom enrolled in a college close to his hometown. He lived in a dorm with his cousin as his roommate. They went home frequently to be part of family gatherings. He had to declare a major when he enrolled, and he decided to major in police science. He thought it sounded good, and one of his friends was majoring in it. He had never really given much thought to choosing a major; his primary decision was whether to attend college or not. He had not had much career guidance in high school, so he really did not have a very clear idea of his interests or his alternatives.

Tom loved college life and became heavily involved in many of the social aspects of a residential college environment. He pledged a fraternity, made many friends, and decided to run for student government office. But he did not do well in his studies. His first-year grades were slightly below a C average. He did even more poorly his second year. He had not realized that police science required such a strong math and science background; math was his weakest subject in high school. At the end of the first semester of his second year, Tom flunked out of college.

Working With Tom

Use the following questions to consider how you are viewing Tom and how you might work with him in career counseling:

1. What are your impressions of Tom?

2. What more would you like to know about him?

3. What hypotheses would you develop about Tom from the perspective of each theory, including gender-focused and culturally appropriate approaches?

4. How will you gather information to test your hypotheses?

5. How does each of these theoretical approaches influence the next step in counseling? What direction would you take from the perspective of each, including gender-focused and culturally appropriate approaches?

EVALUATION OF THE MAJOR THEORIES

One of the most important questions that readers should ask as they consider each of the theories presented in this book is "How well does it work?" The next most important question should be "For whom does it work?" These are critical questions and are answered by the research conducted on each theory by its author(s) and others in the field. The last column of Table 15.1 includes a brief evaluation of the level of empirical support for each theory. This is an overly simplistic summary evaluation, for space does not allow a comprehensive review of the empirical support for each theory. Readers are referred to Brown and Lent (2013), Juntunen and Even (2012) and Blustein (2013) for extensive reviews of the empirical bases for these theories. However, this summary will provide some basis for evaluating the theories. We examined the literature related to each theory on the following criteria: how well the theoretical constructs have been operationalized, how much support those constructs have received, and how applicable each theory is across a wide variety of populations.

The theories in this book have all been developed by scholars dedicated to testing and revising their theories. Consequently, all have stimulated research in an attempt to support their constructs and the relationships among them. It is not surprising that the oldest theories (Holland's, the TWA, and Super's) are the most well researched and, consequently, are the most well established of the theories.

Holland's theory has been operationalized in a number of instruments, among them the SII (Harmon, Hansen, Borgen, & Hammer, 2005) and the Self-Directed Search (Holland, Powell, & Fritzsche, 1994). With hundreds of research studies conducted on it, Holland's theory has been the most extensively examined career theory. One reason is how clearly and easily its constructs have been operationalized (Nauta, 2013). Borgen (1991) notes that "its simplicity makes it eminently useful" (p. 274). For example, research has determined that the RIASEC types exist in both individuals and environments (Nauta, 2013). Hypothesized relationships among constructs also have been supported. For example, congruence is related to satisfaction (Tsabari, Tziner, & Meir, 2005), and the types appear to be related to each other as predicted by the theory (e.g., Armstrong, Allison, & Rounds, 2008; Fouad, Harmon, & Borgen, 1997).

The TWA also has received empirical support, although the constructs have not stimulated as much research as has Holland's theory. Several of the constructs are well operationalized, and one of the hallmarks of TWA is that the authors have developed tools to measure the constructs (e.g., Lofquist & Dawis, 1991). Support for the constructs is somewhat equivocal, although more support has been found for correspondence, satisfaction, and satisfactoriness than for the adjustment style and personality variables. Osipow and Fitzgerald (1996) note that, unlike the extensive research on Holland's theory, empirical support for the TWA has come mostly from its authors and their students with little independent verification. Betz (2008) and Swanson and Schneider (2013), however, review more recent literature on applications of TWA across cross-cultural populations. Betz concludes that the constructs may be useful across developmental stages, including in understanding college retention. Swanson and Schneider conclude that research has demonstrated the "usefulness of TWA in explaining the work experiences of different groups of people" (p. 43).

Super's theory has been generally supported in over five decades of studies. As noted by Borgen (1991), "Super's comprehensive conceptual work has splendidly stood the test of time" (p. 278). Individuals' careers do develop as predicted by Super, and research supports the construct of self-concept implementation and progression through developmental tasks of adolescence and early adulthood (Betz, 2008; Juntunen & Even, 2012). Gottfredson's theory is the newer of the two developmental theories discussed here and is less well operationalized than Super's theory. It has received mixed empirical support, although Gottfredson (2005) notes that research has not tested many areas of the model. Hartung, Porfeli, and Vondracek (2005) reviewed literature in child vocational development and concluded that all four areas (gender, prestige, interests, and socioeconomic status) influence children's vocational choices.

Social cognitive theory, though the newest model in the book, has received a substantial amount of support. It is well operationalized and has stimulated quite a bit of research since Hackett and Betz's (1981) initial introduction and Lent, Brown, and Hackett's (1994) publication of the full social cognitive career theory. Self-efficacy, in particular, has received a great deal of attention and support, as has the application of the theory to diverse groups (Betz, 2008; Juntunen & Even, 2012; Swanson & Gore, 2000).

All the theories were developed with the intention of being applied across a wide variety of populations. However, all have been criticized (e.g., Betz, 2008; Fouad & Kantamneni, 2013; Juntunen & Even, 2012; Worthington, Flores, & Navarro, 2005) for not incorporating gender and culture explicitly into the theory.

All are equally open to criticism for not thoroughly examining how well the theory applies to various populations. In fact, most were originally developed based on research conducted on White, middle-class men. We simply do not know if the theories operate similarly for women and men, for individuals of different racial and ethnic groups, or for gay and lesbian individuals. If they do differ, we do not know specifically how, nor do we know how to incorporate that knowledge into more effective practice.

It is incumbent on researchers and practitioners alike to work together to create a joint research agenda that will more effectively inform practice. First, more research needs to be conducted on the theories themselves and whether the constructs in fact reflect reality. Second, we need to know if the theoretical relationship among constructs differs across populations. Third, we need to know what works for whom and when; in other words, we need to know which particular interventions are effective with specific individuals at distinct times in their lives.

REVISITING COUNSELOR COGNITIONS

We would like to return to the three cases at the very beginning of Chapter 1: Ruth, Harry, and Joel. Ruth is returning to the workforce but is unsure of her options, Harry is worried about losing his job, and Joel is uncertain what he will do after high school. All three are at different stages of their work lives, but all three seek career counseling for help making work and career decisions. And each of these three cases could be viewed as simply helping a client make a work-related decision. However, as we pointed out in Chapters 1 and 14, to be effective, career counseling and personal counseling are often integrated. If we look at each case more holistically, we can see that an integrated perspective may be more helpful to the client. A counselor working with Ruth might want to help her brainstorm options to use her medical technology degree or may help her explore other options, but the counselor might also help her think through how she can adapt to her new role as worker and how her family may react. Harry's counselor would want to help Harry work through his depression and would most likely confront Harry with potential alcohol abuse. The counselor would also help Harry think through how he is doing at work and how he could change his work tasks or change work environments to use his skills better. Joel's counselor might help him consider post-high school options but also help him consider how to talk to his parents about not wanting to go to school.

Each of these three cases, indeed all the cases in this book, highlight how important it is to understand the context in which decisions are made, how race and gender influence decisions, and what work means to each individual. Blustein

(2006) argues that work can have three main purposes in people's lives: survival, relationships, and identity. It is important for career counselors to understand what purpose work plays in clients' lives in helping them make decisions but also what role they want work to play. For example, a client may have worked to earn money for his or her family but may want a future career to have a stronger identity purpose. It is important to look at the context from the clients' perspectives to understand how to help them effectively. We have discussed counselor cognitions throughout this book, using this discussion as a way to highlight the differences among approaches. In this chapter, we have provided an example of a way to integrate those cognitions, and we want to encourage readers to extend their cognitions to reflect this perspective on context.

In Chapter 1, we described how to use career theories to guide your work with clients, primarily through generating and testing hypotheses about clients, and we hope that working with the cases in this text has convinced you of the value of doing so. Developing and implementing a theoretical approach to working with clients involves learning a set of skills. Just like the process of learning any other counseling-related skills, it takes conscious attention and practice.

We recommend that you continue to hone your conceptualization skills by explicitly using them. Only with continued exercise does conceptualization become second nature. Consider the three cases of Ruth, Harry, and Joel. For each case, ask the following questions:

1. How and what am I thinking about this client?

2. What assumptions am I making about the client's career history? What assumptions am I making about the client's current career concerns?

3. How might personal concerns influence the client's career concerns?

4. How does the client's current context (gender, race, family, disability, social class, sexual orientation) influence his or her perceptions of opportunities or barriers of options?

5. Which theoretical approaches are most useful in thinking about this client, and what hypotheses do the approaches suggest?

6. What specific cultural and gender issues are relevant with this client?

7. How do my culture and gender influence how I am thinking about this client?

8. Am I imposing my values on the client?

PARTING WORDS

We are often asked what happened to Leslie. Leslie is not a real person but is based (with her permission) on one of our real clients, although we changed many details to protect her identity. Thus, we cannot say what she ended up doing. We can speculate, however, on the types of decisions she may have made and encourage you to think what she might have decided:

1. Did Leslie change to a different career?

2. Did Leslie seek an additional degree?

3. If Leslie changed careers, what areas might she have considered?

4. Did Leslie decide to continue her work as a high school math teacher?

5. If she decided to continue as a math teacher, how did she resolve her dissatisfaction with her work environment?

6. If she did have children, did she decide to stay home, as her husband expected, or go back to work?

7. How did Leslie decide to balance her various life roles as a worker, daughter, sister, wife, mother, leisurite, citizen?

Finally, we want to return to the fundamental purpose of this book. We continue to be fascinated by the study of career development and by the career issues that clients bring to counseling. We sincerely hope that we have conveyed our excitement and enthusiasm in the pages of this book. We encourage you to allow yourself to be fascinated by career stories. Understanding the role work plays in individuals' lives will serve to make you a better counselor and will help you assist the clients who come to you for counseling.

APPENDIX A: LESLIE'S PROFILES

GENERAL OCCUPATIONAL THEMES **SECTION 1**

The General Occupational Themes (GOTs) measure six broad interest patterns that can be used to describe your work personality. Most people's interests are reflected by two or three Themes, combined to form a cluster of interests. Work activities, potential skills, and values can also be classified into these six Themes. This provides a direct link between your interests and the career and education possibilities likely to be most meaningful to you.

Your *standard scores* are based on the average scores of a combined group of working adults. However, because research shows that men and women tend to respond differently in these areas, your *interest levels* (Very Little, Little, Moderate, High, Very High) were determined by comparing your scores against the average scores for your gender.

THEME DESCRIPTIONS

THEME	CODE	INTERESTS	WORK ACTIVITIES	POTENTIAL SKILLS	VALUES
Investigative	I	Science, medicine, mathematics, research	Performing lab work, solving abstract problems, conducting research	Mathematical ability, researching, writing, analyzing	Independence, curiosity, learning
Social	S	People, teamwork, helping, community service	Teaching, caring for people, counseling, training employees	People skills, verbal ability, listening, showing understanding	Cooperation, generosity, service to others
Conventional	C	Organization, data management, accounting, investing, information systems	Setting up procedures and systems, organizing, keeping records, developing computer applications	Ability to work with numbers, data analysis, finances, attention to detail	Accuracy, stability, efficiency
Realistic	R	Machines, computer networks, athletics, working outdoors	Operating equipment, using tools, building, repairing, providing security	Mechanical ingenuity and dexterity, physical coordination	Tradition, practicality, common sense
Enterprising	E	Business, politics, leadership, entrepreneurship	Selling, managing, persuading, marketing	Verbal ability, ability to motivate and direct others	Risk taking, status, competition, influence
Artistic	A	Self-expression, art appreciation, communication, culture	Composing music, performing, writing, creating visual art	Creativity, musical ability, artistic expression	Beauty, originality, independence, imagination

YOUR HIGHEST THEMES	YOUR THEME CODE
Investigative, Social, Conventional	**ISC**

THEME	CODE	STANDARD SCORE & INTEREST LEVEL	STD SCORE
Investigative	I	VERY HIGH	74
Social	S	HIGH	64
Conventional	C	MODERATE	54
Realistic	R	LITTLE	38
Enterprising	E	VERY LITTLE	36
Artistic	A	VERY LITTLE	34

The charts above display your GOT results in descending order, from your highest to least level of interest. Referring to the Theme Descriptions provided, determine how well your results fit for you. Do your highest Themes ring true? Look at your next highest level of interest and ask yourself the same question. You may wish to highlight the Theme descriptions on this page that seem to fit you best.

Figure A.1   Leslie's Strong Interest Inventory Profile **(Continued)**

BASIC INTEREST SCALES

The Basic Interest Scales represent specific interest areas that often point to work activities, projects, course work, and leisure activities that are personally motivating and rewarding. As with the General Occupational Themes, your interest levels (Very Little, Little, Moderate, High, Very High) were determined by comparing your scores against the average scores for your gender.

As you review your results in the charts below, note your top interest areas and your areas of least interest, and think about how they relate to your work, educational, and leisure activities. Take time to consider any top interest areas that are not currently part of your work or lifestyle and think about how you might be able to incorporate them into your plans.

YOUR TOP FIVE INTEREST AREAS

1. **Research (I)**
2. **Teaching & Education (S)**
3. **Mathematics (I)**
4. **Taxes & Accounting (C)**
5. **Science (I)**

Areas of Least Interest

Culinary Arts (A)
Writing & Mass Communication (A)
Visual Arts & Design (A)

INVESTIGATIVE — Very High

BASIC INTEREST SCALE	STD SCORE & INTEREST LEVEL	STD SCORE
Research	VH	78
Mathematics	VH	73
Science	VH	71
Medical Science	M	54

SOCIAL — High

BASIC INTEREST SCALE	STD SCORE & INTEREST LEVEL	STD SCORE
Teaching & Education	VH	76
Religion & Spirituality	VH	71
Human Resources & Training	M	56
Counseling & Helping	M	56
Social Sciences	M	54
Healthcare Services	L	38

CONVENTIONAL — Moderate

BASIC INTEREST SCALE	STD SCORE & INTEREST LEVEL	STD SCORE
Taxes & Accounting	VH	72
Programming & Information Systems	M	50
Finance & Investing	M	49
Office Management	M	47

REALISTIC — Little

BASIC INTEREST SCALE	STD SCORE & INTEREST LEVEL	STD SCORE
Computer Hardware & Electronics	H	54
Mechanics & Construction	M	50
Nature & Agriculture	M	45
Athletics	M	42
Protective Services	L	40
Military	VL	36

ENTERPRISING — Very Little

BASIC INTEREST SCALE	STD SCORE & INTEREST LEVEL	STD SCORE
Law	L	41
Sales	L	40
Management	L	40
Politics & Public Speaking	L	39
Marketing & Advertising	L	39
Entrepreneurship	L	38

ARTISTIC — Very Little

BASIC INTEREST SCALE	STD SCORE & INTEREST LEVEL	STD SCORE
Performing Arts	VL	36
Visual Arts & Design	VL	35
Writing & Mass Communication	VL	35
Culinary Arts	VL	31

INTEREST LEVELS: VL = Very Little | L = Little | M = Moderate | H = High | VH = Very High

Figure A.1 (Continued)

OCCUPATIONAL SCALES

This section highlights your Profile results on the Occupational Scales of the *Strong*. On the next three pages you will find your scores for 122 occupations. The 10 occupations most closely aligned with your interests are listed in the summary chart below. Keep in mind that the occupations listed in your Profile results are just *some* of the many occupations linked to your interests that you might want to consider. They do not indicate those you "should" pursue. It is helpful to think of each occupation as a single example of a much larger group of occupational titles to consider.

Your score on an Occupational Scale shows how similar your interests are to those of people of your gender who have been working in, and are satisfied with, that occupation. The higher your score, the more likes and dislikes you share with those individuals. The Theme Codes associated with each occupation indicate the GOTs most commonly found among people employed in that occupation.

YOUR TOP TEN STRONG OCCUPATIONS

1. Actuary (CI)
2. Mathematician (IRC)
3. Software Developer (IR)
4. Financial Analyst (CE)
5. Mathematics Teacher (CIR)
6. University Professor (IAR)
7. Medical Technologist (IRC)
8. Biologist (IRA)
9. Bookkeeper (C)
10. Financial Manager (CE)

Occupations of Dissimilar Interest

Public Relations Director (AE)

Graphic Designer (ARI)

Medical Illustrator (AIR)

Art Teacher (ASE)

Advertising Account Manager (AE)

As you read through your Occupational Scales results on this and the following pages, note the names of those occupations for which you scored "Similar." Those are the occupations you might want to explore first. If you have no scores in this range, take a look at those in the midrange and begin there. You might also consider occupations of least interest or for which you scored "Dissimilar"; however, keep in mind that you are likely to have little in common with people in those types of work and probably would contribute to such occupations in a unique way. Your career professional can guide you further in this process.

You can learn about occupations from information found in a public library, in the career library of a college or university near you, in a professional career center, or on the Internet. A recommended online source for occupational information is the O*NET™ database at http://online.onetcenter.org. You can also learn a lot about an occupation by talking to people who are working in that particular occupation. These people can describe their day-to-day work and tell you what they like and dislike about it.

Figure A.1 (Continued)

OCCUPATIONAL SCALES

INVESTIGATIVE – Researching, Analyzing, Inquiring

THEME CODE	OCCUPATIONAL SCALE	DISSIMILAR — MIDRANGE — SIMILAR	STD SCORE
IRC	Mathematician		65
IR	Software Developer		64
IAR	University Professor		62
IRC	Medical Technologist		61
IRA	Biologist		60
IRA	Physicist		59
IRA	Geologist		57
IR	Chemist		55
IR	R&D Manager		52
IRC	Computer Scientist		51
IR	Optometrist		51
IRS	Science Teacher		51
IRA	Respiratory Therapist		46
IAR	Physician		45
IRC	Medical Technician		44
ICR	Pharmacist		44
IA	Geographer		41
IA	Psychologist		39
IES	Dietitian		37
IRA	Chiropractor		36
IAR	Sociologist		36
IRA	Veterinarian		36
IRA	Dentist		22

Similar results (40 and above)
You share interests with women in that occupation and probably would enjoy the work.

Midrange results (30–39)
You share some interests with women in that occupation and probably would enjoy some of the work.

Dissimilar results (29 and below)
You share few interests with women in that occupation and probably would not enjoy the work.

For more information about any of these occupations, visit O*NET™ online at http://online.onetcenter.org.

SOCIAL – Helping, Instructing, Caregiving

THEME CODE	OCCUPATIONAL SCALE	DISSIMILAR — MIDRANGE — SIMILAR	STD SCORE
SE	Special Education Teacher		42
SE	School Counselor		38
S	Elementary School Teacher		36
SA	College Instructor		35
SAI	Rehabilitation Counselor		35
SA	Speech Pathologist		35
SI	Registered Nurse		34
SAE	Foreign Language Teacher		32
SA	Recreation Therapist		30
SCE	Licensed Practical Nurse		28
SA	Social Worker		27
SRC	Physical Education Teacher		26
SEA	Social Science Teacher		26
SEA	School Administrator		25
SAR	Occupational Therapist		24
SAR	Minister		22
SE	Community Service Director		20
SE	Parks & Recreation Manager		17
SIR	Physical Therapist		9

Figure A.1 (Continued)

OCCUPATIONAL SCALES

CONVENTIONAL – Accounting, Organizing, Processing Data

THEME CODE	OCCUPATIONAL SCALE	DISSIMILAR / MIDRANGE / SIMILAR	STD SCORE
CI	Actuary		71
CE	Financial Analyst		62
CIR	Mathematics Teacher		62
C	Bookkeeper		60
CE	Financial Manager		59
CE	Accountant		58
CE	Credit Manager		53
CES	Production Worker		50
C	Computer Systems Analyst		49
CE	Banker		46
C	Health Information Specialist		43
CES	Food Service Manager		42
CES	Business Education Teacher		40
CS	Administrative Assistant		37
C	Computer & IS Manager		37
CSE	Farmer/Rancher		37
CES	Nursing Home Administrator		36
CE	Paralegal		35
CRE	Military Enlisted		27

Similar results (40 and above)
You share interests with women in that occupation and probably would enjoy the work.

Midrange results (30–39)
You share some interests with women in that occupation and probably would enjoy some of the work.

Dissimilar results (29 and below)
You share few interests with women in that occupation and probably would not enjoy the work.

For more information about any of these occupations, visit O*NET™ online at http://online.onetcenter.org.

REALISTIC – Building, Repairing, Working Outdoors

THEME CODE	OCCUPATIONAL SCALE	DISSIMILAR / MIDRANGE / SIMILAR	STD SCORE
RIC	Technical Support Specialist		55
RI	Forester		53
RIC	Network Administrator		52
RI	Engineer		50
RIC	Engineering Technician		45
RSI	Vocational Agriculture Teacher		37
REI	Horticulturist		34
RIS	Radiologic Technologist		29
REI	Military Officer		27
R	Automobile Mechanic		26
RCI	Emergency Medical Technician		26
RC	Landscape/Grounds Manager		24
RIA	Carpenter		22
RIA	Electrician		22
RE	Law Enforcement Officer		19
RIS	Athletic Trainer		12
RIS	Firefighter		11

Figure A.1 (Continued)

OCCUPATIONAL SCALES

ENTERPRISING – Selling, Managing, Persuading

THEME CODE	OCCUPATIONAL SCALE	DISSIMILAR / MIDRANGE / SIMILAR	STD SCORE
EIR	Investments Manager		38
ECS	Housekeeping/Maintenance Manager		37
ECS	Operations Manager		33
ECR	Optician		28
E	Top Executive		26
E	Retail Sales Representative		22
E	Sales Manager		22
EC	Cosmetologist		21
EAI	Technical Sales Representative		19
EAS	Human Resources Manager		18
ECA	Retail Sales Manager		16
ECA	Travel Consultant		16
EA	Marketing Manager		13
ECR	Purchasing Agent		13
E	Life Insurance Agent		10
EC	Buyer		8
EAC	Florist		8
ECR	Restaurant Manager		8
EAS	Flight Attendant		7
E	Realtor		5
EAS	Elected Public Official		4
ERA	Chef		-4
EA	Interior Designer		-5

Similar results (40 and above)
You share interests with women in that occupation and probably would enjoy the work.

Midrange results (30–39)
You share some interests with women in that occupation and probably would enjoy some of the work.

Dissimilar results (29 and below)
You share few interests with women in that occupation and probably would not enjoy the work.

For more information about any of these occupations, visit O*NET™ online at http://online.onetcenter.org.

ARTISTIC – Creating or Enjoying Art, Drama, Music, Writing

THEME CODE	OCCUPATIONAL SCALE	DISSIMILAR / MIDRANGE / SIMILAR	STD SCORE
A	Librarian		31
AI	Urban & Regional Planner		27
A	Musician		26
ASI	ESL Instructor		23
A	Translator		22
AES	Corporate Trainer		19
AR	Artist		18
AIR	Technical Writer		13
ARI	Architect		10
A	Attorney		10
AER	Public Administrator		9
AI	Editor		8
ARE	Photographer		7
AE	Broadcast Journalist		2
ASE	English Teacher		0
A	Reporter		-8
AE	Advertising Account Manager		-9
ASE	Art Teacher		-10
AIR	Medical Illustrator		-10
ARI	Graphic Designer		-13
AE	Public Relations Director		-21

Figure A.1 (Continued)

PERSONAL STYLE SCALES   SECTION 4

The Personal Style Scales describe different ways of approaching people, learning, leading, making decisions, and participating in teams. Personal Style Scales help you think about your preferences for factors that can be important in your career, enabling you to more effectively narrow your choices and examine your opportunities. Each scale includes descriptions at both ends of the continuum, with scores indicating your preference for one style versus the other.

Your scores on the Personal Style Scales were determined by comparing your responses to those of a combined group of working men and women.

> **YOUR PERSONAL STYLE SCALES PREFERENCES**
>
> 1. You are likely to prefer a balance of working alone and working with people
> 2. You seem to prefer to learn through lectures and books
> 3. You probably prefer to lead by example
> 4. You may dislike taking risks
> 5. You probably enjoy participating in teams

**Clear Scores
(Below 46 and above 54)**
You indicated a clear preference for one style versus the other.

Midrange Scores (46–54)
You indicated that some of the descriptors on both sides apply to you.

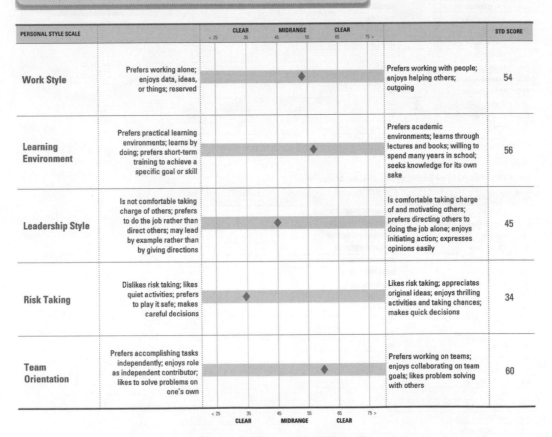

PERSONAL STYLE SCALE			STD SCORE
Work Style	Prefers working alone; enjoys data, ideas, or things; reserved	Prefers working with people; enjoys helping others; outgoing	54
Learning Environment	Prefers practical learning environments; learns by doing; prefers short-term training to achieve a specific goal or skill	Prefers academic environments; learns through lectures and books; willing to spend many years in school; seeks knowledge for its own sake	56
Leadership Style	Is not comfortable taking charge of others; prefers to do the job rather than direct others; may lead by example rather than by giving directions	Is comfortable taking charge of and motivating others; prefers directing others to doing the job alone; enjoys initiating action; expresses opinions easily	45
Risk Taking	Dislikes risk taking; likes quiet activities; prefers to play it safe; makes careful decisions	Likes risk taking; appreciates original ideas; enjoys thrilling activities and taking chances; makes quick decisions	34
Team Orientation	Prefers accomplishing tasks independently; enjoys role as independent contributor; likes to solve problems on one's own	Prefers working on teams; enjoys collaborating on team goals; likes problem solving with others	60

Figure A.1 (Continued)

PROFILE SUMMARY

YOUR HIGHEST THEMES	YOUR THEME CODE
Investigative, Social, Conventional	**ISC**

YOUR TOP FIVE INTEREST AREAS

1. **Research (I)**
2. **Teaching & Education (S)**
3. **Mathematics (I)**
4. **Taxes & Accounting (C)**
5. **Science (I)**

Areas of Least Interest

Culinary Arts (A)

Writing & Mass Communication (A)

Visual Arts & Design (A)

YOUR TOP TEN STRONG OCCUPATIONS

1. **Actuary (CI)**
2. **Mathematician (IRC)**
3. **Software Developer (IR)**
4. **Financial Analyst (CE)**
5. **Mathematics Teacher (CIR)**
6. **University Professor (IAR)**
7. **Medical Technologist (IRC)**
8. **Biologist (IRA)**
9. **Bookkeeper (C)**
10. **Financial Manager (CE)**

Occupations of Dissimilar Interest

Public Relations Director (AE)

Graphic Designer (ARI)

Medical Illustrator (AIR)

Art Teacher (ASE)

Advertising Account Manager (AE)

YOUR PERSONAL STYLE SCALES PREFERENCES

1. **You are likely to prefer a balance of working alone and working with people**
2. **You seem to prefer to learn through lectures and books**
3. **You probably prefer to lead by example**
4. **You may dislike taking risks**
5. **You probably enjoy participating in teams**

RESPONSE SUMMARY

This section provides a summary of your responses to the different sections of the inventory for use in interpretation by your career professional.

ITEM RESPONSE PERCENTAGES

Section Title	Strongly Like	Like	Indifferent	Dislike	Strongly Dislike
Occupations	25	3	12	6	55
Subject Areas	35	0	13	17	35
Activities	38	8	8	15	31
Leisure Activities	39	4	0	21	36
People	31	0	6	0	63
Characteristics	56	11	11	0	22
TOTAL PERCENTAGE	**33**	**4**	**10**	**11**	**42**

Total possible responses: 291   Your response total: 290   Items omitted: 1   Typicality index: 16—Combination of item responses appears inconsistent

Note: Due to rounding, total percentage may not add up to 100%.

Figure A.1 (Continued)

Skills Confidence Inventory®
Profile

LESLIE MORENO

F

LEVELS OF SKILLS CONFIDENCE BY THEME

Your *Skills Confidence Inventory* results describe how you perceive your own capabilities in performing activities related to the same six broad areas represented by the General Occupational Themes. Keep in mind that these results may not reflect your actual abilities; the results reflect how you rate yourself. Your own rating may influence what kinds of activities you try or avoid and may determine what occupations or educational programs you consider as possibilities for exploration.

Your confidence in each of the six areas is shown below in rank order. Your Skills Confidence Theme code summarizes the areas in which you feel most confident performing particular activities. Your Skills Confidence Theme code is ISC.

THEME	CODE	CONFIDENCE SCORE & LEVEL					SCORE (1–5)	TYPICAL SKILL AREAS
		1	2	3	4	5		
Investigative	I				VERY HIGH		4.6	Research, math, science
Social	S			HIGH			3.7	Education, counseling, social service
Conventional	C			HIGH			3.6	Finance, computers, organization
Enterprising	E		LITTLE				2.4	Sales, speaking, management
Artistic	A	VERY LITTLE					1.6	Creative expression, music, design
Realistic	R	VERY LITTLE					1.2	Outdoor work, construction, repair

COMPARISON OF LEVELS OF SKILLS CONFIDENCE AND INTEREST

The chart below compares your skills confidence levels with your interest levels as measured by the *Strong*. Your Skills Confidence Theme code is ISC. Your *Strong* Theme code is ISC. Use this comparison to help you select Themes you'd like to explore further to find satisfying career, educational, and leisure options. Also, refer to Understanding Your Results on the *Skills Confidence Inventory*, available from your career professional, for more information.

THEME	CODE	FURTHER EXPLORATION (if highest level of confidence is moderate) / FURTHER EXPLORATION	PRIORITIES FOR CAREER EXPLORATION
		Less ——————→ More	
Investigative	I	CONFIDENCE / INTEREST	High priority
Social	S	CONFIDENCE / INTEREST	High priority
Conventional	C	CONFIDENCE / INTEREST	High priority
Enterprising	E	CONFIDENCE / INTEREST	Low priority
Artistic	A	CONFIDENCE / INTEREST	Low priority
Realistic	R	CONFIDENCE / INTEREST	Low priority

Total responses out of 60: 60

CPP, Inc. | 800-624-1765 | www.cpp.com

Figure A.2   Leslie's Skills Confidence Inventory Profile

MINNESOTA IMPORTANCE QUESTIONNAIRE
Ranked Form

Name: *LESLIE*
LCT score = 92%

Score
ACHIEVEMENT 1.5

Ability Utilization: I could do something
that makes use of my abilities..............................1.6
Achievement: The job could give me a
feeling of accomplishment...................................1.3

COMFORT −0.4

Activity: I could be busy all the time........................−0.7
Independence: I could work alone on the job.....−0.9
Variety: I could do something different every day....−0.6
Compensation: My pay would compare
well with that of other workers............................0.4
Security: The job would provide for
steady employment..−0.3
Working Conditions: The job would have
good working conditions......................................−0.2

STATUS −0.7

Advancement: The job would provide an
opportunity for advancement...............................0.3
Recognition: I could get recognition
for the work I do...0.0
Authority: I could tell people what to do..................−1.9
Social Status: I could be "somebody" in the
community...0.7

ALTRUISM 1.3

Co-workers: My co-workers would be
easy to make friends with....................................0.8
Social Service: I could do things
for other people..1.1
Moral Values: I could do the work without
feeling that it is morally wrong............................2.1

SAFETY −0.4

Company Policies: The company would
administer its policies fairly...................................0.9
Supervision—Human Relations: My boss
would back up the workers...................................0.0
Supervision—Technical: My boss would train
the workers well...−0.3

AUTONOMY 0.7

Creativity: I could try out some of my own ideas.......0.5
Responsibility: I could make decisions
on my own...0.8
Autonomy: I could plan my work with
little supervision...0.8

Score

Figure A.3   Leslie's Minnesota Importance Questionnaire Profile   **(Continued)**

Minnesota Importance Questionnaire

Correspondence report for *LESLIE*

The MIQ profile is compared with Occupational Reinforcer Patterns (QRPS) for 90 representative occupations. Correspondence is indicated by the C index. A prediction of *Satisfied (S)* results from C values greater than .49, *Likely Satisfied (L)* for C values between .10 and .49, and *Not Satisfied (N)* for C values less than .10. Occupations are clustered by similarity of Occupational Reinforcer Patterns.

	C Index	Pred. Sat.		C Index	Pred. Sat.
CLUSTER A (ACH-AUT-Alt)	.68	S	CLUSTER B (ACH-Com)	.51	S
Architect	.62	S	Bricklayer	.43	L
Dentist	.58	S	Carpenter	.31	L
Family Practitioner (M.D.)	.45	L	Cement Mason	.42	L
Interior Designer/Decorator	.63	S	Elevator Repairer	.31	L
Lawyer	.48	L	Heavy Equipment Operator	.48	L
Minister	.52	S	Landscape Gardner	.49	L
Nurse, Occupational Health	.58	S	Lather	.55	S
Occupational Therapist	.68	S	Millwright	.54	S
Optometrist	.54	S	Painter/Paperhanger	.38	L
Psychologist, Counseling	.72	S	Patternmaker, Metal	.33	L
Recreation Leader	.63	S	Pipefitter	.43	L
Speech Pathologist	.67	S	Plasterer	.37	L
Teacher, Elementary School	.65	S	Plumber	.54	S
Teacher, Secondary School	.66	S	Roofer	.46	L
Vocational Evaluator	.60	S	Salesperson, Automobile	.50	S
CLUSTER C (ACH-Aut-Com)	.60	S	CLUSTER D (ACH-STA-Com)	.48	L
Alteration Tailor	.57	S	Accountant, Certified Public	.49	L
Automobile Mechanic	.47	L	Airplane Co-Pilot, Commercial	.32	L
Barber	.60	S	Cook (Hotel-Restaurant)	.32	L
Beauty Operator	.68	S	Department Head, Supermarket	.19	L
Caseworker	.66	S	Drafter, Architectural	.46	L
Claim Adjuster	.50	S	Electrician	.44	L
Commercial Artist, Illustrator	.46	L	Engineer, Civil	.47	L
Electronics Mechanic	.32	L	Engineer, Time Study	.51	S
Locksmith	.40	L	Firm-Equipment Mechanic I	.33	L
Maintenance Repairer, Factory	.40	L	Line-Installer-Repairer (Telephone)	.08	N
Mechanical-Engineering Technician	.60	S	Machinist	.29	L
Office-Machine Servicer	.41	L	Programmer (Business, Engineering, Science)	.54	S
Photoengraver (Stripper)	.42	L	Sheet Metal Worker	.44	L
Sales Agent, Real Estate	.70	S	Statistical-Machine Servicer	.28	L
Salesperson, General Hardware	.40	L	Writer, Technical Publication	.57	S
CLUSTER E (COM)	.24	L	CLUSTER F (Alt-Com)	.54	S
Assembler, Production	−.05	N	Airplane-Flight Attendant	.57	S
Baker	.18	L	Clerk, General Office, Civil Service	.30	L
Bookbinder	.22	L	Dietitian	.40	L
Bookkeeper I	.28	L	Fire Fighter	.35	L
Bus Driver	.22	L	Librarian	.65	S
Key-Punch Operator	.25	L	Medical Technologist	.61	S
Meat Cutter	.10	L	Nurse, Professional	.46	L
Post-Office Clerk	.19	L	Orderly	.38	L
Production Helper (Food)	.35	L	Physical Therapist	.58	S
Punch-Press Operator	.20	L			

Figure A.3 (Continued)

	C Index	Pred. Sat.		C Index	Pred. Sat.
CLUSTER E (COM)	.24	L	CLUSTER F (Alt-Com)	.54	S
Sales, General (Department Store)	.35	L	Police Officer	.48	L
Sewing-Machine Operator, Automatic	.23	L	Receptionist, Civil Service	.42	L
Solderer (Production Line)	.11	L	Secretary (General Office)	.46	L
Telephone Operator	.19	L	Taxi Driver	.35	L
Teller (Banking)	.24	L	Telephone Installer	.41	L
			Waiter-Waitress	.51	S

Vocational Psychology Research, Department of Psychology
University of Minnesota, Minneapolis MN 55455

Figure A.3 (Continued)

SOURCE: Rounds, J. B., Henley, G. A., Dawis, R. V., Lofquist, L. H., & Weiss, D. J. (1981). *Manual for the Minnesota Importance Questionnaire*. Minneapolis: University of Minnesota. Used with permission.

Individual Analysis of Career Concerns

Name ____Leslie____   Age _____

Compared with _____   Date _____

Consulting Psychologists Press, Inc.
Palo Alto, CA 94303

The ACCI can be self-scored to yield a profile based on the clusters of career development tasks of most concern to you. The procedures for self-scoring and profile analysis are:

1. On the Career Concerns Chart below, enter the distribution of ratings for each of the groups of 5 items in each substage. For example, if for items 1 to 5, you marked 1 for two items, 2 for two items, and 3 for one item, you would enter those numbers in the appropriate spaces on the Crystallization line.

2. Then compute the average score for the substage by dividing the weighted sum by the number of items in the group. For the above example, the weighted sum would be 2+4+3=9, divided by 5, equals 1.8. Enter the weighted sum and average in the appropriate columns. Follow the same procedure for each substage and stage.

3. Circle the number of the response you chose for Item 61.

4. Plot your Career Stage and Substage Profile below by marking with a capital X on the appropriate line the location of each of the four Stage averages, and with a small x each of the Substage averages. Connect the small x's in each Stage to draw the four profiles of your current career concerns. Intraindividual interpretations of average Substage scores are usually more insight-producing than are Stage scores because of present and future orientations and recycling.

5. Convert the raw scores (5-point ratings) into percentiles with the appropriate table in the Manual or from local norms. Percentiles make it possible to compare one person with a group of relevant people, and average ratings on the 5-point scale help when a person compares him or herself using the profile.

6. Record for each Substage the number of items rated either 4 or 5 to show the clustering of major concerns and to help interpret Stage and Substage averages in the Career Concerns Chart below.

CAREER CONCERNS CHART

Items	Career Concerns	None 1	Little 2	Some 3	Cons. 4	Great 5	Weighted Sum	Average
A: EXPLORATION STAGE								
1–5	Crystallization	1	1	3			17	3.4
6–10	Specification		2		3		21	4.2
11–15	Implementation	2	3	3?	3		13	2.6
1–15	TOTAL EXPLORATION	3	6	3?	3		51	3.4
B: ESTABLISHMENT STAGE								
16–20	Stabilizing	1	2	1	1		14	2.8
21–25	Consolidating		4	1			11	2.2
26–30	Advancing		3	2	1		12	2.4
16–30	TOTAL ESTABLISHMENT	1	9	3	1		37	2.5
C: MAINTENANCE STAGE								
31–35	Holding	1	4				9	1.8
36–40	Updating	3	1	1			8	1.6
41–45	Innovating		1	3	3		17	3.4
31–45	TOTAL MAINTENANCE	4	6	2	3		34	2.3
D: DISENGAGEMENT STAGE								
46–50	Deceleration	5					5	1.0
51–55	Retirement Planning	5					5	1.0
56–60	Retirement Living	5					5	1.0
46–60	TOTAL DISENGAGEMENT	15					15	1.0
61	CAREER CHANGE STATUS	1	2	③	4	5 (Circle Response)		

CAREER STAGE AND SUBSTAGE PROFILE

Amount of Current Concern (None 1.0 Little 2.0 Some 3.0 Cons. 4.0 Great 5.0)	%ile	Substages	Number of Concerns Rated 4 (Considerable) or 5 (Great)
		Crystallization	3
		Specification	3
	79	Implementation	--
		Stabilizing	1
		Consolidating	1
	25	Advancing	--
		Holding	--
		Updating	--
	23	Innovating	3
		Deceleration	--
		Retirement Planning	--
	1	Retirement Living	--

97 96 95 94   13 12 11

Figure A.4 Leslie's Adult Career Concerns Inventory Profile

SOURCE: Modified and reproduced by special permission of the Publisher, CPP, Inc., Mountain View, CA 94043 from the Adult Career Concerns Inventory Report Form. Copyright 1988 by CPP, Inc. All rights reserved. Further reproduction is prohibited without the publisher's written consent.

APPENDIX B: NATIONAL CAREER DEVELOPMENT ASSOCIATION *CODE OF ETHICS*

National Career Development Association

Code of Ethics

Revised May 2007

The NCDA Ethics Committee gratefully acknowledges the American Counseling Association (ACA) and its Ethics Committee for permission to adapt their 2005 Code of Ethics. NCDA, one of the founding associations of ACA in 1952, is a current division of ACA. The NCDA Ethics Committee endeavored to follow the structure of ACA's Code so that the two codes would be compatible with each other, while developing, adding, and enhancing profession-specific guidelines for NCDA's membership. More information on ACA's Ethics Code can be found on their website (see the attached web references section).

The NCDA Ethics Committee gratefully acknowledges Cassandra Smisson for her assistance in reviewing the final draft of this code. As of June 2006, Ms. Smisson was pursuing a Ph.D. in Counseling Psych at Florida State University.

2005-2007 NCDA Ethics Committee Members

David M. Reile, Chair, Cheri Butler (Board Liaison) ;Greta Davis; Dennis Engels; Janice Guerriero; Janet Lenz; Julia Makela; Kristin M. Perrone-McGovern; James Sampson; Donald Schutt; Keley Smith-Keller

Nondiscrimination Statement
NCDA opposes discrimination against any individual based on age, culture, mental/physical disability, ethnicity, race, religion/spirituality, creed, gender, actual or perceived gender identity or expression, actual or perceived sexual orientation, marital/partnership status, language preference, socioeconomic status, any other characteristics not specifically relevant to job performance.   (Statement adopted by the NCDA Board of Directors, May 2007)

2007 NCDA Code of Ethics

Introduction & Purpose

While there are many ways to define and think about *ethics*, ethics and ethical behavior are basically about professionalism and transparency. The NCDA Ethics Code has been designed as a guide and resource for career practitioners. While it offers a set of principles that can be applied to wide range of settings and situations, it is not (nor can it be) comprehensive. If you are concerned about whether or not a particular practice is ethical, then you should not engage in that behavior without getting competent advice. More succinctly, when in doubt—don't; at least not without discussing the situation with others. Peer review isn't always going to give you perfect advice; but you can take comfort in knowing that you questioned your behavior before proceeding and allowed others to comment before taking action. There is safety and strength in the depth and breadth of opinions you seek before engaging in activity which may be untried or questionable. The Ethics Committee Members do not hold themselves up as definitive experts in all ethical matters. Further, we are not experts with regard to legal issues and cannot give legal advice. However, we encourage members of the National Career Development Association to contact us with questions. We are committed to working collaboratively to provide guidance where we can and to provide referrals as appropriate. You may reach us at ethics@ncda.org.

The *National Career Development Association (NCDA) Code of Ethics* serves five main purposes:

1. The *Code* enables NCDA to clarify to current and future members, and to those served by their members, the nature of ethical responsibilities held in common by its members.
2. The *Code* helps support the mission of NCDA.
3. The *Code* establishes principles that define ethical behaviors and practices of association members.
4. The *Code* serves as an ethical guide designed to assist members in constructing a professional course of action that best serves those utilizing career services and best promotes the values of the career profession.
5. The *Code* serves as a guide for those receiving career services so that they may understand what to expect from working with a career professional and to understand their rights and responsibilities as consumers of these services.

The *NCDA Code of Ethics* contains nine main sections that address the following areas:
       Section A: The Professional Relationship
       Section B: Confidentiality, Privileged Communication, and Privacy
       Section C: Professional Responsibility
       Section D: Relationships with Other Professionals
       Section E: Evaluation, Assessment, and Interpretation
       Section F: Use of the Internet in Career Services
       Section G: Supervision, Training, and Teaching
       Section H: Research and Publication
       Section I: Resolving Ethical Issues

Each section of the *NCDA Code of Ethics* begins with an Introduction. The Introduction helps set the tone for that particular section and provides a starting point that invites reflection on the ethical guidelines contained in each part of the *NCDA Code of Ethics*. When career professionals are faced with ethical dilemmas that are difficult to resolve, they are expected to engage in a carefully considered ethical decision-making process. Reasonable differences of opinion can and do exist among career professionals with respect to ways in which values, ethical principles, and ethical standards would be applied when they conflict. While there is no specific ethical decision-making model that is most effective, career professionals are expected to be familiar with a credible model of decision-making that can bear public scrutiny and its application. (For one example of an ethical decision-making model from the Ethics Resource Center, see the attached web references section). Through a chosen ethical decision-making process and evaluation of the context of the situation, career professionals are empowered to make decisions that help expand the capacity of people to grow and develop.

NCDA has members in various career services positions (see Career Professionals), as well as in instructional (counselor educators, counseling psychology professors, etc.) and supervisory roles (Director, Associate Director, Career Supervisor, etc.). The term "career professional" will be used throughout this document both as a noun and as an adjective to refer to anyone holding NCDA membership and who is therefore expected to abide by these ethical guidelines. Additionally, a brief glossary is given (see end of document) to provide readers with a concise description of some of the terms used in the *NCDA Code of Ethics*. NCDA Members who are affiliated with other professional associations (i.e., psychologists, school counselors, etc.) should also consult the ethics codes from those organizations and adhere to the highest standard of professional practice.

NCDA acknowledges and supports its members in their quest to achieve the highest academic and professional credentials appropriate to their work. Many NCDA members are trained credentialed counselors, psychologists, and/or educators with masters and/or doctoral-level degrees in counseling, psychology, or related disciplines. NCDA does not encourage or condone replacing these professionals with individuals who have lesser education, training, and/or credentials. However, NCDA acknowledges, respects, and welcomes individuals regardless of their training and educational backgrounds and recognizes the valuable contribution that all of its members make in the field of career development. Thus, NCDA opposes any statement, action, or activity, which implies a "second-class" status to any individuals within our association.

Section A: The Professional Relationship

Introduction
Career professionals encourage client growth and development in ways that foster the interest and welfare of clients and promote formation of healthy relationships. Career professionals actively attempt to understand the diverse cultural backgrounds of the individuals they serve. Career professionals also explore their own cultural identities and how one's cultural identity affects one's values and beliefs about the working relationship.

Career professionals are encouraged to contribute to society by devoting a portion of their professional activity to services for which there is little or no financial return (pro bono publico).

A.1. Welfare of Those Served by Career Professionals
A.1.a. Primary Responsibility
The primary responsibility of career professionals is to respect the dignity and to promote the welfare of the individuals to whom they provide service.

A.1.b. Differentiation Between Types of Services Provided
"Career planning" services are differentiated from "career counseling" services. Career planning services include an active provision of information designed to help a client with a specific need, such as review of a resumé; assistance in networking strategies; identification of occupations based on values, interests, skills, prior work experience, and/or other characteristics; support in the job-seeking process; and assessment by means of paper-based and/or online inventories of interest, abilities, personality, work-related values, and/or other characteristics. In addition to providing these informational services, "career counseling" provides the opportunity for a deeper level of involvement with the client, based on the establishment of a professional counseling relationship and the potential for assisting clients with career and personal development concerns beyond those included in career planning. All career professionals, whether engaging in "career planning" or "career counseling", provide only the services that are within the scope of their professional competence and qualifications. *(See C.2., C.4., E.2.a., F.7.)*

A.1.c. Records
Career professionals maintain records necessary for rendering professional services as required by laws, regulations, or agency or institution procedures. Career professionals include sufficient and timely documentation in their records to facilitate delivery and continuity of services. Career professionals take reasonable steps to ensure that documentation in records accurately reflects client progress and the services provided. If errors are made in records, career professionals take steps to properly note the correction of such errors according to agency or institutional policies. Career professionals are encouraged to purge their files according to the time frame required by federal, state, local, and/or institutional statute, law, regulation, or procedure, particularly when there is no reasonable expectation that a client will benefit from maintaining the records any longer than required. Career professionals are expected to know and abide by all applicable federal, state, local, and/or institutional statutes, laws, regulations, and procedures regarding record keeping. *(See B.6., B.6.g., H.2.j.)*

A.1.d. Career Services Plans

Career professionals and their clients work jointly in devising integrated career services plans (in writing or orally) that offer reasonable promise of success and are consistent with the abilities and circumstances of clients. Career professionals and clients regularly review career plans to assess their continued viability and effectiveness, respecting the freedom of choice of clients. *(See A.2.a., A.2.d.)*

A.1.e. Support Network Involvement

Career professionals recognize that support networks hold various meanings in the lives of clients and consider enlisting the support, understanding, and involvement of others (e.g., family members, friends, and religious/spiritual/community leaders) as positive resources, when appropriate and with client consent.

A.2. Informed Consent in the Professional Relationship

(See B.5., B.6.b., E.3., E.13.b., G.1.c., H.2.a.)

A.2.a. Informed Consent

Clients have the freedom to choose whether to enter into or remain in a professional relationship. To make informed choices, clients need adequate information about the working relationship and the career professional. Career professionals have an obligation to review in writing and orally the rights and responsibilities of both the career professional and the recipient of services prior to the beginning of the working relationship. Further, informed consent is an ongoing part of the professional relationship, and career professionals appropriately document discussions of informed consent throughout the working relationship.

A.2.b. Types of Information Needed

Career professionals clearly explain to clients the nature of all services provided. They inform clients about issues such as, but not limited to, the following: the purposes, goals, techniques, procedures, limitations, potential risks, and benefits of services; the career professional's qualifications, credentials, and relevant experience; continuation of services upon the incapacitation or death of the career professional; and other pertinent information. Career professionals take steps to ensure that clients understand the implications of diagnosis (if applicable), the intended use of tests/assessments and reports, fees, and billing arrangements. Clients have the right to confidentiality and to be provided with an explanation of its limitations (including how supervisors and/or treatment team professionals are involved); to obtain clear information about their records; to participate in the ongoing career services plans; and to refuse any services or modality change and to be advised of the consequences of such refusal.

A.2.c. Developmental and Cultural Sensitivity

Career professionals communicate information in ways that are both developmentally and culturally appropriate. Career professionals use clear and understandable language when discussing issues related to informed consent. When clients have difficulty understanding the language used by career professionals, they provide necessary services (e.g., arranging for a qualified interpreter or translator) to ensure comprehension by clients. The cost for such services, however, may be passed onto clients in accordance with federal, state, local, and/or institutional statute, law, regulation, or procedure. Thus clients should be given the opportunity to seek another career professional or to employ an interpreter or translator of their own choosing. In collaboration with clients, career professionals consider cultural implications of informed consent procedures and, where possible, career professionals adjust their practices accordingly.

A.2.d. Inability to Give Consent

When providing career services to minors or persons unable to give voluntary consent, career professionals seek the assent of clients to services, and include them in decision making as appropriate. Career professionals recognize the need to balance the ethical rights of clients to make choices, their capacity to give consent or assent to receive services, and parental or familial legal rights and responsibilities to protect these clients and make decisions on their behalf.

A.3. Clients Served by Others

When career professionals learn that their clients are in a professional relationship with another mental health professional, they request a written release from clients to inform the other professionals and strive to establish positive and collaborative professional relationships, when necessary and appropriate.

A.4. Avoiding Harm and Imposing Values
A.4.a. Avoiding Harm

Career professionals act to avoid harming their clients, students, trainees, and research participants and to minimize or to remedy unavoidable or unanticipated harm.

A.4.b. Personal Values

Career professionals are aware of their own values, attitudes, beliefs, and behaviors and avoid imposing values that are inconsistent with clients' goals. Career professionals respect the diversity of clients, students, trainees, and research participants.

A.5. Roles and Relationships with Clients
(See G.3., G.10., H.3.)
A.5.a. Current Clients

Sexual or romantic interactions or relationships with current clients, their romantic partners, or their family members are prohibited.

A.5.b. Former Clients

Sexual or romantic interactions or relationships with former clients, their romantic partners, or their family members are prohibited for a period of 5 years following the last professional contact. Career professionals, before engaging in sexual or romantic interactions or relationships with clients, their romantic partners, or client family members after 5 years following the last professional contact, demonstrate forethought and document (in written form) whether the interactions or relationship can be viewed as exploitive in some way and/or whether there is still potential to harm the former client. In cases of potential exploitation and/or harm, the career professional does not enter into such an interaction or relationship.

A.5.c. Nonprofessional Interactions or Relationships (Other Than Sexual or Romantic Interactions or Relationships)

Nonprofessional relationships with clients, former clients, their romantic partners, or their family members should be avoided by career professionals, except when the interaction is potentially beneficial to the client. *(See A.5.d.)*

A.5.d. Potentially Beneficial Interactions

When a nonprofessional interaction with a client or former client may be potentially beneficial to the client or former client, the career professional must document in case records, prior to the interaction (or as soon as feasible), the rationale for such an interaction, the potential benefit, and anticipated consequences for the client or former client and other individuals significantly involved with the client or former client. Such interactions should be initiated with appropriate client consent. Where unintentional harm occurs to the client or former client, or to an individual significantly involved with the client or former client, due to the nonprofessional interaction, the career professional must show evidence of an attempt to remedy such harm. Examples of potentially beneficial interactions include, but are not limited to, attending a formal ceremony (e.g., a wedding/commitment ceremony or graduation); purchasing a service or product provided by a client or former client (excepting unrestricted bartering); hospital visits to an ill family member; and mutual membership in a professional association, organization, or community. *(See A.5.c.)*

A.5.e. Role Changes in the Professional Relationship

When a career professional changes a role from the original or most recent contracted relationship, s/he obtains informed consent from the client and explains the right of the client to refuse services related to the change. Examples of role changes include, but are not limited to:

1. changing from providing individual career services to therapy, relationship or family counseling, or vice versa;
2. changing from a non-forensic evaluative role to a therapeutic role, or vice versa;
3. changing from a career professional to a researcher role (i.e., enlisting clients as research participants), or vice versa; and/or
4. changing from a career professional to a mediator role, or vice versa.

Clients must be fully informed of any anticipated consequences (e.g., financial, legal, personal, or therapeutic) of role changes with a career professional.

A.6. Roles and Relationships at Individual, Group, Institutional, and Societal Levels
A.6.a. Advocacy

When appropriate, career professionals advocate at individual, group, institutional, and societal levels to examine potential barriers and obstacles that inhibit access and/or the growth and development of clients.

A.6.b. Confidentiality and Advocacy

Career professionals obtain consent prior to engaging in advocacy efforts on behalf of a client to improve the provision of services and to work toward removal of systemic barriers or obstacles that inhibit client access, growth, and development.

A.7. Multiple Clients

When a career professional agrees to provide career services to two or more persons who have a relationship, the career professional clarifies at the outset which person or persons are clients and the nature of the relationships the career professional will have with each involved person. If it becomes apparent that the career professional may be called upon to perform potentially conflicting roles, the career professional will clarify, adjust, or withdraw appropriately from one or more roles. *(See A.8.a., B.4.)*

A.8. Group Work *(See B.4.a.)*
A.8.a. Screening

Career professionals screen prospective group participants. To the extent possible, career professionals select members whose needs and goals are compatible with goals of the group, who will not impede the group process, and whose well-being will not be jeopardized by the group experience.

A.8.b. Protecting Clients

In a group setting, career professionals take reasonable precautions to protect clients from physical, emotional, or psychological trauma.

A.9. Fees and Bartering
A.9.a. Accepting Fees From Agency Clients

Career professionals refuse a private fee or other remuneration for rendering services to persons who are entitled to such services through the career professional's employing agency or institution. The policies of a particular agency may make explicit provisions for agency clients to receive career services from members of its staff in private practice. In such instances, the clients must be informed of other options open to them should they seek private career services.

A.9.b. Establishing Fees

In establishing fees for professional career services, career professionals consider the financial status of clients and the locality in which they practice. In the event that the established fee structure is inappropriate for a client, career professionals assist clients in attempting to find comparable services of acceptable cost.

A.9.c. Nonpayment of Fees

If career professionals intend to use collection agencies or take legal measures to collect fees from clients who do not pay for services as agreed upon, they first inform clients of intended actions and offer clients the opportunity to make payment.

A.9.d. Bartering

Career professionals may barter only if the relationship is not exploitive or harmful and does not place the career professional in an unfair advantage, if the client requests it, and if such arrangements are an accepted practice among professionals in the community. Career professionals consider the cultural implications of bartering and discuss relevant concerns with clients and document such agreements in a clear written contract. Career professionals must also be aware of local, state, and/or federal laws, including the tax implications of such an arrangement. Further, career professionals must make the recipients of their services aware of all applicable federal, state, local, and/or institutional statutes, laws, regulations, and procedures and should direct them to seek qualified counsel (i.e., attorney and/or accountant) in determining if such an arrangement is in their best interest.

A.9.e. Receiving Gifts

Career professionals understand the challenges of accepting gifts from clients and recognize that in some cultures, small gifts are a token of respect and a way of showing gratitude. When determining whether or not to accept a gift from clients, career professionals take into account the nature of their relationship, the monetary value of the gift, a client's motivation for giving the gift, and the career professional's motivation for wanting or declining the gift.

A.10. Termination and Referral
A.10.a. Abandonment Prohibited

Career professionals do not abandon or neglect clients to whom they provide career services. Career professionals assist in making appropriate arrangements for the continuation of treatment, when necessary, during interruptions such as vacations, illness, and following termination.

A.10.b. Inability to Assist Clients

If career professionals determine an inability to be of professional assistance to clients, they avoid entering into or continuing the relationship. Career professionals are knowledgeable about culturally and clinically appropriate referral resources and suggest these alternatives. If clients decline the suggested referrals, career professionals may discontinue the relationship.

A.10.c. Appropriate Termination

Career professionals terminate a professional relationship when it becomes reasonably apparent that the client no longer needs assistance, is not likely to benefit from, or is being harmed by continued service provision. Career professionals may terminate the working relationship when in jeopardy of harm by the client, or another person with whom the client has a relationship, or when clients do not pay agreed upon fees. Career professionals provide pre-termination career services and recommend other providers when feasible and necessary.

A.10.d. Appropriate Transfer of Services

When career professionals transfer or refer clients to other practitioners, they ensure that appropriate clinical and administrative processes are completed and open communication is maintained with both clients and practitioners.

Section B: Confidentiality, Privileged Communication, and Privacy

Introduction
Career professionals recognize that trust is a cornerstone of the professional relationship. Career professionals work to earn the trust of clients by creating an ongoing partnership, establishing and upholding appropriate boundaries, and maintaining confidentiality. Career professionals communicate the parameters of confidentiality in a culturally competent manner.

B.1. Respecting Client Rights
B.1.a. Multicultural/Diversity Considerations
Career professionals maintain awareness and sensitivity regarding cultural meanings of confidentiality and privacy. Career professionals respect differing views toward disclosure of information. Career professionals hold ongoing discussions with clients as to how, when, and with whom information is to be shared.

B.1.b. Respect for Privacy
Career professionals respect client rights to privacy. Career professionals solicit private information from clients only when it is beneficial to the working relationship.

B.1.c. Respect for Confidentiality
Career professionals do not share confidential information without client consent or without sound legal or ethical justification.

B.1.d. Explanation of Limitations
At initiation and throughout the professional relationship, career professionals inform clients of the limitations of confidentiality and seek to identify foreseeable situations in which confidentiality must be breached. *(See A.2.b.)*

B.2. Exceptions
B.2.a. Danger and Legal Requirements
The general requirement that career professionals keep information confidential does not apply when disclosure is required to protect clients or identified others from serious and foreseeable harm or when legal requirements demand that confidential information must be revealed. Examples of when career professionals may divulge confidential information may include, but not be limited to, mandated reporting in cases of suspected or actual child or elder abuse, when a client has a communicable and life threatening disease or condition and may infect an identifiable third party, or when notifying a collection agency to recover unpaid fees from a client. Career professionals consult with other professionals, include attorneys, when in doubt as to the validity of an exception. *(See A.9.c., B.2.b., B.2.c & B.2.d.)*

B.2.b. Contagious, Life-Threatening Diseases
When clients disclose that they have a disease commonly known to be both communicable and life threatening, career professionals may be justified in disclosing information to identifiable third parties, if they are known to be at demonstrable and high risk of contracting the disease. Prior to making a disclosure, career professionals confirm that there is such a diagnosis and

assess the intent of clients to inform the third parties about their disease or to engage in any behaviors that may be harmful to an identifiable third party. *(See B.2.a.)*

B.2.c. Court-Ordered Disclosure

When subpoenaed to release confidential or privileged information, career professionals endeavor to inform the client and to obtain written consent from the client or take steps to prohibit the disclosure, or have it limited as narrowly as possible, to minimize potential harm to the client. *(See B.2.d.)*

B.2.d. Minimal Disclosure

To the extent possible, clients are informed before confidential information is disclosed and are involved in the disclosure decision-making process. When circumstances require the disclosure of confidential information, only essential information is revealed. *(See B.2.c.)*

B.3. Information Shared With Others
B.3.a. Subordinates

Career professionals make every effort to ensure that privacy and confidentiality of clients are maintained by subordinates, including employees, supervisees, students, clerical assistants, and volunteers. *(See G.1.c.)*

B.3.b. Treatment Teams

When client treatment involves a continued review or participation by a treatment team, the client will be informed of the team's existence and composition, information being shared, and the purposes of sharing such information.

B.3.c. Confidential Settings

Career professionals discuss confidential information only in settings in which they can reasonably ensure client privacy.

B.3.d. Third-Party Payers

Career professionals disclose information to third-party payers only when clients have authorized such disclosure and in accordance with federal, state, local, and/or institutional statute, law, regulation, or procedure.

B.3.e. Transmitting Confidential Information

Career professionals take precautions to ensure the confidentiality of information transmitted through the use of computers, electronic mail, facsimile machines, telephones, voicemail, answering machines, and other electronic or computer technology.

B.3.f. Deceased Clients

Career professionals protect the confidentiality of deceased clients, consistent with legal requirements and agency or institutional policies.

B.4. Groups and Families
B.4.a. Group Work

In group work, career professionals clearly explain the importance and parameters of confidentiality for the specific group being entered.

B.4.b. Providing Career Services to Multiple Family Members
When providing career services to multiple family members (e.g., spouses/partners, parent and child, etc.), career professionals clearly define who is considered "the client" and discuss expectations and limitations of confidentiality. Career professionals seek agreement and document in writing such agreement among all involved parties having capacity to give consent concerning each individual's right to confidentiality and any obligation to preserve the confidentiality of information known.

B.5. Clients Lacking Capacity to Give Informed Consent
B.5.a. Responsibility to Clients
When providing career services to minor clients or adult clients who lack the capacity to give voluntary, informed consent, career professionals protect the confidentiality of information received in the professional relationship as specified by federal and state laws, written policies, and applicable ethical standards.

B.5.b. Responsibility to Parents and Legal Guardians
Career professionals inform parents and legal guardians about the role of career professionals and the confidential nature of the professional relationship. Career professionals are sensitive to the cultural diversity of families and respect the inherent rights and responsibilities of parents/guardians over the welfare of their children/charges according to law. Career professionals work to establish, as appropriate, collaborative relationships with parents/guardians to best serve the needs and welfare of their clients.

B.5.c. Release of Confidential Information
When providing career services to minor clients or adult clients who lack the capacity to give voluntary consent to release confidential information, career professionals seek permission from an appropriate third party to disclose information. In such instances, career professionals inform clients consistent with their level of understanding and take culturally appropriate measures to safeguard client confidentiality.

B.6. Records
B.6.a. Confidentiality of Records
Career professionals ensure that records are kept in a secure location and that only authorized persons have access to records.

B.6.b. Permission to Record
Career professionals obtain permission from clients prior to recording sessions through electronic or similar means (i.e., audio or video recording).

B.6.c. Permission to Observe
Career professionals obtain permission from clients prior to allowing observation of sessions, review of session transcripts, or viewing recordings of sessions with supervisors, subordinates, faculty, peers, or others within a training environment.

B.6.d. Client Access

Career professionals provide reasonable access to records and copies of records when requested by competent clients. Career professionals limit the access of clients to their records, or portions of their records, only when there is compelling evidence that such access would cause harm to the client and in accordance with federal, state, local, and/or institutional statute, law, regulation, or procedure. Career professionals document the request of clients and the rationale for withholding some or all of the record in the files of clients. In situations involving multiple clients, career professionals provide individual clients with only those parts of records that related directly to them and do not include confidential information related to any other client.

B.6.e. Assistance with Records

When clients request access to their records, career professionals provide assistance and consultation in interpreting such records.

B.6.f. Disclosure or Transfer

Unless exceptions to confidentiality exist, career professionals obtain written permission from clients to disclose or transfer records to legitimate third parties. Steps are taken to ensure that receivers of career services records are sensitive to their confidential nature. *(See A.3., E.4.)*

B.6.g. Storage and Disposal After Termination

Career professionals store records following termination of services to ensure reasonable future access, maintain records in accordance with all applicable federal, state, local, and/or institutional statutes, laws, regulations, and procedures governing records, and dispose of client records and other sensitive materials in a manner that protects client confidentiality. When records are of an artistic nature, career professionals obtain client (or guardian) consent with regard to handling of such records or documents. Career professionals are encouraged to purge their files according to the time frame required by federal, state, local, and/or institutional statute, law, regulation, or procedure, particularly when there is no reasonable expectation that a client will benefit from maintaining the records any longer. Career professionals are expected to know and abide by all applicable federal, state, local, and/or institutional statutes, laws, regulations, and procedures regarding record keeping and disposal. *(See A.1.c.)*

B.6.h. Reasonable Precautions

Career professionals take reasonable precautions to protect client confidentiality in the event of the career professional's termination of practice, incapacity, or death. *(See C.2.h.)*

B.7. Research and Training
B.7.a. Institutional Approval

When institutional approval is required, career professionals provide accurate information about their research proposals and obtain approval prior to conducting their research. They conduct research in accordance with the approved research protocol.

B.7.b. Adherence to Guidelines

Career professionals are responsible for understanding and adhering to state, federal, agency, or institutional policies or applicable guidelines regarding confidentiality in their research practices.

B.7.c. Confidentiality of Information Obtained in Research

Violations of participant privacy and confidentiality are risks of participation in research involving human participants, however, investigators maintain all research records in a secure manner. They explain to participants the risks of violations of privacy and confidentiality and disclose to participants any limits of confidentiality that can reasonably be expected. Regardless of the degree to which confidentiality will be maintained, investigators must disclose to participants any limits of confidentiality that can reasonably be expected. *(See H.2.e.)*

B.7.d. Disclosure of Research Information

Career professionals do not disclose confidential information that reasonably could lead to the identification of a research participant unless they have obtained prior consent of the person. Use of data derived from professional relationships for purposes of training, research, or publication is confined to content that is disguised to ensure the anonymity of the individuals involved. *(See H.2.a., H.2.d.)*

B.7.e. Agreement for Identification

Identification of clients, students, or supervisees in a presentation or publication is permissible only when they have reviewed the material and agreed to its presentation or publication. *(See H.4.d.)*

B.8. Consultation

B.8.a. Agreements

When acting as consultants, career professionals seek agreements among all parties involved concerning each individual's rights to confidentiality, the obligation of each individual to preserve confidential information, and the limits of confidentiality of information shared by others.

B.8.b. Respect for Privacy

Information obtained in a consulting relationship is discussed for professional purposes only with persons directly involved with the case. Written and oral reports present only data germane to the purposes of the consultation, and every effort is made to protect client identity and to avoid undue invasion of privacy.

B.8.c. Disclosure of Confidential Information

When consulting with colleagues, career professionals do not disclose confidential information that reasonably could lead to the identification of a client or other person or organization with whom they have a confidential relationship unless they have obtained the prior consent of the person or organization or the disclosure cannot be avoided. They disclose information only to the extent necessary to achieve the purposes of the consultation. *(See D.2.d.)*

Section C: Professional Responsibility

Introduction
Career professionals provide open, honest, and accurate communication in dealing with the public and other professionals. They practice in a nondiscriminatory manner within the boundaries of professional and personal competence and have a responsibility to abide by the *NCDA Code of Ethics.* Career professionals actively participate in local, state, and national associations that foster the development and improvement of the provision of career services. Career professionals promote change at the individual, group, institutional, and societal levels that improves the quality of life for individuals and groups and removes potential barriers to the provision or access of appropriate services being offered. Career professionals have a responsibility to the public to engage in ethical practice. In addition, career professionals engage in self-care activities to maintain and promote their emotional, physical, mental, and spiritual well-being to best meet their professional responsibilities.

C.1. Knowledge of Standards
Career professionals have a responsibility to read, understand, and follow the *NCDA Code of Ethics* and adhere to all applicable federal, state, local, and/or institutional statutes, laws, regulations, and procedures.

C.2. Professional Competence

C.2.a. Boundaries of Competence
Career professionals practice only within the boundaries of their competence, based on their education, training, supervised experience, state and national professional credentials, and appropriate professional experience. Career professionals gain knowledge, personal awareness, sensitivity, and skills pertinent to working with a diverse client population. *(See E.2., G.2., G.11.c.)*

C.2.b. New Specialty Areas of Practice
Career professionals practice in specialty areas new to them only after obtaining appropriate education, training, and supervised experience. While developing skills in new specialty areas, career professionals take steps to ensure the competence of their work and to protect others from possible harm. *(See G.6.e.)*

C.2.c. Qualified for Employment
Career professionals accept employment only for positions for which they are qualified by education, training, supervised experience, state and national professional credentials, and appropriate professional experience. Career professionals hire for professional positions only individuals who are qualified and competent for those positions.

C.2.d. Monitor Effectiveness
Career professionals continually monitor their effectiveness as professionals and take steps to improve when necessary. Career professionals in private practice take reasonable steps to seek peer supervision, as needed, to evaluate their efficacy as career professionals.

C.2.e. Consultation on Ethical Obligations
Career professionals take reasonable steps to consult with other career professionals or related practitioners when they have questions regarding their ethical obligations or professional activities.

C.2.f. Continuing Education
Career professionals recognize the need for continuing education to acquire and maintain a reasonable level of awareness of current scientific and professional information in their fields of activity. They take steps to maintain competence in the skills they use, are open to new procedures, and keep current with the populations with whom they work.

C.2.g. Impairment
Career professionals are alert to the signs of impairment from their own physical, mental, or emotional problems and refrain from offering or providing professional services when such impairment is likely to harm a client or others. They seek assistance for problems that reach the level of professional impairment, and, if necessary, they limit, suspend, or terminate their professional responsibilities until such time as it is determined that they may safely resume their work. Career professionals assist colleagues or supervisors in recognizing their own professional impairment. They provide consultation and assistance, when warranted, with colleagues or supervisors showing signs of impairment and intervene as appropriate to prevent imminent harm to clients. *(See A.10.b., G.8.b.)*

C.2.h. Incapacitation or Termination of Practice
When career professionals leave a practice, they follow a prepared plan for transfer of clients and files. Career professionals prepare and disseminate to an identified colleague or "records custodian" a plan for the transfer of clients and files in case of their incapacitation, death, or termination of practice. *(See A.1.c., A.10., B.6.g.)*

C.3. Advertising and Soliciting Clients

C.3.a. Accurate Advertising
When advertising or otherwise representing their services to the public, career professionals identify their credentials in an accurate manner that is not false, misleading, deceptive, or fraudulent. *(See C.4.)*

C.3.b. Testimonials
Career professionals who use testimonials do not solicit them from individuals who may be vulnerable to undue influence.

C.3.c. Statements by Others
Career professionals make reasonable efforts to ensure that statements made by others about them or the services they provide are accurate.

C.3.d. Recruiting Through Employment
Career professionals do not use their places of employment or institutional affiliations to recruit or gain clients, supervisees, or consultees for their private practices, unless they have permission.

If permitted to solicit for their private practices, career professionals must make potential clients, supervisees, or consultees aware of the free or low-cost services already provided by them or others through their place of employment or institutional affiliation. *(See A.9.a)*

C.3.e. Products and Training Advertisements
Career professionals who develop products related to their profession or conduct workshops or training events ensure that the advertisements concerning these products or events are accurate and disclose adequate information for consumers to make informed choices.

C.3.f. Promoting to Those Served
Career professionals do not use individual consultation, teaching, training, or supervisory relationships to promote their products or training events in a manner that is deceptive or would exert undue influence on individuals who may be vulnerable. However, educators may adopt textbooks and/or other materials they have authored or developed for instructional purposes.

C.4. Professional Qualifications

C.4.a. Accurate Representation
Career professionals claim or imply only professional qualifications actually completed and correct any known misrepresentations of their qualifications by others. Career professionals truthfully represent the qualifications of their professional colleagues. Career professionals clearly distinguish between paid and volunteer work experience and accurately describe their continuing education and specialized training. *(See A.1.b, C.2.a, E.9.c.)*

C.4.b. Credentials
Career professionals claim only licenses or certifications that are current and in good standing.

C.4.c. Educational Degrees
Career professionals clearly differentiate between earned and honorary degrees.

C.4.d. Implying Doctoral-Level Competence
Career professionals clearly state their highest earned degree in counseling or a closely related field. Career professionals do not imply doctoral-level competence when possessing only a master's degree in counseling or a related field. Career professionals do not use the title "Dr." nor refer to themselves as "Dr." in a counseling or career services context when their doctorate is not in counseling or a related field.

C.4.e. Program Accreditation Status
Career professionals clearly state the accreditation status of their degree programs at the time the degree was earned.

C.4.f. Professional Membership
Career professionals clearly differentiate between current, active memberships and former memberships in associations.

C.5. Nondiscrimination

Career professionals do not condone or engage in discrimination against any individual based on age, culture, mental/physical disability, ethnicity, race, religion/spirituality, creed, gender, gender identity, sexual orientation, marital/partnership status, language preference, socioeconomic status, any other characteristics not specifically relevant to job performance, or any basis prohibited by law. Career professionals do not discriminate against clients, students, employees, supervisees, or research participants in a manner that has a negative impact on these persons.

C.6. Public Responsibility

C.6.a. Sexual Harassment

Career professionals do not engage in or condone sexual harassment. Sexual harassment is defined as sexual solicitation, physical advances, or verbal or nonverbal conduct that is sexual in nature, that occurs in connection with professional activities or roles, and that either
1. is unwelcome, is offensive, or creates a hostile workplace or learning environment, and career professionals know or are told this; or
2. is sufficiently severe or intense to be perceived as harassment to a reasonable person in the context in which the behavior occurred. Sexual harassment can consist of a single intense or severe act or multiple persistent or pervasive acts.

C.6.b. Reports to Third Parties

Career professionals are accurate, honest, and objective in reporting their professional activities and judgments to appropriate third parties, including courts, health insurance companies, those who are the recipients of evaluation reports, and others. *(See B.3., E.4.)*

C.6.c. Media Presentations

When career professionals provide advice or comment by means of public lectures, demonstrations, radio or television programs, prerecorded tapes, technology-based applications, printed articles, mailed material, or other media, they take reasonable precautions to ensure that
1. the statements are based on appropriate professional literature and practice,
2. the statements are otherwise consistent with the *NCDA Code of Ethics,* and
3. the recipients of the information are informed that a professional relationship has not been established.

C.6.d. Exploitation of Others

Career professionals do not exploit others in their professional relationships. *(See A.5.b., A.9.d.)*

C.6.e. Scientific Bases for Treatment Modalities

Career professionals use techniques/procedures/modalities that are grounded in theory, are generally considered to be established professional practice in the fields of counseling and career development, and/or have an empirical or scientific foundation. Career professionals who do not must define the techniques/procedures as "unproven" or "developing" and explain the potential risks and ethical considerations of using such techniques/procedures and take steps to protect clients from possible harm. *(See A.4.a.)*

C.7. Responsibility to Other Professionals

C.7.a. Personal Public Statements
When making personal statements in a public context, career professionals clarify that they are speaking from their personal perspectives and that they are not speaking on behalf of all career professionals or the profession. *(See C.6.c.)*

Section D: Relationships with Other Professionals

Introduction
Career professionals recognize that the quality of their interactions with colleagues can influence the quality of services provided to clients. They work to become knowledgeable about colleagues within and outside the profession. Career professionals develop positive working relationships and systems of communication with colleagues to enhance services to clients.

D.1. Relationships with Colleagues, Employers, and Employees

D.1.a. Different Approaches
Career professionals are respectful of approaches to career services that differ from their own. Career professionals are respectful of traditions and practices of other professional groups with which they work.

D.1.b. Forming Relationships
Career professionals work to develop and strengthen interdisciplinary relations with colleagues from other disciplines to best serve clients.

D.1.c. Interdisciplinary Teamwork
Career professionals who are members of interdisciplinary teams delivering multifaceted services to clients keep the focus on how to best serve the clients. They participate in and contribute to decisions that affect the well-being of clients by drawing on the perspectives, values, and experiences of the profession and those of colleagues from other disciplines. *(See B.3.b.)*

D.1.d. Confidentiality
When career professionals are required by law, institutional policy, or extraordinary circumstances to serve in more than one role in judicial or administrative proceedings, they clarify role expectations and the parameters of confidentiality with their colleagues. *(See A.5.e, B.1.c., B.1.d., B.2.c., B.2.d., B.3.b.)*

D.1.e. Establishing Professional and Ethical Obligations
Career professionals who are members of interdisciplinary teams clarify professional and ethical obligations of the team as a whole and of its individual members. When a team decision raises ethical concerns, career professionals first attempt to resolve the concern within the team. If they cannot reach resolution among team members, career professionals pursue other avenues to address their concerns consistent with client well-being.

D.1.f. Personnel Selection and Assignment
Career professionals select competent staff and assign responsibilities compatible with their knowledge, skills, and experiences.

D.1.g. Employer Policies
The acceptance of employment in an agency or institution implies that career professionals are in agreement with its general policies and principles. Career professionals strive to reach agreement

with employers as to acceptable standards of conduct that allow for changes in institutional policy conducive to the growth and development of clients.

D.1.h. Negative Conditions

Career professionals alert their employers of inappropriate policies and practices. They attempt to effect changes in such policies or procedures through constructive action within the organization. When such policies are potentially disruptive or damaging to clients or may limit the effectiveness of services provided and change cannot be achieved, career professionals take appropriate further action. Such action may include referral to appropriate certification, accreditation, or state licensure organizations, or voluntary termination of employment.

D.1.i. Protection from Punitive Action

Career professionals take care not to harass or dismiss an employee who has acted in a responsible and ethical manner to expose inappropriate employer policies or practices.

D.2. Consultation

D.2.a. Consultant Competency

Career professionals take reasonable steps to ensure that they have the appropriate resources and competencies when providing consultation services. Career professionals provide appropriate referral resources when requested or needed. *(See C.2.a.)*

D.2.b. Understanding Consultees

When providing consultation, career professionals attempt to develop with their consultees a clear understanding of problem definition, goals for change, and predicted consequences of interventions selected.

D.2.c. Consultant Goals

The consulting relationship is one in which consultee adaptability and growth toward self-direction are consistently encouraged and cultivated.

D.2.d. Informed Consent in Consultation

When providing consultation, career professionals have an obligation to review, in writing and orally, the rights and responsibilities of career professionals and consultees. Career professionals use clear and understandable language to inform all parties involved about the purpose of the services to be provided, relevant costs, potential risks and benefits, and the limits of confidentiality. Working in conjunction with the consultee, career professionals attempt to develop a clear definition of the problem, goals for change, and predicted consequences of interventions that are culturally responsive and appropriate to the needs of consultees. *(See A.2.a., A.2.b.)*

Section E: Evaluation, Assessment, and Interpretation

Introduction
Career professionals use assessment instruments as one component of the career services process, taking into account the client's personal and cultural context. Career professionals promote the well-being of individual clients or groups of clients by developing and using appropriate career, educational, and psychological assessment instruments.

E.1. General

E.1.a. Assessment
The primary purpose of educational, psychological, and career assessments is to provide measurements that are valid and reliable in either comparative or absolute terms. These include, but are not limited to, measurements of ability, personality, interest, intelligence, achievement, skills, values, and performance. Career professionals recognize the need to interpret the statements in this section as applying to both quantitative and qualitative assessments.

E.1.b. Client Welfare
Career professionals do not misuse assessment results and interpretations, and they take reasonable steps to prevent others from misusing the information these tools provide. They respect the client's right to know the results, the interpretations made, and the bases for career professionals' conclusions and recommendations.

E.2. Competence to Use and Interpret Assessment Instruments

E.2.a. Limits of Competence
Career professionals utilize only those testing and assessment services for which they have been trained and are competent in administering and interpreting. Career professionals using technology-assisted test interpretations are trained in the construct being measured and the specific instrument being used prior to using its technology-based application. Career professionals take reasonable measures to ensure the proper use of psychological and career assessment techniques by persons under their supervision. *(See G.1.)*

E.2.b. Appropriate Use
Career professionals are responsible for the appropriate application, scoring, interpretation, and use of assessment instruments relevant to the needs of the client, whether they score and interpret such assessments themselves or use technology or other services.

E.2.c. Decisions Based on Results
Career professionals responsible for decisions involving individuals or policies that are based on assessment results have a thorough understanding of educational, psychological, and career measurement, including validation criteria, assessment research, and guidelines for assessment development and use.

E.3. Informed Consent in Assessment

E.3.a. Explanation to Clients
Prior to assessment, career professionals explain the nature and purposes of assessment and the specific use of results by potential recipients. The explanation will be given in the language of the client (or other legally authorized person on behalf of the client), unless an explicit exception has been agreed upon in advance. Career professionals consider the client's personal or cultural context, the level of the client's understanding of the results, and the impact of the results on the client. *(See A.2.)*

E.3.b. Recipients of Results
Career professionals consider the examinee's welfare, explicit understandings, and prior agreements in determining who receives the assessment results. Career professionals include accurate and appropriate interpretations with any release of individual or group assessment results. *(See B.2.c., B.5.)*

E.4. Release of Data to Qualified Professionals
Career professionals release assessment data in which the client is identified only with the consent of the client or the client's legal representative. Such data are released only to persons recognized by career professionals as qualified to interpret the data and in accordance with all applicable federal, state, local, and/or institutional statutes, laws, regulations, and procedures. *(See B.1., B.3., B.5.c., B.6.e.)*

E.5. Diagnosis

E.5.a. Proper Diagnosis
Career professionals take special care to provide proper diagnosis and do so only when making a diagnosis is appropriate and when properly trained. Assessment techniques (including personal interview) used to determine client care (e.g., locus of treatment, type of treatment/services, or recommended follow-up) are carefully selected and appropriately used.

E.5.b. Cultural Sensitivity
Career professionals recognize that culture affects the manner in which clients' problems are defined. Clients' socioeconomic and cultural experiences are considered when making a diagnosis. *(See A.2.c.)*

E.5.c. Historical and Social Prejudices in the Diagnosis of Pathology
Career professionals recognize historical and social prejudices in the misdiagnosis and pathologizing of certain individuals and groups and the role career professionals can play in avoiding the perpetuation of these prejudices through proper diagnosis and provision of services.

E.5.d. Refraining From Diagnosis
Career professionals may refrain from making and/or reporting a diagnosis if they believe it would cause harm to the client or others.

E.6. Instrument Selection

E.6.a. Appropriateness of Instruments
Career professionals carefully consider the validity, reliability, psychometric limitations, and appropriateness of instruments when selecting assessments.

E.6.b. Referral Information
If a client is referred to a third party for assessment, the career professional provides specific referral questions and sufficient objective data about the client to ensure that appropriate assessment instruments are utilized. *(See B.3.)*

E.6.c. Culturally Diverse Populations
Career professionals are cautious when selecting assessments for culturally diverse populations to avoid the use of instruments that lack appropriate psychometric properties for the client population. *(See A.2.c., E.5.b.)*

E.7. Conditions of Assessment Administration

E.7.a. Administration Conditions
Career professionals administer assessments under the same conditions that were established in their standardization. When assessments are not administered under standard conditions, as may be necessary to accommodate clients with disabilities, or when unusual behavior or irregularities occur during the administration, those conditions are noted in interpretation, and the results may be designated as invalid or of questionable validity.

E.7.b. Technological Administration
Career professionals ensure that administration programs function properly and provide clients with accurate results when technological or other electronic methods are used for assessment administration.

E.7.c. Unsupervised Assessments
Unless the assessment instrument is designed, intended, and validated for self-administration and/or scoring, career professionals do not permit inadequately supervised use of any assessment.

E.7.d. Disclosure of Favorable Conditions
Prior to administration of assessments, conditions that produce the most favorable assessment results are made known to the examinee.

E.8. Multicultural Issues/Diversity in Assessment
Career professionals use, with caution, assessment techniques that were normed on populations other than that of the client. Career professionals recognize the possible effects of age, color, culture, disability, ethnic group, gender, race, language preference, religion, spirituality, sexual orientation, and socioeconomic status on test administration and interpretation, and place test results in proper perspective with other relevant factors. *(See A.2.c., E.5.b.)*

E.9. Scoring and Interpretation of Assessments

E.9.a. Reporting
In reporting assessment results, career professionals indicate reservations that exist regarding validity or reliability due to circumstances of the assessment or the inappropriateness of the norms for the person tested.

E.9.b. Research Instruments
Career professionals exercise caution when interpreting the results of research instruments not having sufficient technical data to support respondent results. The specific purposes for the use of such instruments are stated explicitly to the examinee.

E.9.c. Assessment Services
Career professionals who provide assessment scoring and interpretation services to support the assessment process confirm the validity of such interpretations. They accurately describe the purpose, norms, validity, reliability, and applications of the procedures and any special qualifications applicable to their use. The public offering of an automated test interpretation service is considered a professional-to-professional consultation. The formal responsibility of the career professional is to the individual/organization requesting the assessment, but the ultimate and overriding responsibility is to the client. *(See E.1.b., E.2.)*

E.10. Assessment Security
Career professionals maintain the integrity and security of tests and other assessment techniques consistent with legal and contractual obligations. Career professionals do not appropriate, reproduce, or modify published assessments or parts thereof without acknowledgment and permission from the publisher.

E.11. Obsolete Assessments and Outdated Results
Career professionals do not use data or results from assessments that are obsolete or outdated for the current purpose. Career professionals make every effort to prevent the misuse of obsolete measures and assessment data by others.

E.12. Assessment Construction
Career professionals use established scientific procedures, relevant standards, and current professional knowledge for assessment design in the development, publication, and utilization of educational and psychological assessment techniques.

E.13. Forensic Evaluation: Evaluation for Legal Proceedings

E.13.a. Primary Obligations
When providing forensic evaluations, the primary obligation of career professionals is to produce objective findings that can be substantiated based on information and techniques appropriate to the evaluation, which may include examination of the individual and/or review of records. Career professionals are entitled to form professional opinions based on their professional knowledge and expertise that can be supported by the data gathered in evaluations. Career

professionals will define the limits of their reports or testimony, especially when an examination of the individual has not been conducted.

E.13.b. Consent for Evaluation
Individuals being evaluated are informed in writing that the relationship is for the purposes of an evaluation, not to provide career services. Entities or individuals who will receive the evaluation report are identified. Written consent to be evaluated is obtained from those being evaluated unless a court orders evaluations to be conducted without the written consent of individuals being evaluated. When children or vulnerable adults are being evaluated, informed written consent is obtained from a parent or guardian. *(See A.2. B.2.c., B.5.)*

E.13.c. Client Evaluation Prohibited
Career professionals do not evaluate current or former clients for forensic purposes. Career professionals do not accept as clients, individuals they are evaluating or have previously evaluated for forensic purposes.

E.13.d. Avoid Potentially Harmful Relationships
Career professionals who provide forensic evaluations avoid potentially harmful professional or personal relationships with family members, romantic partners, and close friends of individuals they are evaluating or have evaluated in the past. *(See A.5.)*

Section F: Use of the Internet in the Provision of Career Services

Introduction
Career professionals have always been at the forefront in using new technologies to assist in serving clients. More and more, technology (and specifically the Internet) is being used to provide and/or support services offered by career professionals. However, the Internet should typically be only one component of the career services process and then its use must be evaluated based on the client's personal and cultural context. Above all, career professionals must practice ethically and continually promote the well-being of individual clients or groups of clients.

F.1. General

F.1.a. Benefits and Limitations
Career professionals inform clients of the benefits and limitations of using information technology applications in their professional relationship and in business/billing procedures. Such technologies include but are not limited to computer hardware and software, telephones, the Internet, online assessment instruments, and other communication devices.

F.1.b. Capability to Utilize and Benefit from Technology-Assisted Services
When providing technology-assisted distance career services, career professionals determine that clients are intellectually, emotionally, and physically capable of using, and are likely to benefit from, the application and that the application is appropriate for the needs of clients. Where possible, career professionals utilize multiple methods of contact (i.e., telephone, video conference, and email), in assessing the best means of providing career services to a particular client.

F.2. Technology Applications

F.2.a. Types of Technology-Assisted Services
Multiple means of online provision of career services currently exist, the most common of which are email, newsgroups, bulletin boards, instant messaging, chat rooms, blogs (web logs), web cams (video cameras) and websites offering a wide variety of services. Telephone or audiovisual linkages supported by the Internet continue to grow in popularity as the technology improves and the costs decline. Based on readily-available capabilities at the time of this writing, the Internet could be used in at least four ways to provide and/or support career services. These include:

1. Delivering information about occupations, the world of work, career planning, and job searching. This may include occupational/job descriptions, employment prospects, skills requirements, estimated salary, resume writing, job interviewing techniques, etc. Delivery may come through one or a combination of media including text, still images, graphics, and/or video. In providing these services, the standards for information development and presentation are the same as those for other print and audiovisual materials as stated in other NCDA documents.
2. Providing assessments and/or online searches of academic, occupational, or other databases to identify career, educational, or other alternatives. In providing these

services, other standards developed by NCDA (i.e., *Section E of this Code*) and the Association of Computer-based Systems for Career Information (ACSCI) apply.

3. Delivering interactive career services. This use assumes that clients, either as individuals or as part of a group, have intentionally placed themselves in direct communication with a career professional. Standards for using the Internet for these purposes are addressed in this section.
4. Providing a database of job openings. Guidelines for this application are included in this section as well.

F.2.b. Alternative Services

When technology-assisted distance career services are deemed inappropriate by the career professional or client, career professionals provide appropriate alternatives, including face to face service and/or a referral to career professionals who can provide in person services. *(See A.10)*

F.2.c. Access

Career professionals ensure reasonable access to computer applications when providing technology-assisted distance career services. If they are unable to do so they provide an alternative method of service delivery, including referrals to career professionals who would be able to provide face-to-face services. *(See A.10)*

F.2.d. Laws and Statutes

Career professionals ensure that the use of technology services with clients is in accordance with all applicable federal, state, local, and/or institutional statutes, laws, regulations, and procedures, particularly when the services offered via technology cross state and/or national boundaries.

F.2.e. Outside Assistance

Career professionals seek business, legal, and technical assistance (when necessary and appropriate) when using technology applications, particularly when the use of such applications crosses state or national boundaries.

F.2.f. Informed Consent & Confidentiality

As part of the process of establishing informed consent and defining confidentiality and its limits, career professionals who provide technology-assisted distance career services:

1. Provide information to clients about their credentials.
2. Work with clients to establish goals and determine if a technology-assisted distance modality is appropriate.
3. Where applicable, define the fees for service and billing procedures.
4. Provide clients with information regarding where and how they can report any behavior on the part of the career professional that they consider unethical.
5. Where feasible, address issues related to maintaining the confidentiality of electronically transmitted communications (e.g., the use of encryption).
6. Inform clients of the inherent difficulty of maintaining absolute confidentiality when conducting electronically transmitted communication.

7. Urge clients to be aware of all authorized or unauthorized users (including family members and fellow employees) who may have access to any technology clients use in the professional relationship.
8. Inform clients of pertinent legal rights and limitations governing the practice of a profession over state lines or international boundaries, when necessary and appropriate.
9. Inform clients if and for how long archival storage of transaction records will be maintained.
10. Discuss the possibility of technology failure and alternate methods of service delivery.
11. Inform clients of emergency procedures, such as calling 911 or a local crisis hotline, when the career professional is not available, should circumstances warrant.
12. Discuss time zone differences, local customs, and cultural or language differences that might impact service delivery.
13. Establish a method for verifying identity.
14. Obtain the written consent of the legal guardian or other authorized legal representative prior to rendering services in the event the client is a minor child, an adult who is legally incompetent, or an adult incapable of giving informed consent.

F.3. Qualifications of Developer or Provider

Websites and other services designed to assist clients with career planning and job searching should be developed with content input from career professionals. The service should clearly state the qualifications and credentials of the developers.

F.4. Access and Understanding of Environment

Career professionals have an obligation to be aware of free and/or low cost public access points to the Internet within the community, so that a lack of financial resources does not create a significant barrier to clients accessing career services or information, assessments, or instructional resources over the internet.

F.5. Content of Career Services on the Internet

F.5.a. Appropriateness of Internet Content

The content of a website or other online career information or planning services should be reviewed for the appropriateness of offering the material in this medium. Some types of content have been extensively tested for online delivery including searching databases by relevant variables; displaying occupational information; developing a resumé; assessing interests, abilities, personality, and other characteristics and linkage of these to occupational titles; relating school majors to occupational choices; and the completing of forms such as a financial needs assessment questionnaire or a job application.

When a website offers content or a service that has not been extensively tested for online delivery, is not grounded in theory, is not generally considered to be established professional practice in the fields of counseling and career development, and/or does not have an empirical or scientific foundation, career professionals must define the content or service as "unproven" or "developing" and explain the potential risks and ethical considerations of using such content or service and take steps to protect clients from possible harm.

F.5.b. Maintaining Internet Sites
Career professionals maintaining sites on the Internet do the following:

1. Regularly check that electronic links are working and are professionally appropriate.
2. Provide electronic links to relevant state licensure and professional certification boards to protect consumer rights and facilitate addressing ethical concerns.
3. Provide a site that is accessible to persons with disabilities, when feasible.
4. Provide translation capabilities (when feasible) for clients who have a different primary language while also acknowledging the imperfect nature of such translations.
5. Assist clients in determining the validity and reliability of information found on the Internet and in other technology applications.
6. If a website includes links to other websites, the career professional who creates this linkage is responsible for ensuring that the services to which the site is linked meet all applicable ethical standards. If this is not possible, career professionals should post a disclaimer explaining that the linked site may not meet all applicable ethical standards and (if known) which standards are not met by the site.

F.6. Ongoing Client Support
When providing technology-assisted distance career services, career professionals periodically monitor clients' progress. Should career professionals determine that little or no progress is being made toward stated goals, career professionals will discuss the need for a referral to a face-to-face service provider. Career professionals will assist clients in identifying appropriate providers and will facilitate the transition. *(See A.10., E.6.b., F.2.b.)*

F.7. Use of Assessment
When using assessments on the Internet, career professionals are responsible for knowing and abiding by other standards developed by NCDA (i.e., *Section E of this Code*) and the Association of Computer-based Systems for Career Information (ACSCI). Where applicable and possible, career professionals should:

1. determine if the assessments have been tested for online delivery and ensure that their psychometric properties are the same as in print form; or the client must be informed that the assessments have not yet been tested for this mode of delivery.
2. abide by the same ethical guidelines as if administering and interpreting these assessments in person or in print form.
3. make every effort to protect the confidentiality of client results.
4. refer clients to qualified career professionals in his or her geographic area, if there is evidence that the client does not understand the assessment results.
5. determine if the assessments have been validated for self-help use or that appropriate counseling intervention is provided before and after completion of the assessment resource if the resource has not been validated for self-help use.

F.8. Internet Job Posting and Searching
All job postings must represent a valid opening for which those searching on the Internet have an opportunity to apply. It is encouraged that job postings be removed from the database within 48 hours of the time that the announced position is filled. Names, addresses, resumés, and other

information that may be gained about individuals should not be used for any purposes other than provision of further information about job openings.

F.9. Unacceptable Behaviors on the Internet
Career professionals have a responsibility to act in an ethical manner at all times. Because a behavior is not expressly prohibited, this does not imply that it is ethical. The following behaviors are deemed unacceptable for career professionals:

1. Use of a false e-mail identity when interacting with clients and/or other professionals. When acting in a professional capacity on the Internet, career professionals have a duty to identify themselves honestly.
2. Accepting a client who will not identify him/herself and/or is unwilling to arrange for a telephone conversation as well as online interchange.
3. Anonymously monitoring chat rooms, web logs (blogs), bulletin board services, and/or other web-based communities and offering career planning and related services when no request has been made for such services. This includes sending out mass unsolicited e-mails to individuals with whom you do not have an already established professional relationship. Career professionals may advertise their services but must do so observing proper online "netiquette" and standards of professional conduct.

Section G: Supervision, Training, and Teaching

Introduction
Career professionals foster meaningful and respectful professional relationships and maintain appropriate boundaries with supervisees and students. Career professionals have theoretical and pedagogical foundations for their work and aim to be fair, accurate, and honest in their assessments of students.

G.1. Supervision and Client Welfare

G.1.a. Client Welfare
A primary obligation of supervisors is to monitor the services provided by other career professionals or students for whom they have responsibility. Supervisors also monitor client welfare and supervisee performance and professional development. To fulfill these obligations, supervisors meet regularly with supervisees to review case notes, samples of work, or live observations. Supervisees have a responsibility to understand and follow the *NCDA Code of Ethics*.

G.1.b. Credentials
Supervisors work to ensure that clients are aware of the qualifications of the supervisees who render services to clients. *(See A.2.b.)*

G.1.c. Informed Consent and Client Rights
Supervisors make supervisees aware of client rights including the protection of client privacy and confidentiality in the professional relationship. Supervisees provide clients with professional disclosure information and inform them of how the supervision process influences the limits of confidentiality. Supervisees make clients aware of who will have access to records of the professional relationship and how these records will be used. *(See A.2.a., A.2.b., B.1.d. D.3.)*

G.2. Supervisor Competence

G.2.a. Supervisor Preparation
Prior to offering supervision services, career professionals are trained in supervision methods and techniques. Career professionals who offer supervision services regularly pursue continuing education activities including both career services and supervision topics and skills. *(See C.2.a., C.2.f.)*

G.2.b. Multicultural Issues/Diversity in Supervision
Supervisors are aware of and address the role of multiculturalism/diversity in the supervisory relationship.

G.3. Supervisory Relationships

G.3.a. Relationship Boundaries with Supervisees
Supervisors clearly define and maintain ethical professional, personal, and social relationships with their supervisees, although they avoid and/or keep to a minimum nonprofessional

relationships with current supervisees. If supervisors must assume other professional roles (e.g., clinical and administrative supervisor, instructor, etc.) with supervisees, they work to minimize potential conflicts and explain to supervisees the expectations and responsibilities associated with each role. They do not engage in any form of nonprofessional interaction that may compromise the supervisory relationship.

G.3.b. Sexual Relationships
Sexual or romantic interactions or relationships with current supervisees are prohibited.

G.3.c. Harassment
Supervisors do not condone or subject supervisees to harassment, sexual or otherwise. *(See C.6.a.)*

G.3.d. Close Relatives and Friends
Supervisors avoid accepting close relatives, romantic partners, or friends as supervisees.

G.3.e. Potentially Beneficial Relationships
Supervisors are aware of the power differential in their relationships with supervisees. If they believe nonprofessional relationships with a supervisee may be potentially beneficial to the supervisee, they take precautions similar to those taken by career professionals when working with clients. Examples of potentially beneficial interactions or relationships include attending a formal ceremony; hospital visits; providing support during a stressful event; or mutual membership in a professional association, organization, or community. Supervisors engage in open discussions with supervisees when they consider entering into relationships with them outside of their supervisory roles. Before engaging in nonprofessional relationships, supervisors discuss with supervisees and document the rationale for such interactions, potential benefits or drawbacks, and anticipated consequences for the supervisee. Supervisors clarify the specific nature and limitations of the additional role(s) they will have with the supervisee. *(See A.5.d.)*

G.4. Supervisor Responsibilities

G.4.a. Informed Consent for Supervision
Supervisors are responsible for incorporating into their supervision the principles of informed consent and participation. Supervisors inform supervisees of the policies and procedures to which they are to adhere and the mechanisms for due process appeal of individual supervisory actions.

G.4.b. Emergencies and Absences
Supervisors establish and communicate to supervisees procedures for contacting them or, in their absence, alternative on-call supervisors to assist in handling crises.

G.4.c. Standards for Supervisees
Supervisors make their supervisees aware of professional and ethical standards and legal responsibilities. Supervisors of post-degree career professionals encourage these individuals to adhere to professional standards of practice. *(See C.1.)*

G.4.d. Termination of the Supervisory Relationship

Supervisors or supervisees have the right to terminate the supervisory relationship with adequate notice. Reasons for withdrawal are provided to the other party. When cultural, professional, or other issues are crucial to the viability of the supervisory relationship, both parties make efforts to resolve differences. When termination is warranted, supervisors make appropriate referrals to possible alternative supervisors.

G.5. Supervision Evaluation, Remediation, and Endorsement

G.5.a. Evaluation

Supervisors document and provide supervisees with ongoing performance appraisal and evaluation feedback and schedule periodic formal evaluative sessions throughout the supervisory relationship.

G.5.b. Limitations

Through ongoing evaluation and appraisal, supervisors are aware of the limitations of supervisees that might impede performance. Supervisors assist supervisees in securing remedial assistance when needed. They recommend dismissal from training programs, applied practice settings, or state or voluntary professional credentialing processes when those supervisees are unable to provide competent professional services. Supervisors seek consultation and document their decisions to dismiss or refer supervisees for assistance. They ensure that supervisees are aware of options available to them to address such decisions. *(See C.2.g.)*

G.5.c. Multiple Roles/Relationships with Supervisees

If supervisees request counseling, career services, or any other professional service which a supervisor may ordinarily offer, the supervisor will provide the supervisee with acceptable referrals. Career professionals do not typically engage in multiple roles/relationships with supervisees. If supervisors must provide a service to a supervisee in addition to providing supervision, they work to minimize potential conflicts and explain to supervisees the expectations and responsibilities associated with each role. In addition, the supervisor must address participation in multiple roles/relationships with the supervisee in terms of the impact of these issues on clients, the supervisory relationship, and professional functioning. *(See G.3.a.)*

G.5.d. Endorsement

Supervisors endorse supervisees for certification, licensure, employment, or completion of an academic or training program only when they believe supervisees are qualified for the endorsement. In addition, supervisors do not withhold endorsement of qualified supervisees for certification, licensure, employment, or completion of an academic or training program for any reason unrelated to their fitness as a student or professional. Regardless of qualifications, supervisors do not endorse supervisees whom they believe to be impaired in any way that would interfere with the performance of the duties associated with the endorsement.

G.6. Responsibilities of Educators

G.6.a. Educators
Educators who are responsible for developing, implementing, and supervising educational programs are skilled as teachers and practitioners. They are knowledgeable regarding the ethical, legal, and regulatory aspects of the profession, are skilled in applying that knowledge, and make students and supervisees aware of their responsibilities. Educators conduct education and training programs in an ethical manner and serve as role models for professional behavior. *(See C.1., C.2.a., C.2.c.)*

G.6.b. Integration of Study and Practice
Educators establish education and training programs that integrate academic study and supervised practice.

G.6.c. Teaching Ethics
Educators make students and supervisees aware of the ethical responsibilities and standards of the profession and the ethical responsibilities of students to the profession. Educators infuse ethical considerations throughout the curriculum. *(See C.1.)*

G.6.d. Peer Relationships
Educators make every effort to ensure that the rights of peers are not compromised when students or supervisees lead career groups or provide supervision. Educators take steps to ensure that students and supervisees understand they have the same ethical obligations as educators, trainers, and supervisors.

G.6.e. Innovative Theories and Techniques
When educators teach techniques/procedures that are innovative, without an empirical foundation, or without a well-grounded theoretical foundation, they define the techniques/procedures as "unproven" or "developing" and explain to students the potential risks and ethical considerations of using such techniques/procedures. *(See C.6.e.)*

G.6.f. Field Placements
Educators develop clear policies within their training programs regarding field placement and other clinical experiences. Educators provide clearly stated roles and responsibilities for the student or supervisee, the site supervisor, and the program supervisor. They confirm that site supervisors are qualified to provide supervision and inform site supervisors of their professional and ethical responsibilities in this role. In addition, educators do not accept any form of professional services, fees, commissions, reimbursement, or remuneration from a site for student or supervisee placement.

G.6.g. Professional Disclosure
Before initiating career services in a field placement, students disclose their status and explain how this status affects the limits of confidentiality. Educators ensure that the clients at field placements are aware of the services rendered and the qualifications of the students and supervisees rendering those services. Students and supervisees obtain client permission before

they use any information concerning the professional relationship in the training process. *(See A.2.b.)*

G.7. Student Welfare

G.7.a. Orientation
Educators recognize that orientation is a developmental process that continues throughout the education and training of students. Faculty provide prospective students with information about the educational program's expectations including but not necessarily limited to:

1. the type and level of skill and knowledge acquisition required for successful completion of the training;
2. training program goals, objectives, and mission, and subject matter to be covered;
3. bases for evaluation;
4. training components that encourage self-growth or self-disclosure as part of the training process;
5. the type of supervision settings and requirements of the sites for required clinical field experiences;
6. student and supervisee evaluation and dismissal policies and procedures; and
7. up-to-date employment prospects for graduates.

G.7.b. Self-Growth Experiences
Education programs delineate requirements for self-disclosure or self-growth experiences in their admission and program materials. Educators use professional judgment when designing training experiences they conduct that require student and supervisee self-growth or self-disclosure. Students and supervisees are made aware of the ramifications their self-disclosure may have when career professionals whose primary role as teacher, trainer, or supervisor requires acting on ethical obligations to the profession. Evaluative components of experiential training activities explicitly delineate predetermined academic standards that are separate from and do not depend on the student's level of self disclosure. Educators may require trainees to seek professional help to address any personal concerns that may be affecting their competency.

G.8. Student Responsibilities

G.8.a. Standards for Students
Students have a responsibility to understand and follow the *NCDA Code of Ethics* and adhere to all applicable federal, state, local, and/or institutional statutes, laws, regulations, and procedures governing professional staff behavior at the agency or placement setting. Students have the same obligation to clients as those required of career professionals. *(See C.1.)*

G.8.b. Impairment
Students refrain from offering or providing career services when their physical, mental, or emotional problems are likely to harm a client or others. They are alert to the signs of impairment, seek assistance for problems, and notify their program supervisors when they are aware that they are unable to effectively provide services. In addition, they seek appropriate

professional services for themselves to remediate the problems that are interfering with their ability to provide services to others. *(See A.1.a., C.2.d., C.2.g.)*

G.9. Evaluation and Remediation of Students

G.9.a. Evaluation
Career professionals clearly state to students, prior to and throughout the training program, the levels of competency expected, appraisal methods, and timing of evaluations for all areas of competency. Educators provide students with ongoing performance appraisal and evaluation feedback throughout the training program.

G.9.b. Limitations
Educators, through ongoing evaluation and appraisal, are aware of and address the inability of some students to achieve the level of competencies needed for successful continued performance. Educators

1. assist students in securing remedial assistance when needed,
2. seek professional consultation and document their decision to dismiss or refer students for assistance, and
3. ensure that students have recourse in a timely manner to address decisions to require them to seek assistance or to dismiss them and provide students with due process according to institutional policies and procedures.

G.9.c. Counseling for Students
If students request counseling or if counseling services are required as part of a remediation process, educators provide acceptable referrals.

G.10. Roles and Relationships Between Educators and Students
G.10.a. Sexual or Romantic Relationships
Sexual or romantic interactions or relationships with current students are prohibited.

G.10.b. Harassment
Educators do not condone or subject students to harassment, sexual or otherwise. *(See C.6.a.)*

G.10.c. Relationships with Former Students
Educators are aware of the power differential in the relationship between faculty and students. Faculty members foster open discussions with former students when considering engaging in a social, sexual, or other intimate relationship. Faculty members discuss with the former student how their former relationship may affect the change in relationship.

G.10.d. Nonprofessional Relationships
Educators avoid nonprofessional or ongoing professional relationships with students in which there is a risk of potential harm to the student or that may compromise the training experience or grades assigned.

G.10.e. Career Services
Educators do not serve as career professionals to current students unless this is a brief role associated with a training experience or in their role as an academic advisor.

G.10.f. Potentially Beneficial Relationships
Educators are aware of the power differential in the relationship between faculty and students. If they believe a nonprofessional relationship with a student may be potentially beneficial to the student, they take precautions similar to those taken by career professionals when working with clients. Examples of potentially beneficial interactions or relationships include, but are not limited to, attending a formal ceremony; hospital visits; providing support during a stressful event; or mutual membership in a professional association, organization, or community. Educators engage in open discussions with students when they consider entering into relationships with students outside of their roles as teachers and supervisors. They discuss with students the rationale for such interactions, the potential benefits and drawbacks, and the anticipated consequences for the student. Educators clarify the specific nature and limitations of the additional role(s) they will have with the student prior to engaging in a nonprofessional relationship. Nonprofessional relationships with students should be time-limited and initiated with student consent. *(See G.3.e)*

G.11. Multicultural/Diversity Competence in Education and Training Programs

G.11.a. Faculty Diversity
Educators are committed to recruiting and retaining a diverse faculty. Additionally, educators do not condone or engage in discrimination based on age, culture, mental/physical disability, ethnicity, race, religion/spirituality, creed, gender, actual or perceived gender identity or expression, actual or perceived sexual orientation, marital/partnership status, language preference, socioeconomic status, any other characteristics not specifically relevant to job performance, or any basis prohibited by law.

G.11.b. Student Diversity
Educators actively attempt to recruit and retain a diverse student body. Educators demonstrate commitment to multicultural/diversity competence by recognizing and valuing diverse cultures and types of abilities students bring to the training experience. Educators provide appropriate accommodations that enhance and support diverse student well-being and academic performance.

G.11.c. Multicultural/Diversity Competence
Educators actively infuse multicultural/diversity competency in their training and supervision practices. They actively train students to gain awareness, knowledge, and skills in the competencies of multicultural practice. Educators include case examples, role-plays, discussion questions, and other classroom activities that promote and represent various cultural perspectives.

Section H: Research and Publication

Introduction
Career professionals who conduct research are encouraged to contribute to the knowledge base of the profession and promote a clearer understanding of the conditions that lead to a healthy and more just society. Career professionals support efforts of researchers by participating fully and willingly whenever possible. Career professionals minimize bias and respect diversity in designing and implementing research programs.

H.1. Research Responsibilities

H.1.a. Use of Human Research Participants
Career professionals plan, design, conduct, and report research in a manner that is consistent with pertinent ethical principles, all applicable federal, state, and local statutes, laws, regulations, and/or procedures, host institutional regulations, and scientific standards governing research with human research participants. For one source of online training regarding information about the rights and welfare of human participants in research, see the attached web references section.

H.1.b. Need for Research and Review
Career professionals have an obligation to contribute to periodic evaluations of the services they provide to their clients. The interventions, techniques, and methods of service delivery they use should be evaluated to establish evidence-based practice. Career professionals also have an obligation to periodically review the evaluation and research literature in their area of expertise so that the career services they provide to their clients reflect established best practice.

H.1.c. Deviation from Standard Practice
Career professionals seek consultation and observe stringent safeguards to protect the rights of research participants when a research problem suggests a deviation from standard or acceptable practices.

H.1.d. Independent Researchers
When independent researchers do not have access to an Institutional Review Board (IRB), they should consult with researchers who are familiar with IRB procedures to provide appropriate safeguards.

H.1.e. Precautions to Avoid Injury
Career professionals who conduct research with human participants are responsible for the welfare of participants throughout the research process and should take reasonable precautions to avoid causing injurious psychological, emotional, physical, or social effects to participants.

H.1.f. Principal Researcher Responsibility
The ultimate responsibility for ethical research practice lies with the principal researcher. All others involved in the research activities share ethical obligations and responsibility for their own actions.

H.1.g. Minimal Interference
Career professionals take reasonable precautions to avoid causing disruptions in the lives of research participants that could be caused by their involvement in research.

H.1.h. Multicultural/Diversity Considerations in Research
When appropriate to research goals, career professionals are sensitive to incorporating research procedures that take into account cultural considerations. They seek consultation when appropriate.

H.2. Rights of Research Participants *(See A.2)*

H.2.a. Informed Consent in Research
Individuals have the right to consent to become research participants. In seeking consent, career professionals use language that

1. accurately explains the purpose and procedures to be followed.
2. identifies any procedures that are experimental or relatively untried.
3. describes any attendant discomforts and risks.
4. describes any benefits or changes in individuals or organizations that might be reasonably expected.
5. discloses appropriate alternative procedures that would be advantageous for participants.
6. offers to answer any inquiries concerning the procedures.
7. describes any limitations on confidentiality.
8. describes the format and potential target audiences for the dissemination of research findings.
9. instructs participants that they are free to withdraw their consent and to discontinue participation in the project at any time without penalty.

H.2.b. Deception
Career professionals do not conduct research involving deception unless alternative procedures are not feasible and the prospective value of the research justifies the deception. If such deception has the potential to cause physical or emotional harm to research participants, the research is not conducted, regardless of prospective value. When the methodological requirements of a study necessitate concealment or deception, the investigator explains the reasons for this action as soon as possible during the debriefing.

H.2.c. Student/Supervisee Participation
Researchers who involve students or supervisees in research make clear to them that the decision regarding whether or not to participate in research activities does not affect one's academic standing or supervisory relationship. Students or supervisees who choose not to participate in educational research are provided with an appropriate alternative to fulfill their academic or other requirements.

H.2.d. Client Participation
Career professionals conducting research involving clients make clear in the informed consent process that clients are free to choose whether or not to participate in research activities. Career

professionals take necessary precautions to protect clients from adverse consequences of declining or withdrawing from participation.

H.2.e. Confidentiality of Information

Information obtained about research participants during the course of an investigation is confidential. When the possibility exists that others may obtain access to such information, ethical research practice requires that the possibility, together with the plans for protecting confidentiality, be explained to participants as a part of the procedure for obtaining informed consent.

H.2.f. Persons Not Capable of Giving Informed Consent

When a person is not capable of giving informed consent, career professionals provide an appropriate explanation to, obtain agreement for participation from, and obtain the appropriate consent of a legally authorized person.

H.2.g. Commitments to Participants

Career professionals take reasonable measures to honor all commitments to research participants.

H.2.h. Explanations After Data Collection

After data are collected, career professionals provide participants with full clarification of the nature of the study to remove any misconceptions participants might have regarding the research. Where scientific or human values justify delaying or withholding information, career professionals take reasonable measures to avoid causing harm.

H.2.i. Informing Sponsors

Career professionals inform sponsors, institutions, and publication channels regarding research procedures and outcomes. Career professionals ensure that appropriate bodies and authorities are given pertinent information and acknowledgment.

H.2.j. Disposal of Research Documents and Records

Within a reasonable period of time following the completion of a research project or study, career professionals take steps to destroy records or documents (audio, video, digital, and written) containing confidential data or information that identifies research participants in accordance with all applicable federal, state, local, and/or institutional statutes, laws, regulations, and procedures. When records are of an artistic nature, researchers obtain participant consent with regard to handling of such records or documents. Career professionals are encouraged to purge their files according to the time frame required by federal, state, local, and/or institutional statute, law, regulation, or procedure, particularly when there is no reasonable expectation that anyone will benefit from maintaining the records any longer. *(See B.6.a, B.6.g.)*

H.3. Relationships with Research Participants (When Research Involves Intensive or Extended Interactions)

H.3.a. Nonprofessional Relationships
Nonprofessional relationships with research participants should be avoided as these interactions may set up dual relationships and role confusion that may be harmful to the emotional health of participants.

H.3.b. Relationships with Research Participants
Sexual or romantic interactions or relationships between career professionals/researchers and current research participants are prohibited.

H.3.c. Harassment and Research Participants
Researchers do not condone or subject research participants to harassment, sexual or otherwise. *(See C.6.a.)*

H.3.d. Potentially Beneficial Interactions
When a nonprofessional interaction between the researcher and the research participant may be potentially beneficial, the researcher must document, prior to the interaction (when feasible), the rationale for such an interaction, the potential benefit, and anticipated consequences for the research participant. Such interactions should be initiated with appropriate consent of the research participant. Where unintentional harm occurs to the research participant due to the nonprofessional interaction, the researcher must show evidence of an attempt to remedy such harm.

H.4. Reporting Results

H.4.a. Accurate Results
Career professionals plan, conduct, and report research accurately. They provide thorough discussions of the limitations of their data and alternative hypotheses. Career professionals do not engage in misleading or fraudulent research, distort data, misrepresent data, or deliberately bias their results. They explicitly mention all variables and conditions known to the investigator that may have affected the outcome of a study or the interpretation of data. They describe the extent to which results are applicable for diverse populations.

H.4.b. Obligation to Report Unfavorable Results
Career professionals report the results of any research of professional value. Results that reflect unfavorably on institutions, programs, services, prevailing opinions, or vested interests are not withheld.

H.4.c. Reporting Errors
If career professionals discover significant errors in their published research, they take reasonable steps to correct such errors in a correction erratum, or through other appropriate publication means.

H.4.d. Identity of Participants

Career professionals who supply data, aid in the research of another person, report research results, or make original data available take due care to disguise the identity of respective participants in the absence of specific authorization from the participants to do otherwise. In situations where participants self-identify their involvement in research studies, researchers take active steps to ensure that data is adapted/changed to protect the identity and welfare of all parties and that discussion of results does not cause harm to participants.

H.4.e. Replication Studies

Career professionals are obligated to make available sufficient original research data to qualified professionals who may wish to replicate a study.

H.5. Publication

H.5.a. Recognizing Contributions

When conducting and reporting research, career professionals are familiar with and give recognition to previous work on the topic, observe copyright laws, and give full credit to those to whom credit is due.

H.5.b. Plagiarism

Career professionals do not plagiarize; that is, they do not present another person's work as their own.

H.5.c. Review/Republication of Data or Ideas

Career professionals fully acknowledge and make editorial reviewers aware of prior publication of ideas or data where such ideas or data are submitted for review or publication.

H.5.d. Contributors

Career professionals give credit through joint authorship, acknowledgment, footnote statements, or other appropriate means to those who have contributed significantly to research or concept development in accordance with such contributions. The principal contributor is listed first, and minor technical or professional contributions are acknowledged in notes or introductory statements.

H.5.e. Agreement of Contributors

Career professionals who conduct joint research with colleagues or students/supervisees establish agreements in advance regarding allocation of tasks, publication credit, and types of acknowledgment that will be received.

H.5.f. Student Research

For articles that are substantially based on students' course papers, projects, theses, or dissertations, and on which students have been the primary contributors, they are listed as principal authors.

H.5.g. Duplicate Submission
Career professionals submit manuscripts for consideration to only one journal at a time. Manuscripts that are published in whole or in substantial part in another journal or published work are not submitted for publication without acknowledgment and permission from the previous publication.

H.5.h. Professional Review
Career professionals who review material submitted for publication, research, or other scholarly purposes respect the confidentiality and proprietary rights of those who submitted it. Career professionals use care to make publication decisions based on valid and defensible standards. Career professionals review article submissions in a timely manner and based on their scope and competency in research methodologies. Career professionals who serve as reviewers at the request of editors or publishers make every effort to review only materials that are within their scope of competency and use care to avoid personal biases.

Section I: Resolving Ethical Issues

Introduction
Career professionals behave in a legal, ethical, and moral manner in the conduct of their professional work. They are aware that client protection and trust in the profession depend on a high level of professional conduct. They hold other career professionals to the same standards and are willing to take appropriate action to ensure that these standards are upheld. Career professionals work to resolve ethical dilemmas with direct and open communication among all parties involved and seek consultation with colleagues and supervisors when necessary. Career professionals incorporate ethical practice into their daily work. They engage in ongoing learning and development regarding current topics in ethical and legal issues in the profession.

I.1. Standards and the Law

I.1.a. Knowledge
Career professionals understand the *NCDA Code of Ethics* and other applicable ethics codes from professional organizations or from certification and licensure bodies of which they are members and/or which regulate practice in a state or territory. Career professionals ensure that they are knowledgeable of and follow all applicable federal, state, local, and/or institutional statutes, laws, regulations, and procedures. Lack of knowledge or misunderstanding of an ethical responsibility is not a defense against a charge of unethical conduct.

I.1.b. Conflicts Between Ethics and Laws
If ethical responsibilities conflict with laws, regulations, or other governing legal authorities, career professionals make known their commitment to the *NCDA Code of Ethics* and take steps to resolve the conflict. If the conflict cannot be resolved by acknowledging and discussing the pertinent principles in the *NCDA Code of Ethics*, career professionals must adhere to the requirements of all applicable federal, state, local, and/or institutional statutes, laws, regulations, and procedures.

I.2. Suspected Violations

I.2.a. Ethical Behavior Expected
Career professionals expect colleagues to adhere to the *NCDA Code of Ethics*. When career professionals possess knowledge that raises doubts as to whether another career professional is acting in an ethical manner, they take appropriate action, as noted in I.2.b-I.2.g.

I.2.b. Informal Resolution
When career professionals have reason to believe that another career professional is violating or has violated an ethical standard, they attempt first to resolve the issue informally with the other career professional if feasible, provided such action does not violate confidentiality rights that may be involved.

I.2.c. Reporting Ethical Violations
If an apparent violation has substantially harmed, or is likely to substantially harm, a person or organization and is not appropriate for informal resolution or is not resolved properly, career

professionals take further action appropriate to the situation. Such action might include referral to state or national committees on professional ethics, voluntary national certification bodies, state licensing boards, law enforcement or other appropriate institutional authorities. This standard does not apply when an intervention would violate confidentiality rights or when career professionals have been retained to review the work of another career professional whose conduct is in question.

I.2.d. Consultation
When uncertain as to whether a particular situation or course of action may be in violation of the *NCDA Code of Ethics,* career professionals consult with others who are knowledgeable about ethics and the *NCDA Code of Ethics,* with colleagues, and/or with appropriate authorities.

I.2.e. Organizational Conflicts
If the demands of an organization with which career professionals are affiliated pose a conflict with the *NCDA Code of Ethics,* career professionals specify the nature of such conflicts and express to their supervisors or other responsible officials their commitment to the *NCDA Code of Ethics.* When possible, career professionals work toward change within the organization to allow full adherence to the *NCDA Code of Ethics.* In doing so, they are mindful of and address any confidentiality issues.

I.2.f. Unwarranted Complaints
Career professionals do not initiate, participate in, or encourage the filing of ethics complaints that are made with reckless disregard or willful ignorance of facts that would disprove the allegation.

I.2.g. Unfair Discrimination Against Complainants and Respondents
Career professionals do not deny persons employment, advancement, admission to academic or other programs, tenure, or promotion based solely upon their having made or their being the subject of an ethics complaint. This does not preclude taking action based upon the outcome of such proceedings or considering other appropriate information.

I.3. Cooperation with Ethics Committees
Career professionals assist in the process of enforcing the *NCDA Code of Ethics.* Career professionals cooperate with investigations, proceedings, and requirements of the NCDA Ethics Committee or ethics committees of other duly constituted associations or licensing/certifications boards having jurisdiction over those charged with a violation. Career professionals are familiar with the *NCDA Policy and Procedures for Processing Complaints of Ethical Violations* and use it as a reference for assisting in the enforcement of the *NCDA Code of Ethics.*

Glossary of Terms

NOTE: NCDA has members in various career services positions (see Career Professionals), as well as in instructional (counselor educators, counseling psychology professors, etc.) and supervisory roles (Director, Associate Director, Career Supervisor, etc.). The term "career professional" will be used throughout this document both as a noun and as an adjective to refer to anyone holding NCDA membership and who is therefore expected to abide by these ethical guidelines.

Advocacy – promotion of the well-being of individuals and groups, and the career counseling profession within systems and organizations. Advocacy seeks to remove barriers and obstacles that inhibit access, growth, and development.

Assent – to demonstrate agreement, when a person is otherwise not capable or competent to give formal consent (e.g., informed consent) to a career counseling service or plan.

Career Counselor – a professional (or a student who is a career counselor-in-training) engaged in a career counseling practice or other career counseling-related services. Career counselors fulfill many roles and responsibilities such as career counselor educators, researchers, supervisors, practitioners, and consultants.

Career Professionals – this term includes career counselors, career coaches, career consultants, career development facilitators, and anyone else who is a member of NCDA and provides career counseling, career advice/advising, career coaching, career planning, job search assistance, and/or related services.

Career Services – all activities delivered by career professionals to individuals, groups and organizations. Services may include, but are not necessarily limited to, career counseling, career planning, assessment, job search assistance, skills practice, workshops and training, homework assignments, bibliographies, journaling, and overall career program development.

Career Services Plan – a document created by a career professional and a client that outlines goals, steps, time frames and outcome measures whereby a client can learn and apply an orderly process for reaching career goals.

Client(s) – individuals seeking or referred to the services of a career professional. Clients willfully enter into a defined professional relationship with a career professional or are included by means of informed consent by a parent or guardian.

Educator – a professional engaged in developing, implementing, and supervising the educational preparation of students and/or supervisees.

Supervisor – a professional who engages in a formal relationship with a practicing career professional or a student for the purpose of overseeing that individual's career services work and/or clinical skill development.

Culture – membership in a socially constructed way of living, which incorporates collective values, beliefs, norms, boundaries, and lifestyles that are co-created with others who share similar worldviews comprising biological, psychosocial, historical, psychological, and other factors.

Distance Career Services – The use of technology (including but are not limited to computer hardware and software, telephone, the Internet, online assessment instruments, and other communication devices) to provide career services to clients who are not located in the same room with the career professional.

Diversity – the similarities and differences that occur within and across cultures, and the intersection of cultural and social identities.

Documents – any written, digital, audio, visual, or artistic recording of the work within the career services relationship between career professional and client.

Dual Relationships – relationships and/or interactions with clients, students, supervisees, and/or research participants that involve the career professional in more than one professional role or a combination of professional and nonprofessional roles.

Examinee – a recipient of any professional career service that includes educational, psychological, and career appraisal utilizing qualitative or quantitative techniques.

Forensic Evaluation – any formal assessment conducted for court or other legal proceedings.

Multicultural/Diversity Competence – a capacity whereby career professionals possess cultural and diversity awareness and knowledge about self and others, and how this awareness and knowledge is applied effectively in practice with clients and client groups.

Netiquette – the etiquette of online/internet communication.

Professional Relationship – a relationship in which the roles of client and career professional are defined, activities and services are selected, and fees are charged to a client, an employer, or a referring organization.

Student – an individual engaged in formal educational preparation as a career professional.

Supervisee – a career professional or student whose career services work and/or clinical skill development is being overseen in a formal supervisory relationship by a qualified trained professional.

Supervisor – Career professionals who are trained to oversee the work of other career professionals and students/supervisees.

Teaching – all activities engaged in as part of a formal educational program for career professionals.

Training – the instruction and practice of skills related to the work of career professionals. Training contributes to the ongoing proficiency of students and career professionals.

Working Relationship – a current agreement between a career professional and a client in which the roles, responsibilities and activities of both career professional and client are clearly defined.

Web References

ACA's Ethics Code: http://www.counseling.org/Resources

Introduction: An ethical decision-making model from the Ethics Resource Center
http://www.ethics.org/resources/decision-making-model.asp

H.1.a. Use of Human Research Participants
http://cme.cancer.gov/clinicaltrials/learning/humanparticipant-protections.asp

Appendix C: Sample O*Net Summary (Mental Health Counselor)

Summary Report for:
21-1014.00 - Mental Health Counselors

Counsel with emphasis on prevention. Work with individuals and groups to promote optimum mental and emotional health. May help individuals deal with issues associated with addictions and substance abuse; family, parenting, and marital problems; stress management; self-esteem; and aging.

Sample of reported job titles: Behavior Analyst, Behavior Support Specialist (BSS), Case Manager, Clinician, Correctional Counselor, Counselor, Mental Health Counselor, Mental Health Specialist, Mental Health Therapist, Therapist

Tasks

- Maintain confidentiality of records relating to clients' treatment.
- Encourage clients to express their feelings and discuss what is happening in their lives, helping them to develop insight into themselves or their relationships.
- Collect information about clients through interviews, observation, or tests.
- Assess patients for risk of suicide attempts.
- Fill out and maintain client-related paperwork, including federal- and state-mandated forms, client diagnostic records, and progress notes.
- Prepare and maintain all required treatment records and reports.
- Counsel clients or patients, individually or in group sessions, to assist in overcoming dependencies, adjusting to life, or making changes.
- Guide clients in the development of skills or strategies for dealing with their problems.
- Perform crisis interventions with clients.
- Develop and implement treatment plans based on clinical experience and knowledge.

Tools & Technology

Tools used in this occupation:

Blood pressure cuff kits — Sphygmomanometers

Desktop computers

Electronic medical thermometers — Digital medical thermometers

Notebook computers

Scanners — Flatbed scanners

Technology used in this occupation:

Electronic mail software — Email software; Microsoft Outlook

Internet browser software — Microsoft Internet Explorer *; Netscape Navigator; Web browser software

Medical software — Client information database systems; Patient electronic medical record EMR software

Office suite software — Microsoft Office software

Spreadsheet software — Microsoft Excel

* Software developed by a government agency and/or distributed as freeware or shareware.

Figure C.1   Sample O*Net Health Summary

Knowledge

Psychology — Knowledge of human behavior and performance; individual differences in ability, personality, and interests; learning and motivation; psychological research methods; and the assessment and treatment of behavioral and affective disorders.

Therapy and Counseling — Knowledge of principles, methods, and procedures for diagnosis, treatment, and rehabilitation of physical and mental dysfunctions, and for career counseling and guidance.

Customer and Personal Service — Knowledge of principles and processes for providing customer and personal services. This includes customer needs assessment, meeting quality standards for services, and evaluation of customer satisfaction.

Sociology and Anthropology — Knowledge of group behavior and dynamics, societal trends and influences, human migrations, ethnicity, cultures and their history and origins.

English Language — Knowledge of the structure and content of the English language including the meaning and spelling of words, rules of composition, and grammar.

Education and Training — Knowledge of principles and methods for curriculum and training design, teaching and instruction for individuals and groups, and the measurement of training effects.

Clerical — Knowledge of administrative and clerical procedures and systems such as word processing, managing files and records, stenography and transcription, designing forms, and other office procedures and terminology.

Philosophy and Theology — Knowledge of different philosophical systems and religions. This includes their basic principles, values, ethics, ways of thinking, customs, practices, and their impact on human culture.

Law and Government — Knowledge of laws, legal codes, court procedures, precedents, government regulations, executive orders, agency rules, and the democratic political process.

Administration and Management — Knowledge of business and management principles involved in strategic planning, resource allocation, human resources modeling, leadership technique, production methods, and coordination of people and resources.

Skills

Active Listening — Giving full attention to what other people are saying, taking time to understand the points being made, asking questions as appropriate, and not interrupting at inappropriate times.

Social Perceptiveness — Being aware of others' reactions and understanding why they react as they do.

Service Orientation — Actively looking for ways to help people.

Speaking — Talking to others to convey information effectively.

Critical Thinking — Using logic and reasoning to identify the strengths and weaknesses of alternative solutions, conclusions or approaches to problems.

Judgment and Decision Making — Considering the relative costs and benefits of potential actions to choose the most appropriate one.

Monitoring — Monitoring/Assessing performance of yourself, other individuals, or organizations to make improvements or take corrective action.

Writing — Communicating effectively in writing as appropriate for the needs of the audience.

Reading Comprehension — Understanding written sentences and paragraphs in work related documents.

Persuasion — Persuading others to change their minds or behavior.

Abilities

Oral Comprehension — The ability to listen to and understand information and ideas presented through spoken words and sentences.

Oral Expression — The ability to communicate information and ideas in speaking so others will understand.

Problem Sensitivity — The ability to tell when something is wrong or is likely to go wrong. It does not involve solving the problem, only recognizing there is a problem.

Inductive Reasoning — The ability to combine pieces of information to form general rules or conclusions (includes finding a relationship among seemingly unrelated events).

Written Comprehension — The ability to read and understand information and ideas presented in writing.

Written Expression — The ability to communicate information and ideas in writing so others will understand.

Deductive Reasoning — The ability to apply general rules to specific problems to produce answers that make sense.

Speech Clarity — The ability to speak clearly so others can understand you.

Speech Recognition — The ability to identify and understand the speech of another person.

Fluency of Ideas — The ability to come up with a number of ideas about a topic (the number of ideas is important, not their quality, correctness, or creativity).

Figure C.1 (Continued)

Work Activities

Assisting and Caring for Others — Providing personal assistance, medical attention, emotional support, or other personal care to others such as coworkers, customers, or patients.

Documenting/Recording Information — Entering, transcribing, recording, storing, or maintaining information in written or electronic/magnetic form.

Establishing and Maintaining Interpersonal Relationships — Developing constructive and cooperative working relationships with others, and maintaining them over time.

Getting Information — Observing, receiving, and otherwise obtaining information from all relevant sources.

Performing for or Working Directly with the Public — Performing for people or dealing directly with the public. This includes serving customers in restaurants and stores, and receiving clients or guests.

Updating and Using Relevant Knowledge — Keeping up-to-date technically and applying new knowledge to your job.

Resolving Conflicts and Negotiating with Others — Handling complaints, settling disputes, and resolving grievances and conflicts, or otherwise negotiating with others.

Thinking Creatively — Developing, designing, or creating new applications, ideas, relationships, systems, or products, including artistic contributions.

Developing Objectives and Strategies — Establishing long-range objectives and specifying the strategies and actions to achieve them.

Making Decisions and Solving Problems — Analyzing information and evaluating results to choose the best solution and solve problems.

Work Context

Structured versus Unstructured Work — To what extent is this job structured for the worker, rather than allowing the worker to determine tasks, priorities, and goals?

Contact With Others — How much does this job require the worker to be in contact with others (face-to-face, by telephone, or otherwise) in order to perform it?

Telephone — How often do you have telephone conversations in this job?

Freedom to Make Decisions — How much decision making freedom, without supervision, does the job offer?

Face-to-Face Discussions — How often do you have to have face-to-face discussions with individuals or teams in this job?

Indoors, Environmentally Controlled — How often does this job require working indoors in environmentally controlled conditions?

Spend Time Sitting — How much does this job require sitting?

Frequency of Decision Making — How frequently is the worker required to make decisions that affect other people, the financial resources, and/or the image and reputation of the organization?

Electronic Mail — How often do you use electronic mail in this job?

Impact of Decisions on Co-workers or Company Results — How do the decisions an employee makes impact the results of co-workers, clients or the company?

Job Zone

Title	Job Zone Five: Extensive Preparation Needed
Education	Most of these occupations require graduate school. For example, they may require a master's degree, and some require a Ph.D., M.D., or J.D. (law degree).
Related Experience	Extensive skill, knowledge, and experience are needed for these occupations. Many require more than five years of experience. For example, surgeons must complete four years of college and an additional five to seven years of specialized medical training to be able to do their job.
Job Training	Employees may need some on-the-job training, but most of these occupations assume that the person will already have the required skills, knowledge, work-related experience, and/or training.
Job Zone Examples	These occupations often involve coordinating, training, supervising, or managing the activities of others to accomplish goals. Very advanced communication and organizational skills are required. Examples include librarians, lawyers, aerospace engineers, wildlife biologists, school psychologists, surgeons, treasurers, and controllers.
SVP Range	(8.0 and above)

Figure C.1 (Continued)

Education

Percentage of Respondents	Education Level Required
64	Master's degree
34	Bachelor's degree
1	Associate's degree

Interests

Interest code: **SIA**

Social — Social occupations frequently involve working with, communicating with, and teaching people. These occupations often involve helping or providing service to others.

Investigative — Investigative occupations frequently involve working with ideas, and require an extensive amount of thinking. These occupations can involve searching for facts and figuring out problems mentally.

Artistic — Artistic occupations frequently involve working with forms, designs and patterns. They often require self-expression and the work can be done without following a clear set of rules.

Work Styles

Self Control — Job requires maintaining composure, keeping emotions in check, controlling anger, and avoiding aggressive behavior, even in very difficult situations.

Concern for Others — Job requires being sensitive to others' needs and feelings and being understanding and helpful on the job.

Integrity — Job requires being honest and ethical.

Stress Tolerance — Job requires accepting criticism and dealing calmly and effectively with high stress situations.

Dependability — Job requires being reliable, responsible, and dependable, and fulfilling obligations.

Cooperation — Job requires being pleasant with others on the job and displaying a good-natured, cooperative attitude.

Initiative — Job requires a willingness to take on responsibilities and challenges.

Persistence — Job requires persistence in the face of obstacles.

Independence — Job requires developing one's own ways of doing things, guiding oneself with little or no supervision, and depending on oneself to get things done.

Achievement/Effort — Job requires establishing and maintaining personally challenging achievement goals and exerting effort toward mastering tasks.

Work Values

Relationships — Occupations that satisfy this work value allow employees to provide service to others and work with co-workers in a friendly non-competitive environment. Corresponding needs are Co-workers, Moral Values and Social Service.

Achievement — Occupations that satisfy this work value are results oriented and allow employees to use their strongest abilities, giving them a feeling of accomplishment. Corresponding needs are Ability Utilization and Achievement.

Independence — Occupations that satisfy this work value allow employees to work on their own and make decisions. Corresponding needs are Creativity, Responsibility and Autonomy.

Related Occupations

19-3031.03	Counseling Psychologists
21-1011.00	Substance Abuse and Behavioral Disorder Counselors
21-1012.00	Educational, Guidance, School, and Vocational Counselors
21-1013.00	Marriage and Family Therapists ⊛ Bright Outlook
21-1021.00	Child, Family, and School Social Workers ⊛
21-1023.00	Mental Health and Substance Abuse Social Workers ⊛
25-1066.00	Psychology Teachers, Postsecondary

Figure C.1 (Continued)

Wages & Employment Trends

National

Median wages (2012)	$19.27 hourly, $40,080 annual
Employment (2010)	120,000 employees
Projected growth (2010-2020)	▄▄▄▄ Much faster than average (29% or higher)
Projected job openings (2010-2020)	69,400
Top industries (2010)	Health Care and Social Assistance
	Government

Source: Bureau of Labor Statistics 2012 wage data 🔗 and 2010-2020 employment projections 🔗. "Projected growth" represents the estimated change in total employment over the projections period (2010-2020). "Projected job openings" represent openings due to growth and replacement.

Sources of Additional Information

Disclaimer: Sources are listed to provide additional information on related jobs, specialties, and/or industries. Links to non-DOL Internet sites are provided for your convenience and do not constitute an endorsement.

- Mental Health Counselors and Marriage and Family Therapists 🔗. Bureau of Labor Statistics, U.S. Department of Labor. *Occupational Outlook Handbook, 2012-13 Edition.*

Figure C.1 (Continued)

REFERENCES

American Counseling Association. (2005). *ACA code of ethics.* Retrieved from http://www.counseling.org/Resources/CodeOfEthics/TP/Home/CT2.aspx

American Psychological Association. (2003). Guidelines on multicultural education, training, research, practice, and organizational change for psychologists. *American Psychologist, 58,* 377–402.

American Psychological Association. (2010). *Ethical principles of psychologists and code of conduct.* Retrieved from http://www.apa.org/ethics/code/principles.pdf

American Psychiatric Association. (2013). *Diagnostic and statistical manual of mental disorders* (5th ed.). Washington, DC: American Psychiatric Publishing.

American School Counseling Association. (2004). *The ASCA National Model: Framework for School Counselors.* Alexandria, VA: American School Counseling Association.

Amundson, N., Harris-Bowlsbey, J. G., & Niles, S. G. (2009). *Essential elements of career counseling: Processes and techniques* (2nd ed.). Upper Saddle River, NJ: Pearson Prentice Hall.

Arbona, C. (1996). Career theory and practice in a multicultural context. In M. L. Savickas, & W. B. Walsh (Eds.), *Handbook of career counseling theory and practice* (pp. 45–54). Palo Alto, CA: Davies-Black.

Armstrong, P. I., Allison, W., & Rounds, J. (2008). Development and initial validation of brief public domain RIASEC marker scales. *Journal of Vocational Behavior, 73*(2), 287–299. doi:10.1016/j.jvb.2008.06.003

Arthur, M. B., & Rousseau, D. (Eds.). (1996). *The boundaryless career.* Oxford, UK: Oxford University Press.

Association for Assessment in Counseling and Evaluation. (2003a). *Responsibilities of users of standardized tests (RUST)* (3rd ed.). Retrieved from http://aac.ncat.edu/documents/rust.html

Association for Assessment in Counseling. (2003b). *Standards for multicultural assessment.* Retrieved from http://aac.ncat.edu/Resources/documents/STANDARDS%20FOR%20MULTICULTURAL%20ASSESSMENT%20FINAL.pdf

Bandura, A. (1977). Self-efficacy: Toward a unifying theory of behavioral change. *Psychological Review, 84,* 191–215.

Bandura, A. (1986). *Social foundations of thought and action.* Englewood Cliffs, NJ: Prentice Hall

Bandura, A. (1997). *Self-efficacy: The exercise of control.* New York: Freeman.

Betz, N. E. (1989). Implications of the null environment hypothesis for women's career development and for counseling psychology. *The Counseling Psychologist, 17*(1), 136–144. doi:10.1177/0011000089171008

Betz, N. E. (1992). Career assessment: A review of critical issues. In S. D. Brown, & R. W. Lent (Eds.), *Handbook of counseling psychology* (2nd ed., pp. 453–484). New York: Wiley.

Betz, N. E. (2005). Women's career development. In S. D. Brown, & R. W. Lent (Eds.), *Career development and counseling: Putting theory and research to work* (pp. 253–277). Hoboken, NJ: Wiley.

Betz, N. E. (2008). Advances in vocational theories. In S. D. Brown, & R. W. Lent (Eds.), *Handbook of counseling psychology* (4th ed., pp. 357–374). New York: Wiley.

Betz, N. E., Borgen, F. H., & Harmon, L. W. (1996). *Skills Confidence Inventory.* Palo Alto, CA: Consulting Psychologists Press.

Betz, N. E., & Schifano, R. S. (2000). Evaluation of an intervention to increase realistic self-efficacy and interests in college women. *Journal of Vocational Behavior, 56,* 35–52.

Bingham, R. P., & Ward, C. M. (1994). Career counseling with ethnic minority women. In W. B. Walsh, & S. Osipow (Eds.), *Career counseling with women* (pp. 165–195). Hillsdale, NJ: Lawrence Erlbaum.

Blanchard, C. A., & Lichtenberg, J. W. (2003). Compromise in career decision making: A test of Gottfredson's theory. *Journal of Vocational Behavior, 62,* 250–271.

Blustein, D. L. (1997). A context-rich perspective of career exploration across the life roles. *Career Development Quarterly, 45,* 260–274.

Blustein, D. L. (2006). *The psychology of working: A new perspective for career development, counseling, and public policy.* Mahwah, NJ: Erlbaum.

Blustein, D. L. (2008). The role of work in psychological health and well-being: A conceptual, historical, and public policy perspective. *American Psychologist, 63,* 228–240.

Blustein, D. L. (2011). A relational theory of working. *Journal of Vocational Behavior, 79*(1), 1–17. doi:10.1016/j.jvb.2010.10.004

Blustein, D. L. (2013). *Oxford handbook of the psychology of working.* New York: Oxford University Press.

Blustein, D. L., Chaves, A. P., Diemer, M. A., Gallagher, L. A., Marshall, K. G., Sirin, S., & Bhati, K. S. (2002). Voices of the forgotten half: The role of social class in the school-to-work transition. *Journal of Counseling Psychology, 49,* 311–323.

Blustein, D. L., & Fouad, N. A. (2008). Changing face of vocational psychology: The transforming world of work. In W. B. Walsh (Ed.), *Biennial review of counseling psychology* (pp. 129–155). New York: Routledge/Taylor & Francis.

Blustein, D. L., Medvide, M. B., & Kozan, S. (2012). A tour of a new paradigm: Relationships and work. *Counseling Psychologist, 40*(2), 243–254.

Blustein, D. L., Schultheiss, D. E. P., & Flum, H. (2004). Toward a relational perspective of the psychology of careers and working: A social constructionist analysis. *Journal of Vocational Behavior, 64,* 423–440.

Blustein, D. L., & Spengler, P. M. (1995). Personal adjustment: Career counseling and psychotherapy. In W. B. Walsh, & S. H. Osipow (Eds.), *Handbook of vocational psychology* (2nd ed., pp. 295–320). Hillsdale, NJ: Lawrence Erlbaum.

Borgen, F. H. (1991). Megatrends and milestones in vocational behavior: A 20-year counseling psychology retrospective. *Journal of Vocational Behavior, 39,* 263–290.

Bowen, M. (1978). *Family therapy in clinical practice.* New York: Jason Aronson.

Bowman, S. L. (1993). Career intervention strategies for ethnic minorities. *The Career Development Quarterly, 42*(1), 14–25.

Bozarth, J. D., & Fisher, R. (1990). Person-centered career counseling. In W. B. Walsh, & S. H. Osipow (Eds.), *Career counseling* (pp. 45–78). Mahwah, NJ: Lawrence Erlbaum.

Brown, D., & Brooks, L. (1985). Career counseling as a mental health intervention. *Professional Psychology: Research and Practice, 16,* 860–867.

Brown, D., & Brooks, L. (1991). *Career counseling techniques.* Needham Heights, MA: Allyn & Bacon.

Brown, M. T., Fukunaga, C., Umemoto, D., & Wicker, L. (1996). Annual review, 1990–1996: Social class, work, and retirement behavior. *Journal of Vocational Behavior, 49,* 159–189.

Brown, S. D., & Lent, R. W. (1996). A social cognitive framework for career choice counseling. *Career Development Quarterly, 44,* 354–366.

Brown, S. D., & Lent, R. W. (2013). *Career development and counseling: Putting theory and research to work* (2nd ed.). New York: Wiley.

Brown, S. D., & Ryan Krane, N. E. (2000). Four (or five) sessions and a cloud of dust: Old assumptions and new observations about career counseling. In S. D. Brown, & R. W. Lent (Eds.), *Handbook of counseling psychology* (3rd ed., pp. 740–766). New York: Wiley.

Bureau of Labor Statistics. (2011). Charting the projections 2010–2020: A special issue. *Occupational Outlook Quarterly.* Retrieved from http://www.bls.gov/opub/ooq/2011/winter/winter2011ooq.pdf

Bureau of Labor Statistics. (2012). *Labor force characteristics by race and ethnicity, 2011.* Retrieved from http://www.bls.gov/cps/cpsrace2011.pdf

Byars-Winston, A., Kantamneni, N., & Mobley, M. (2012). The changing economic order: Implications of economic disparities for counseling psychologists. In N. A. Fouad, J. A. Carter, & L. M. Subich (Eds.),

APA handbooks in psychology. APA handbook of counseling psychology, Vol. 2. Practice, interventions, and applications (pp. 255–283). Washington, DC: American Psychological Association. doi:10.1037/13755-011

Caporoso, R. A., & Kinselica, M. S. (2004). Career counseling with clients who have a severe mental illness. *Career Development Quarterly, 52*, 235–245.

Chartrand, J. M. (1991). The evolution of trait-and-factor career counseling: A person X environment fit approach. *Journal of Counseling and Development, 69*, 518–524.

Chronister, K. M., Harley, E., Aranda, C. L., Barr, L., & Luginbuhl, P. (2012). Community-based career counseling for women survivors of intimate partner violence: A collaborative partnership. *Journal of Career Development, 39*(6), 515–539. doi:10.1177/0894845311401618

Cottone, R. R., & Tarvydas, V. M. (2007). *Counseling ethics and decision making* (3rd ed.). Upper Saddle River, NJ: Pearson.

Davidson, M. M., Nitzel, C., Duke, A., Baker, C. M., & Bovaird, J. A. (2012). Advancing career counseling and employment support for survivors: An intervention evaluation. *Journal of Counseling Psychology, 59*(2), 321–328. doi:10.1037/a0027965

Davidson, S. L., & Gilbert, L. A. (1993). Career counseling is a personal matter. *Career Development Quarterly, 42,* 149–153.

Dawis, R. V. (1992). The individual differences tradition in counseling psychology. *Journal of Counseling Psychology, 39,* 7–19.

Dawis, R. V. (1996). The theory of work adjustment and person-environment-correspondence counseling. In D. Brown, L. Brooks, & Associates (Eds.), *Career choice and development* (3rd ed., pp. 75–120). San Francisco: Jossey-Bass.

Dawis, R. V. (2005). The Minnesota theory of work adjustment. In S. D. Brown, & R. W. Lent (Eds.), *Career development and counseling: Putting theory and research to work* (pp. 3–23). New York: Wiley.

Dawis, R. V., & Lofquist, L. H. (1984). *A psychological theory of work adjustment.* Minneapolis: University of Minnesota Press.

DeBell, C. (2001). Ninety years in the world of work in America. *Career Development Quarterly, 50,* 77–88.

DeBell, C. (2006). What all applied psychologists should know about work. *Professional Psychology: Research and Practice, 37,* 325–333.

Deci, E. L., & Ryan, R. M. (1985). *Intrinsic motivation and self-determination in human behavior.* New York: Plenum.

Degges-White, S., & Shoffner, M. F. (2002). Career counseling with lesbian clients: Using the Theory of Work Adjustment as a framework. *Career Development Quarterly, 51,* 87–96.

Dewey, C. R. (1974). Exploring interests: A nonsexist method. *Personnel and Guidance Journal, 52,* 311–315.

Dolliver, R. H. (1969). An adaptation of the Tyler Vocational Card Sort. *Personnel and Guidance Journal, 45,* 916–920.

Donnay, D. A. C., & Borgen, F. H. (1999). The incremental validity of vocational self-efficacy: An examination of interest, self-efficacy, and occupation. *Journal of Counseling Psychology, 46,* 432–447.

Duckworth, J. (1990). The counseling approach to the use of testing. *The Counseling Psychologist, 18,* 198–204.

Emmel, A., & Cosca, T. (2010). The 2010 SOC: A classification system gets an update. *Occupational Outlook Quarterly.* Retrieved from http://www.bls.gov/opub/ooq/2010/summer/art02.pdf

Erikson, E. H. (1968). *Identity: Youth and crisis.* New York: Norton.

Evans, K. M. (2012). Career counseling with couples and families. In D. Capuzzi, & M. D. Stauffer (Eds.), *Career counseling: Foundations, perspectives, and applications* (2nd ed., pp. 467–495). New York: Routledge/Taylor & Francis Group.

Fassinger, R. E. (2005). Theoretical issues in the study of women's career development: Building bridges in a brave new world. In W. B. Walsh, & M. L. Savickas (Eds.), *Handbook of vocational psychology* (3rd ed., pp. 85–124). Mahwah, NJ: Lawrence Erlbaum.

Feldman, D. C. (1996). The nature, antecedents, and consequences of underemployment. *Journal of Management, 22,* 385–407.

Feldman, D. C., Leana, C. R., & Bolino, M. C. (2002). Underemployment and relative deprivation among re-employed executives. *Journal of Occupational and Organizational Psychology, 75,* 453–471.

Figler, H. (2007). The annual career checkup. In H. Figler, & R. N. Bolles (Eds.), *The career counselor's handbook* (2nd ed.). Berkeley, CA: Ten Speed Press.

Flattau, P. E., Bracken, J., Van Atta, R., Bandeh-Ahmadi, A., de la Cruz, R., & Sullivan, K. (2006). *The National Defense Education Act of 1958: Selected outcomes*. Washington, D.C.: Science and Policy Institute.

Flores, L. Y., & Heppner, M. J. (2002). Multicultural career counseling: Ten essentials for training. *Journal of Career Development, 28*(3), 181–202.

Fouad, N. A. (2007). Work and vocational psychology: Theory, research and practice. *Annual Review of Psychology, 58*, 543–564.

Fouad, N. A., & Bingham, R. (1995). Career counseling with racial/ethnic minorities. In W. B. Walsh & S. H. Osipow (Eds.), *Handbook of vocational psychology* (2nd ed., pp. 331–366). Hillsdale, NJ: Lawrence Erlbaum.

Fouad, N. A., & Brown, M. T. (2000). Role of race and social class in development: Implications for counseling psychology. In S. D. Brown, & R. W. Lent (Eds.), *Handbook of counseling psychology* (3rd ed., pp. 379–408). Hoboken, NJ: Wiley.

Fouad, N. A., & Byars-Winston, A. M. (2005). Cultural context of career choice: Meta-analysis of race/ethnicity differences. *Career Development Quarterly, 53,* 223–233.

Fouad, N. A., & Bynner, J. (2008). Work transitions. *American Psychologist, 63*, 241–251.

Fouad, N. A., Cotter, E. W., Fitzpatrick, M. E., Kantamneni, N., Carter, L., & Bernfeld, S. (2010). Development and validation of the Family Influence Scale. *Journal of Career Assessment, 18*(3), 276–291. doi:10.1177/1069072710364793

Fouad, N. A., Harmon, L. W., & Borgen, F. H. (1997). Structure of interests of employed male and female members of U.S. racial-ethnic minority and nonminority groups. *Journal of Counseling Psychology, 44,* 339–345.

Fouad, N. A., & Jackson, M. A. (2013). Vocational psychology: Strengths, weaknesses, threats and opportunities. In W. B. Walsh, M. L. Savickas, & P. J. Hartung (Eds.). *Handbook of vocational psychology* (4th ed., pp. 305–320). New York: Routledge.

Fouad, N. A., & Kantamneni, N. (2008). Contextual factors in vocational psychology: Intersections of individual, group, and societal dimensions. In S. D. Brown & R. W. Lent (Eds.), *Handbook of counseling psychology* (4th ed., pp. 408–425). Hoboken, NJ: John Wiley.

Fouad, N.A., & Kantamneni, N. (2009). Cultural validity of Holland's theory. In J. Ponterotto, J. M. Casas, L. A. Suzuki, & C. M. Alexander (Eds.), *Handbook of multicultural counseling* (3rd ed., pp. 703–714). Thousand Oaks, CA: Sage.

Fouad, N. A., & Kantamneni, N. (2013). The role of race and ethnicity in career choice, development, and adjustment. In S. D. Brown, & R. W. Lent (Eds.), *Career counseling and development: Putting theory and research to work* (2nd ed., pp. 215–244). New York: Wiley.

Freeman, J. (1979). The Sex Discrimination Act and the APU Occupational Interests Guide: A reply to Closs. *British Journal of Guidance & Counselling, 7*(2), 212–217. doi:10.1080/03069887900760231

Garb, H. N. (1998). *Studying the clinician: Judgment research and psychological assessment.* Washington, DC: American Psychological Association.

Gelfand, M. J., Erez, M., & Aycan, Z. (2007). Cross-cultural organizational behavior. *Annual Review of Psychology, 58*, 479–514.

Gibson, D. E. (2004). Role models in career development: New directions for theory and research. *Journal of Vocational Behavior, 65*, 134–156.

Giordano, J., & McGoldrick, M. (1996). European families: An overview. In M. McGoldrick, J. Giordano, & J. K. Pearce (Eds.), *Ethnicity and family therapy* (pp. 427–441). New York: Guilford.

Gold, J. M., & Scanlon, C. R. (1993). Psychological distress and counseling duration of career and noncareer clients. *Career Development Quarterly, 42,* 186–191.

Goldsmith, A., & Diette, T. (2012). Exploring the link between unemployment and mental health outcomes. Retrieved from http://www.apa.org/pi/ses/resources/indicator/2012/04/unemployment.aspx

Gomez, M. J., Fassinger, R. E., Prosser, J., Cooke, K., Mejia, B., & Luna, J. (2001). Voces abriendo caminos (voices foraging paths): A qualitative study of the career development of notable Latinas. *Journal of Counseling Psychology, 48*, 286–300.

Gore, P. A., Leuwerke, W. C., & Kelly, A. R. (2013). Structure, sources and uses of occupational information. In S. D. Brown, & R. W. Lent (Eds.), *Career counseling and development: Putting theory and research to work.* (2nd ed., pp. 507–538). New York: Wiley.

Gottfredson, G. D. (1999). John L. Holland's contributions to vocational psychology: A review and evaluation. *Journal of Vocational Behavior, 55,* 15–40.

Gottfredson, G. D., & Holland, J. L. (1996). *Dictionary of Holland occupational codes* (3rd ed.). Palo Alto, CA: Consulting Psychologists Press.

Gottfredson, L. S. (1996). A theory of circumscription and compromise. In D. Brown, & L. Brooks (Eds.), *Career choice and development: Applying contemporary theories to practice* (3rd ed., pp. 179–232). San Francisco: Jossey-Bass.

Gottfredson, L. S. (2005). Applying Gottfredson's theory of circumscription and compromise in career guidance and counseling. In S. D. Brown, & R. W. Lent (Eds.), *Career development and counseling: Putting theory and research to work* (pp. 71–100). Hoboken, NJ: Wiley.

Gottfredson, L. S., & Lapan, R. T. (1997). Assessing gender-based circumscription of occupational aspirations. *Journal of Career Assessment, 5,* 419–441.

Guindon, M. H., & Giordano, F. G. (2012). Career counseling in mental health and private practice settings. In D. Capuzzi, & M. D. Stauffer (Eds.), *Career counseling: Foundations, perspectives, and applications* (2nd ed., pp. 399–428). New York: Routledge/Taylor & Francis Group.

Gysbers, N. C., Heppner, M. J., & Johnston, J. A. (2009). *Career counseling: Process, issues, and techniques* (3rd ed.). Alexandria, VA: American Counseling Association.

Hackett, G. (1993). Career counseling and psychotherapy: False dichotomies and recommended remedies. *Journal of Career Assessment, 1,* 105–117.

Hackett, G., & Betz, N. E. (1981). A self-efficacy approach to the career development of women. *Journal of Vocational Behavior, 18,* 326–339.

Hackett, G., Lent, R. W., & Greenhaus, J. H. (1991). Advances in vocational theory and research: A 20-year retrospective. *Journal of Vocational Behavior, 38,* 3–38.

Hall, D. T. (1976). *Careers in organizations.* Pacific Palisades, CA: Goodyear.

Hansen, J. C. (2005). Assessment of interests. In S. D. Brown, & R. W. Lent (Eds.), *Career development and counseling: Putting theory and research to work* (pp. 281–304). New York: Wiley.

Hansen, J. C. (2013). Nature, importance and assessment of interests. In S. D. Brown, & R.W. Lent (Eds.), *Career development and counseling: Putting theory and research to work* (2nd ed., pp.387–416). Hoboken, NJ: Wiley.

Hare-Mustin, R. T., & Marecek, J. (1988). The meaning of difference: Gender theory, postmodernism, and psychology. *American Psychologist, 43,* 455–464.

Harmon, L. W., Hansen, J. C., Borgen, F. H., & Hammer, A. C. (2005). *Strong Interest Inventory: Applications and technical guide.* Palo Alto, CA: Consulting Psychologists Press.

Hartung, P. J. (2013). The life-span, life-space theory of careers. In S. D. Brown, & R. W. Lent (Eds.), *Career development and counseling: Putting theory and research to work* (2nd ed., pp 83–114). New York: Wiley.

Hartung, P. J., Porfeli, E. J., & Vondracek, F. W. (2005). Child vocational development: A review and reconsideration. *Journal of Vocational Behavior, 66,* 385–419.

Hartung, P. J., & Taber, B. J. (2008). Career construction and subjective well-being. *Journal of Career Assessment, 16,* 75–85.

Hartung, P. J., Vandiver, B. J., Leong, F. T. L., Pope, M., Niles, S. G., & Farrow, B. (1998). Appraising cultural identity in career development assessment and counseling. *Career Development Quarterly, 46,* 276–293.

Haverkamp, B. E. (2013). Education and training in assessment for professional psychology: Engaging the "reluctant student." In K. F. Geisinger, B. A. Bracken, J. Carlson, J. C. Hansen, N. R. Kuncel, S. P. Reise, & M. C. Rodriguez (Eds.), *APA handbook of testing and assessment in psychology, Vol. 2: Testing and assessment in clinical and counseling psychology* (pp. 63–82). Washington, DC: American Psychological Association. doi: 10.1037/14048-005

Haverkamp, B. E., & Moore, D. (1993). The career-personal dichotomy: Perceptual reality, practical illusion, and workplace integration. *Career Development Quarterly, 42,* 154–160.

Heppner, M. J. (2013). Women, men, and work: The long road to gender equity. In S. D. Brown, & R.W. Lent (Eds.), *Career counseling and development: Putting theory and research to work* (2nd ed., pp. 215–244). New York: Wiley.

Heppner, M. J., & Heppner, P. P. (2003). Identifying process variables in career counseling: A research agenda. *Journal of Vocational Behavior, 62,* 429–452.

Heppner, P. P., & Lee, D.-G. (2009). Problem-solving appraisal and psychological adjustment. In S. J. Lopez, & C. R. Snyder (Eds.), *Oxford library of psychology. Oxford handbook of positive psychology* (2nd ed., pp. 345–355). New York: Oxford University Press.

Herr, E. L. (1997). Super's life-span, life-space approach and its outlook for refinement. *Career Development Quarterly, 45,* 238–246.

Herr, E. L., Cramer, S. H., & Niles, S. G. (2004). *Career guidance and counseling through the lifespan: Systematic approaches* (6th ed.). Needham Heights, MA: Allyn & Bacon.

Holland, J. L. (1994). *The occupations finder.* Odessa, FL: Psychological Assessment Resources.

Holland, J. L. (1996a). Exploring careers with a typology: What we have learned and some new directions. *American Psychologist, 51,* 397–406.

Holland, J. L. (1996b). Integrating career theory and practice: The current situation and some potential remedies. In M. L. Savickas, & W. B. Walsh (Eds.), *Handbook of career counseling theory and practice.* Palo Alto, CA: Davies-Black.

Holland, J. L. (1997). *Making vocational choices: A theory of vocational personalities and work environments* (3rd ed.). Odessa, FL: Psychological Assessment Resources.

Holland, J. L., & Gottfredson, G. D. (1994). *CASI: Career Attitudes and Strategies Inventory: An inventory for understanding adult careers.* Odessa, FL: Psychological Assessment Resources.

Holland, J. L., Powell, A. B., & Fritzsche, B. A. (1994). *The Self-Directed Search professional user's guide.* Odessa, FL: Psychological Assessment Resources.

Hochschild, A. R. (1989). *The second shift: Working parents and the revolution at home.* New York: Viking Penguin.

Humes, K. R., Jones, N. A., & Ramirez, R. R. (2011). Overview of race and Hispanic origin: 2010. Retrieved from www.census.gov/population/race/publications/

Ihle, K. H., Fouad, N. A., Gibson, P., Henry, C., Harris-Hodge, E., Jandrisevits, M., . . . Metz, A. J. (2005). The impact of cultural variables on vocational psychology: Examination of the Fouad and Bingham (1995) culturally appropriate career counseling model. In R. T. Carter (Ed.), *Handbook of racial/ cultural psychology* (pp. 262–285). New York: Wiley.

Janis, I. L., & Mann, L. (1977). *Decision making: A psychological analysis of conflict, choice, and commitment.* New York: Free Press.

Joint Committee on Testing Practices. (2004). *Code on fair testing practices in education.* Washington, DC: Author. Retrieved from http://www.apa.org/science/FinalCode.pdf

Juntunen, C. L. (2006). The psychology of working: The clinical context. *Professional Psychology: Research and Practice, 37*(4), 342–350. doi:10.1037/0735-7028.37.4.342

Juntunen, C. L., Ali, S. R., & Pietrantonio, K. R., (2013). Social class, poverty, and career development. In S. D. Brown & R.W. Lent (Eds.), *Career counseling and development: Putting theory and research to work* (2nd ed., pp. 245–274). New York: Wiley.

Juntunen, C. L., Barraclough, D. J., Broneck, C. L., Seibel, G. A., Winrow, S. A., & Morin, P. M. (2001). American Indian perspectives on the career journey. *Journal of Counseling Psychology, 48,* 274–285.

Juntunen, C. L., Cavett, A. M., Clow, R. B., Rempel, V., Darrow, R. E., & Guilmino, A. (2006). Social justice through self-sufficiency: Vocational psychology and the transition from welfare to work. In R. L. Toporek, L. H. Gerstein, N. A. Fouad, G. Roysircar, & T. Israel (Eds.), *Handbook for social justice in counseling psychology: Leadership, vision, and action* (pp. 294–309). doi:10.4135/9781412976220.n21

Juntunen, C. L., & Even, C. E. (2012). Theories of vocational psychology. In N. A. Fouad, J. A. Carter, & L. M. Subich (Eds.), *APA handbooks in psychology. APA handbook of counseling psychology, Vol. 1. Theories, research, and methods* (pp. 237–267). doi:10.1037/13754-009

Kapes, J. T., Mastie, M. M., & Whitfield, E. A. (1994). *A counselor's guide to career assessment instruments.* Alexandria, VA: National Career Development Association.

Katz, J. H. (1985). The sociopolitical nature of counseling. *The Counseling Psychologist, 13,* 615–624.

Kenny, M. E., Blustein, D. L., Chaves, A., Grossman, J. M., & Gallagher, L. A. (2003). The role of perceived barriers and relational support in the educational and vocational lives of urban high school students. *Journal of Counseling Psychology, 50,* 142–155.

Kenny, M. E., & Walsh-Blair, L. Y. (2012). Educational development: Applications. In N. A. Fouad, J. A. Carter, & L. M. Subich (Eds.), *APA handbooks in psychology. APA handbook of counseling psychology, Vol. 2. Practice, interventions, and applications* (pp. 29–55). Washington, DC: American Psychological Association. doi:10.1037/13755-002

Kim, U., Yang, K.-S., Hwang, K.-K. (2006). Contributions to indigenous and cultural psychology: Understanding people in context. In U. Kim, K.-S. Yang, & K.-K. Hwang (Eds.), *Indigenous and cultural psychology: Understanding people in context.* (pp. 3–25). New York, NY: Springer Science + Business Media.

Kjos, D. (1995). Linking career counseling to personality disorders. *Journal of Counseling & Development, 73*(6), 592–597.

Kohatsu, E. L. (Ed.). (2005). *Acculturation: Current and future directions* (Vol. 1). Hoboken, NJ: Wiley.

Krieshok, T. S., & Black, M. D. (2009). Assessment and counseling competencies and responsibilities: A checklist for counselors. In E. A. Whitfield, R. W. Feller, & C. Wood (Eds.). *A counselor's guide to career assessment instruments* (5th ed., pp. 61–64). Broken Arrow, OK: National Career Development Association.

Krumboltz, J. D. (1994). Improving career development theory from a social learning perspective. In M. L. Savickas, & R. W. Lent (Eds.), *Convergence in career development theories* (pp. 9–31). Palo Alto, CA: Consulting Psychologists Press.

Lapan, R. T. (2004). *Career development across the K–16 years: Bridging the present to satisfying and successful futures.* Alexandria, VA: American Counseling Association.

Lapan, R. T., Turner, S. L., & Pierce, M. E. (2012). College and career readiness: Policy and research to support effective counseling in schools. In N. A. Fouad, J. A. Carter, & L. M. Subich (Eds.), *APA handbook of counseling psychology.* Washington, DC: American Psychological Association.

Lent, R. W. (2013). Social cognitive career theory. In S. D. Brown, & R. W. Lent (Eds.), *Career development and counseling: Putting theory and research to work* (2nd ed., pp. 151–146). Hoboken, NJ: Wiley.

Lent, R. W., Brown, S. D. (2013). Understanding and facilitating career development in the 21st century. In S. D. Brown & R.W. Lent (Eds.), *Career counseling and development: Putting theory and research to work* (2nd ed., pp. 1–28). New York: Wiley.

Lent, R. W., Brown, S. D., & Hackett, G. (1994). Toward a unifying social cognitive theory of career and academic interest, choice, and performance. *Journal of Vocational Behavior, 45,* 79–122.

Lent, R. W., Brown, S. D., & Hackett, G. (1996). Career development from a social cognitive perspective. In D. Brown, L. Brooks, & Associates (Eds.), *Career choice and development* (3rd ed., pp. 373–422). San Francisco: Jossey-Bass.

Lent, R. W., Brown, S. D., & Hackett, G. (2000). Contextual supports and barriers to career choice: A social cognitive analysis. *Journal of Counseling Psychology, 47,* 36–49.

Lent, R. W., Brown, S. D., & Hackett, G. (2002). Social cognitive career theory. In D. Brown (Ed.), *Career choice and development* (4th ed., pp. 255–311). San Francisco: Jossey-Bass.

Lewis, P., & Rivkin, D. (1999). *Development of the O*Net interest profiler.* Retrieved from http://www .onetcenter.org/dl_files/IP.pdf

Liu, W. M., & Ali, S. R. (2008). Social class and classism: Understanding the psychological impact of poverty and inequality. In S. D. Brown, & R. W. Lent (Eds.), *Handbook of counseling psychology* (4th ed., pp. 159–175). New York: Wiley.

Lofquist, L. H., & Dawis, R. V. (1991). *Essentials of person-environment-correspondence counseling.* Minneapolis: University of Minnesota Press.

Long, B. S., Kahn, S. E., & Schutz, R. W. (1992). A causal model of stress and coping: Women in management. *Journal of Counseling Psychology, 39, 337–439.*

Lucas, M. S. (1992). Problems expressed by career and non-career help seekers: A comparison. *Journal of Counseling and Development, 70,* 417–420.

Lucas, M. S. (1996). Building cohesiveness between practitioners and researchers: A practitioner-scientist model. In M. L. Savickas, & W. B. Walsh (Eds.), *Handbook of career counseling theory and practice* (pp. 81–88). Palo Alto, CA: Davies-Black.

Lyons, H. Z., Brenner, B. R., & Fassinger, R. E. (2005). A multicultural test of the theory of work adjustment: Investigating the role of heterosexism and fit perceptions in the job satisfaction of lesbian, gay, and bisexual employees. *Journal of Counseling Psychology, 52,* 537–548.

Lyons, H. Z., & O'Brien, K. M. (2006). The role of person-environment fit in the job satisfaction and tenure intentions of African American employees. *Journal of Counseling Psychology, 53,* 387–396.

Magee, I. M., & Whiston, S. C. (2010). Casting no shadow: Assessing vocational overshadowing. *Journal of Career Assessment, 18*(3), 239–249. doi: 10.1177/10690 72710364790

McAdams, D. P., & Olson, B. D. (2010). Personality development: Continuity and change over the life course. *Annual Review of Psychology, 61*, 517–542.

McCloy, R., Waugh, G., Medsker, G., Wall, J., Rivkin, D., & Lewis, P. (1999). Development of the O*Net computerized Work Importance Profiler. Retrieved from http://www.onetcenter.org/dl_files/Dev CWIP.pdf

McWhirter, E. H. (1997). Perceived barriers to education and career: Ethnic and gender differences. *Journal of Vocational Behavior, 50*, 124–140.

Merriam-Webster Dictionary (2013). *Definition of work.* Retrieved from http://www.merriam-webster .com/dictionary/work.

Metz, A. J., & Jones, J. (2013). Ability and aptitude assessment in career counseling. In S. D. Brown & R.W. Lent (Eds.), *Career development and counseling: Putting theory and research to work* (2nd ed., pp. 449–476). Hoboken, NJ: Wiley.

Miller, S. A., Dillon, A., & Swanson, J. L. (2007, May). *Genograms as sources of support, inspiration, and meaningful adolescent self-exploration.* Paper presented at the eighth biennial conference of the Society for Vocational Psychology, Akron, Ohio.

National Association of Colleges and Employers (2013). *Professional competencies for college and university career services practitioners.* Retrieved from http://www.naceweb.org/career-services/ professional-competencies.aspx

National Career Development Association (NCDA). (2007). *NCDA Code of Ethics.* Retrieved from http:// ncda.org/aws/NCDA/asset_manager/get_file/3395

National Career Development Association (NCDA). (2009). Multicultural career counseling minimum competencies. Retrieved from http://www.ncda.org/aws/NCDA/pt/sp/guidelines

National Career Development Association (2011). *Career development: A policy statement of the National Career Development Association.* Retrieved from http://www.ncda.org/aws/NCDA/pt/sp/guidelines

National Career Development Association (2013). *Guidelines for the preparation and evaluation of career and occupational information literature.* Retrieved from http://www.ncda.org/aws/NCDA/asset_ manager/get_file/3399

National Career Development Association/Association for Assessment in Counseling and Education. (2010). Career counselor assessment and evaluation competencies. Retrieved from http://www.ncda .org/aws/NCDA/asset_manager/get_file/18143/aace-ncda_assmt_eval_competencies

Nauta, M. M. (2010). The development, evolution, and status of Holland's theory of vocational personalities: Reflections and future directions for counseling psychology. *Journal of Counseling Psychology, 57*(1), 11–22. doi:10.1037/a0018213

Nauta, N. M. (2013). Holland's theory of vocational choice and adjustment. In S. D. Brown, & R. W. Lent (Eds.), *Career development and counseling: Putting theory and research to work* (2nd ed., pp 55–82). New York: Wiley.

Niles, S. G., & Harris-Bowlsbey, J. H. (2009). *Career development interventions in the 21st century.* Upper Saddle River, NJ: Merrill.

O'Brien, K. M. (2001). The legacy of Parsons: Career counselors and vocational psychologists as agents of social change. *Career Development Quarterly, 50*(1), 66–76.

Okiishi, R. W. (1987). The genogram as a tool in career counseling. *Journal of Counseling and Development, 66*, 139–143.

Osborne, W. L., Brown, S., Niles, S., & Miner, C. U. (1997). *Career development, assessment, and counseling: Applications of the Donald E. Super C-DAC approach.* Alexandria, VA: American Counseling Association.

Osipow, S. H. (1996). Does career theory guide practice or does career practice guide theory? In M. L. Savickas, & W. B. Walsh (Eds.), *Handbook of career counseling theory and practice* (pp. 403–409). Palo Alto, CA: Davies-Black.

Osipow, S. H., & Fitzgerald, L. (1996). *Theories of career development* (4th ed.). Needham Heights, MA: Allyn & Bacon.

Parsons, F. (1989). *Choosing a vocation.* Garrett Park, MD: Garrett Park Press. (Original work published 1909).

Paul, K. I., & Moser, K. (2009). Unemployment impairs mental health: Meta-analyses. *Journal of Vocational Behavior, 74*(3), 264–282.

Pfeiffer, A. M., Whelan, J. P., & Martin, J. M. (2000). Decision-making bias in psychotherapy: Effects of hypothesis source and accountability. *Journal of Counseling Psychology, 74*, 429–436.

Phillips, S. D., Friedlander, M. L., Kost, P. P., Specterman, R. V., & Robbins, E. S. (1988). Personal versus vocational focus in career counseling: A retrospective outcome study. *Journal of Counseling and Development, 67,* 169–173.

Phillips, S. D., & Jome, L. M. (2005). Vocational choices: What do we know? What do we need to know? In W. B. Walsh, & M. L. Savickas (Eds.), *Handbook of vocational psychology* (3rd ed., pp. 127–153). Mahwah, NJ: Erlbaum.

Prince, J. P. (2013). Career development of lesbian, gay, bisexual and transgender individuals. In S. D. Brown & R.W. Lent (Eds.), *Career counseling and development: Putting theory and research to work* (2nd ed., pp. 275–298). New York: Wiley.

Quintana, S. M., Chew, A., & Schell, G. (2012). Counseling psychology theory and research on race and ethnicity: Implications for a psychological science of diversity. In N. A. Fouad, J. A. Carter, & L. M. Subich (Eds.), *APA handbooks in psychology. APA handbook of counseling psychology, Vol. 1. Theories, research, and methods* (pp. 453–489). Washington, DC: American Psychological Association. doi:10.1037/13754-017

Reed, J. R., Patton, M. J., & Gold, P. B. (1993). Effects of turn-taking sequences in vocational test interpretation interviews. *Journal of Counseling Psychology, 40*, 144–155.

Richardson, M. S. (1993). Work in people's lives: A location for counseling psychologists. *Journal of Counseling Psychology, 40*, 425–433.

Richardson, M. S. (1996). From career counseling to counseling/psychotherapy and work, jobs, and career. In M. L. Savickas, & W. B. Walsh (Eds.), *Handbook of career counseling theory and practice* (pp. 347–360). Palo Alto, CA: Davies-Black.

Richardson, M. S. (2009). Another way to think about the work we do: Counselling for work and relationship. *International Journal for Educational and Vocational Guidance, 9*(2), 75–84.

Richardson, M. S. (2012). Counseling for work and relationship. *The Counseling Psychologist, 40*(2), 190–242. doi:10.1177/0011000011406452

Richardson, M. S. (2013). Counseling for work and relationship. *The Counseling Psychologist, 40,* 190–242.

Richardson, M. S., Constantine, K., & Washburn, M. (2005). New directions for theory development in vocational psychology. In W. B. Walsh, & M. L. Savickas (Eds.), *Handbook of vocational psychology* (3rd ed., pp. 51–84). Mahwah, NJ: Lawrence Erlbaum.

Richie, B. S., Fassinger, R. E., Linn, S. G., Johnson, J., Prosser, J., & Robinson, S. (1997). Persistence, connection, and passion: A qualitative study of the career development of highly achieving African American–Black and White women. *Journal of Counseling Psychology, 44*(2), 133–148. doi:10.1037/0022-0167.44.2.133

Roberts, R. K., Swanson, N. G., & Murphy, L. R. (2004). Discrimination and occupational mental health. *Journal of Mental Health, 13*(2), 129–142. doi:10.1080/09638230410001669264

Robertson, H. C. (2013). Income and support during transition from a military to civilian career. *Journal of Employment Counseling, 50*(1), 26–33. doi:10.1002/j.2161-1920 .2013.00022.x

Robitschek, C., & DeBell, C. (2002). The reintegration of vocational psychology and counseling psychology: Training issues for a paradigm shift. *The Counseling Psychologist, 30*, 801–814.

Rottinghaus, P. J., & Hauser, P. M. (2013). Assessing additional constructs affecting career choice and development. In S. D. Brown, & R.W. Lent (Eds.), *Career development and counseling: Putting theory and research to work* (2nd ed., pp.477–506). Hoboken, NJ: Wiley.

Rounds, J. B., & Armstrong, P. I. (2005). Assessment of needs and values. In S. D. Brown, & R. W. Lent (Eds.), *Career development and counseling: Putting theory and research to work* (pp. 305–329). New York. Wiley.

Rounds, J. B., Henley, G. A., Dawis, R. V., Lofquist, L. H., & Weiss, D. J. (1981). *Manual for the Minnesota Importance Questionnaire.* Minneapolis: University of Minnesota.

Rounds, J. B., Su, R. Lewis, P., & Rivkin, D. (2010). *O*Net interest profiler short form psychometric characteristics: Summary.* Retrieved from http://www.onetcenter.org/dl_files/IPSF_Psychometric .pdf

Rounds, J. B., & Tracey, T. J. (1990). From trait-and-factor to person-environment fit counseling: Theory and process. In W. B. Walsh, & S. H. Osipow (Eds.), *Career counseling: Contemporary topics in vocational psychology* (pp. 1–44). Hillsdale, NJ: Lawrence Erlbaum.

Ryan Krane, N. E., & Tirre, W. C. (2005). Ability assessment in career counseling. In S. D. Brown, & R. W. Lent (Eds.), *Career development and counseling: Putting theory and research to work* (pp. 330–352). New York: Wiley.

Ryan, R. M., & Deci, E. L. (2000). Self-determination theory and the facilitation of intrinsic motivation, social development and well-being. *American Psychologist, 55,* 68–78.

Salomone, P. R. (1996). Tracing Super's theory of vocational development: A 40-year retrospective. *Journal of Career Development, 22,* 167–184.

Savickas, M. L. (1994a). Measuring career development: Current status and future directions. *Career Development Quarterly, 43,* 54–62.

Savickas, M. L. (1994b). Vocational psychology in the postmodern era: Comment on Richardson (1993). *Journal of Counseling Psychology, 41*(1), 105–107. doi:10.1037/ 0022-0167.41.1.105

Savickas, M. L. (1997). Career adaptability: An integrative construct for life-span, life-space theory. *Career Development Quarterly, 45,* 247–259.

Savickas, M. L. (2002). A developmental theory of vocational psychology. In D. Brown (Ed.), *Career choice and development* (4th ed., pp. 149–205). San Francisco: Jossey-Bass.

Savickas, M. L. (2005). The theory and practice of career construction. In S. D. Brown, & R. W. Lent (Eds.), *Career development and counseling: Putting theory and research to work* (pp. 42–70). Hoboken, NJ: Wiley.

Savickas, M. L. (2011). *Career counseling.* Washington, DC: American Psychological Association.

Savickas, M. L. (2012). Life design: A paradigm for career intervention in the 21st century. *Journal of Counseling and Development, 90,* 13–19.

Savickas, M. L. (2013). Career construction theory and practice. In S. D. Brown, & R. W. Lent (Eds.), *Career development and counseling handbook: Putting theory and research to work* (2nd ed., pp. 147–183). New York: Wiley.

Savickas, M. L., Nota, L., Rossier, J., Dauwalder, J., Duarte, M. E., Guichard, J., . . . & van Vianen, A. E. M. (2009). Life designing: A paradigm for career construction in the 21st century. *Journal of Vocational Behavior, 75,* 239–250.

Savickas, M. L., & Walsh, W. B. (Eds.). (1996). *Handbook of career counseling theory and practice.* Palo Alto, CA: Davies-Black.

Schenck, P. M, Anctil, T. M., Smith, C. K., & Dahir, C. (2012). Coming full circle: Reoccurring career development trends in schools. *Career Development Quarterly, 60,* 221–230.

Schermerhorn, J. R., Hunt, J. G., & Osborn, R. N. (2008). *Organizational behavior* (10th ed.). New York: Wiley.

Schultheiss, D. E. P. (2006). The interface of work and family life. *Professional Psychology: Research and Practice, 37,* 334–341.

Seligman, L. (1994). *Developmental career counseling and assessment* (2nd ed.). Thousand Oaks, CA: Sage.

Sharf, R. S. (1997). *Applying career development theory to counseling* (2nd ed.). Pacific Grove, CA: Brooks/Cole.

Sheu, H.-B., Lent, R. W., Brown, S. D., Miller, M. J., Hennessy, K. D., & Duffy, R. D. (2010). Testing the choice model of social cognitive career theory across Holland themes: A meta-analytic path analysis. *Journal of Vocational Behavior, 76*(2), 252–264. doi:10.1016/j.jvb.2009.10.015.

Shirom, A. (2003). Job-related burnout: A review. In J. C. Quick, & L. E. Tetrick (Eds.), *Handbook of occupational health psychology* (pp. 245–264). Washington, DC: American Psychological Association.

Spengler, P. M., Blustein, D. L., & Strohmer, D. C. (1990). Diagnostic and treatment overshadowing of vocational problems by personal problems. *Journal of Counseling Psychology, 37*(4), 372–381. doi: 10.1037/0022-0167.37.4.372

Spengler, P. M., White, M. J., Ægisdóttir, S., Maugherman, A. S., Anderson, L. A., Cook, R. S., . . . Rush, J. D. (2009). The meta-analysis of clinical judgment project: Effects of experience on judgment accuracy. *The Counseling Psychologist, 37*(3), 350–399. doi:10.1177/0011000006295149

Spokane, A. R. (1996). Holland's theory. In D. Brown, L. Brooks, & Associates (Eds.), *Career choice and development* (3rd ed., pp. 33–74). San Francisco: Jossey-Bass.

Spokane, A. R., & Cruza-Guet, M. C. (2005). Holland's theory of vocational personalities in work environments. In S. D. Brown, & R. W. Lent (Eds.), *Career development and counseling: Putting theory and research to work* (pp. 24–41). New York: Wiley.

Subich, L. M. (1993). How personal is career counseling? *Career Development Quarterly, 42,* 120–131.

Subich, L. M. (2005). Career assessment with culturally diverse individuals. In W. B. Walsh, & M. L. Savickas (Eds.), *Handbook of vocational psychology: Theory, research, and practice* (3rd ed., pp. 397–421). Mahwah, NJ: Lawrence Erlbaum.

Sue, D. W., & Sue, D. (2013). *Counseling the culturally diverse: Theory and practice* (6th ed.). New York: Wiley

Super, D. E. (1953). A theory of vocational development. *American Psychologist, 8,* 185–190.

Super, D. E. (1957). *The psychology of careers.* New York: HarperCollins.

Super, D. E. (1980). A life-span, life-space approach to career development. *Journal of Vocational Behavior, 13,* 282–298.

Super, D. E. (1983). Assessment in career counseling: Toward truly developmental counseling. *Personnel and Guidance Journal, 61,* 555–562.

Super, D. E., Osborne, W. L., Walsh, D. J., Brown, S. D., & Niles, S. G. (1992). Developmental career assessment and counseling: The C-DAC. *Journal of Counseling and Development, 71,* 74–80.

Super, D. E., Savickas, M. L., & Super, C. M. (1996). The life-span, life-space approach to careers. In D. Brown, L. Brooks, & Associates (Eds.), *Career choice and development* (3rd ed., pp. 121–178). San Francisco: Jossey-Bass.

Super, D. E., Thompson, A. S., & Lindeman, R. H. (1988). *Adult Career Concerns Inventory: Manual for research and exploratory use in counseling.* Palo Alto, CA: Consulting Psychologists Press.

Suzuki, L. A., Onoue, M. A., Fukui, H., & Ezrapour, S. (2012). Foundations of counseling psychology: Assessment. In N. A. Fouad, J. A. Carter, & L. M. Subich (Eds.), *APA handbook of counseling psychology, Vol. 1. Theories, research, and methods* (pp. 167–199). doi:10.1037/13754-007

Swanson, J. L. (1995). The process and outcome of career counseling. In W. B. Walsh, & S. H. Osipow (Eds.), *Handbook of vocational psychology* (2nd ed., pp. 217–259). Hillsdale, NJ: Lawrence Erlbaum.

Swanson, J. L. (2012). Work and psychological health. In N. A. Fouad, J. A. Carter, & L. M. Subich (Eds.), *APA handbooks in psychology. APA handbook of counseling psychology, Vol. 2. Practice, interventions, and applications* (pp. 3–27). doi:10.1037/13755-001

Swanson, J. L. (2013). Traditional and emerging career development theory and the psychology of working. In D. L. Blustein (Ed.), *Handbook of the psychology of working* (pp. 49–67). New York: Oxford University Press.

Swanson, J. L., & Chu, S. P. (2000). Applications of person-environment psychology to the career development and vocational behavior of adolescents and adults. In M. E. Martin Jr., & J. L. Swartz-Kulstad (Eds.), *Person-environment psychology and mental health: Assessment and intervention* (pp. 143–168). Mahwah, NJ: Lawrence Erlbaum.

Swanson, J. L., & D'Achiardi, C. (2005). Beyond interests, needs/values, and abilities: Assessing other important career constructs over the life span. In S. D. Brown, & R. W. Lent (Eds.), *Career development and counseling: Putting theory and research to work* (pp. 353–380). New York: Wiley.

Swanson, J. L., Daniels, K. K., & Tokar, D. M. (1996). Assessing perceptions of career-related barriers: The Career Barriers Inventory. *Journal of Career Assessment, 4,* 219–244.

Swanson, J. L., & Gore, P. A. (2000). Advances in vocational psychology theory and research. In S. D. Brown, & R. W. Lent (Eds.), *Handbook of counseling psychology* (3rd ed., pp. 233–269). New York: Wiley.

Swanson, J. L., & Schneider, M. (2013). Minnesota theory of work adjustment. In S. D. Brown, & R. W. Lent (Eds.), *Career development and counseling: Putting theory and research to work* (2nd ed., pp. 29–53). New York: Wiley.

Triandis, H. C., & Gelfand, M. J. (2012). A theory of individualism and collectivism. In P. A. M. Van Lange, A. W. Kruglanski, & E. T. Higgins (Eds.), *Handbook of theories of social psychology* (Vol. 2, pp. 498–520). Thousand Oaks, CA: Sage.

Tsabari, O., Tziner, A., & Meir, E. I. (2005). Updated meta-analysis on the relationship between congruence and satisfaction. *Journal of Career Assessment, 13*(2), 216–232. doi:10.1177/1069072704273165

Turner, S. L., & Lapan, R. T. (2005). Promoting career development and aspirations in school-age youth. In S. D. Brown, & R. W. Lent (Eds.), *Career development and counseling: Putting theory and research to work* (pp. 417–440). Hoboken, NJ: Wiley.

Varghese, F. P. (2013). Vocational interventions with offenders: Interdisciplinary research, theory, and integration. *The Counseling Psychologist, 41,* 1011–1039.

Velez, B. L., & Moradi, B. (2012). Workplace support, discrimination, and person–organization fit: Tests of the theory of work adjustment with LGB individuals. *Journal of Counseling Psychology, 59*(3), 399–407. doi:10.1037/a0028326

Walborn, F. S. (1996). *Process variables: Four common elements of counseling and psychotherapy.* Pacific Grove, CA: Brooks/Cole.

Walsh, W. B., & Osipow, S. H. (Eds.). (1995). *Handbook of vocational psychology* (2nd ed.). Hillsdale, NJ: Lawrence Erlbaum.

Walsh, W. B., Price, R. H., & Craik, K. H. (1992). Person-environment psychology: An introduction. In W. B. Walsh, K. H. Craik, & R. H. Price (Eds.), *Person-environment psychology: Models and perspectives* (pp. vii–xi). Mahwah, NJ: Lawrence Erlbaum.

Ward, C. M., & Bingham, R. P. (1993). Career assessment of ethnic minority women. *Journal of Career Assessment, 1,* 246–257.

Watkins, C. E., Jr., & Campbell, V. L. (1990). Testing and assessment in counseling psychology: Contemporary developments and issues. *The Counseling Psychologist, 18,* 189–197.

Watkins, C. E., Jr., & Savickas, M. L. (1990). Psychodynamic career counseling. In W. B. Walsh, & S. H. Osipow (Eds.), *Career counseling* (pp. 79–116). Mahwah, NJ: Lawrence Erlbaum.

Welfel, E. R. (2013). Ethics in counseling and psychotherapy: Standards, research, and emerging issues (5th ed.). Belmont, CA: Brooks/Cole.

Whiston, S. C. (2005). *Principles and applications of assessment in counseling* (2nd ed.). Belmont, CA: Brooks/Cole.

Whiston, S., & Blustein, D. L (2013). The impact of career interventions: Preparing our citizens for the 21st century jobs (Policy Brief). National Career Development Association (www.ncda.org) and the Society for Vocational Psychology (www.div17.org/vocpsych/)

Whiston, S. C., Brecheisen, B. K., & Stephens, J. (2003). Does treatment modality affect career counseling effectiveness? *Journal of Vocational Behavior, 62,* 390–410.

Whiston, S., Fouad, N. A., & Juntunen, C. L. (in press). *Guidelines for integrating the role of work and career into professional practice* (Report). Task Force of the Society for Vocational Psychology, Society of Counseling Psychology.

Whiston, S. C., & Rahardja, D. (2008). Vocational counseling process and outcome. In S. D. Brown, & R. W. Lent (Eds.), *Handbook of counseling psychology* (4th ed., pp. 444–461). New York: Wiley.

Whiteley, J. M. (1984). Counseling psychology: A historical perspective. *The Counseling Psychologist, 12,* 3–109.

Williams, C. M., & Subich, L. M. (2006). The gendered nature of career related learning experiences: A social cognitive career theory perspective. *Journal of Vocational Behavior, 69*(2), 262–275. doi:10.1016/j.jvb.2006.02.007

Williams, C. P., & Savickas, M. L. (1990). Developmental tasks of career maintenance. *Journal of Vocational Behavior, 36,* 166–175.

Wood, C., & Hays, D. G. (2013). *A counselor's guide to assessment instruments* (6th ed.). Broken Arrow, OK: National Career Development Association.

Worthington, R. L., Flores, L. Y., & Navarro, R. L. (2005). Career development in context: Research with people of color. In S. D. Brown, & R. W. Lent (Eds.), *Career development and counseling: Putting theory and research to work* (pp. 225–252). New York: Wiley.

Young, R. A., & Collin, A. (2004). Introduction: Constructivism and social constructionism in the career field. *Journal of Vocational Behavior, 64,* 373–388.

Zunker, V. (2008). *Career, work, and mental health: Integrating career and personal counseling.* Thousand Oaks, CA: Sage.

Zytowski, D. G. (2001). Frank Parsons and the Progressive Movement. *Career Development Quarterly, 50,* 57–65.

INDEX

ABOUT THE AUTHORS

Jane L. Swanson, PhD, is Professor of Psychology at Southern Illinois University Carbondale. She received her PhD from the University of Minnesota in 1986. She is a Fellow of the Society of Counseling Psychology (Division 17) of the American Psychological Association and has served as Chair of the Society for Vocational Psychology and on the boards of the Society of Counseling Psychology and the Association for Assessment in Counseling. Dr. Swanson has served on several journal editorial boards and as Associate Editor of the *Journal of Vocational Behavior.* She has published extensively on topics related to career and vocational psychology, such as career assessment, career barriers, measurement of vocational interests, and career interventions. Dr. Swanson is also experienced as a career counselor and facilitator, including founding and directing a university career counseling agency, developing and delivering career interventions for high school students, and training and supervising career counselors.

Nadya A. Fouad, PhD, is a Distinguished Professor and Chair of the Department of Educational Psychology at the University of Wisconsin–Milwaukee and faculty member in the Counseling Psychology program. She is the immediate past editor of *The Counseling Psychologist.* She was recipient in 2003 of the John Holland Award for Outstanding Achievement in Career and Personality Research, the 2009 APA Distinguished Contributions to Education and Training Award, the 2009 Janet Helms Award for Mentoring and Scholarship, the 2010 Paul Nelson Award by the Council of Chairs of Training Councils, and the Lifetime Achievement Award from the Council of Counseling Psychology Training Programs. She cochaired the writing committee for the 2003 APA Multicultural Guidelines with Patricia Arredondo; they are currently working on a 2014 revision to the Guidelines. Her research focuses on the work-related decisions of women and ethnic minorities. She has worked most recently on "Stemming the Tide" with her colleague Romila Singh, focusing on understanding why women leave engineering.